SURVIVAL AND WITNESS AT EUROPE'S BORDER

SURVIVAL AND WITNESS AT EUROPE'S BORDER

The Afterlives of a Disaster

Karina Horsti

CORNELL UNIVERSITY PRESS   **ITHACA AND LONDON**

First published 2023 by Cornell University Press

Library of Congress Cataloging-in-Publication Data

Names: Horsti, Karina, author.
Title: Survival and witness at Europe's border : the afterlives of a disaster / Karina Horsti.
Description: Ithaca [New York] : Cornell University Press, 2023. | Includes bibliographical references and index.
Identifiers: LCCN 2022060673 (print) | LCCN 2022060674 (ebook) | ISBN 9781501771378 (hardcover) | ISBN 9781501771408 (paperback) | ISBN 9781501771385 (pdf) | ISBN 9781501771392 (epub)
Subjects: LCSH: Eritreans—Europe—Social conditions—21st century. | Shipwrecks—Mediterranean Sea—History—21st century. | Lampedusa Island (Italy)—Emigration and immigration—Social aspects.
Classification: LCC DT16.5 .H67 2023 (print) | LCC DT16.5 (ebook) | DDC 910.91458/22—dc23/eng/20230111
LC record available at https://lccn.loc.gov/2022060673
LC ebook record available at https://lccn.loc.gov/2022060674

Contents

Acknowledgments

I would like to thank those who shared their experiences and thoughts on survival with me. I am deeply grateful for the trust of Bisrat, Kebrat, Adhanom, Solomon, Amanuel, Teddy, Ambasanger, Aregai, Mohamed, Tadese, Semhar, and many others whose names I can't mention. I learned so much from them. *Msgana! Nkulom netom temokrom zekafeluni lbawi msgana yeqrb. Kabakum bzuh temahire eyie.* I also thank people in Sicily and Lampedusa who participated in the research and provided information. I am particularly grateful to Vito Fiorino, Constantino and Rosa Maria Baratta, Mauro Buccarello, Paola la Rosa, the Askavusa collective, Mariangela Galante and Nicola Coppola.

Ilaria Tucci has been an invaluable research assistant and coanalyst throughout the project. I thank her for translating multiple Italian dialects and body languages, and for her precise observations. I also thank Anna Blom who produced and directed the *Remembering Lampedusa* documentary films, which provided a humane perspective to the disaster. I'm grateful for Adal Neguse for codirecting the films and interviewing survivors. My work would not have been possible without his committed and insightful participation throughout the research and the writing processes. I also thank Adal for coanalysis and attentive assistance in translations.

There are many individuals, networks, and institutions that supported my research over the years. The research has been funded by the Academy of Finland and the Kone Foundation. I am grateful for the Department of Social Sciences and Philosophy and my supportive colleagues at the University of Jyväskylä, particularly Päivi Pirkkalainen, Outi Fingerroos, and Miikka Pyykkönen. During the project, I have been a visiting scholar at London School of Economics and Political Science, New York University, Melbourne University, and Nordic Africa Institute, Uppsala. I thank Radha Hegde, Marita Sturken, Nikos Papastergiadis, Lilie Chouliaraki, Myria Georgiou, Redie Bereketeab, and Cristiano Lanzano for engaging with my work and for making my visits so valuable. I also thank the people who invited me to present the research leading to this book at events they organized and who discussed ideas with me in those events, particularly Raelene Wilding, Amanda Lagerkvist, Philipp Seuferling, Heike Graf, Anna Roosvall, Christina Lohmeier, Christian Pentzold, Pierluigi Musarò, Jopi Nyman, Johan Schimanski, Tuuli Lähdesmäki, Eveliina Lyytinen, Maria Rovisco, and Kate Zambon. The book began to take shape during the Border Memories workshops

I organized in 2016 and 2017 (funded by the Joint Committee for Nordic Research Councils), and I thank all participants. Another inspiring group of scholars I wish to thank gathered at the Hamburg Foundation for the Advancement of Research and Culture in 2019, invited by Klaus Neumann. In addition, I am grateful for artists HM Jokinen and Jan Ijäs, curators Cajsa Rundström and Johannes Olsson, and Maritiman Maritime Museum for collaboration. I have shared numerous important conversations with colleagues about the book's topic, and I would like to thank everyone, particularly Randi Marselis, Anitta Kynsilehto, Anna-Kaisa Kuusisto, Saara Pellander, Noora Kotilainen, Mari Maasilta, Kaarina Nikunen, Miyase Christensen, Alexa Robertson, Carolina Boe, Tanja Thomas, Margreth Lünenborg, Débora Medeiros, Anne McNevin, Annalisa Mangiaracina, Vicki Squire, Federica Mazzara, and Gianluca Gatta. Klaus Neumann read drafts of this book and discussed them with me. I am grateful for his time, generosity, and attention to detail, even after reading various versions of the same chapters. Special thanks to him for suggesting the term afterlife early in the project.

I have been fortunate to have thoughtful editors, and I would like to thank them. Christina Saarinen proofread the English language and made helpful suggestions that improved the text and the choice of terms. Jim Lance at Cornell University Press believed in the book early on and has been encouraging in the final stages of the publication process together with Clare Jones. I am also grateful for the anonymous readers of the manuscript whose comments and suggestions were crucial.

My friends and family have understood the importance of research and writing for me, and I would like to thank my mother Terhi, the father of my daughters Mikko, and my daughters Aino, Seela, and Milma for their support.

Abbreviations

AP	The Associated Press
DDA	Direzione Distrettuale Antimafia
ECR	The European Conservatives and Reformists Group
EFDD	Europe of Freedom and Direct Democracy Group
ELF	The Eritrean Liberation Front
EPLF	The Eritrean People's Liberation Front
EU	European Union
FRONTEX	European Border and Coast Guard Agency
GARIWO	Gardens of the Righteous Worldwide
ICMP	International Commission on Missing Persons
INTERPOL	The International Criminal Police Organization
IOM	International Organization for Migration
LABANOF	Laboratorio di Antropologia e Odontologia Forense dell'Università degli Studi di Milano
LIBE	The European Parliament's Committee on Civil Liberties, Justice, and Home Affairs
MEP	Member of the European Parliament
NGO	Non-Governmental Organization
NI	Non-Inscrits
RAI	Radiotelevisione Italiana
SAR	Search and Rescue
UN	United Nations
UNHCR	The United Nations High Commissioner for Refugees
UNITED	United for Intercultural Action

SURVIVAL AND WITNESS
AT EUROPE'S BORDER

FIGURE 1. Key locations mentioned in the text.

Introduction

A large bundle of numbered keys jingle in a man's hand as he walks briskly from a car parked on the street toward a three-story apartment building. The man has soft, curly hair and a full, black beard. He is in his late twenties or early thirties. It's hard to say—his appearance is both relaxed and serious, young and old at the same time. The verdant neighborhood has the typical quiet atmosphere of a Scandinavian suburb built in the 1950s. The man wears sandals, the trees are green, and flowers have been planted by the building's entrance. The man looks like as if he might have roots in Ethiopia or Eritrea, but he doesn't come across as someone who has recently arrived in Europe. He's dressed unremarkably in jeans and a light green polo shirt, and he enters the building confidently, as if it's his territory.

> "Hej, Karl! Do you remember me?" the man says in Swedish. "I'm from Aleris Home Care."
> "Yes, yes," an elderly voice says.
> "I was thinking of helping you with lunch."
> "No, no, no."
> "I can help you to warm up your meal."
> "No, no, no, nothing right now. I'm watching the horse races."

The viewer is not brought inside, instead hearing the conversation with only a view of the building from the outside. Karl, the elderly client, remains unseen, but the man with the keys is already familiar to the viewer. The scene is from a short film about Adhanom Rezene, and before the encounter with the old man, we have already seen Adhanom giving a hug to a woman and picking up a toddler in the hallway of a small apartment before leaving for work. A white crucifix hangs from his neck, and on the wall in the background is a poster of a saint on a white horse. Adhanom seems sympathetic and kind—the kind of person anyone would be happy to let in to help with lunch. The woman comes into the shot only briefly, but it's obvious she is the little girl's mother, and Adhanom is the father. The woman is about the same age as Adhanom, and she too seems to have roots in the Horn of Africa. The soft early morning sun makes the couple and their home glow: they are a beautiful, happy family.

Adhanom holds the keys not only to Karl's, but also to many other elderly people's homes in Stockholm. The film's story, however, is not about these visits—it is about Adhanom being forced to leave his home and the family that raised him. In Eritrea, "life had no future," Adhanom says in the film. His voice is heard over scenes of traveling through Stockholm, taking the *pendeltåg*—the local train—and driving the care service's car. He narrates his escape from Eritrea's compulsory, indefinite military service and from the Isaias Afwerki regime that imprisoned him multiple times. Adhanom describes how he survived a shipwreck in the Mediterranean Sea while crossing from Libya to the Italian island of Lampedusa on a smuggler's boat in 2013. At least 366 of his fellow passengers drowned. A cross and the words "God Help Me" are tattooed on his arm. When the camera focuses on the tattoos, their roughness is evident: they were obviously done in conditions where help was truly needed.

The film *Remembering Lampedusa/Love* (directed by Anna Blom and Adal Neguse) is being shown on a large television screen inside the crew accommodations of the *HSwMS Småland*, a destroyer in service of the Swedish military from the 1950s until 1979. Adhanom's story and the visuals of his life and work in Sweden have a particular resonance here inside the warship. Before entering the cool, dark space, smelling of iron and old motor oil, visitors will have walked along the decks of the 396-foot ship, seen defunct missiles, and scaled steep, narrow stairs up and down. One encounters Adhanom's story rather unexpectedly in the course of following the arrows and signs indicating the route through the large ship. Adhanom's memories of crossing borders to seek refuge from a present-day conflict stand both in contrast to and as a continuation of Sweden's maritime and war history. *Småland* guarded borders that no longer exist in the Baltic Sea, an association that illuminates the ephemerality of present-day borders. Today, Sweden, alongside the other European Union member states, militarily guards Europe's external border in the Mediterranean Sea, preventing people from certain countries, people like Adhanom, from crossing it safely. One day, that border too will cease to exist.

The Cold War–era ship is docked at the Maritiman maritime museum in Gothenburg, which advertises *Småland* as the largest Scandinavian warship preserved in a museum. Below deck, visitors can choose to see the film and hear Adhanom tell his story in Tigrinya, with subtitles in Swedish, English, German, or Italian. Adhanom's film, screened inside the Swedish destroyer, I argue, illustrates well how memories of the disaster travel beyond Lampedusa and live on, becoming a part of the history of the places they reach. Memories of border deaths are inherently part of the history of Europe, including in places beyond the Mediterranean region. In the film, Adhanom recounts his journey from Eritrea to its disastrous encounter with Europe's border in the Mediterranean Sea. Adhanom risked his life for the chance to have a future, he explains in the film. He narrates the entire journey: his escape from Eritrea to a refugee camp in Ethiopia, his trip through Sudan and Libya, and finally, the dangerous sea-border crossing on a smuggler's boat to Italy—or rather, almost to Italy. The boat capsized only a kilometer from the Italian island of Lampedusa.

Into a story otherwise told in Tigrinya, Adhanom inserts a Swedish word, *ensam* (alone, lonely). He has never experienced such loneliness before coming to Sweden, he says, and it seems he has no word for it in Tigrinya. Adhanom talks about the irony of caring for the elderly in Sweden while his own parents get old in Eritrea. "Money is the only thing you can help them with. But there's more to being human than just money," he says and pauses.

The film is part of the exhibition *Remembering Lampedusa*, which recounts the migrant disaster that Adhanom survived in the early morning of October 3, 2013. An overcrowded fishing boat carrying mainly Eritrean refugees from the shore of Libya was approaching the Italian island of Lampedusa when the Tunisian captain, Khaled Bensalem, turned off the engine. In the dark of the night, they waited to be noticed by other boats and to be rescued. As Adhanom recalls in the film: "A ship came and went around us. It had a big searchlight. We said to one another, 'Stay calm, they are here to rescue us.' But once they saw us, they left. Or did they see us? I couldn't tell because of the bright light. We waited, and another ship came and went." Water started to seep into the boat, and to attract the attention of the islanders and nearby boats, Bensalem set a blanket on fire. The people on the boat panicked, and the commotion on board caused the boat to list. It sank "like the *Titanic*, the bow went last," as another survivor, Solomon Gebrehiwet, recalled elsewhere.[1]

Adhanom is one of 155 people who clung to empty water bottles to stay afloat or managed to swim until they were chanced upon by a group of Lampedusans on an overnight fishing trip three hours later. The bodies of 366 people were recovered over the next few days, including those of all sixteen young children and all but six of the women on board.

The Lampedusa disaster put the issue of migrant border deaths on the public agenda in Europe. Human rights activists had been trying to raise awareness of the watery graveyard the Mediterranean had become since Europe began changing its immigration, visa, and border policies after the Schengen Convention of 1990 (UNITED 2022). The disaster was just one of thousands of migrant disasters, similar in many ways to those that happened before and after it. However, it was also a disaster like no other—its corporeality and proximity to the iconic island of Lampedusa resulted in an unprecedented mediatization and secured its prominence in the European imagination. Since the disaster, the Central Mediterranean route through the Strait of Sicily has continued to be the deadliest migration corridor in the world, with almost 19,000 reported deaths in 2014–2021 (IOM 2022).

This book examines the afterlives of the October 3, 2013, disaster, known in Italy as *la strage di Lampedusa*, the massacre of Lampedusa. It examines how the disaster continues to reappear in the public sphere through two domains, representation and memorialization. It then analyzes the politics, subjectivities, and relationships that emerge through the disaster's afterlives. How does the disaster shape not only the lives of individuals, families, and communities, but also the European Union, which created the conditions in which the natural forces of the sea kill certain people?

This book continues the line of research that has been opened by critical migration scholars who argue that borders and practices of bordering are productive: they generate subjects and subjectivities (Mezzadra and Neilson 2013; Anderson, Sharma and Wright 2011; McNevin 2011). I examine how four types of witnesses engage with the disaster through representations and memorializations: Most people witnessed the disaster from a distance, through the media. Then, there were those who witnessed the corporeal aftermath of the mass death with their own eyes in Lampedusa or in Sicily, where the dead were buried. Some of these eyewitnesses and mediated witnesses refused to remain bystanders and felt a responsibility to act upon what they saw. They refused to live on as if a disaster like the *strage di Lampedusa* was an unintended yet unavoidable consequence of the bordering of Europe. I also follow survivors who lived through the disaster, who have an embodied experience of it. Finally, I consider the family members of victims, who bear witness to the human consequences of the disaster in their intimate lives and relationships.

Survivors and relatives of victims are specific kinds of witnesses not only because of their intimate relationship with the disaster and the dead but also because of the specific transnational conditions in which the afterlives of the disaster unfold. Families are often dispersed and divided by borders. Survivors and relatives must navigate not only the institutional and social environments of

Europe, where they reside or where the dead bodies are managed, but also their diasporic communities and relationships with the state they left behind.

In the analysis of afterlives, I am specifically interested in how victims, survivors, and relatives of victims are represented in mediated images and narratives and what kinds of roles they are given by others in memorials and commemorative rituals. I am also interested in how survivors and relatives interact with representations and memorializations—how they insert their identities, politics, and agency into the scenes of the event's myriad afterlives. This methodological approach is influenced by critical refugee studies, which emphasize the agency, sociality, and subjectivity of refugees (see, e.g., Nguyen 2012; Espiritu 2014; Hong 2016), and by the autonomy of migration approach, which shifts the focus in migration studies from apparatuses of control to the autonomous ways in which migrants operate in spite of restrictions (see, e.g., Papadopoulos and Tsianos 2013; de Genova 2017). Focusing on agency is not an attempt to romanticize survival or trauma, but rather a way to learn how people live on and find their own ways to act politically and critically from the position of survivorship.

The book is based on multisited research, with the commemorations held on the anniversary of the disaster in Lampedusa functioning as an important site. I attended commemorations in Lampedusa in 2014, 2015, 2017, 2018, and 2021. There I came to know thirteen survivors of the disaster, as well as the families of three victims. Nine of the survivors became involved in my ethnographic research, and I regularly visited six of them in Sweden, where they had settled. The survivors most closely involved in this research are all men, which is in part due to the fact that only six women survived. Two women gave interviews for the research, but they are not among those who have been keen on staying in touch about the project over the years. Two of the survivors knew English well, and I was able to communicate with them directly from early on. The other survivors and I began conversing in Swedish about two years after we first met in 2014. Before that, I had mainly relied on the interpreting skills of Adal Neguse, the brother of one of the victims of the 2013 disaster.

Not having a common language with survivors in the beginning was the most difficult aspect of the study. I also had to rely on translations and interpretations of Italian. Because I am from Finland, I was always an outsider, lacking to some degree in my capacity to understand the languages and cultures at each of the sites—Sweden, Germany, Italy, and online. While this limited my research, I believe it also helped me to create a sympathetic relationship with people I observed. Sometimes, our shared Nordic context created a bond when survivors or relatives of victims and I encountered situations in Italy that were unfamiliar to us in Sweden and Finland.

In this multifaceted research, conversations with Eritrean Europeans have been central in my analysis of mainstream media, social media, diasporic media, art, film, and literature. I have also analyzed different types of official documents, for example, Italian parliamentary debates in 2016 about the establishment of October 3 as a National Day of Remembrance for the Victims of Immigration. I searched European Union databases for instances where the October 3, 2013, disaster was mentioned. During my visits to Lampedusa, I met with rescuers and other Lampedusans, including the activists of the Askavusa collective and the island's political and religious leaders. I conducted interviews with Eritrean human rights activists in Europe and visited cemeteries in Sicily where the dead are buried, talking with locals there about their practices of attending migrant graves. Teddy, a young man in his twenties from Hamburg, invited me to accompany him to a cemetery in Sicily, where he was searching for his older brother's grave. Some of the people I interviewed wish to be identified in this book by their own names. Others have decided to use pseudonyms.

Adal Neguse and I first met in Lampedusa in October 2014, but it was on our ways home from Italy that we had our first long conversation, while waiting for our connecting flights in Rome. Adal told me he had watched the morning news on October 3, 2013, while getting ready to go to work at his job at a health care services provider in Stockholm. By then, he had been living in Sweden for ten years, after having arrived as a resettlement refugee from a camp in Sudan. The news worried him, particularly because he had woken up around 2 a.m. and been unable to go back to sleep. Adal feared the worst. He had sent money to his younger brother Abraham, who was waiting in Libya to be smuggled to Europe. Adal called the smuggler, who assured him that Abraham had not been on the boat that sank. Adal did not trust the smuggler and decided to fly to Lampedusa immediately to find out if his brother had been on the boat. He showed Abraham's photo to survivors at the reception center on the island, and one woman nodded her head. Abraham was dead.

My conversation with Adal at the airport, which we carried out in Swedish, made me reflect for the first time on how disasters at Europe's borders were not so distant from my own lifeworld in Finland. Adal and I stayed in touch, and he became an important coresearcher and a dear friend. I was struck by how little, despite our globalized world, was communicated in the media and academic literature about relatives' and survivors' experiences of migrant disasters. They were hardly visible—at least as complete human beings—in depictions of disasters and their aftermath. Survivors of disasters disappeared from the public domain after the initial news reports, where they were usually depicted as objects of care, exhausted, and wrapped in emergency foil blankets. What happened to these people afterward? Who were they? Who did they become? These questions were seldom considered. And yet, Adal's story demonstrated that survivors and relatives were the people most intimately affected by such disasters.

Adal's motivation to engage with me had a lot to do with his frustration with his own experiences of being interviewed by the Swedish media. Journalists were rarely interested in disappearances at the border, which nonetheless characterize the everyday life of Eritreans in Sweden. People in Adal's community regularly search for missing relatives or collect donations to pay ransoms to kidnappers. They struggle with being apart from their loved ones who remain in Eritrea or live as refugees in Ethiopia or Sudan. After gaining residence permits or citizenship, the first thing many Eritreans do is travel to Ethiopia to meet their relatives. Life is simultaneously in Europe and elsewhere.

Adal was also keen on finding out what had happened during the fatal journey and why the rescue had failed; collaborating in the research that led to this book made some of that investigation possible. Adal and I initiated the documentary film project *Remembering Lampedusa* with Anna Blom, one result of which was the film about Adhanom described above. Adal's interviews with four survivors for the film project, which he codirected with the filmmaker Anna Blom, comprise the main research material of chapter 8 in this book. Adal characterizes the film project as a work of mourning for his brother. The questions that led to teasing out the meaning of survival for the disaster's survivors originate from Adal's curiosity and need to understand the whole picture of the disaster. Throughout my research, Adal has been an invaluable expert as well as a coresearcher and a thinking partner who has patiently kept asking, "How's the book going?"[2]

One important decision made in writing this book that emerged from my collaboration with Adal regards the use of names. When referring to Eritreans and Ethiopians, I adhere to the naming traditions of these cultures. There is no tradition of surnames in these countries; the father's first name is taken as a second name. First names have a particular importance, as the Italian Ethiopian filmmaker Dagmawi Yimer (2015) has pointed out: "Naming our children is a way of telling the world about our hopes, our dreams, our beliefs, or about the people and things we respect" (Yimer 2015, 15). While I often refer to Europeans by surname only, I refer to Eritreans and Ethiopians by first name. The only exception to this is the references, where for consistency and in keeping with academic practice, I use second names.

Lampedusa as a Symbol of the Border

The continuation of life after a rupture—an event that interrupts and calls into question what one perceives to be normal—is always an individual experience and can vary in its level of severity. Surviving a mass disaster in which one's life was in danger and others lost their lives is not the same as witnessing the disaster from a distance. However, these different types of witnessing need to be discussed in conjunction with one another. Border deaths continue to affect communities beyond the border, particularly the communities where the survivors of a disaster settle—the communities *with which they survive*. The survivors of the Lampedusa disaster are now residents—and, in some cases, citizens—of Sweden, Norway, Denmark, Germany, the Netherlands, and Italy. In many cases, they were in fact en route to meet siblings, cousins, or partners who were citizens of these countries when the disaster occurred. The disaster's memory thus travels across Europe with the survivors, and with the relatives and friends of the victims.

While locations as peripheric as Lampedusa are arguably convenient for dealing with ethically compromising matters (Mountz 2020), memories and representations travel far beyond them. Lampedusa can also be seen as a *traumascape*, *trauma site*, or *wounded place*, in the terms of Maria Tumarkin (2005), Patrizia Violi (2012), and Karen Till (2008), who by using the vocabulary of trauma studies have highlighted that traces of horrific events continue to live on in the places where the events occurred. However, though such spaces might be used for the externalization of responsibility and of the consequences of border deaths, this does not mean that the event is completely forgotten. On the contrary, Lampedusa can function as a repository where the difficult memory can be discussed from a safe distance. The critical political question, however, remains: How does such a process transform the border and the practice of bordering that has created the wound?

Lampedusa, like other iconic islands situated in global border zones, such as Lesbos in the Aegean Sea and Christmas Island in the Indian Ocean, has come to symbolize bordering, securitization, and humanitarianism in the global imaginary of migration (Mountz 2020). By the time of the disaster, the island had already become a stage for Europe's securitized border plays and spectacles (Friese 2010; Cuttitta 2014; Brambilla 2015; Ritaine 2016; Gatta 2018). In 2011, Italy's nationalist-populist prime minister, Silvio Berlusconi, used Lampedusa as the staging site to respond to the so-called humanitarian emergency that arose when thousands of young people left North Africa during the Arab Spring uprisings (BBC 2011). However, the island has also gained symbolic value as a site for healing, hope, resistance, and hospitality (Kushner 2016; Horsti and Neumann 2019; Mazzara 2019; Squire 2020; Scarabicchi 2020). Pope Francis made his first papal visit outside of Rome to the island in July 2013 to say Mass and throw a wreath of flowers into the sea in memory of those who had died during migration journeys (Vatican 2013). The power of Lampedusa's role in the social imaginary is reflected in its ability to become "an empty signifier" (Friese 2019, 26) that can travel to other locations in Europe, giving meaning to a variety of phenomena. For example, it has brought visibility to less visible bordering in city spaces, as the migrant protests *Lampedusa in Berlin* and *Lampedusa in Hamburg* demonstrate (see, e.g., Bak Jørgensen 2019). Lampedusa has even become a reference to the present-day continuation of colonialism (see, e.g., Saucier and Woods 2014).

The bordering of Europe produced the *strage di Lampedusa*, but the disaster would also transform the border, leading to an intensification of the nexus between the humanitarian and securitizing border regimes in Italy (Albahari 2015, 180; Cuttitta 2015; 2018b, 638; Crawley et al. 2016). By October 3, 2013, this nexus of increasing security technology and the depiction of migration as a security threat, combined with the language and practice of humanitarianism, had gained currency in Europe. For example, in their public communications, the European Border and Coast Guard Agency Frontex shifted its framing of migrants as criminals and a threat toward framing them as victims of smugglers (Horsti 2012). This reframing allowed Frontex to cast its border control actions as "saving lives." Such discursive simulation of the language of humanitarianism aims to neutralize Frontex's actions, masking political and national interests (Horsti 2012; Pallister-Wilkins 2015; Perkowski 2018).

After Berlusconi, a border policy tending toward humanitarianism prevailed in Italy to varying degrees until 2018, when a right-wing government came to power and criminalized the private, donation-based search and rescue operations that had been collaborating with the Italian military and border guards (Caccia, Heller, and Mezzadra 2020; Cusumano and Villa 2020). A major example of the intensified nexus of securitized-humanitarian border policy took place within a month of the Lampedusa disaster: on October 18, 2013, Italy launched a year-long naval and air operation called Mare Nostrum (Our Sea) "to tackle the humanitarian emergency in the Strait of Sicily" (Marina Militare 2020; see also, e.g., Albahari 2015; Heller and Pezzani 2018, 34). Over the course of the operation, the Italian Navy and other Italian border authorities, in collaboration with Frontex, rescued 150,000 people. For the Italian Navy, which oversaw the operation, Mare Nostrum had the twofold purpose of "safeguarding human life at sea and bringing to justice human traffickers and migrant smugglers" (Marina Militare 2020), illustrating the rationale of the securitized humanitarianism at the border. This *humanitarian bordering* was an active constructing of the securitized border using the discourse and practices of humanitarianism.

The international mediatization of the disaster also prompted major civil society initiatives, including civil search and rescue operations in the Mediterranean Sea. The founders of the Migrant Offshore Aid Station (MOAS), a civil search and rescue operation in Malta established in 2014, have repeatedly identified the Lampedusa disaster as their moment of mobilization (see, e.g., Catrambone 2020;

MOAS 2014, 10). The first German donation-based search and rescue initiative, Sea-Watch, launched its first mission from Lampedusa in 2015. According to Sea-Watch's press relations representative, Lampedusa added a symbolic dimension to the organization's image and mission (Neugebauer 2016). The island and the disaster had gained symbolic value that could be transferred to the launch of civil rescue operations in a competitive and commodified field of solidarity.

Furthermore, the unprecedented corporeality of the disaster revealed to both forensic experts and the public the significant lack of forensic investigation into the identities of dead migrants across the Mediterranean countries of Europe. Italian forensic experts and the Italian government's Office of the Commissioner for Missing Persons launched a pilot project that applied the forensic methods used in criminal investigations and other types of disasters to the victims of the Lampedusa disaster (Olivieri et al. 2018; M'charek and Casartelli 2019, 739; Bertoglio et al. 2020).

Border Deaths and New Subjectivities

Border deaths have gained scholarly attention in recent years. Such scholarship has focused on three themes: the production and contestation of the border, humanitarianism and solidarity, and the experiences of those who risk crossing borders and of their relatives, who struggle with the disappearance or deaths of their loved ones.

Critical border scholars emphasize that the EU's restrictive migration and visa policies are structures that produce deaths at the border—the sea is made into a weapon that kills (e.g., Albahari 2015; Cuttitta 2015; Squire 2020; Tazzioli 2015; Mezzadra and Neilson 2013). The border regime not only produces the killing, but also criminalizes those who make the crossing, producing a category of people who can be exploited and even disposed of (Mezzadra and Neilson 2013). Border deaths do not *happen*, but are *made* in a complex, diffused, and contested context (Weber and Pickering 2011).

Significant scholarly attention has also been paid to European civil society actors who have acted in response to the deaths. Their actions range from countersurveillance operations and civil rescue at sea borders to counting and listing deaths (Stierl 2016; Squire 2020; Neumann 2020). The role of artistic and activist performances that aim to raise public awareness about the deaths and contest the border regime have also been examined (Horsti 2016a; 2019a; 2021; Stierl 2016; Rygiel 2016; Lewicki 2017; Mazzara 2019; Squire 2020). Burials and commemoration of dead strangers by local and activist communities in border zones has been theorized as a form of transgressive politics (e.g., Kobelinsky, Furri, and

Noûs 2021; Squire 2020; Rygiel 2014; 2016). These responses to border deaths vary in their critical stance toward the governments that control the border. Some NGOs that carry out SAR operations or arts-based engagements adopt a neutral stance regarding the politics that produce the bordering, in fact depoliticizing bordering by facilitating the border work of agents such as Frontex. At the other end of the spectrum are civil rescue operations and artistic actions that take a more politicized and confrontational approach to border authorities (Cuttitta 2018b; Neumann 2020; Esperti 2020). Critical scholars have also examined how solidarity actions, just like border control actions, are commodified in order to compete for attention and resources with other causes (Andersson 2014; Nikunen 2019).

Ethnographic research has highlighted why people choose to take the risk of crossing borders (Perl 2016; Proglio 2020). For example, many Eritreans are escaping the repressive regime in their home country that aims to control the most intimate spheres of life—family, work, personal finances, and religion—causing an experience of "social death" (Ayalew Mengiste 2018; 2019; Belloni 2019). Many also did not see a future as UNHCR-recognized refugees in Sudan and Ethiopia. However, these decisions to take risks are not just individual decisions but are influenced by peers and relatives (Belloni 2019, 32–33).

The identification of dead migrant bodies—or more accurately, the low success rate of identification efforts—and the uncertainty that the families of those who have disappeared cope with have also recently gained scholarly attention (M'charek and Casartelli 2019; Kobelinsky 2020). A project focusing on the documentation of border deaths found that almost two-thirds of the people found dead at southern EU borders from 1990 to 2013 have not been identified by the local authorities charged with investigating their deaths (Last 2015). In a social sense, their death is not complete, and their families live on in an ambiguous state of uncertainty—in legal, social, and psychological terms (Boss 1999; Robins 2010). Between death and life, there is disappearance (Schindel 2020; Distretti 2020), and through raising the framework of disappearance, scholars have added a transnationalized dimension to deaths at the European border. The term *disappearance* creates an association with conflicts, protests, and the struggle for justice elsewhere, namely, with *desaparecidos* in Latin America. It directs attention to the families of the disappeared and, in doing so, helps to reveal how states often treat migrant deaths and disappearances differently than those involving Europeans. This perspective of disappearance illuminates how border deaths, more than a humanitarian issue, are a human rights concern.

This book follows on from the existing rich scholarship on border deaths by paying close attention to what happens to those who witness the disaster either in person or through mediation and to those who survive the death of another. While research on border deaths has proliferated in recent years and the generative force of bordering is highlighted in critical research, there is still little knowledge about the subjectivities that border deaths produce. My point of departure is one disaster and its aftermath, which I examine through two domains of the disaster's public afterlife: mediated representations and memorializations. My method of focusing on one disaster is explorative. The disaster has produced a kaleidoscope of afterlives, which take on different forms depending on the position of the witness: a variety of pasts and futures intersect in the present moment when people make meanings of the disaster. There is no single afterlife but a variety of afterlives. The variegated nature of the disaster requires an exploratory approach that allows me to identify the multiple practices, relationships, and subjectivities in the afterlives of the disaster. The issues raised in this in-depth exploration nonetheless resonate with the broader phenomenon of border deaths.

Afterlife and Survival

The domains of representation and memorialization constitute what I call an event's *afterlife*. In this book, the term refers not to life after death, but to the reappearance, continuation, or reanimation of an event, place, person, idea, or object. The use of the term *afterlife* to mean reappearance or reanimation can be traced to the 1910s and the art historian Aby Warburg's notion of *Nachleben*, which is translated as "afterlife" or "survival" (Didi-Huberman 2002). Warburg demonstrated how art and culture comprise an appropriation, circulation, and interpretation of earlier figures or themes. For example, he showed how antiquity reappears and lives on in later styles of art. Walter Benjamin (2009) built on Warburg's work in developing a related term, *Fortleben*, that has also been translated as "afterlife" in English. He argued that literary works have a life of their own and live on after publication as they transform and appear in different contexts, such as in translation. Benjamin's use of *Fortleben* refers to a complete artwork, a literary text. In contrast, a disaster is never complete and does not live on or transform in the same way a complete work might. In the case of the Lampedusa disaster, there is not even a shared understanding of how such a deadly disaster could occur so close to a strategic, militarized island.

In his book *Forms of Talk*, Erving Goffman presented the idea of a "referential afterlife" (1981, 46). His conceptualization of afterlife emphasizes shared understanding and cultural resonance as important qualifiers for being able to give rise to an afterlife. Further, he adds the aspect of limited temporality, the period in which an event can make sense to those who share the same communicative space. For example, when writing about self-correction, Goffman says:

> Once a gaffe of some kind has been made, it can have a referential after-life of considerable duration; an hour or a day later, when topic and context give some assurance that those present will be able to understand what incident is being referred to, the speaker in passing can gratuitously inject an ironic allusion, showing that chagrin has been sustained, which demonstration reaches back a goodly distance for its referent. (Goffman 1981, 46)

This short quote references both the contextual resonance and the temporality of an afterlife: the referential power of an event has limited duration and can therefore fade away. Nevertheless, the memory of an event may be actively sustained. Diana Taylor (2003) differentiates between two kinds of technologies to sustain cultural memory: the repertoire and the archive (Taylor 2003). Archival memory exists as apparently enduring material, such as texts, photographs, documents, and objects. Repertoire, on the other hand, is embodied memory and knowledge that is enacted through forms such as orality and dance. While archival memory might seem more enduring, it can be destroyed, manipulated, or controlled in more straightforward ways than embodied memory. Rituals such as commemorative ceremonies are part of a repertoire that transmits memory and shapes the afterlife of the event being commemorated.

In response to Goffman's idea of a referential afterlife, Gary Alan Fine and Terence Mcdonnell (2007) argue that an event may leave traces that can be rediscovered, though the period of shared recollection has passed. They analyze such traces in the domain of law, which Taylor would categorize as archival memory. However, repertoires can also transmit unacknowledged or hidden traces. The origins of a ritual may be investigated after the original referential connection has faded. In both cases, what matters is the motivation to find and interpret those referential connections. In their analysis, Fine and Mcdonnell (2007) argue that for a memory of an event to be rediscovered, the event must be meaningful for the memory entrepreneurs who engage with its traces. The event needs to resonate culturally and be relevant to a group's collective identity in the present.

My use of the term *afterlife* takes three important premises from this literature. First, the *life* in the term *afterlife* implies that events, objects, places, memories, people, and stories live on: they do not remain the same and are not merely replicated, but continue on as life does, undergoing transformation and change. This is central to surviving the disaster or the death of a loved one, and to the disaster's memory in the public domain. The disaster's meaning continues to transform, depending on who engages with its representation and memorialization, and on where and when they do so. There is a certain, finite period when a disaster can function as a referent, Goffman would argue. Nevertheless, the technologies of collective memory—Taylor's archive and repertoire—can extend referential afterlives or can help people to reconnect after a period of forgetting.

Second, events revive or survive oblivion because engaging with them is meaningful for the people who make sense of them in a new context, temporal or otherwise. This is central to memories' recovery after their referential afterlife (Fine and Mcdonnell 2007). An agent is involved in this process, such as Benjamin's translator, whose transformation of a literary work indicates the work's *Fortleben* stage, or Warburg's artist, who is "an organ of social memory" (Warburg 1999, 715). In this transformation, some meaning may be lost while new meaning is added. In an event's afterlife, select parts or qualities of the event live on, while others may be ignored or forgotten.

The third important insight is that the notion of afterlife references the actuality of a distinct past in the present. In this sense, the concept of afterlife contains an immediate paradox because death at Europe's borders is an ongoing occurrence. While this one, singular disaster—the disaster of October 3, 2013—can be conceived of as an event that has afterlives, the phenomenon of border deaths has continued.

The problem of understanding afterlife as something that exists once the precipitating event or condition has definitively concluded is discussed by Susana Draper (2012) in her analysis of the transformation of Latin American cities in the transition from dictatorship to neoliberal freedom. Draper traces how dictatorship continues to speak in places and spaces under neoliberalism; the presence of dictatorship is not completely gone in a "post-dictatorship" society. Similarly, Saidiya Hartman (2007, 6) conceptualizes the continuation of limited life chances in Black communities in the United States as the "afterlife of slavery." My position, which sees afterlife as the continuation of an event, is similar to Draper's and Hartman's uses of the term. Like the memory of dictatorship in Latin America, the Lampedusa disaster can draw forth other pasts, allowing them to emerge in the public domain. I will discuss how Italy's colonial rule in Eritrea, the history of Italian emigration, and earlier deadly borders of Europe, such as the Berlin Wall, reappear as specters in the representations and memorializations of the Lampedusa disaster.

In addition, other scholars have pointed out that people's actions can be shaped by the idea that the present may come to haunt the future, as Adam's (2010) notion of the present as the future's past suggests. That the present is haunted by past incidents reminds us of the possibility that the disaster could become a "ghostly matter" (Gordon 2008): the social forces that produce the murderous border today may continue to haunt societies in the future. Those who engage with the disaster's memory may do so for the sake of how their actions will be judged in the future. They imagine the afterlife of *la strage di Lampedusa* unfolding in front of them and act accordingly.

Analyzing the afterlives of the disaster brings attention to several aspects of survival: how survivors *continued their lives*, how other people touched by the disaster *survived the rupture* in their own lives, and how relatives and friends of the victims *survived their loved ones*. This book develops the concept of survival to rethink border deaths beyond the structures and processes that produce the murderous border and constitute the focus of critical migration studies. It demonstrates how the process of survival transforms people and societies—survival is productive. There is no return to what was before. The participation in a common world of those who survived the disaster at Europe's border, as well as public awareness of the deaths of its victims, can lead to new subjectivities. The people most intimately affected by the disaster have continued their lives in Europe. As the story of Adhanom in the beginning of this book illustrates, the survivors and relatives of the victims are the neighbors, friends, and coworkers of other Europeans, and their memories of what they went through have spread to the communities in which they live. Survivors have started families, and though their children have been born in Europe, they are affected by what their parents went through.

The perspective of survival therefore adds an important temporal aspect to border deaths—it demonstrates that the present will one day be the future's past (Adam 2010). This awareness of temporality allows us to imagine possible futures, potentially prompting a vision of a convivial future society: a society shared by both those whose governments created the border and those who managed to cross it. Further, we anticipate that in the future, others may examine and judge the present, just as we currently examine the violent events of the past. The specters haunting the present are not only from the past but also from the future.

The cognizance of the future that the notion of survival entails resonates with theories of haunting. In social theory, haunting is understood as repressed or unresolved inequality, oppression, or social violence coming into view. In Avery Gordon's (2008) terms, a "ghostly matter" is an issue that was supposed to be over and done with but instead comes alive and requires corrective action. This "something-to-be-done" aspect (Gordon 2008, xvii) of haunting opens a view to the future. Haunting is not only about the past's reappearance in the present but also a demand to transform the future. Haunting creates an awareness that the present can give rise to ghosts who will reappear to future generations.

Jacques Derrida's (1994) understanding of haunting is also directed to the future, although his understanding of specters is more ambiguous than Gordon's. In Derrida's hauntology, a specter does not return to deliver a message or reveal a secret, as Colin Davis (2007, 88) points out. For Derrida, haunting is a productive opening of meaning: "a structural openness or address directed towards the living by the voices of the past or the not-yet formulated possibilities of the future" (Davis 2007, 13).

The analysis of different types of witnesses in this book shows that those who engage with the disaster are haunted by specters of the past or the future. They *bear witness*, which in addition to seeing something means actively taking responsibility and acting on that basis (Durham Peters 2001; Felman 2000; Tait 2011). Something needs to be done. Certainly, there are people who do not engage with the disaster's memory for one reason or another, who might have *seen* but do not *bear witness*. As my method is to follow the afterlives of the disaster in the public domain of representations and memorializations, these positions are outside the scope of this study.

Civil Imagination and Citizenship

Citizenship studies provides a basis for analyzing and theorizing the identities and subject positions generated by border deaths in the public domain. Researchers on irregular migration have theorized various forms of resistance and contestation through the framework of citizenship—taken not as a status, but as acts and practices of belonging to the communities in which they live, regardless of formal status (McNevin 2011; Hegde 2016, 24–26). Different forms of citizenship emerge through visible "acts of citizenship" (Isin and Nielsen 2008), events through which subjects resist their positioning as outsiders and constitute themselves as citizens, as well as more processual practices people use to correct failures in state responsibilities.

Citizenship understood as constitutive acts or practices is citizenship constituted in a relationship: between an individual or a social group and the state, between an individual and a social group or community, or between people. These relationships are interconnected, mutually constitutive, and changing. In the context of border deaths, as this book will demonstrate, different forms of citizenship are constituted at the scales of individuals, communities, states, and the European Union.

Relational citizenship (Pols 2016; Reineke 2022; M'charek and Casartelli 2019) between people is constituted in different forms, often when the state fails in its responsibilities. Following the Lampedusa disaster, different types of witnesses constituted various forms of relational citizenship. Throughout the book, I explore how civic engagement, based on attentiveness to the particularities of the disaster, to the dead as individuals or *persons-as-such* (Edkins 2011), and to the victims' living relatives, constituted a relational citizenship of attentiveness. In addition, attentiveness to one's own self-interest or "capacity to do harm" (Nguyen 2016, 73) emerged in the research as crucial for a citizenship with the transformative potential to move beyond the oppressive structures that produce border deaths.

These relational forms of citizenship develop between living individuals who are mutually engaged in a relationship, but the living can also constitute a civil relationship with the dead, as researchers participating in forensic initiatives to identify dead migrants in Italy (M'charek and Casartelli 2019) and at the US-Mexico border (Reineke 2022) have argued. These forms of citizenship transgress boundaries such as citizen/noncitizen and in-group/out-group (see, e.g., Rygiel 2014; 2016; Stierl 2016), and as I argue in chapters 1 and 4, require a capacity to imagine conviviality in which strangers are part of the same world—a capacity for what Ariella Azoulay (2012) terms "civil imagination." Some forms of relational citizenship are likely typical in disaster situations. For example, writing of early 1900s disasters in the US-Canada borderlands, Jacob A. C. Remes (2016) theorizes the solidarity between working class survivors of the Salem Fire of 1914 and Halifax Explosion of 1917 as "disaster citizenship."

All of the forms of citizenship that I analyze in this book are to some extent conditional. Italian prime minister Enrico Letta granted posthumous citizenship to the victims of the Lampedusa disaster (Ansa 2013), but that was merely a symbolic act of benevolence. None of the rights that come with formal citizenship status were granted to the dead (or through them, to their relatives). Quite the opposite, even relatives who had formal citizenship in Sweden, Germany, or other European countries were not treated as full citizens in respect to their rights to decide on the burial of their dead relatives. Some survivors and relatives of the victims contested the ways in which not only European states, but also their country of origin, Eritrea, treated them. For example, in chapter 7, I discuss survivor citizenship, a position from which survivors made political claims against both the Eritrean regime and European states. They contested Eritrea's refusal to commemorate the victims, and by calling on the memories of the dead, they demanded the rights of refugees on the move. In chapter 9, I discuss forensic citizenship, which opens the possibility of contesting the lack of rights afforded to the dead and the victims' relatives. These citizenship positions of contestation are nevertheless conditioned by gender norms and expectations of acceptable refugeeness. They are also very much conditioned by the diasporic community and the citizenship developed in relation to the state they left, Eritrea. Diasporic citizenship shapes and conditions the constitution of civil agency in the afterlives of the disaster among survivors and relatives of the victims.

They Left Eritrea, but Eritrea Did Not Leave Them

Almost everyone in the boat sailing for Lampedusa had roots in Eritrea, a multiethnic country in the Horn of Africa. This creates a specific context for the disaster and its afterlives. Some of the people had made their journey from Eritrea over the course of a couple of months, but others had spent longer periods, even years, as UNHCR-recognized refugees in Sudan or Ethiopia. Understanding the context of Eritrea—why people leave the country, and the origins of the conflicts that drive mobility—is relevant to understanding the disaster and its afterlives. In addition, it is necessary to know how survivors and relatives of victims in Europe are still conditioned by the state they left and by Eritrean diasporas in Europe, both "old" and "new." They may have left Eritrea, but Eritrea has not left them. In this section, I provide the necessary background related to Eritreans' mobility and diasporic condition.

The Eritrean diaspora is considerable in relation to the country's population of about 3.5 million: at least a third of all Eritreans have migrated to other countries. In Europe, the highest numbers of Eritrean refugees are in Germany, Switzerland, Sweden, the Netherlands, the United Kingdom, and Norway (UNHCR 2021). However, Europe is often not the first destination from which Eritreans seek protection: 34 percent of those interviewed by UNHCR in Italy in 2017 had sought international protection before arriving in Italy, and 57 percent had stayed in refugee camps in Ethiopia or Sudan. However, these places had not provided sufficient security or prospects for a meaningful life for those who decided to risk their lives on a people smugglers' route to Libya and across the Central Mediterranean to Italy. Many of those arriving in Italy (in 2017, 64 percent of men and 84 percent of women interviewed by UNHCR) have close family already living in Europe (UNHCR 2019, 26).

In Eritrea, the two main religious groups, Muslims and Orthodox Christians, are equal in number, but among migrants who reach Europe, there are more Christians. In Europe, Eritreans work mainly in the service sector: in health care and elderly care, cleaning, restaurants, and as bus and taxi drivers (Ayalew Mengiste 2018; Mohammad 2021, 41). Diasporic communities are central in people's everyday lives, and friends and spouses are usually found among Eritreans. While there is a strong nationalism among Eritreans, the diaspora is nonetheless divided. Transnational diasporic online platforms have facilitated the construction of alternative perspectives on Eritrean history, politics, and identity (Bernal 2014, 47; Mohammad 2021). Religion, class, and ethnicity, as well as level of integration in the country of settlement constitute different Eritrean diasporic identities (Redeker Hepner 2009, 193). Political views about the Eritrean regime create major divisions in the Eritrean diaspora. However, people who have critical views about some aspects of the regime might at the same time support other aspects. For example, they might be against the open-endedness of the national service but praise Isaias Afwerki for foreign policy. Another division is between the old diaspora, people who left during the struggle for independence, and the new diaspora, those who left during the post-independence Isaias Afwerki regime. In addition, the Eritrean diaspora is diverse in terms of ethnicity, religion, and class. Migrants' new countries of settlement and attachment to them also shapes diasporic identities. Abdulkader Saleh Mohammad (2021, 44) argues that there has been an increase in ethnic and cultural minority identities among people in Eritrea and the Eritrean diaspora, and that this increase is a subtle protest against the majority ethnic group Tigrinyan's dominance in the Eritrean regime, secularism, and the lack of integration in host countries in Europe.

Present-day Eritrean refugee mobility has its roots in decades of repression, starting from the creation of the country as a result of Italian colonialization in 1890. Colonialism in Eritrea, first by Italy (1889–1941), then by the British military administration (1941–52), followed by Ethiopia (1952–91), ended with the defeat of the Ethiopian army in 1991 and a declaration of independence in 1993 after a popular referendum (Tronvoll and Mekonnen 2014, 4).

Italy had used its *Colonia Eritrea* for raw materials and as a source of colonial soldiers (Negash 1987). Nevertheless, Italy also introduced modern infrastructure and urban centers that resulted in a higher level of development in Eritrea compared to Ethiopia, which was not colonized (Bereketeab 2016, 18–19). After the Allied defeat of Mussolini's fascist Italy in 1941, the British military administration ruled the territory of Eritrea until the United Nations decided to submit to the demands of the Ethiopian Empire and federated Eritrea to Ethiopia in 1952. Ethiopia justified the federation on the basis of cultural, ethnic, historical, and geographical affiliations (Bereketeab 2016, 1–2). However, the UN never secured the establishment of any federal institutions.

Armed resistance to Ethiopia began to form in Eritrea, first as the Eritrean Liberation Front (ELF) in 1961. In 1962, Ethiopia annexed Eritrea as a province. The Eritrean People's Liberation Front (EPLF), a left-wing nationalist group, split from ELF in 1970 and led the resistance. At this time, the liberation struggle gained force, and intellectuals and students, including those in diaspora, began to support the guerilla war. During the various phases of thirty years of armed resistance in Eritrea, there were internal conflicts among the resistance. EPLF was led by Isaias Afwerki, who became Eritrea's first president after independence in 1993. EPLF transformed into People's Front for Democracy and Justice (PFDJ) in 1994, and this continues to be the only legal political party in Eritrea.

During the liberation struggle, Eritreans had formed a unified nationalism under the idea of "the common good," in which individual interests were sacrificed for independence, and despite internal conflicts, ethnic, political, and religious differences were suppressed in what Eritreans perceived as a "just war" against Ethiopian rulers (Kahsay 2022; Plaut 2016). However, the intolerance of diverse views maintained by Eritreans during the war has continued since independence (Bereketeab 2016).

The Eritrean strategy in the liberation struggle was self-reliance, not depending on Cold War superpowers, but Eritrean fighters did make tactical alliances with Ethiopian rebel movements and, at times, with other states in the region, such as Somalia and Sudan (Weldemichael 2013, 287). Neither the United Nations nor the Organization of African Unity (since 2002, the African Union) showed sympathy to the Eritrean cause; the organizations refrained from seeing the situation as colonialism (Reid 2009; Bereketeab 2016, 18–19; Bereketeab 2009, 117). Ethiopia had gained clout on the African continent and in the international arena, particularly as it was the only African country that had not been a European colony. Finally, the weakening and collapse of the Soviet Union, which had been arming Ethiopia, made a referendum for the independence of Eritrea possible (Weldemichael 2013, 191, 287).

Soon after independence, in 1998–2000, Eritrea and Ethiopia fought a border war over disputed territory, including the town of Badme. The conflict continued at a stalemate, and the Isaias regime used the fighting to justify the continuation of the country's state of exception. Military training is now compulsory for everyone, and after six months most Eritreans between the ages of eighteen and forty-seven (for women) or fifty-four (for men) are obligated to take part in open-ended national service either in the military or in the civil sector (Home Office 2021). This is, according to human rights organizations, forced labor (Human Rights Watch 2021; Kibreab 2009). Mandatory national service is the main reason young people leave Eritrea (Kahsay 2022, 422).

In 2018, Ethiopia's new prime minister, Abiy Ahmed, offered peace to Eritrea, and as a result, the UN Security Council also lifted sanctions against Eritrea. However, Ethiopian forces did not leave Badme until 2021, after the Eritrean armed forces had fought alongside the Ethiopian army against the Tigray People's Liberation Front in the Tigray region of Ethiopia. Despite the 2018 peace agreement, the UN special rapporteur for the situation of human rights in Eritrea concluded in 2022 that there had been no improvement in Eritrea regarding human rights and that the Eritrean army had extended their human rights violations beyond Eritrea's borders during the fighting in Ethiopia (Kahsay 2022).

In the struggle for Eritrean independence, the diaspora was central in funding and supporting the armed resistance. Sending money to EPLF and raising awareness of the conflict were important activities in the diaspora across the world. When the referendum for independence was held, the liberating forces made sure that the diaspora population was involved and would continue its formal attachment to the new nation. The diaspora politics of common sacrifice that had been formed during the liberation struggle continued as a strategy of the Eritrean state.

Through its embassies, the Eritrean state continues to govern the diaspora—people who are, in fact, often citizens of other countries. Eritreans are expected to and often coerced into paying 2 percent of their income to the Eritrean government as Recovery and Rehabilitation Tax, a general "diaspora tax." This is calculated on the basis of Eritreans' tax returns in the countries where they live and earn money. Eritrea does not recognize the renunciation of Eritrean citizenship, and while diasporic Eritreans use their citizenship in their country of residence for all other travel, they can simultaneously hold Eritrean identity cards that permit them to enter the country without a visa. The use of consular and other services, and access to some social events depend on paying the tax, which many Eritreans, nevertheless, refuse to do (DSP 2017.) Some Eritreans in diaspora fear that their relatives in Eritrea can be discriminated against if they do not pay, for instance, by restricting access to remittances (DSP 2017, 13). Sacrificial citizenship, "the social contract between Eritreans and the state in which the citizen's role is to serve the nation and sacrifice themselves for the survival and well-being of the nation" (Bernal 2014, 33), reflected in the (presently indefinite) national service, extends to financial sacrifice for those living in diaspora.

The discourse of national sacrifice also produces the idea of "traitors"—those who do not participate in the national struggle. People who flee Eritrea and seek asylum in another country are in the eyes of the regime seen as traitors, which shapes refugees' subjectivities as they build new lives and networks (Tronvoll and Mekonnen 2014, 119; Mohammad 2021, 45). The regime has had a "shoot to kill" policy at the border targeting those who attempt to leave the country without documents (Keetharuth 2013, 9; Kahsay 2022, 422). Nevertheless, those "traitors" who have not been actively involved in oppositional politics abroad can make amends in the eyes of the regime by signing a "letter of regret" and paying the regime 2 percent of the income they have earned since exiting the country (DSP 2017, 13; EASO 2019, 9).

European countries have tried to collaborate with Eritrea, particularly in recent years, to prevent the irregular arrival of refugees in Europe, even at the cost of truly supporting human rights. Martin Plaut (2016, 86–101) documents a number of incidents in which the European Union and individual nation-states have made compromises regarding human rights in Eritrea. Nevertheless, Eritrea's continuous human rights violations against citizens who desert the national service or engage in oppositional politics prevents the European Union from deporting people to Eritrea. The asylum acceptance rate for Eritreans is among the highest in Europe at about 90 percent (Eurostat 2017; EASO 2021).

Human rights violations against individuals who oppose the regime, desert the national service, or belong to religious minorities have been widely documented and reported by human rights organizations, European Parliament, and the United Nations. The Eritrean regime's systematic violations of human rights include extrajudicial killings, enforced disappearances, arbitrary detention, torture, and lack of freedom of expression and assembly (United Nations Office of the High Commissioner for Human Rights 2019; see also Tronvoll and Mekonnen 2014, 169–78, 109–18; Höfner and Tewolde-Berhan 2017; Human Rights Watch 2018; Amnesty International 2021, 155–56). While multiple oppositional political groups, media outlets, and human rights activists voice alternative views outside Eritrea, large sections of the diaspora do not publicly acknowledge the regime's human rights violations. Some genuinely support the regime while others are afraid of the long arm of the Eritrean government, which may deny their right to embassy services, block access to Eritrea, or harm their relatives in Eritrea (Plaut 2016, 128–30; Mohammad 2021, 45).

Structure of the Book

I begin my examination of the representation of the events that took place in Lampedusa on October 3, 2013, by building the case for using the term *disaster* to describe the drowning of hundreds of people. The naming of an event is a central framing device that directs one's understanding when asking "what is it that is going on here," as Goffman (1972, 8) would put it. In naming events, certain explanations are made more appealing than others. I discuss how terms such as *shipwreck* or *tragedy* produce categorically different political and ethical registers than the Italian word *strage* (which translates as "massacre") or the English term *disaster*. With the use of these terms, certain responses and responsibilities become more likely than others. The way the disaster was framed prompted mediated spectators to engage with the disaster, and as chapter 2 demonstrates, representation and memorialization were the domains in which spectators could perform their compassion as resistance to indifference.

Chapter 2 examines the visual representation of the disaster, focusing on photographs that became iconic. Images of hundreds of coffins, arranged neatly in an airport hangar, appeared a few days after the disaster. These photographs demonstrated the massive number of fatalities and represented the very *presence of death*. The images created a spectacle out of the harmonious arrangement of coffins, which contradicted the imagery of unorganized masses of dead bodies in the sea that the public might expect. I demonstrate that there is an alternative to this dignified, yet depersonalized, visuality, a different visuality that represents the disaster not as the presence of death but as the *absence of life*. I trace two routes to this alternative representation: one in which family members and survivors of the Lampedusa disaster insert photographs of the dead into the mainstream media, and another in which journalists imaginatively read existing photographs. These methods visualized what the disaster had made absent: human beings with social lives and relationships. The methods were generated by a capacity for "civil imagination" and call on the public to imagine the world convivially.

I continue to engage with the complexity of representing both the massive scale of the disaster and the absence of individual lives in chapter 3. I contrast the dominant representation of the disaster—the enumeration of victims—with practices that emphasize the individuality and irreplaceability of each person. Representing the victims by listing their names and displaying their photographs is a means of making their number visible and comprehensible. After the Lampedusa disaster, the survivors compiled a list of victims' names. The list later enabled others to recite and visualize victims' names in art, rituals, and memorials. The labor of compiling this list of names was the survivors' first act of *survivor citizenship*, a concept I develop in chapter 7. This subjectification of the victims, carried out by survivors, was an act of "civic forensics," a form of civil agency and belonging that asserts the right to identification and nondisappearance. Another critical means to counter the distancing and sanitizing representation produced by enumeration is to select one name to represent the entire group of victims. While 366 are too many to know and remember one by one, it is possible to remember one individual. In the Lampedusa disaster, the name of one young woman, Yohanna, often stands in for all of the victims.

After these three chapters that consider the critical potential of representations and the problematics of generalities and particularities, I turn to analyzing memorialization, both memorializing "others" and memorializing "one's own." The next three chapters focus on how "others" are memorialized; the people who initiated the memorials and rituals examined here did not have a personal relationship with the victims, nor were the victims members of their community or citizens of their country. By examining select instances of memorialization at the local, national, and European scale, I ask who memorializes, and how and why.

What functions do the different forms of memorialization have for identities, politics, and societies? Survival in this context refers to the experience of living on after an event that disrupts the social and moral order of things. The people I discuss in this section are either eyewitnesses or mediated witnesses of the disaster and its consequences. It is a different kind of a survival than surviving the disaster or the death of a loved one—such experiences connect with memorializing "one's own" and form the core of the third part of the book.

In chapter 4, I examine how Sicilians responded to the disaster with memorializing and why some of them "adopted" the dead into their community by creating memorials and performing burial rituals. Three hundred sixty-six dead bodies were transported from Lampedusa to be buried in several different cemeteries in Sicily. In some communities, locals cared for the graves and created memorials in their cemeteries. I examine how cemeteries can be seen as communicative spaces where community and identity are performed. In the context of border deaths, they can also function as spaces where a new kind of civil sphere is created through encounters between locals and the relatives of victims who mourn at victims' graves. This transcultural sphere facilitates the challenging of established certainties, such as the nation-state and borders, and serves as a space in which anticipated distinctions such as citizen/noncitizen, kin/non-kin, and in-group/out-group are transgressed.

In chapter 5, I discuss how Lampedusans memorialized the disaster after the dead were taken away and buried in Sicily. This chapter, like the previous one, focuses on those who eye-witnessed the materiality of the unknown dead bodies, either directly or in their coffins. Lampedusans have created two memorials to remember the disaster's victims, while also making an intervention into the memory politics of border deaths and migration politics more generally. In doing so, they have further contributed to the public imagery of the island as an iconic representation of Europe's border.

In chapter 6, I expand my analysis of memorials and commemorations from islands in the Mediterranean Sea to the national scale in Italy and beyond, to the scale of Europe. I examine why the Italian Parliament and Senate established October 3 as the National Day of Remembrance for the Victims of Immigration in 2016. I also discuss how some members of the European Parliament in Brussels have memorialized the day in order to raise the issue of border deaths as a European concern. In addition, I return to a particular local scale of memorialization, discussing how the disaster's memory resonates with anti-fascist activists in Dresden, Germany, prompting them to commemorate deaths that happened thousands of miles away. Analysis of memory politics at these more distant scales of the afterlives of the disaster shows how specters from the past and the future shape the meaning of the disaster and responses to it, not only in the border zone but also beyond it. Depending on the context of memorialization, other borders and contestations of borders in the past, such as the Berlin Wall, Italian labor migration, and anti-fascist Italian exiles haunt the present understanding of border deaths.

While the common understanding is that memorializing of border deaths emerges in response to a lack of memorialization—in other words, to the public "ungrievability" (Butler 2009) of the victims—my analysis shows that memorializations are instead often prompted by other memorials and rituals: people often respond to how others remember dead strangers. Memorials attract rituals, and rituals may elicit a need to create longer-lasting memorials. These three chapters also demonstrate that memorializing strangers in public has a purpose and significance for the communities that remember—often more so than for the victims and their families. I show that memorializing the Lampedusa disaster has served two functions: one therapeutic, to help cope with having witnessed mass death and its aftermath (often through mediation); and the other instrumental, to make a political point or to create community.

While rituals and memorials in Lampedusa, Sicily, and beyond were mainly tailored for European publics, they nevertheless increased the capacity of survivors and families of the victims to memorialize in a way that was more public and political than would have otherwise been feasible. Therefore, to conclude my discussion of the public memorialization of border deaths with a criticism of Eurocentric interests would not do justice to what survivors and relatives of the victims have done within the commemorative sphere.

The last three chapters examine a different scale of remembering: that of survivors and victims' relatives in the context of Eritrean diaspora. By examining memorializing from the perspective of a minority ("Eritrean Europeans"), I move beyond the previous chapters' focus on the commemorative performances of the majority ("Europeans") and how they constitute subjectivities in relation to border deaths to a refugee-centered perspective that acknowledges the creative agency, hopes, and politics of refugees. Chapter 7 argues for a *survivor citizenship*, an identity of survivorship created by making political, moral, and social claims in the context of memorializing. However, the afterlife of the disaster, like life itself, has been complex and sometimes contradictory. Through their actions, survivors both unsettle and affirm the expectations of the majority, and both refute and uphold European attempts to define the public meanings of the disaster. They also negotiate a complex form of diasporic citizenship in both refuting and upholding the expectations of diasporic communities and the Eritrean regime, the long arm of which reaches them even in exile.

Chapter 8 goes deeper into the process of survival through analyzing interviews with those who survived the disaster. I discuss what survival means for the survivors and how some of them draw on the legacy of the victims to actively and ethically participate in the world. These experiences shape survivor citizenship. In addition, I examine mediated experiences of survival in literature and film. For example, when border-crossers return to Lampedusa, the place where their state of survival started, they make visible how survivors have proceeded from the position of victim by actively participating in the world around them.

Relatives of the victims are featured in most chapters, as they have an important critical role in both representations and memorializations. Their relationship with the victims makes the humanity of the dead understandable. Chapter 9, however, centers the victims' relatives, whose mourning and memorialization practices, though intimate, nevertheless take place in a mediated everyday life. The chapter demonstrates how digitally mediated memorialization blurs the distinctions between private and public, local and global, planned and spontaneous, and formal and vernacular. I examine how digital media practices shape transnational relationships in the specific context of border deaths and disappearances. As the sister of one victim told me, surviving the death of a loved one in these specific circumstances is not the same as surviving a death with a different cause. This chapter shows the distinct ambiguity of border deaths, which can be attributed to two interwoven elements: uncertainties related to the body and death rituals, and uncertainties deriving from the context of migration.

The concluding chapter brings together the main arguments on how the afterlives form and generate survival through an examination of the public life of one survivor, Kebrat, and her engagement with representations and memorializations. The reappearance of various versions of her story in cultural productions—theater, literature, and music—has created a public platform from which she speaks for the cause of refugees and constitutes a survivor citizenship. Her platform is nevertheless conditional: she negotiates how she will insert the issues that are important to her into the public domain.

Taken together, the book's three parts—representation, memorializing "others," and memorializing "one's own"—present a holistic analysis of the afterlife of one of the most mediatized migrant disasters in Europe. The Lampedusa disaster is but one of thousands, and yet the continuation of its memory in the public domain in representations and memorializations makes it specific. The disaster has come to symbolize the present era of the bordering of Europe—a time in which the natural forces of the sea are being used by Europe in its attempts to shield its territory. Letting people die has become a means of creating Europe.

The stories in this book feature people and communities across Europe who have refused to remain bystanders in this constellation of bordering, in which they witness the spectacle of mass death in person or through mediation. The Lampedusa disaster disrupted and disrupts their world and what they consider a normal order of things. They act in response, in order to survive the rupture, in order to live on in a shared world that has revealed its inequality. This book brings their thoughts and actions into conjunction with those most intimately touched by the disaster—those who survived the disaster or the death of a loved one. In considering both of these positions, I underline how the perspective of survival can envision a way forward from the horrific present, which is not sustainable. It illuminates both the temporal and the social dimension in which allowing the death of migrants happens. Those who survive a disaster at Europe's border, and their children, are or become members of the societies that have so determinedly tried to prevent their cohabitation. They are Europeans, in the very essence of the idea. They have family and friends across the continent and vivid memories of different parts of Europe. They regularly travel from their new homes in Northern Europe to Europe's external border zone in the South to visit memorial sites and remember those whom Europe's borders killed, and in doing so, they create and maintain relationships among themselves and with others who refuse to be bystanders. They create a new transcultural civil sphere and constitute new subjectivities as they navigate and sometimes contest expectations from diaspora, Eritrean state, and Europe. This book examines these relationalities and considers their transformative potential. Afterlives of a disaster shape the life of the living—those who continue to make the world.

WORDS

Alessandro Marino: "*Capitaneria*, we are in the middle of the sea facing Tabaccara. Guys, come immediately, there are five hundred people in the water. *Clandestini* [illegals] are telling us that there are five hundred people in the water."
Coast Guard: "Yes, received, *Gamar*. You need to tell me if it is a boat or a rubber dinghy. Motorboat *Gamar*, this is *Capitaneria* of Lampedusa, do you receive me?"
Alessandro Marino: "Look, we're rescuing. Guys, there are plenty of people in the water."

(Emergency call, October 3, 2013)

The panicky voice of a primary eyewitness, Lampedusan Alessandro Marino, in his phone call to the Harbor Master in Lampedusa, communicated the first recorded depiction of the scene. In the call, Marino does not name the event.[1] What he sees are "plenty of people in the water," "Five hundred persons in the water." The people in need of rescue are not yet framed as victims nor have they become survivors—they are *persone* ("people" and "persons"), and *clandestini* ("illegals"). Human beings are about to die in front of the caller's eyes, and, therefore, they are in immediate need of rescue. It is impossible to ignore what is happening or turn away at that moment; these people must be rescued. Marino does not seek the *capitaneria*'s permission to rescue, in fact, his friends are rescuing as he is calling. There is a sense of urgency—he has no time to answer the question "is it a boat or a rubber dinghy?" and say that the boat is nowhere to be seen.

The lack of distance is the key to the relationship of rights and duties in this scene. Marino sees drowning persons with his own eyes and is able to reach and help some of them. This conjunction of knowing about the disaster and the possibility of acting at the scene defines the situation as one in which involvement is not only possible but necessary. He calls the coast guard while his friends rescue those they can reach.

It is "the necessity inherent in the situation" (Boltanski 1999, 9) that applies in the event that Marino encounters. The necessity prompts people to help in a situation they have chanced upon, even if they had not wished to be in that situation. Political, religious, and general motives are not important in situations defined by such an immediate closeness to death. Marino rescues and calls for help although he names the people in need of help *clandestini*, illegals. It does not matter whether their being there is justified or legal. It does not matter what Marino's political views on migration might be. If they had not intervened in the scene, Marino and others would have violated Article 98 of the United Nations Convention of the Law of the Sea (UN 1982). While under international law they had a duty to rescue (Pusterla 2020, 4), they risked violating domestic laws that criminalized facilitating entry of immigrants (Basaran 2014, 375–76). The drowning people had a right to be rescued, but only because the crew of *Gamar* was nearby. This right follows from their universal right to life under both international human rights law and European law (Mann 2020, 605–7). However, Vito Fiorino (2017), the owner of the leisure boat *Gamar* who was with Marino and six others that night, emphasized several times to me in an interview that when they chanced upon the disaster the group of friends did not debate whether or not to pull the drowning people to their boat. They acted spontaneously, Fiorino said. The necessity inherent in the situation guided their action.

While making the emergency call, Marino does not have a name for the event that he describes as "plenty of people in the water." The only clue that he gives to the coast guard is the word *clandestini*, which opens up a space of shared understanding what the situation is about. The naming of the event comes later, and at a distance. Naming events is one central device through which people make sense of the world. They select and elevate some aspects of what they perceive and make them more salient; they frame events and situations. Erving Goffman in *The Presentation of Self in Everyday Life* maintained that when people come to situations they look for clues that help them to contextualize and interpret what is going on (Goffman 1990, 1). This interpretation is largely based on their previous knowledge, and it is culturally shared. The term *clandestini* is a clue that prompts the coast guard's question "is it a boat or a rubber dinghy?"

By naming events, people make certain reasoning devices more appealing than others, devices that explain the causes of the event and the possible solutions. Other devices that characterize a discourse are images, symbols, and metaphors. Theorists of media framing, such as William A. Gamson and Andre Modigliani (1989), have argued that competing discourses evolve and transform over time around any relevant policy issue. Frames are organizing ideas of a discourse, and the media is a central field where framings evolve. Journalists, photographers, political and religious leaders, activists, and other public figures frame events, interpreting them to the public. The media's and their sources' naming of what happened at sea near Lampedusa on October 3, 2013, conveys how the different agents gave salience to certain causes and responses and produced certain kinds of interpretative packages to understand death at the border. The different namings also highlight or hide certain figures and actors in the scene more than others. The construction and visibility of these figures is connected to the naming of the event.

Naufragio, tragedia, strage

The disaster became a key event in the Italian media: it was high on the news agenda and shaped the coverage of immigration news in general for a while (Zerback et al. 2020). The Italian media defined the disaster by using three terms in particular: *naufragio, tragedia,* and *strage*—terms that evoke different emotional, moral, and political registers. *Naufragio*, shipwreck, is the most neutral term. A ship—an object, a thing—has sunk. *Tragedia*, tragedy, assumes that there are emotions and affects involved in the event. It is unexpected, dramatic, catastrophic—an unfortunate event that is emotionally out of the ordinary. The emphasis is on the suffering. A shipwreck is certainly unfortunate, but it might be without great suffering. However, like shipwreck the term tragedy does not imply that there is necessarily an agent, a perpetrator. A shipwreck and a tragedy could be accidental whereas *strage*—massacre or carnage—implies there is a perpetrator. A massacre does not just happen but is made. In addition, a massacre necessarily has dead victims whereas a tragedy or a shipwreck could happen without a loss of life.

The disaster in Lampedusa came to be known as a *strage* in relation to four aspects—the place, the space, the date, and the category of victims: *strage di Lampedusa* (the place where it happened, e.g., *La Stampa*, October 6, 2013); *strage nel mare* (space where it happened: the sea, e.g., *Repubblica Bari*, October 5, 2013; Spagnolo 2013); *strage del 3 ottobre* (the date when it happened, e.g., *La Repubblica Palermo* October 12, 2013); and *strage di migranti* (the category of people who died: migrants, e.g., *La Stampa*, October 4, 2013; Galeazzi 2013). In addition, Giorgio Napolitano, the then president of the Republic, called the disaster "*strage di innocenti*" (Breda 2013), which is a biblical reference to the "massacre of innocents": Herod the Great's infanticide as reported in the Gospel of Matthew.

In Italian, *strage* is used to describe genocides and terrorist attacks but also natural catastrophes such as earthquakes. Central to the term is the intentional mass killing of humans or animals. In this sense, its dictionary definition is a synonym for *massacro*, which also translates as massacre in English. *Strage* would remind Italians of terrorist attacks such as the *strage di Bologna*, a neofascist bombing at the Bologna railway station on August 2, 1980, and another bomb attack known as *strage di piazza Fontana* of December 12, 1969, in Milan (Roghi 2020).

In both these disasters perpetrators were sought although in the latter case it took decades. Therefore, the choice of the term *strage* also implies that what happened was human-made like the other *stragi* had been. In the context of border deaths at sea the media had not used the term *strage* widely before the Lampedusa disaster. Nevertheless, it was not the first migrant boat disaster to be known as a *strage*. The sinking of a ship carrying at least 283 migrants on the night of December 25–26, 1996, near Portopalo of Sicily is known as *strage di Natale*, the Christmas Massacre or *strage di Portopalo* (Balzarotti and Miccolupi 2016).

The emergence of the word *strage* in common discourse in the context of border deaths reflects the period of the humanitarian-security nexus in Italian politics that began when Enrico Letta of the center-left Democratic Party became prime minister in April 2013. Letta's Catholic ethos replaced his predecessor Silvio Berlusconi's anti-migration rhetoric (Crawley et al. 2016, 69). An example of the general use of the term *strage* in the context of border deaths is the debate in the Italian Senate on May 24, 2016, when a number of senators used the term in reference to the October 3, 2013, disaster when discussing the bill to establish a Day of Remembrance to commemorate migrant dead. Laura Fasiolo of the Democratic Party, for example, called it the *"prima grande strage di Lampedusa,"* "the first big massacre of Lampedusa" and Salvatore Torrisi of the Popular Alternative referred to it as *"strage dei 366 migranti,"* "massacre of 366 migrants" (Senato della Repubblica 2016).

The common usage of the term *strage* characterizes the brief window of a more humanitarian approach in bordering—a policy and practice that oscillates between humanitarianism and securitizing (Cuttitta 2018a and b). In 2018, when the right-wing Lega politician Matteo Salvini became minister of the interior, criminalization of civil rescue in the Mediterranean Sea became one of the government's trademarks (Caccia, Heller, and Mezzadra 2020).

Rebeca Andreina Papa (2014) has observed that the Italian media—across different political leanings—had in 2013 begun to represent migrants as victims rather than threats. Reporting of the Lampedusa disaster, the Italian mainstream media, she argues, replaced the previously commonly used terms *clandestini* and *immigranti*, illegals and immigrants, with terms that shifted attention to the right to seek protection: *richiedenti asilo* and *rifugiati*, asylum seekers and refugees (Andreina Papa 2014, 86). The framing of migrants as victims was common also in the German and Belgian media's coverage of the disaster (Zerback et al. 2020, 759). The media in Italy framed those crossing the border by boats as victims of the conditions they had fled, and of the Italian and European immigration and border policies. Among media sources that emphasized the role of Italy in the disaster was the Congolese-born minister of integration at the time, Cécile Kyenge, who criticized Italian laws that criminalized irregular migration dating back to the Bossi-Fini law of 2002 and the Maroni "security package" of 2008 (Cetin 2015, 386; Polch 2013). The conditions in Eritrea—the country that almost all of the people in the boat originated from—were described in the Italian media in general terms of poverty and conflict rather than in detailed contextualization (Andreina Papa 2014).

The prevalence of the term *strage* in the Italian media can also be seen as a result of a professional conversation among scholars, activists, and some journalists about language use in migration-related reporting. Two of the major outcomes of these discussions are the Carta di Roma, a journalists' code of conduct signed in 2008 and the foundation of the Association of Carta di Roma in 2011 (Carta di Roma 2020; Bellu 2014). The journalists' association provides guidelines about responsible journalism related to immigration issues. It does not address the naming of migrant disasters and border deaths specifically but the Code of Ethics sensitizes journalists to the connotations of language use and the choice of words in relation to migration. Critical migration scholars in Italy, such as Gianluca Gatta, have also replaced *naufragio* and *tragedia* with *strage* in their academic and popular articles deliberately so that the border deaths would be conceived as produced phenomena instead of naturally occurring accidents (see, e.g., Gatta 2014; Vassallo Paleologo n. d.).

Vergogna, le parole de scusi

On October 3, 2013, Pope Francis—a major media figure in Italy and globally—called the disaster *vergogna*, disgrace, which was widely reported in the global media (Yardley and Povoledo 2013). The media across Europe picked up on the idea and highlighted terms that translate as shame, shameful, or disgrace in the headlines. The German *Süddeutsche Zeitung*'s headline on October 6 was: "*Europas Schande*," "Europe's shame." *Le Monde* titled its weekend front page on October 5, 2013 "*Lampedusa: l'indifférence coupable de l'Europe*," "Lampedusa: Europe's culpable indifference," which echoed the pope's speech during his first pastoral visit outside of Rome, in Lampedusa earlier that year, in July 2013. The pope had then used the phrase "globalizzazione dell'indifferenza," "globalization of indifference," in his address on border deaths (Pope Francis 2013b).

Vergogna and the English words shame and disgrace describe emotions. Someone feels ashamed or someone angrily accuses another person, as in "shame on you." The headlines in *Süddeutsche Zeitung* and *Le Monde* do not impose the feeling of shame on external others but include their readers among those who should feel ashamed. They do not see the disaster as having been caused by Italy or any other particular country but by Europe collectively. Importantly, such discourse constitutes an actor on the scene, Europe: a community that is able to do wrong but also one that can have emotions and take responsibility.

The pope's words, "It is a disgrace!" do not explicitly indicate any entity such as Europe or a group of people who should feel ashamed about the disaster. He spoke in the name of humanity, and he addressed everyone. "It is a disgrace! Let us pray together to God for those who lost their lives: men, women, children, for their relatives and for all refugees. Let us unite our efforts so that similar tragedies are not repeated! Only through the concerted collaboration of everyone can we help to prevent them" (Pope Francis 2013a). On the one hand, this all-encompassing definition of those who are responsible for the disgrace calls everyone to think of their own involvement. On the other, it does not distinguish between actors and therefore, when everyone is implicated, no one is specifically responsible. No one, necessarily, is a perpetrator.

However, the word "indifference" in the pope's ceremony in Lampedusa earlier in 2013 ("globalization of indifference") was again quoted in the news about the October 3 disaster (e.g., Galeazzi 2013), and that framing directs attention to a responsible figure—not an active perpetrator but an indifferent bystander who knows about mass deaths at the border and sees them happening (through mediation) but turns away from the suffering of others. The idea that indifference is globalized refers to the way in which migrant deaths at one border (Lampedusa) epitomize deaths at borders globally. The phrase "globalization of indifference" in relation to the October 3 disaster demands bystanders of border violence globally to take responsibility.

Italian prime minister Enrico Letta took the discourse of shame and disgrace politically further, to an (almost) apology. A video clip of his speech at the press conference in Lampedusa on the October 9, 2013, is titled on his website: "*A Lampedusa una tragedia immane, l'Italia chiede scusa*" (Letta 2013a). "A huge tragedy in Lampedusa, Italy asks for forgiveness." In Lampedusa, at a press conference alongside European leaders José Manuel Barroso, Cecilia Malmström, and Italian interior minister Angelino Alfano, Letta stated on October 9, 2013: "The words we have said to all those we have met in recent days are also the words of apology for the defaults of our country in respect to a tragedy like this and the tragedies that these events entail and have entailed" (Letta 2013b).

While the headline on Letta's webpage claims "Italy asks for forgiveness," he actually did not issue an apology. He did not perform an action. Letta did not say, for example: "Italy apologizes" or "I deliver the apology of the state." Instead, he interpreted what had been done and said by Italian leaders as *parole di scusi*, words of regret. He referred to three actions of the Italian government as *parole di scusi*: first, the national day of mourning that had been held on October 4, on the day of San Francesco, the patron saint of Italy; second, the visits to Lampedusa by the representatives of parliament and the government; and third, the state funeral to be held for the victims that he announced in the press conference. These actions, together with "the words we have said," were the *parole di scusi*, words of regret.

There is a crucial difference: apologetic discourse or gesture is not the same as an apology which is a speech act—words that sincerely perform an action (Austin 1975). An apology is directed at someone—someone asks to be forgiven and someone else accepts an apology. After the Grenfell tower fire that killed at least seventy-nine people in London in 2017, Prime Minister Theresa May apologized in the immediate aftermath of the fire: "That was a failure of the state—local and national—to help people when they needed it most. As Prime Minister, I apologize for that failure" (Murphy 2017). After the collapse of a motorway bridge in Genoa and the death of forty-three people in 2018, Italy organized a state funeral but did not apologize. The apology was expected from Atlantia, the company that maintained the bridge. It only apologized in 2020 for fear of losing its construction deals with the government. The apology then was directed to "the families of the victims and to all Italians" (Landini and Suzzi 2020).

Public apologies by a state are a recurring feature of historical justice movements (Neumann and Thompson 2015). Apologies for historical injustices are either followed up by corrective measures such as reparations or perceived to be an end in itself—done in lieu of material reparations. In state apologies for past wrongs, the core elements include definition of what has been wronged and to whom the apology is directed. Enrico Letta was not clear what exactly were the "defaults of our country" that the "words of regret" were aimed to correct (Letta 2013a). Nor did he seek an apology from a specific group of people, such as the victims' families and the survivors. In fact, the apology (if one interprets Letta's words as such) might as well have been directed to the Lampedusans or the Italian people who suffered as witnesses of mass death.

Even the actions that Letta interpreted as *parole di scusi* were not performed in the presence of those related to the victims. For example, the way in which the "state funeral" was organized in Agrigento, Sicily (which I examine in more detail in chapter 4) reflected a symbolic performance for Italians rather than a ritual that would have been meaningful for the survivors of the disaster or the surviving family members of the dead. Italian-based representatives of the Eritrean government—the regime that many people on the boat had fled—were invited to the official memorial ceremony. Diasporic human rights activists who oppose the regime protested their presence (Estefanos 2016). Against the wishes of survivors and many victims' families, the dead had already been buried in various cemeteries in Sicily, and without their relatives having been present. Even those family members who were among the survivors of the disaster were prevented from participating in the ceremony. Letta claimed the funeral was *"in una logica di compartecipazione a una sofferenza drammatica,"* "in a logic of sharing a dramatic suffering" (Letta 2013a). The logic of "a shared suffering" directed attention to the ones who share a dramatic emotion. It could have referred to the Lampedusans who filtered the shock and sadness created through witnessing of mass death through the media. They suffered on behalf of a European mediated audience as they performed their witness testimonies in the media (about media witnessing, see Frosh and Pinchevski 2008; 2014). Without mourners the massive dying at Europe's borders would have seemed disturbingly undignified. Nevertheless, relatives of the victims and survivors and their grief remained invisible.

Letta himself acted two important performances of *parole di scusi*. One was to symbolically grant Italian citizenship to the dead. On the national day of mourning, October 4, 2013, he declared: "The hundreds who lost their lives off Lampedusa yesterday are Italian citizens as of today" (Ansa 2013). It was a speech act but only a symbolic one. Letta was not in a position to actually grant citizenship to dead people. The speech did not result in any other actions, duties, or rights that a granting of a formal citizenship would normally entail. For example, the surviving children of the dead did not inherit the citizenship of their parents. Furthermore, the survivors of the disaster were excluded from citizenship, even at a symbolic level. They were not granted any performative role in the official memorial ceremony that took place in Agrigento, Sicily.

In death, migrants were worthy of inclusion into the body politic—they turned into "innocents" as in Napolitano's *"strage di innocenti"* (Breda 2013), human beings of no history or sins. They were innocent to the extent that it did not even matter that Italy was not their actual destination. But as living survivors, the migrants were not eligible; on the contrary, they were potential criminals, suspected of having violated the law as they had crossed the border without documentation. They were confined in the *centro accoglienza* (the so-called Welcome Center) in Lampedusa. Not even their relationality to the dead (the "citizens") was acknowledged. The purification of the victims as "innocents," to mere biological human bodies, qualified them for Italian "citizenship."

Some of the Italian media interpreted Letta's phrase *parole di scusi* as an apology and even amplified it by making an analogy to a public state apology made on the same day, October 9, 2013, in front of a community that had lost more than 1,900 members in a dam disaster fifty years ago in Longarone, Veneto, in North Italy (Brambilla 2013; L'Ancora Online 2013). The president of the Italian senate, Pietro Grasso, issued the apology on behalf of the state in a service that commemorated the victims of a tsunami created by a landslide at the Vajont Dam. In its reporting of the state apology L'Ancora Online drew a parallel to Letta's *parole di scusi*: "Eyes are downcast, evidently embarrassed, along the avenues of a cemetery in the mountains of Veneto. A knee bends, and a hand reaches for a small white coffin, on the southernmost island of Sicily. At the two geographical extremes of Italy, almost at the same time, on October 9, 2013, apologetic words come from the top of the state" (L'Ancora Online 2013).

The newspaper's parallel refers to Letta's performative pose of bending one knee and pausing to look at and touch a white coffin holding a child's body at the Lampedusa airport hangar where hundreds of coffins had been arranged for a commemorative service on October 9, 2013. This performative pose is the second gesture of "words of regret" that Letta performed himself in addition to granting citizenship to the victims. It can be seen as a visual metaphor for asking forgiveness. The performance of kneeling at the coffin might call to mind Willy Brandt's *Kniefall* in Poland during the commemoration of the Warsaw Ghetto Uprising on December 7, 1970.[2] Brandt performed an impromptu gesture of forgiveness rather than a planned and choreographed state apology.

In Veneto, the analogy between the two disasters and two (presumed) state apologies was made also in the ceremony itself. The mayor of Longarone, Roberto Padrin, announced a one-minute silence for the victims of the Lampedusa shipwreck (Ribattuta 2013). *Corriere della Sera* described the act as "the most moving moment" in the memorial service that commemorated those who had died in the dam disaster fifty years earlier (Ribattuta 2013).

The analogy with the Vajont Dam disaster opened a rare opportunity to conceive the shipwreck as a produced disaster rather than an accident. The community of Longarone had waited for fifty years for the state apology to conclude the

FIGURE 2. Still image of Enrico Letta's performative pose. © European Union, 2013. EC—Audiovisual Service/ I-082382 (9 October 2013), director: Catherine Vandezande.

series of downplaying and cover-ups of the human responsibility for the tsunami. The state and the authorities had claimed for years that it was a natural disaster. Documentary films and international television series revealed the human involvement in the disaster decades after.

The minute of silence for the Lampedusa victims during the commemoration of the Vajont Dam disaster was an act of solidarity from the community of Longarone that recognized the victims of the Lampedusa disaster and the living family members. The Longarone community memorialized the deaths of their own and of others, simultaneously. In doing so, they recognized that there are survivors of a disaster and surviving family members of the victims that live on after a disaster. They avoided ignorance in the sense that they not only commemorated their own dead and received the long-awaited state apology for their own community, but expanded this civil recognition to others who (by coincidence) were dealing with the loss of their loved ones at the same time. This commemorative act created a critical rupture in the state apology. In the context of the history of the Longarone region and an apology that was received after fifty years, the issues of injustice and human responsibility were brought to the fore in their community. The parallels between the two disasters are a reminder that injustices are not necessarily forgotten, and that they continue to haunt. Through the analogy between the two disasters, the Longarone community created solidarity across time and space and cultivated an imagination of a common world where the mourning relatives and suffering communities here and there, then and now, shared the right to justice. The community constituted a relational form of citizenship between people who shared similar experiences of loss due to disaster and the state's neglect of their rights. The transgression of anticipated distinctions between the groups cultivated a shared identification, a disaster citizenship.

Disaster

While I agree with those journalists and scholars in Italy who use the term *strage* that it is a more appropriate naming for border deaths than tragedy and shipwreck, I have decided to call what happened on October 3, 2013, a "disaster." Massacre, in English, would not capture the process that leads to mass death at the border, because of its reference to direct killing. Admittedly, like the other available words in the register, such as accident, shipwreck, and tragedy, everyday connotations of the term disaster also fail directly to address the productive and processual nature of the event and the existence of responsible agents. The Oxford English Dictionary defines disaster as "a sudden accident or a natural catastrophe that causes great damage or loss of life." In itself, the term does not imply responsibility, agency, or deaths in the same ways "massacre" would. The survivors and relatives of the victims call the disaster *hadega* or *Lampedusa's hadega*, which is Tigrinya and means "incident."

In academic literature, defining the term "disaster" is complicated, as the anthropologists Anthony Oliver-Smith and Susanna M. Hoffman (2002) note. However, they identify the key characteristic as a conjunction of two factors: a vulnerable human population and a potentially destructive agent. Both factors are embedded in natural and social systems that unfold as processes over time. According to Oliver-Smith and Hoffman, the core of the anthropological study of disasters is therefore to examine disasters not as suddenly occurring events, but as processes that are produced in a specific context with its historical, social, political, economic, and cultural ties. As an academic concept, disaster includes the notion of agency and responsibility and the understanding that the effects of a disaster are felt unequally. Oliver-Smith and Hoffman emphasize that a single destructive agent affects populations disproportionally: some are more vulnerable than others, and this vulnerability, too, is a production. A disaster is multidimensional and involves multiple subjectivities.

These conditional conjunctures have been critically examined in the anthropology of humanitarianism (e.g., Ferguson 1994; De Waal 1997). A central critique laid out by scholars has been that states and international organizations, including those providing disaster relief, have ignored the politics underlying disasters. Solutions to disasters such as famines, for example, have been technical rather than political. This technocratic approach universalizes disasters and interventions rather than recognizing their particularities and specific historical, political, and cultural conjunctions.

While the term "disaster" may evoke popular connotations that contribute to the tendency to understand border deaths as unexpected events needing technocratic solutions, other connotations of the word support the use of the term. It is known to describe not only adverse events resulting from natural processes but also those that result from deliberate human actions and inactions, such as fires, explosions, collapses, and massacres. Furthermore, the term "disaster" refers not only to the massive number of deaths but also to the lack of attention to human life. The word disaster in the context of October 3, 2013, can also imply a *disaster of humanity*, a disaster of responsibility and ethics. This meaning of disaster also encompasses bystanders—indifference to the mass deaths at Europe's borders is a disaster of humanity. Such definition of a disaster requires what Ariella Azoulay (2012) calls "civil imagination," a discourse that "insists on delineating the full field of vision in which the disaster unfolds so as to lay bare the blueprint of the regime" (Azoulay 2012, 2).

When people drowned off Lampedusa, it seemed that they were killed by the sea, with no trace of a human perpetrator. On the surface, it looked like an accident. But the perpetrators and the bystanders were many, and they were both in the vicinity and far away from the sinking boat. The actions and inactions that led to the deaths had long temporal and spatial roots, but there were also very immediate human involvements that produced death. Various perpetrators would be called out on media platforms, in courtrooms, and in activist demonstrations. Human rights, border, and migration activists demanded that Italian and European political leaders take responsibility for the structures and conditions that produced border deaths. Activists were also involved in supporting a civil court case against Sicilian fishermen who had failed to provide assistance to the ship. Eritrean oppositional and human rights activists in Europe accused the Eritrean regime, while diasporic groups that supported the regime blamed the "West" and members of the diaspora who had encouraged Eritreans to follow their aspirations for a better life.

Criminals who operated human smuggling networks were on everyone's list of perpetrators. Italy invested significantly in investigating human smuggling, using the elite anti-Mafia unit with the Palermo prosecutor's office in the investigation. In research on the smuggling networks that facilitated the fatal journey of October 3, 2013, Paolo Campana (2018) identified 292 actors—spanning from the Horn of Africa and Libya to Sicily, the rest of Italy, and finally to Northern European countries, Canada, and the United States (Campana 2018, 2, 7).

In the years to come, the ones who were sentenced were the facilitators—the Tunisian "captain" Khaled Bensalem (eighteen years in prison in 2014) and the six Eritreans living in Italy who were sentenced to prison for human trafficking (up to six years and four months in 2016) (DDA 2014; *Il Fatto Quotidiano* 2016). In 2016, Italian authorities, the Sudanese police and the British National Crime Agency arrested a man thought to be one of the most wanted human traffickers, Medhanie Yehdego Mered ("the General"), in Sudan. Eritrean diaspora and media outlets in Europe, notably the *Guardian* and the Swedish public service broadcaster SVT, revealed the mistaken identity, and Medhanie Tesfamariam Berhe was released in 2019 (Tondo 2019).

In addition, a civil court case initiated in 2017 concerning the fishing crew of the *Aristeus* of Mazara del Vallo, Sicily, led to seven fishermen receiving sentences of five to eight years in prison in 2020 for failing to provide assistance or notify authorities about a boat in distress (Tribunale di Agrigento 2020, 3–4). The case against the crew of the *Aristeus* was raised by two human rights NGOs: Gandhi Charity, founded by Eritrean Italian human rights activist Alganesh Fessaha, and Progetto Diritti, which provided support to relatives of the victims. The *Aristeus* case was then disputed in the courts (final decision pending at the appeal stage[3]).

The fishermen and the smugglers, however, were the easy targets that could be held accountable. Not even Khaled Bensalem denied his responsibility. Crying in a televised interview on RAI TG2 he said, in Italian: "I am responsible but the whole tragedy is not my fault. It's not my fault (Bensalem 2014)." Bensalem recounted the events in the television interview, similar to the testimonies of the Eritrean survivors that in 2020 appeared in the court proceedings against the *Aristeus* crew (Tribunale di Agrigento 2020) and Adhanom's testimony quoted in the beginning of this book: the appearance of two ships that came close and directed their spotlight on the migrant boat while it was still afloat. Bensalem implies that there were others who saw the boat in distress but turned away. Investigations on why the migrant boat was not detected when it approached Lampedusa and stopped less than a kilometer off the island at midnight did not lead to charges against authorities or to public investigation.

This continues to perplex many of those who have investigated the disaster—lawyers, activists, journalists, and cultural producers, such as filmmakers and writers. Lampedusan collective Askavusa produced a documentary film with a local filmmaker, Antonio Maggiore, in 2015 titled *I giorni della tragedia* (The Days of the Tragedy) and published a civil investigative report *Lampedusa 3 Ottobre 2013: Il naufragio della verità* (Lampedusa 3 October 2013: The Sinking of the Truth) (as of this writing, Askavusa has updated the document twice, on 3 October in 2017 and 2018). In Germany, Antonio Umberto Riccò wrote two plays *Ein Morgen vor Lampedusa* (That Morning off Lampedusa, 2014) and *Das Boot ist voll!* (The Boat Is Full!, 2018) that discuss the contradictions in the public narratives of the disaster and shed suspicion that the authorities hide failures in the search and rescue operation. Elsewhere, I have analyzed these cultural interventions as "civil investigation" to capture a form of agency to correct an injustice. In reference to Ariella Azoulay's (2012) notion of "civil imagination," I argue that civil investigation is both a product and a producer of civil imagination—a capacity to see the world in terms of conviviality (Horsti 2021).

Lampedusa is a militarized island with radars that monitor movements at the sea border. An Eritrean who had lived in Italy for ten years by the time of the disaster and who was a member of the initial investigating team of Italian authorities told me in a telephone interview that the first investigation's main aim was to identify the facilitator who operated the migrant boat and smugglers with whom migrants had had contact along their journey. Other aspects, notably, the eyewitness testimonies of survivors who were on the two large vessels were not of primary importance in the investigation.

The processes that make the border murderous and the agents who are involved in the making of the border are far removed from the circumstances under which the necessity to rescue would actualize. It is therefore more difficult to personify the responsible agents and to demand that they take responsibility. When tracing the responsibility for the disaster, one could begin with the Isaias Afwerki regime, which many on the boat were escaping from. In my conversations with survivors, almost everyone said Eritrea's indefinite national service was why they left the country. National service prevented them from partaking in what one survivor called a "normal life": doing work for reasonable pay and having a family with whom one can spend time. Some had also been confined for their oppositional opinions. (See similar results in Crawley and Blitz 2019; Belloni 2019, 103–5.)

Survivors' blame of the regime was complex, however, and their views reflected the diversity of opinion and affiliation which Mohammed (2021) has described in the Eritrean diaspora more broadly. While open-ended national service was reason to leave, some survivors also noted that Eritrea had been sanctioned by the international community and pushed into isolation. Eritrea's national service was introduced in 1994, after independence, as the "school of the nation" to serve military purposes but also to rebuild the country after the war of independence. In fact, some survivors felt somewhat guilty for having left the country, as one of them told me almost ten years after the disaster, "for selfish reasons." Some survivors, however, blamed the regime for the disaster, and had become only more vocal as time passed.

Second, the people on the boat had been forced to choose this dangerous route because few countries accept resettlement refugees through UNHCR programs (Fleming 2013). For example, in 2017, UNHCR expected Europe to accept over 300,000 refugees in need of resettlement but the actual admission of refugees through the resettlement program was 17,413 persons (UNHCR 2018). The needs vs. submissions rate was just 6 percent. In 2013, only 1,027 Eritreans were resettled in Europe through the UNCHR program (UNHCR 2021). The people on the boat were very likely to have been recognized as refugees: Eritreans were the second-highest nationality in asylum recognition rates in Europe in 2008–2018 (Hatton 2021, 6).

Third, the people had chosen this Central Mediterranean route, the deadliest border crossing zone in the world (IOM 2022), because intensified bordering of Europe prevented safer mobility. Physical barriers and surveillance have been erected to prevent border crossing elsewhere, and legal means of mobility, namely the family reunification process, have been tightened (Block 2015; Jeholm and Bissenbakker 2019; Pellander 2021; Pannia 2021). Digital border surveillance has also played a role in producing vulnerability. Some of those on the boat had mobile phones, including Bensalem, but they threw them into the sea when they saw the lights of the island and the other boats nearby. They were afraid of being identified, which would require them to seek asylum in Italy. Without their phones, they could not call for help when water started entering the boat. These are the structural, national and international, invisible, and not-easily-personifiable processes that produced the disaster. Activists, critical politicians, and journalists are among those who stress that other European governments, alongside the government of Italy, were responsible for the lack of safe passage and withholding the right to seek asylum.

The violence of the border is far removed from the agents that are implicated in it. In this sense, border deaths are caused by what Rob Nixon (2011) has termed slow violence: "a violence that occurs gradually and out of sight, a violence of delayed destruction that is dispersed across time and space, an attritional violence that is typically not viewed as violence at all" (Nixon 2011, 2). Nixon developed the idea of slow violence by considering the pain and suffering that result from environmental neglect or disaster. Similarly, drowning off Lampedusa seems "to happen" rather than "is made." In a scenario of mass deaths characterized by slow violence, the only potential perpetrators are those who can be identified as proactively creating conditions for the disaster (smugglers) or bystanders who do not respond to their duty of rescue under the Law of the Sea (fishermen). The states that prevented the people from traveling safely are removed from the scenario of death by temporal and spatial distance.

These multiple human, technological, and institutional agents and actions, in Lampedusa and far away, in the moment of the disaster and long before, produced the disaster in conjunction with one another. The attributes of violence and injustice are invisible: water, wind, and waves to carry out the slow violence. Maurizio Albahari (2015) calls such processes "crimes of peace": results of "ambitions, laborious, and resilient administrative, political, and ideological work of maintaining a 'system' that has proven crumbling and volatile and that keeps proving unjust, violent, and unequal" (Albahari 2015, 21). The disaster was produced by structural inequality, failed administration, bad policy, and unreasonable law. The states could prevent these "crimes of peace," but they do not do so in the name of sovereignty. The process is similar to "a regime-made disaster" that Ariella Azoulay (2012, 1–5) examines in the context of the Israeli government's destruction of Palestinian lives and homes. Destruction is "part of an organized, regulated and motivated system of power that is nourished by the institutions of the democratic state," Azoulay (2012, 2) argues.

Disasters at the European border are the product of a power asymmetry that makes certain populations vulnerable to the destructive agency of natural forces. While the violence is very familiar to some populations, to others it remains invisible. The Mediterranean Sea features as a space of leisure or a space of livelihood for some, while it is at the same time "a death-world"—to use Achille Mbembe's term—for others. In the context of colonialism, Mbembe argued, death worlds are "unique forms of social existence in which vast populations are subjected to conditions of life conferring upon them the status of living dead" (Mbembe 2003, 40). This condition explains why it was so unproblematic for Letta to incorporate the innocent dead into the body politic as "citizens" while leaving the survivors confined and the children of the dead "citizens" without the rights normally given to citizens. In the European imagination, migrants were not alive as social and relational beings before drowning in the sea.

In one sense, then, the disaster in Lampedusa was a massacre of migrants, a "*strage di migranti*": people categorized as migrants were massacred by actors that were spatially and temporally removed from the actual scene. Citizens of Europe—the opposite of noncitizens—were not massacred. However, through the massacre, it was possible to incorporate dead migrants into the body of citizens, as Letta's declaration demonstrates. This incorporation required imagining the migrants as innocents, giving them a bare humanity without past or future, without relationality or a social life. This posthumous citizenship was not a citizenship in any meaningful sense. Rather, it was a performance, constituting a position of benevolence by the one who granted this "citizenship," Italy.

In another sense, however, *strage* is a much broader disaster, not only limited to the realm of migrants and symbolic unreal "citizens" but one that expands to Europe more broadly. This is the meaning that my work underlines by choosing to use the term disaster to name the drowning of at least 366 people near Lampedusa. Foremost, it is crucial to note that the disaster impacted most severely those who had to take the dangerous route and the victims' families. But, in addition, it affected communities and societies in Europe and beyond, and those communities are not separate from other communities but connected. The notion of "Europe" also includes diasporic citizens and residents who lost their relatives. In order to understand the whole picture of the disaster, one needs to see beyond the dichotomy between noncitizens and citizens and terms such as "*strage di migranti*" or "migrant disaster." There are multiple connections that unite Europe and the refugees who were on the boat: colonial history, economic exploitation, military involvement, and present-day diasporic family ties.

I propose that the disaster be conceived of as the outcome of a network of interconnected actors that emerged in the scene of the disaster, long before it, and in the afterlives that developed from it. To name the October 3, 2013, event a disaster is an attempt to gain a holistic vision of it: an understanding of the event not as a suddenly occurring event but as a process in the conjuncture of European morality and responsibility, the repressive regime in Eritrea and its global entanglements, and as the outcome of a failure of global responsibility in refugee protection. To understand the disaster in these terms requires seeing others not as separate from "our" life but as people who coexist in the same world governed by the same regimes that have produced the violent border. To recognize the disaster as a process leading to killing is to recognize the people on the boat as people of a shared world entitled to a life.

2

IMAGES

The dominant visual structure in the immediate framing of the disaster in the Italian and international media produced an asymmetrical relationship between spectators and arriving people, whether they arrived alive or dead. News photographs of the disaster employed three types of visual structures that created a hierarchy between the refugees and the European rescuers. First, the photographs depict the survivors and the dead as *masses of strangers*, which is a typical visual representation of migration globally (see, e.g., Gilligan and Marley 2010; Bleiker et al. 2013; Horsti 2016b). In one photograph that was widely disseminated, at least seventeen survivors are gathered in a small Guardia Costiera search and rescue vessel, half-naked and wrapped in emergency blankets. The figures seem otherworldly—extraterrestrial—in their shiny silver and gold foil blankets. They make up a completely different category of beings compared to the active agents in the scene: the photographers, onlookers, and rescuers on the dock, who are situated in the foreground of the image. The agents in uniform are recognizable figures in any disaster scene. We see them in action and their gaze is meaningful, while the survivors are still, isolated from everyone around them. The European agents represent functionality and rationality in a time of emergency, whereas the half-naked figures wrapped in foil seem strange and dysfunctional.

The composition of the image invites the viewer to look at the scene *from the authorities' perspective*, another visual structure commonly used in depictions of migration (see, e.g., Horsti 2016b; Musarò 2017; Giubilaro 2018). In the foreground of the photograph of the otherworldly survivors, a man stands on the dock, his back to the camera. He is looking at the group of survivors in the vessel in front of him, and the text on the back of his vest identifies him as a representative of the Sicilian health authority. He wears latex gloves on his hands, giving the impression that the group wrapped in foil is potentially dangerous. He is there not only to care for those who have been pulled from the sea, but also to protect us, who are taking in the scene from his perspective. The otherworldliness of the survivors is a spectacle, framed simultaneously as both threatening and vulnerable. They are extraterrestrial, not alive in the social sense, which makes them simultaneously a threat and a victim. Their vulnerability does not derive from their interdependence with other human beings but from their "innocence"— they have yet to become part of the social reality that the European spectator acknowledges. They are pure victims, innocents, as the president of the Italian Republic Giorgio Napolitano framed them by calling the disaster "the massacre of innocents," "*Strage di innocenti*" (Breda 2013).

In another photograph depicting the rescue, a male survivor on a stretcher is wrapped tightly in golden foil. Two medics on the right side of the photograph are looking at the man on the stretcher, while in the background, two other paramedics are at work. The image resembles the way figures are arranged in religious paintings—suffering Jesus in the middle—and it illustrates a third visual strategy: the European rescuer as *moral agent*. In this photograph, the medics' gaze is focused on one single survivor, making him differently visible in comparison to the survivors depicted as a group in the other image. Nevertheless, the active and moral agents in this photograph are again the Italian representatives of some agency, perhaps medical or humanitarian. There are no images in which the survivors exhibit agency or exercise authority, in which they belong to the civic sphere as people capable of ethical or rational action.

Lampedusan civilians also rescued people with their own fishing vessels and would become important agents in the mediated narrative of the disaster. They did not, however, appear together with survivors or the dead in the first images from the scene of the disaster. In photographs and in filmed interviews, the Lampedusan civilian rescuers appeared separately from the Eritrean survivors. On October 4, the day after the disaster, *La Repubblica* published a series of eight portraits of the civilian first responders, which also appeared as a slide show on their website. The faces of the rescuers are lit by a bright flash, and they gaze directly at the camera. The portraits' aesthetic centers the emotions and personalities of the named civilian rescuers, while the survivors remain invisible as emotional and personal beings.

This asymmetrical structure, constituted through the three visual strategies, dominated the early media representation. It is typical for the news coverage of migrant disasters and dangerous border crossings in Europe more broadly (see, e.g., Gilligan and Marley 2010; Horsti 2016b; Musarò 2017; Giubilaro 2018). However, the unusual number of retrieved bodies, the proximity to the island, and the local people's demands to commemorate them resulted in an unusual visuality of migrant death at the border in the following news coverage. The iconic images of the Lampedusa disaster are not among the ones shot on the day, but those taken two and six days later. On October 5 and 9, press photo agencies disseminated a variety of images depicting the more than one hundred wooden coffins that were organized in rows inside the Lampedusa airport hangar.

In this chapter, I examine these iconic images and discuss how they appealed to different agents who engaged with the disaster and its memory. The conscious display of coffins en masse produced different emotions and politics for Lampedusans, the Italian government, European Union leaders, and the Eritrean diaspora. This chapter also discusses how mass death at the border is represented through images in alternative ways. I pay specific attention to visual means of representing *the absence of life*—rather than *the presence of death*. What kinds of visual structures can resist and counteract the dominant asymmetrical relationship? How can the dead, survivors, and the relatives of the victims be represented as persons—human beings with agency? I argue for *the visual politics of interdependency*: seeing the dead in relation to the living brings the humanity of the disaster to the fore.

The Presence of Death in Iconic Images

The Lampedusa disaster was unusual because of its corporeality: hundreds of dead bodies were retrieved from the sea. Neither before nor since has there been another postwar maritime disaster in the European waters involving the immediate recovery and management of so many dead migrant bodies—usually, they disappear into the sea. The proximity of the disaster to the island also meant that many Lampedusans witnessed the management of the dead. Just as the proximity of the drowning necessitated rescue (as discussed in chapter 1), the physical presence of dead bodies necessitated rituals. Stefano Nastasi (2017), the local priest at the time, explained to me how the parish had ordered flowers to be laid on the coffins and how they organized a memorial service at the airport hangar. "The Church had to go to the dead because there were too many of them to bring to the church," he said (Nastasi 2017). The Lampedusan community expected the dead to be treated in a dignified manner, which included a memorial service where the bodies were present. The bodies were hidden inside coffins but as everyone I interviewed about the service recalls without my asking, the corporeality of a mass death was sensible in the horrific smell that filled the airport hangar on a warm October day.

A photograph distributed by Reuters on October 5 (and a similar one distributed by the European Commission Audiovisual Service on October 9) depict the scene in the airport hangar. In order to get a general view, the Reuters photographer, Antonio Parrinello, climbed up on a ladder to take the picture of the coffins from an elevated perspective. Wooden caskets in varying shades of brown are arranged in three rows, with some space left between them. A single red rose or gerbera has been placed on each coffin. In the background, photographers take pictures of the four small white coffins lined up alongside the adult-sized brown ones. Two of the photographers have kneeled down to focus their lenses on the teddy bears and lilies placed on top of the children's coffins. Behind the photographers, men and women in uniform stand in two straight lines that are parallel to the rows of coffins. The choreography of the scene creates a commemorative aura and sense of importance in a space that could otherwise be considered unsuitable for memorial services: it is a place to park airplanes. The officers in uniform are turned toward the coffins, and one might think that they are there to pay their respects to the dead. However, at the far right of the image is another row of people whose backs are turned to the coffins—and the photographic moment suggests that the people in uniform are standing in line to honor or welcome someone who is about to enter the stage formed by the space between the groups. The image suggests that while the coffins themselves are a spectacle, another spectacle, for which the coffins will serve as a backdrop, is about to begin.

The arrangement of the coffins in rows represents the *presence of death*—the presence of many dead in an orderly fashion. The horrific smell of corpses that everyone who was present recalls is not visible. For the European public, the arrangement may be reminiscent of war cemeteries. Such official memorials are built to remind the public of the "duty to remember," but as Marc Augé (2004) argues, they are not only about memory. Oblivion stands side by side with memory, and one technology of "forgetting by remembering" is the beautification of horror. Describing the cemeteries for World War II victims in Normandy, Augé notes that "the impressive spectacle of the army of the dead immobilized in the white crosses standing at attention" does not evoke memories of horrific battles or the fear felt by the men. Instead, the emotions aroused by the cemeteries are simply "born from the harmony of forms" (Augé 2004, 89).

In present-day mass disasters, the dead are often mourned and buried individually and separately by their families. Visualizations of "the many" are not always welcomed by the institutions that send soldiers to war. During the thirty-year liberation struggle against Ethiopia, the Eritrean People's Liberation Front (EPLF) kept guerilla fighters' deaths a secret. During, and long after, the border

FIGURE 3.   General scene in the airport hangar. © European Union, 2013.
EC—Audiovisual Service/ P-024114/00-14 (9 October 2013), photographer:
Roberto Salomone.

war of 1998–2000, the Eritrean government did not release accurate numbers of deaths nor the identities of the war dead. To this day, the dead of both wars are remembered as a homogeneous group of "martyrs" (Bernal 2014, 122). Victoria Bernal (2014, 122–23) argues that calling the war dead martyrs and the establishment of Martyrs' Day as a national memorial allows the state to claim all losses for itself while obscuring the private dimensions of loss experienced by Eritreans. The state simultaneously commemorates the dead and hides the actual numbers and identities of those who died; in doing so, it prevents families from mourning an individual lost life.

For eighteen years the United States prohibited the publication of photographs of the transfer of soldiers' remains at the Dover Air Force Base in Delaware. The administrations of both Presidents George H. W. Bush and George W. Bush feared that seeing the many casualties, more so than simply hearing their number, might turn the public against the wars in the Gulf, Iraq, and Afghanistan. Their claim was that allowing media representatives on site would violate the privacy of the families and degrade what they called "dignified transfers" (Alinder 2012, 197, 180). One argument in favor of the ban was that images of many identical coffins could be instrumentalized and politicized by the antiwar movement. Critics claimed that the ban drew attention away from the human cost of war (e.g., Ralph Begleiter quoted in Alinder 2012, 197). The ban was lifted by the Obama administration in 2009, with the condition that the families of the dead would have to consent to the publication of an image where their relative's coffin was visible. This requirement had the effect of making it difficult for photographers to capture an image containing many coffins.

Managing the production of visual knowledge of war dead is one form of states' power to manage not only citizens' lives but also their deaths. In reference to Achille Mbembe's (2003, 2019) concept of necropolitics, which formulates how violence constitutes states, cultures, and subjectivities, the management of the visuality of war dead can be conceptualized as a form of *visual necropolitics*— politics that use visual representation to further states' power over death.

In the mediated flow of staged images from the Lampedusa airport hangar, there were no concerns about demonstrating the size of the disaster for the global public nor hurting the feelings of the relatives. On the contrary, the indication that performers would enter the stage with the coffins suggested that the arrangement was to be looked at and photographed. The spectacle was realized four days later when a group of high-profile performers entered the scene. More coffins had been added to the arrangement in the hangar on October 9, 2013, and there was no longer any space between the rows. New fresh flowers had been placed on each brown casket, and lilies and teddy bears on the now eight small white caskets in front. Both the European Commission Audiovisual Services and the office of the Italian prime minister released photographs of José Manuel Barroso, the president of the European Commission; Cecilia Malmström, the EU commissioner for home affairs; Enrico Letta, the prime minister of Italy; and Lampedusa's mayor, Giusi Nicolini, standing together looking at the coffins.[1]

The display of coffins is the setting of a formal act of commemoration: Nicolini wears a tricolor sash, Barroso is photographed laying flowers on one of the white coffins, Letta puts one knee down on the concrete floor as he stops to look at and touch a child victim's coffin. The European Commission press office titled its images "Paying tribute to the victims." The actors in the scene "pay tribute," but the intentional placement of coffins for appearances sake has an active role to play, too. The coffins are deliberately arranged to have an emotional effect.

The moment in the hangar is referenced in both Barroso's and Malmström's speeches at a press conference later the same day. "I will never forget the sight of 280 coffins today," Malmström (2013) said. Barroso (2013) commented that the "image of hundreds of coffins will never leave my mind. It is something I think one cannot forget. Coffins of babies, coffins with the mother and the child who was born at that very moment. This is something that profoundly shocked and deeply saddened me." Barroso returns to the image again in a speech in the

FIGURE 4.   European and Italian leaders "pay tribute to the victims."
© European Union, 2013. EC—Audiovisual Service/ P-024114/00-01
(9 October 2013), photographer: Roberto Salomone.

European Parliament on October 23, 2013: "As you know, I was in Lampedusa two weeks ago at the invitation of the Italian authorities, and of course I was profoundly touched by what I saw. The images will remain impressed on me forever." Interestingly, it is not clear what "image" remains impressed—the "image" of the arrangement that he saw or the "image" of the arrangement of the coffins that he had surely seen as a press photograph before arriving on Lampedusa, an image that he traveled to witness with his own eyes.

In orchestrating the visual event, Lampedusa mayor Giusi Nicolini aimed to make an emotional impact that would sway the government in Rome and the leaders of the European Union. The official visitors to Lampedusa not only viewed the arrangement of the coffins, but became part of it as participants in a commemorative *tableau vivant*. For Nicolini, this was one of the highlights of her political career, an event she recalled in an interview with *La Repubblica* after she failed to win a second term in 2017: "Five years ago, in the collective imagination, this island was the gateway to hell, not to Europe. We had to break up the isolation, demand a solid response from the institutions. Barroso came here, too—we made him bow before the coffins" (Nicolini in Lauria 2017). For Nicolini, the arrangement of coffins and the commemorative performance it generated served many functions: they were a continuation of her outspoken solidarity with migrants and their families. The year before, in November 2012, she had sent an open letter to the European Union that was covered widely across the media and among activists. In the letter Nicolini called for attention to border deaths:

> I am scandalised by Europe's silence, which can only be exacerbated by the fact it has just recently been awarded the Nobel Prize for Peace yet continues to stay silent over a tragedy that is now reaching figures more commonly associated with war. I am becoming more and more convinced that European policy on immigration sees this toll of human lives as a means to moderate the flow, if not as an actual deterrent. If the journey by boat is the only possibility of hope that these people have, I believe that Europe should be ashamed and disgraced by the deaths, which occur at sea. (Nicolini 2012)

Nicolini's role in the arrangement of the commemorative spectacle in 2013 continued her earlier political stance on the bordering of Europe. Lampedusans were with her when it came to commemoration, albeit perhaps for a different reason. The display of the coffins was a means to demonstrate solidarity with the survivors, Nastasi (2017) told us in the interview. In addition, shops closed for a day, flags were lowered to half-mast, and a candlelight vigil was held. These actions demonstrated that Lampedusans treat the dead with dignity. And, as contradictory as it may seem, the spectacle of the harmonious arrangement of coffins countered any imagery that may have existed in the public imagination of unorganized masses of dead bodies floating in the sea. In her 2017 interview with *La Repubblica*, Nicolini said that she had succeeded at countering images of Lampedusa as a "gateway to hell" and as "a holiday destination where one swims with the dead."

The display of the coffins was also a powerful tool for Italian leaders, who used it to effectively communicate their agenda: to reframe irregular border crossings as a European rather than an Italian problem and to demonstrate the unfairness of the Dublin III Regulation. The arrangement of the coffins also supported Enrico Letta's announcement that a state funeral would be held for the victims and the "words of apology"—the phrase that he used in the speech for the press the same day he was photographed paying tribute to the victims. As I discuss in chapter 1, Letta avoided making the actual speech act of apology. Nevertheless, his performative pose of bending one knee and pausing to look at and touch the white coffin holding a child's body can be seen as a visual metaphor for an apology.

The politicians' "tribute to the victims" (in the words of the European Commission), and Letta's "words of apology" (as he called them) were insufficient to be considered an apology in a sense of reparative justice (Neumann and Thompson

2015, 15–17). Victims' families and the survivors were not directly addressed, nor did they receive reparations. Rather than acts of justice, they were performances of benevolence. Issues of justice were entirely absent from the public agenda. And while reparations were not offered to the victims of the disaster, they were, in fact, offered to Italy: in his speech in Lampedusa, Barroso announced 30 million euros in EU support for the country. The announcement was made in both English and Italian at the press conference that followed the politicians' performance of paying tribute.

For European leaders, the visual arrangement and commemorative acts in Lampedusa offered an opportunity to demonstrate European unity. Migration had long been an issue of division in the European Union. The Dublin regulation was one topic of long controversy—the Mediterranean countries resented that asylum seekers are required to submit their applications in the first country of arrival in the European Union and that other countries in the EU can forcibly deport people back to their first country of arrival. Reemergence of internal borders within the borderless Schengen area of twenty-six European countries was making a comeback in certain regions, such as the border between Italy and France (Horsti 2018; Tazzioli 2020). In addition, nationalist far right parties were gaining support among the European electorate, which alarmed the media. Tougher border and migration control was the main issue on their agenda (Mudde 2016). While these threats of division would be on full display in 2015 during the European refugee reception crisis, they were emerging already in October 2013.

In Lampedusa, Barroso and Malmström presented the European Union as a responsible institution, capable of emotion and possessing agency. They arrived in Lampedusa to symbolically restore order and dignity amid the chaos of mass death. The solutions they offered followed the pattern of the humanitarianized securitization and militarization of the European border (as discussed in the Introduction). In their speeches, they extended their gratitude to countries that accept refugees, to humanitarian NGOs, and to the Lampedusans. They praised the European border agency, Frontex, and the proposed European Border Surveillance System, Eurosur, which the European Parliament would vote to implement the next day.

Both Malmström and Barroso offered their condolences to the families of the victims in the speeches they gave in Lampedusa. While their speeches were otherwise given in English, Malmström and Barroso expressed their condolences in Italian, together with their thanks to the Lampedusan people for their hospitality and to the Italian authorities for their invitation.[2] It seemed that the victims belonged to the Italians. There was no mention of Eritrea nor of the fact that many on the boat were on their way to live with relatives who were already settled in various countries in Europe and who were citizens of Sweden, Germany, and Norway. It would have made more sense for Malmström to deliver her condolences in Swedish, which is, after all, her native language. It is also the language of the country to which most people on the boat were heading. But a transnational understanding of the disaster was not conceivable for European and Italian leaders. They treated it as a disaster that had struck Italy and the Italian people—and, by extension, Europe. However, they treated it as a European or Italian disaster only to the extent that Europeans had to witness (mostly through mediation) and manage the mass disaster. They did not recognize and acknowledge how the disaster touched Europeans also at an intimate level: it touched those European Eritreans who lost loved ones.

The politicians' geographically narrow understanding of the disaster was also evident in that none of the victims' family members or friends was present, whether in person or symbolically, in the photographic events that were staged at the hangar. The coffins remained anonymous: essentially identical and lacking any relationship to one another or to any living person. There were no personalized elements on the coffins, such as photographs or names. Meanwhile, the survivors, many of whom were related to the dead, were being detained in a reception center for the crime of having entered Italy illegally, a provision that had been introduced by the Italian government's "security package" of 2008 (Maccanico 2009, 3). They were consciously removed from the scene of commemoration, from Letta's verbal and gestured "words of apology," and from Barroso's and Malmström's condolences.

A society's sense of civilization is measured by how it cares for the burial of the poorest (Laqueur 2015, 314–15), and in Lampedusa that sense was being performed at local, national, and European scales. Lampedusans put flowers onto the coffins, the government of Italy provided the caskets and sent the prime minister and the interior minister to pay their respects, and the European Union representatives also arrived to mourn. The body bags had been visible in the media internationally on the day of the disaster, and therefore, mediation of mourning rituals and the dignified arrangement of the coffins were to communicate a sense of civility and sympathy of the agents who were responsible for the aftermath of the disaster either by their presence or by the polity that they represented.

Solidarity and Visibility

The survivors were able to view the coffins on at least two occasions, although those moments were not visible in the mainstream media. The first was a memorial ceremony arranged at the airport hangar with Lampedusans. No photographs depicting the joint memorial service of the two mourning communities were circulated in media spheres. The reason for this is that by October 5, Lampedusans had become tired of the presence of the press. This was typical of the islanders, as clearly expressed in an ironic mural that used to be at the entrance of the military port through which rescued migrants enter the island. The mural read: "Un sorriso per la stampa" ("Smile for the press"). Nastasi (2017) explained to me that he ordered the media out of the hangar before the survivors and locals came in. He wanted to create an intimate memorial service for those who had witnessed the disaster and its aftermath.

What remained circulating in the mediated sphere afterward were images of Lampedusans commemorating the disaster only among themselves. Images of two scenes of commemoration performed by Lampedusans were disseminated through the media; none of these images include survivors. The first were of the Lampedusans' candlelight procession, and the second were of Salvatore Martello, the chairman of the Lampedusan fishermen's association (Consorzio dei pescatori) who would in 2017 be elected mayor of Lampedusa, throwing a wreath bearing the words "Pescatori di Lampedusa" into the sea. In interviews, Martello declared that "Fishermen save lives"—an effort to counter the suspicion based on the survivors' testimonies that a fishing boat passed the migrant boat in distress without making an emergency call.

The decision not to mediate the commemorative event that brought together the islanders and the survivors, albeit important for the people who were present at the service, further removed the survivors from the public scene of mourning. The display of coffins is dignified in itself—a beautiful and harmonious way to honor the dead—but simultaneously, it beautifies horror for the European public, to paraphrase Marc Augé. Coffins as such can potentially serve as representations of individuals, as they are familiar objects that resonate with relationships and familial closeness. But they only accommodate this function if we know who is inside. To the public eye, the caskets remained distanced from the people to whom the dead mattered as individuals. Instead, the coffins represent the presence of death, the biological end of life.

The memorial service at the airport hangar was a memorable experience for three male survivors in their early twenties whom I interviewed in Stockholm in November 2015. During the focus group interview, they recalled how Lampedusans had mourned and cried with them—a topic other survivors too brought up in conversations with me. In Stockholm, we looked at the press photographs of the coffins and watched television footage of a group of about twenty survivors walking toward the hangar. The survivors whom I had come to know were barely identifiable in the footage, as their habitus had changed so much in their two years in Europe. In the footage, they were thin and dressed identically in jumpsuits issued by the reception center. Now, their frames had filled in, and they each had an individual style. The survivors explained that at the time, they had not known what was awaiting them in the hangar. They had only realized what was happening when they saw the rows of coffins. That was the moment when television cameras stayed outside. Many collapsed in shock, the three survivors told me. They cried and consoled one another and embraced the Lampedusans who were at the ceremony.

Since 2014, photographs of the coffins in the hangar in Lampedusa have reappeared each year on the anniversary of the disaster in social media messages and in YouTube memorial videos shared across the global Eritrean diaspora. For those who knew the victims or who survived the disaster, the images convey a different meaning than they do for the general public. For them, the images cannot be seen as a representation of nonpersons: of the many, of the presence of death, of the mere end of biological life. They *know* a person in one of those coffins, though they cannot be sure which.

I spent October 3, 2016, in London with the sister of a victim of the disaster. Every now and again, she showed me condolences she kept receiving on her phone from people who knew that her brother had died in the disaster. Many of those messages included a news photograph of the display of the coffins. These images also appeared on other sites and in Viber groups she followed, such as a group for those who used to live in the same neighborhood in Asmara, Eritrea's capital. Often, the photographs had been modified with editing tools: texts such as *RIP*, *Lampedusa 3 October 2013*, and *May God receive you in heaven*, as well as images of burning candles and decorative frames, had been added to the photographs of the coffins.

The continuous use of the images demonstrates that the arrangement of coffins created by Lampedusans has had an afterlife among the Eritrean diaspora. Digital press photographs are easy to circulate and to turn into memory objects that function as signs of solidarity and care. Furthermore, the images of the coffins had a specific aesthetic and cultural plasticity: different meanings could be attached to them. Just as the images served multiple purposes for the Italians, so they did for the Eritrean diaspora. The images have not only been used as digitalized objects of memorialization, but they have also had a political function. The human rights advocates Elsa Chyrum (2016) in London and Meron Estefanos (2016) in Stockholm confirmed in interviews with me that these photographs are the iconic visual representation of the disaster for Eritreans in Eritrea and in the diaspora. Those who oppose the Eritrean government frame the display of coffins as a testimony to the regime's suppression of human rights, while supporters of the regime claim that it attests to how the West "lures the young" to leave the country.

Depicting Grief

The second opportunity for the survivors to view the coffins was on October 12, when the coffins were loaded onto the Italian navy ships to be taken to Agrigento, Sicily. The European and Italian leaders had left the scene by then, and the journalists, filmmakers, and photographers who documented what happened at the port were for the most part working independently. The scene at the port differs from the earlier, dignified arrangement of the coffins in the hangar. One of the survivors described the scene at the port to me a year later in Stockholm: "The worst thing was that they moved the coffins with a machine, like the dead were commodities. We had heard people saying that in Europe, there is respect for human beings, so we expected respect for the dead. It was awful to see that. We tried to prevent them from moving the dead that way. They said they didn't have enough staff and space to carry the coffins to the ship. We offered to carry all the coffins, but we were not allowed to."

This undignified treatment of the dead keeps reappearing in the Eritrean diasporic media as a key topic of discussion and a site of memory. Other Eritrean Europeans have asked survivors why they did not intervene and prevent the undignified treatment of the dead. On October 3, 2020, the Eritrean Swedish activist Semhar Ghebreselassie moderated a four-hour live discussion on the Global Yiakl Facebook site, one of the many sites for young Eritreans of the diasporic resistance. A person who worked as a translator for the Italian government during the disaster recalled the scene at the port in the Global Yiakl program—he recalled how survivors and relatives of the victims from Europe were screaming, throwing themselves on the coffins so that the Italian authorities would not lift the coffins by the crane. "There was no order, it was chaos," he said.[3] An Italian Eritrean activist by the name of Abraham shifts attention from the Italian authorities to the Eritrean authorities of the embassy in Rome: "I've never seen Eritrean bodies being moved like this, like they are dirt. It is a disgrace, and it makes me sad. This happened because of the Eritrean authorities [in Italy]. It is their duty, not the duty of Italians. This [undignified treatment of the bodies] is the work of the ambassador sent by the Eritrean government."

The survivors and ten to twenty family members who were in Lampedusa searching for missing relatives created a scene of mourning on the dock as a crane lifted the coffins onto the ship. In the video footage and in photographs of the scene, the distinction between family members and survivors is obvious from the clothes they wear. The family members are dressed in typical European clothes, while the survivors are still wearing jumpsuits. Together they kneel on the concrete dock to pray and sing. Some had printed photographs of the dead and attached them to the coffins. Others cried loudly and threw themselves on the coffins, and the mourners hugged and consoled one another. The survivors were allowed to carry some of the children's coffins. The relatives filmed and photographed personalized coffins and vernacular mourning rituals so that other relatives and friends would be able to see how they had memorialized the dead. For the Eritreans, digitally shared photographs of the scene function as visual evidence of death and the ritual closure. I return to the scene at the harbor in chapter 8 where I examine the survivors' and relatives' practices of memorialization.

In the European public sphere, the images of the events at the dock were mainly disseminated through independent journalism and documentary films such as Morgan Knibbe's *Those Who Feel the Fire Burning* (2014) and in Tim Baster and Isabelle Merminod's (2013) photo essay in the *New Internationalist*. Associated Press chose nine photographs of the events taken by the Lampedusan photographer Mauro Buccarello. The photographs disseminated through international press agencies mainly depict Italian officials in protective masks and gloves, coffins hanging in the air from the crane, and the tight arrangement of the coffins on the deck of the ship. Mauro Buccarello, too, was appalled by the use of the crane. In an interview, he told me that by focusing on the machinery, he wanted to communicate how Europe attempted to distance itself from the dead migrants (Buccarello 2015).

One of the images distributed by AP stands out. Rather than depicting the coffins as potentially toxic "commodities" it shows a crying Eritrean European woman, wearing a green velvet sweater, who has thrown herself on a coffin. An enlarged photograph of the victim has been attached to the coffin, and a flower laid beneath it. The woman is being held by three Eritrean European men. The photograph offers an alternative imaginary of the disaster: instead of a massive number of anonymous deaths, it depicts an individual lost life, who is mourned by the woman. Buccarello's photograph conveys the social relationship that has been severed by death.

Buccarello is a native Lampedusan who has often been the first person on the scenes of migrant disasters, gaining him the attention of the Associated Press. He discussed the photographs of the transfer of the coffins with me one afternoon in October 2015 over a cup of coffee in a café on Via Roma in Lampedusa. He explained that he had felt unsure about sending the photograph of the mourning woman to the Associated Press because he had not had the woman's consent for publication. In fact, the caption written by the agency incorrectly identifies her as "a survivor." He ultimately decided to submit the image, however, because none of his other photos captured the grief he had witnessed.[4]

While the scene at the dock was perceived as unorganized and undignified by Buccarello and Eritreans alike, it nevertheless allowed survivors and family members to take an active role and to perform grief and mourning through

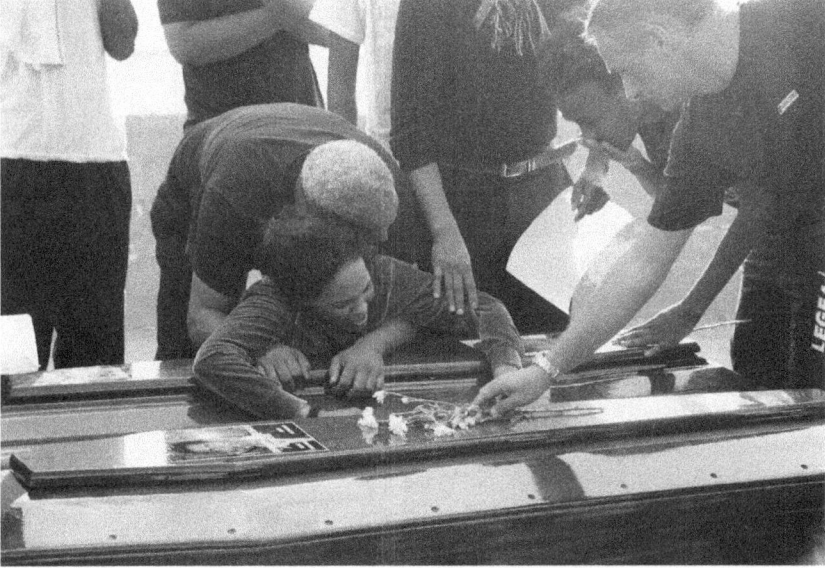

FIGURE 5.   A relative of a victim grieves in Lampedusa. This photo is of the same series of shots as the one distributed by the Associated Press. © Mauro Buccarello, 2013. Photo by Mauro Buccarello.

spontaneous forms of remembering. These practices—and their documentation and mediation across transnational diasporic families—are crucial in dealing with the social aspects of death in a situation where burial and funeral are not feasible (as is further explored in chapter 8).

Personification of the Victims

In the images of the scene at the dock, photographs of disaster victims taped on the coffins were instrumental in personifying the dead. Another instance of the personification of the victims through a photograph emerged from an encounter between a journalist and Adal Neguse who was in Lampedusa searching for his lost brother. Grazia Longo of *La Stampa* interviewed Adal (with whom I would later work as part of this project) days after the disaster. In the photo published with Longo's story, Adal stands on the main street in Lampedusa holding a photo of his younger brother in front of his chest; Adal's face is pixelated to protect his identity.[5] The story explains that he had learned about the disaster on television on the morning of October 3 and then traveled to Lampedusa to search for his brother. By the time of the interview, Adal had received confirmation from the survivors that his brother had been on the boat, but no one had seen him since the disaster.

A quote from Adal was selected as the headline of the article: "I paid for my brother Abraham's trip: Return his body. Eritrean who moved to Sweden: He wanted to follow me." With this headline, a complex emotional register is applied to the disaster unlike that of any other news story covering the event: a register of loss, grief, and guilt. The photograph, the title, and the story combine to produce a representation of the absence of a life and of a person, as well as of a relationship between two brothers.

The details provided in the *La Stampa* story present a more complicated, transnational, and detailed geography of the disaster than what appeared in dominant media representations. The story of Adal and Abraham connected Eritrea and Sweden to the scene of the disaster in Lampedusa. Adal, as an Eritrean Swede, is emotionally involved in the disaster: he mourns his brother and feels guilty for having partly paid for his journey. The brothers' story reveals the problematics of diasporic relationships. Adal can also evoke memories of the colonial past— a specter from Italy's *Colonia Eritrea* claims for rights in Italy and makes the ancient connections visible. The narrative of the two brothers also reveals the Europeanness of the disaster: it connects Sweden to Italy and Europe to Eritrea. The photograph and the story demonstrate that the disaster is European not only at the political level, but also on a very personal, intimate level.

Adal Neguse's pose in *La Stampa*, holding the picture of his brother, is a well-known visual arrangement across social movements globally. The Mothers of the Plaza de Mayo in Argentina, *Les Mamans des Disparus Tunisiens* in Tunisia, the Association of Parents of Disappeared Persons in Kashmir, and the *Asociación Comité de Familiares de Migrantes Fallecidos y Desaparecidos de El Salvador* are known for carrying photographs of the dead, disappeared, or missing and are often photographed in that pose at protests. Displaying these photographs represents the act of missing or grieving someone; it communicates that the protesters are people who are capable of such feelings and emphasizes the personhood of those who have been lost. The images also appeal: Where is my loved one, and what happened to him or her? They are evidence that the people depicted in them existed, and the public display is evidence that the people mattered. Those who bear photos of the disappeared refuse to forget and to keep the photographs in the private realm. They turn the gaze of the disappeared once more on those who are responsible for the violence.

Photographs of the disappeared can be understood as being part of "the file" that Ather Zia (2019, 157) writes about in her ethnography of mothers and half-widows of the forced disappeared in Kashmir. The women collect information about their loved ones that the Indian forces have made to disappear. The desire to archive and document "traces 'the absence'" of a person and seeks to make the disappeared persons and their histories physically visible and present. The disappeared are sometimes treated as dead and at other times as if they were alive. Thus, their archival presence is a haunting presence.

Aesthetically, the image of Adal Neguse in *La Stampa* belongs to the global protest genre and the transnational category of enforced disappearance (Schindel 2020), therefore creating critical potential in the representation of this specific disaster. Adal carried the image with him in Lampedusa because he wanted to show it to survivors and rescuers in case someone recognized the brother. He did not perform a mode of affective politics per se—he was not displaying the photograph as a protest to claim rights for the dead or the families. Nevertheless, as an image, printed in *La Stampa*, the pose of holding the photograph of a disappeared transforms into a political act. Adal turns the gaze of his brother back onto those who are responsible for his death and for the undignified treatment of his body after death. In the headline, Adal makes a claim: return his body. It is an act of forensic citizenship: Adal generates pressure on Italian and European authorities to carry out their responsibility to identify those who died at the border and to investigate disappearances.

Visualizing the Invisible

It is standard news practice in disaster reporting to publish personal photographs of the victims from before the disaster. In the case of massacres, in particular, the media considers visualizing the attack with photographs of the victims to be an important ethical practice. After the right-wing extremist attack in Christchurch, New Zealand, in March 2019, photographs of the dead were circulated widely so as to demonstrate the loss of socially significant lives. Simultaneously, the perpetrator's presence in the media was deliberately erased: his Facebook livestream was removed (although unsuccessfully) and the authorities pixelated his face in courtroom footage (Deutsche Welle 2019).

The lack of such representation of the victims of migrant disasters therefore deviates from the news coverage routinely produced in other kinds of mass deaths.[6] The Italian mainstream media did, however, use two other strategies to visualize the victims or their absence. While they did not publish photographs of the victims, they provided images to inspire the reader to *imagine* the victims.

The first instance was in *La Repubblica*, which reprinted sixty mug shots of the 153 photos that had been taken of survivors at the reception center in Lampedusa.[7] The faces have been blurred beyond identification: only the hair, shoulders, and chest of each person are visible. Italian journalists were aware that publishing photographs of the survivors might harm their relatives in Eritrea or risk their opportunity to seek asylum elsewhere in Europe.[8] On the left side of each mug shot, a hand holds a number. The sixty black-and-white passport-size photos are printed in a grid on the upper portion of the newspaper page, and below is a headline: "The void, the fear, the exhaustion in the eyes of the 153 invisibles." The mug shots visualize what is not there—"the void," as the title suggests. The text explains: "The survivors talk about a cargo of five hundred lives. The photo album ends at 153. The difference is the magnitude of the massacre. Its evidence is in the absence."

The 153 mug shots visualize what *is* there, but only the journalist, Gabriele Romagnoli, sees them clearly. He describes for his readers the emotions on the faces of the survivors, focusing on the five women—the women "corresponding to the numbers 42, 107, 108, 132, 149." In Romagnoli's poetic reading, the women seem not fully alive; he seems unsure whether life is possible after having witnessed the horror of the disaster:

> The first [woman's face] communicates loss, mouth half open, an empty gaze fixed on something that no longer exists. The eyes have retreated to see the near past, survival is nominal, *de facto* but not *de jure*. The second and the third communicate the echo of a challenge that was lost: we will try again. But they have already done it, so it is gone, we will regain that which we lost. The fourth pleads with the only language she has, that of the eyes. She has raised her hands; she has surrendered. She says, repeats: do not let me go. The fifth lies on a stretcher, doesn't look into the camera lens, doesn't even look toward it. We could say that she never really reached the shore; we could think she lost something more valuable than that which remained, even though she stayed alive. (Romagnoli 2013)

The day following the disaster, three Italian newspapers, *La Stampa*, *La Repubblica*, and *Corriere della Sera*, published personal photographs that had been discovered among the debris of the disaster and in the wallets and pockets of the dead (for a collection of newspaper pages see Cosentino n.d.). Each picture depicts two or more young people posing in a photographer's studio. Everyone is holding someone, either by the hand or with arms around someone's shoulders; two photos depict a man and a woman holding one another, possibly a husband and a wife. The poses and the smiles communicate that the people in the photos care about one another: they are friends, siblings, or a couple. The subjects in the photos have been arranged in front of a studio backdrop: curtains, a copy of a religious painting, a large image of a flowering plant. In one photograph published on

La Repubblica's website, a group of ten young men and one woman is too large for the backdrop and spills over its edges; they fill the whole space of the studio, revealing the backdrop as a backdrop and exposing the studio setting. Fitting everyone into the same frame was prioritized over maintaining the illusion of the studio.

Four years after the disaster, Grazia Longo, a *La Stampa* journalist, told me that she still remembered the night she obtained the seven photographs *La Stampa* would publish on the front page above the headline *L'ecatombe di Lampedusa*, "The massacre of Lampedusa." It is not exactly clear from our conversation who gave her the photos, and she never attempted to return them to the survivors. The photos were still at her home, she said. Longo recalled that she saw the photos at around 8 p.m. on October 3 and then called the head of *La Stampa*'s editorial office in Turin. Unlike other Italian and European newspapers, *La Stampa* decided to use the found photos as their sole front-page visual element depicting the disaster. This deviated from the dominating representation that depicted the disaster as an asymmetrical relation between extraterrestrial strangers and moral Europeans, as I argued in the beginning of this chapter. Longo explained the unique decision: "*La Stampa* has a style of publishing not only news but also stories. Behind a story there are people's lives—in this case, lives that cannot be reduced to a number or the category of 'migrant' who has arrived in Italy. They were people of flesh and blood." The importance of the photos, she said, was that they represented the human aspect, "the dignity of the people who died" and "the world where they came from" (Longo 2017).

In their articles about the found photographs, journalists invited the public to imagine the victims' lives and hopes. They read the subjects' clothes and expressions as signs that the refugees were not that different from "us" in the West—as signs that the people in the images were capable of aspiring to freedom and Westernness. Goffredo Buccini in *Corriere della Sera* even used the English words "campus" and "sneakers" to underline the Western aspirations present in his reading of the photographs.

> They have American jeans and jackets. Shirts hanging loose, like campus guys. Sneakers to go far in and eyes full of hope. Their dream is in the clothes they wear: the promise of a secured meal that brings well-being, the desire to look like us, to escape from horror and fear onto our shores. In the photos they look into the camera lens, but it goes beyond—their gaze is fixed on the future they pursued here on the other side of the sea. (Buccini 2013)
>
> There are friends, dressed well, and they seem like movie stars. She in white, he in jeans and a soccer player's shirt, between two yellow curtains and a backdrop of fake plants. (Longo 2013)

The Italian media framed the found photographs as portraits of the dead, although the people in the pictures may not have been on the boat at all. Geoffredo Buccini calls the pictures "photos of the ghosts of Lampedusa" (Buccini 2013). The subtitle of Grazia Longo's story frames the pictures as *foto di vite spezzate*, "photos of broken lives" and *foto dei fantasmi del mare*, "photos of the ghosts of the sea." In her article, she states: "These little wet photographs, soaked with salt water, are all that remains of those who did not make it." She interprets the expressions of the people in the photographs as an omen of the disaster: "They don't smile, as if they could foresee what awaits them" (Longo 2013).

Photographs as Objects

In our interview, Grazia Longo (2017) reflected that she was particularly fascinated by the idea that by publishing the found photographs, the newspaper could illustrate the victims' "world." That world was elsewhere and in another temporality. The aesthetics of the soft, faded Eritrean studio photographs contrasted with the sharp quality of the other news photographs, producing a sense of a different time, an unspecified "then." In none of the newspapers that published found photographs did the journalists reflect on the fact that the people on the boat were coming from Eritrea, a former colony of Italy. The different temporality and space—the "there" and the "then"—remained unspecified, a haunting presence of a silenced past.

In *Corriere della Sera*, *La Repubblica*, and *La Stampa*, the photographs are reprinted not just as images, but in their entirety, as objects. The edges of the photos are visible, and in *La Repubblica*, the little picture lies in the palm of someone's hand. The public is directed to look at the pictures as printed photographs—objects that could be in an album or a wallet. It is not only the images that communicate the relationality of the victims, but also the objects themselves—that someone carried these photographs along on the journey. The journalists' language also cues the reader that the photographs should be seen as objects: the photos are described as *portafortuna*, "lucky charms" (Buccini 2013) and *figurini*, "collectibles" (Longo 2013).

Studio photographs are taken as mementos: they illuminate the passing of time and an awareness of the *has-been* or *having-been-there* nature of photographs. Susan Sontag (1977) even maintains that photographs are always already "memento mori," reminders of the eventual death. Roland Barthes (1977, 159) has argued in his comparison of photography to painting and moving images that photography has the distinct ability to create an awareness of temporality. However, a studio photograph often represents a *timeless past*, particularly if there are no clues about when and for what occasion the picture was taken. This quality of studio photographs, along with the fictional placelessness created by the use of backdrops, encourages the use of imagination in interpreting the images. The literary style that the journalists adopted when writing about the found studio photographs illustrates how the found photographs invite or require imagination.

The found studio photographs are not posed family portraits, but instead, document friendships: the subjects are all young and of the same generation. This particular genre of studio photography may remind the European public of school photographs. Marianne Hirsch (1997) points out that family photographs can contain conventional elements that make them meaningful for those not in the picture, as well. In her analysis of mediated witnessing of the Rwandan genocide, Kaarina Nikunen (2019, 115) describes how family photographs seen in an installation at the Kigali Genocide Memorial affect her differently from news images of the dead bodies. She recognizes the format and the function of such photographs: the mundane surroundings of home communicate how the people lived and were loved (Nikunen 2019, 116). Jens Ruchatz (2008, 372) argues that photographs can be "read" by anyone, and in those readings, generic conventions overtake the images' specific meanings. The aesthetic of studio photography, like the aesthetic of a family album photograph, accentuates the images' universality and enhances viewers' ability to identify with the people depicted and imagine their life stories.

Compared to the dominant visuality of migrant disasters that I examined at the beginning of this chapter, the found photographs alter the gazes of the migrant and the viewer. In general, migrant disasters and "Third World problems" such as famine and forced displacement are represented visually either through images of anonymous people suffering en masse—"a sea of humanity" representing "anonymous corporeality," in the terms of Liisa Malkki (1996)— or through emotional close-ups, usually of women and children who embody a suitable victimhood and compel the spectator to stay with the sufferer (Chouliaraki 2006, 123). In migrant disasters, the gaze of the viewer aligns with that of the photographer, who shoots from the perspective of European rescuers: coast guard, military, or humanitarian agents. It has been rare that the gaze is turned toward the European bordering agents. However, this pattern has been interrupted by NGOs such as the German Sea-Watch that maintain the position of countersurveillance at maritime borders and cultivate "a disobedient gaze"— that unveils "that which it attempts to hide—the political violence it is founded on and the human rights violations that are its structural outcome" (Pezzani and Heller 2013, 294). In addition, mobile phone footage filmed by migrants during the journey, rescue, or push back operations have been mediated in social and mainstream media (Bennett 2018).

In the dominant visualities that produce a hierarchy where the migrants are the objects of both the action and the gaze of the European authority, the migrants are looked at without their knowledge or consent. In contrast, a studio photograph invites a more horizontal gaze from the viewer. The subject poses and looks into the camera self-consciously in a photographic situation that is familiar to the viewer: the subjects have prepared for the camera and negotiated with the photographer about how they wish to be seen. Importantly, they do not pose with a European spectator in mind. In these pictures, the people are not objects of the gaze of the European authorities, but instead agents who ask to be looked at in a specific role: as someone's friend, brother, sister, or cousin.

Page 5 of *Corriere della Sera* (Cosentino n.d.) on October 4, 2013, illustrates this contrast between the two types of gazes. At the center of the page is a still from a coast guard video, shot from a helicopter. In the deep blue sea below, a body floats in the crosshairs of the camera's viewfinder. With this image, the newspaper reader is invited to see the scene of death from the coast guard's perspective, through their lens. The dead migrant floats in the sea alone, an object without dignity and in relationship to none. Chiara Giubilaro analyses the image as "a violent asymmetry between those with the right to see and represent and those who are excluded from it" (Giubilaro 2018, 107). On three sides of the image of the drowned body are four found photographs depicting a group of friends, a couple, and two individuals. These images are laid out differently—as photographs with their white frames—whereas the image of the dead body is without frames.

The found photographs represent relationality—friendship, kinship, or love— but by *re-presenting* the photos as objects, the media attempted to transform them from personal photographs or mementos into publicly meaningful objects and images. From among the debris of the disaster site, the photographs were recovered and turned into publicly valuable objects: *mediated relics of the disaster*. The relics remain—survive—though the people they belonged to have died. The meaning the relics convey to mediated spectators is that those who died were social beings. These photographs did not end up in the numbered plastic bags holding the material remains of each victim for future identification. They also do not end up in the trash. Instead, they were retrieved by the divers and public health authorities who managed the dead and passed the photographs along to journalists, who then created public stories about them. Those managing the disaster identified a broader public and cultural significance of the photographs, beyond their being forensic evidence. The photographs evoke thoughts of the lives that the people on the boat might have lived—a civil imagination (Azoulay 2012) that conceives of the migrants as persons. However, while this presents an opening for an alternative narrative and representation of the dead, neither the media nor the public took that potential any further. There were no follow-up stories or investigations into who the people in the photographs were, no biographies. The objects held the potential to connect people—if they were considered as personal belongings that could be returned to their owners.

The dominant representation of the dead focused on coffins and body bags, *the presence of death*. The European agents were active in managing the dead— finding and retrieving them, providing coffins and burial places. The hierarchical visual structure, in which Europeans dominated, carried through into images of mourning the disaster. The survivors remained nonpersons, agents without social lives or ethical agency. The arrangement of the coffins, which became the iconic visual representation of the disaster, visualized and aestheticized the "many"—ultimately, the numerical quantity of the dead. The dominant representation produced a visual necropolitics in which Italy managed the deaths of its "non-citizens" as a homogeneous category of innocents with neither individuality nor relationships to Europe (whether past, present, or future). They were not represented as inheritors of *Colonia Eritrea*, as relatives of present-day Europeans, or as future Europeans.

The iconic arrangement of the coffins had no visual trace of those inside the coffins. The singularity of the dead was erased not only by the representation of a massive number of dead but also by the sanitized similarity of the coffins. Nothing in the images themselves revealed that they represented border deaths or victims who originated from Eritrea. The colonial past of Italian Eritrea was not visible in any way, nor were the victims' present-day connections with the European countries that were their destinations and where they had relatives. This generic aesthetic and "Italianness" was so profound that later the coffins passed as representative of mass death of Italians. During the COVID-19 spring of 2020, suddenly, these iconic photographs of the October 3, 2013, disaster appeared in social media internationally to visualize the death toll caused by the virus in the Lombardia region in Northern Italy. The images were tagged with #protectourfamilies, #stayhome that framed them as visual proof of the deadliness of the virus. Reuters (2020) and Agence France Press (Mason 2020) corrected the false association in their fact checking sites. In almost seven years, the referential afterlife of the iconic images of the Lampedusa disaster had faded from the public imagination (at least outside of Italy). The images were no longer immediately associated with the original event. Interestingly, the misrepresentation of the images prompted the news agencies to make news about the false context, and in doing so, they recalled the details of the Lampedusa disaster in the context of the pandemic. Global publics were reminded of the border deaths that had taken place almost seven years earlier.

In this chapter, I have identified several critical ways photographs were used to represent not the *presence of any death*, but rather the *absence of an irreplaceable life*. Family members and survivors of the Lampedusa disaster were influential in creating a critical alternative representation of the disaster: they chose photographs of the victims and attached them to the coffins at the Lampedusa harbor before the authorities transported the dead to Sicily. Adal Neguse displayed a photograph of his brother in an aesthetic format familiar from its use in global social movements, creating a parallel with forced disappearances and providing a visual opening for the register of forensics and the right to identification. These practices produced an alternative visual politics, that of human interdependency.

The other examples of alternative and potentially critical visuality that I have discussed in this chapter—the blurred mug shots and the found studio photographs—are ethically more complicated than the photographs of the dead that the relatives consciously displayed to the public. No consent was obtained from the people who owned them or were pictured in them. Their presence in the public sphere required journalists to interpret the images for their audiences. They *imagined* who the victims were and what the survivors thought. Nevertheless, these photographs intervened in and disrupted the dominant visual hierarchy of the disaster. They opened a potentially critical gaze toward the disaster: recognizing absence in the case of the mug shots, and the humanity and personality of the victims in the found photos. The found photographs in particular represented agency, friendship, and solidarity, providing a different and more human register for imagining *who* the dead were.

ENUMERATION, NAMING, PHOTOS

Counting and naming are the two most common forms of acknowledging the victims of any disaster. When the victims' names are known, the media and the mourners also bring forward photographs of the dead as a means of knowing *who* they were. In the case of the Lampedusa disaster, there is a relative lack of interest in the European public domain in the exact death toll and the names of the dead. This reveals that the victims of this disaster—or of this kind of disaster—were not treated the same way as the victims of other kinds of disasters in the European public sphere. This is an example of what Judith Butler (2009, 1) terms the ungrievability of certain bodies, meaning that within particular epistemological frameworks, some lives are not conceived as livable lives at all, and therefore, cannot be lost. Ungrievability is a notion that many scholars of border deaths have used in arguing that there is a differentiated public response to migrant deaths in comparison to other deaths (see Stierl 2016; Rygiel 2016; Stümer 2018). They argue that public performances of mourning can be a means to resist ungrievability and produce a critical politics to confront fatal bordering.

Similarly, in the words of Pope Francis (2013b), differential treatment of border deaths is an example of "globalized indifference" to the suffering of certain people: "In this globalized world, we have fallen into globalized indifference. We have become used to the suffering of others: it doesn't affect me; it doesn't concern me; it's none of my business!" This chapter examines how the victims of the Lampedusa disaster were represented by numbers, names, and photographs, and how those representations were assembled. I am specifically interested in the potentialities and limitations of these modes of representation. How do they shape the afterlife and memorialization of the disaster? How does the memory of the disaster survive oblivion in the public domain through these modes of representation?

Quantifying the Dead

No matter how the disaster is named—whether it is a tragedy, a massacre (*strage*), or a shipwreck—the dominant representation is a number, a count of the victims. No one definitive figure represents the Lampedusa disaster, however. Instead, several different numbers have been cited: 366, 367, 368, 369, 373. When the *Guardian* published what it called "the List," a fifty-two-page list of refugee deaths, on June 20, 2018, in a supplement marking World Refugee Day, the Lampedusa disaster took up just one line: "03/10/13, 373, N.N., Africa, drowned after boat on way from Libya to Italy caught fire and sank in the Mediterranean Sea; 155 rescued." The more commonly used figures start from 366, the official number of deaths (DDA 2014). Three hundred sixty-six refers to the number of bodies that were discovered on the boat and nearby. The 367th was a baby that divers discovered still attached to his mother by the umbilical cord, Lampedusans told me.

It is common in cases of mass deaths, such as in wars, for the precise number of missing persons or deaths to be a subject of controversy, with the number itself becoming a matter of contestation. In the case of the Lampedusa victims, however, the differing figures appear to be uncontested, and it seems that the exactness of the number is inconsequential to the agents who have engaged with the disaster in the public sphere: the difference between 367 and 368 or between 367 and 369 is not important to them. The number stands for a category—the victims of the October 3 shipwreck—and the individual, one increment in that sum, loses its significance. The essence of the figure, like the figure representing border deaths in general (the 34,361 in the *Guardian*'s "List," for example) is not the number's exactness, but its greatness—the many.

That the numbers are indeterminate is common knowledge among those who engage with border deaths. Nevertheless, NGOs, academics, journalists, governments, and the International Organization for Migration (IOM) continue to attempt to count border deaths and to represent them with numbers, which when used, seem exact and appear to be facts. In 1993, United for Intercultural Action (UNITED) became the first civil society actor to attempt to count border deaths, doing so with the goal of directing critical attention to the deaths. The Italian journalist Gabriele del Grande started counting deaths in 2006 for the *Fortress Europe* blog, and the University of Amsterdam started to compile the database

Border Deaths in 2012. The Turkish artist Banu Cennetoğlu (2018), who has engaged with UNITED's "List of Deaths" through art, explains the justification for counting deaths: "The governments don't keep these records for the public; they don't want the public to see these records because it exposes their policies. So, you have NGOs trying to put the data together, and that data is incomplete and fragile, but then again someone has to do it." The motivation of civil society organization for counting the dead was to seek accountability.

Border activists and artists have used the "List of Deaths" to make border deaths visible in multiple ways, helping to visualize "the many." Cennetoğlu printed the list in the style of a train schedule and displayed it at the Basel central railway station in 2011. At the Museum of Modern Art in New York, the list was spread out on the walls of a gallery. And at least two newspapers—*Der Tagesspiegel* in Berlin and the *Guardian* in the United Kingdom—have published the list as a supplement for their readers. Such materiality makes the number concrete: "the many" feels heavy in the form of a thick newspaper supplement, and it cannot be passed by with a single glance when the pages are spread across several yards of wall. However, as with the figure representing the victims of the Lampedusa disaster, the exactness of the number of dead on the "List of Deaths" does not seem to be the main concern for those compiling the list or engaging with it. It is unimportant even in a material sense, as is clear from the lines in the list. The Lampedusa disaster, with 373 dead, occupies only one row, whereas some other disasters are spread over multiple rows, with each N.N. or name being given its own row.

Nathaniel White, a documentary photographer, has taken a closer look at the "List of Deaths" in his 2017 project *Routes*, in which he traces the exact locations where people have died or gone missing. Aerial photographs—again, a great number of them—contrast the everydayness of the landscape (a motorway, the sea, a field, a building) and violent death. By attending to one detail, the location of death, his intention is to focus on the singularity of each death. "The number thirty thousand and something dead doesn't tell me anything, doesn't touch me," White (2018) told me.

The work of critical border activists to document and expose the massive scale of border deaths, which, as Cennetoğlu explained, was a response to governments not revealing the extent of death, was relevant throughout the 1990s and the first decade of the 2000s. The situation changed, however, after the Lampedusa disaster. One outcome of the disaster was that in 2014, the year after the Lampedusa disaster, the International Organization for Migration (IOM) started compiling lists and providing figures on a regular basis. Quantification became the dominant way of representing border deaths across the field, from activists to governmental agencies.[1]

The Lampedusa disaster was a key moment in this respect: it suddenly seemed that governments in Europe were no longer avoiding the issue of border deaths, but rather highlighting their magnitude. The IOM made the monthly count a recurring news item (IOM 2022). Media could regularly report the figures and whether they had increased or decreased, like they did on stock markets. To the public, it began to look like European policies could manage and control migration, and a critical tool in creating this impression were the numbers. Previously, the main indicator for monitoring migration and policy had been statistics on asylum applications; now, fatality metrics were also operationalized as an optic for viewing migration and bordering. It was paradoxical that the IOM, which was part of the technology of border management and which represented the governments that had produced the fatal conditions, had become so interested in counting deaths.

While the IOM has adopted a practice invented by civil society actors, the rationale behind its counting and the politics that it produces are different. First, the IOM argues that deaths are attributable to greedy people smugglers, omitting any reference to the responsibility borne by European migration policies and border controls. Second, the IOM only counts deaths that occur during crossings of Europe's external border and omit counting deaths resulting from bordering *inside* Europe, to avoid assigning any direct responsibility to European states. UNITED, on the contrary, also counts deaths in detention centers and suicides resulting from the threat of deportation. In an analysis of the transfer of tools from "civil society counterstatistics to intergovernmental recuperation" of border death metrics, Charles Heller and Antoine Pécoud (2020) argue that the IOM neutralizes the critical politics of counting, and in fact, uses statistics on border deaths to reinforce the very structures and practices that produce them.

While activists' counterstatistics have critical power in their demands for accountability, as they show the murderous effects of bordering, statistics are tricky. They are central to the logic of governmentality. Power and resistance to power are mutually constitutive, as Heller and Pécoud's (2020, 484) Foucauldian discussion underlines.

In other contexts, scholars have brought critical attention to the knowledge acquired through fatality metrics and the power of metrics, for example, in waging war and in human rights activism. Yến Lê Espiritu (2014, 2, 178) exposes a schizophrenic fascination with counting the confirmed Vietnamese "kills" to chart the United States progress in the Vietnam war while simultaneously weaving a "fabric of erasure" and an "organized blankness" of these deaths. The dead were numbers but not people with "faces and names, family and friends, personal histories and beliefs." They were people "whose lives do not count" (Espiritu 2014, 178). Jennifer Hyndman (2007), who examines fatality metrics in relation to the Iraq War, argues that metrics are incapable of accounting for the destruction of life and livelihood. They risk being "a disembodied, abstract process, the methodology of which has been as contentious as the deaths themselves" (Hyndman 2007, 36). Such a distant and sanitized gaze on death can dehumanize the consequences of war. Martina Tazzioli (2015) argues that counting deaths at EU borders reinforces a governmental gaze on the border by creating the sense that the border and its fatality are issues of management. In contrast to the removed and distanced spatiality produced by metrics, Hyndman searches for an alternative, feminist perspective. She argues for "more accountable, embodied ways of seeing and understanding the intersection of power and space. Instead of mapping and quantifying, the understanding of the fatal border requires knowledge of the human consequences: the destruction of life" (Hyndman 2007, 36).

Jenny Edkins (2011, 7) presents a similar critique to quantifying when she writes about missing persons. Figures count groups of people, alive or dead, not for *who* they are, but for *what* they are, she argues. The bodies are counted in order to produce an object suitable for some purpose: administration, remembering, or documenting. The number serves simply as a reference to a category, such as *migrant victims of the October 3 shipwreck*. It answers the question, what happened. Three hundred sixty-six, or 367, or 368, or 369 people categorized as migrants drowned. But this performance of knowledge, of an exact-sounding figure, doesn't generate the question, *who* died. If that were asked, we would have to know who the 369th person was. What was her name?

Knowing One Name

One counterhegemonic strategy to the distant knowledge provided by fatality metrics is to ask *who* died. Hannah Arendt (1998, 97) wrote in *The Human Condition* that the chief characteristic of human life, as opposed to animal life, is that it can be told as a story. This distinguishes *bios*, the mortal individual life, from the merely biological *zoe*. Every life story, every biography, starts with a name. Knowing a person starts with knowing their name.

After the Lampedusa disaster, the need for names was obvious to the Eritrean diasporic community and to those in Eritrea who were searching for someone. But that was a matter of practicality, not representation. There were also others who were not looking for a specific name among the dead, but nevertheless asked this question in search of an ethical representation of the disaster. In the few representations of the Lampedusa disaster that actually named an individual victim, Yohanna was the most frequent choice. She was chosen not because she was representative of typical migrant victims, but because her story was like no other. She became known as the woman who gave birth in a sinking boat. Giving birth is an experience to which many can relate: in giving birth she is similar to me, because I know what it feels like to be in labor. But in giving birth to a baby while her boat was sinking, knowing of a certain death, she is like no one else.

The Italian divers who brought the bodies to the surface told the media stories of what they had seen. One diver recounted that he had found the body of a newborn boy, still connected to his mother by the umbilical cord. The story was repeated across the international media as a horrific detail of the disaster. Though the story circulated globally, it was Meron Estefanos, an Eritrean human rights activist and journalist in Stockholm, who first set out to discover the woman's name. She traveled to Lampedusa to find out who the woman was and reported the full story on her radio program *Voices of Eritrean Refugees*, which aired on the Tigrinya-language station Radio Erena, based in Paris.

I met Meron Estefanos in her home in Stockholm where she told me she had felt compelled to find out the name and the story of the "woman who drowned while giving birth," as she was known in the media (Estefanos 2016). In Lampedusa, Meron found out from survivors that the woman had been called Yohanna and that she had been eight months pregnant. She also found the woman's fiancé, who had survived the disaster. By telling the story of Yohanna and interviewing her fiancé, Mehbratom, Meron wanted to produce one story that could stand for many others. She explained: "Three hundred sixty-eight died, they say. It is just a number. It doesn't add up. But by telling an individual's story, I am able to reach the pain that they went through. Rather than giving figures, I want to touch people's hearts. It could have been you if the circumstances were different."

Once Meron had made Yohanna's name public to the Eritrean diaspora, the story of Yohanna inspired more writing and performance. Poetry provided a form where the disaster's memory could be processed and transmitted among Eritreans in Eritrea and in diaspora. Traditionally, oral poems are recited to tell stories and to remember the deceased. A type of oral poetry, *aulò*, can convey critical judgment about issues and provide information, in addition to emotional expression (Brioni 2014). One widely circulated poem after the disaster is Ribka Sibhatu's (2016) Italian language poem "In Lampedusa," in which the name of Yohanna is central. The poem tells how Yohanna gave birth to a son, and Mehbratom cried "among the floating corpses": *Yohanna! Yohanna! Yohanna!*.

The horror of the baby being born and dying in the same instant, and of Yohanna suffering the pain of labor and drowning simultaneously becomes the narrative that speaks for all of the victims, who are represented by a figure. "A woman died while giving birth! / 368 people died!" Ribka's poem exclaims. Yohanna's pain symbolizes the pain of the 368.

Another Eritrean diasporic writer, Selam Kidane, also underlines the nonac-knowledgment of the new life as she draws on the story of Yohanna in her poem "Ode to Yohanna's Baby":

> On
> The vast dark sea
> His mother feebly fighting to stay afloat
> A baby boy was born
> No one saw his eyes
> Open briefly
> Then shut
>   (Kidane 2014, excerpt of the English-
> language poem "Ode to Yohanna's Baby")

Except for Meron Estefanos's interview with Mehbratom, the uses of the name of Yohanna do not trigger any retelling of her life beyond the experience of giving birth and dying simultaneously. The poems are not based on Yohanna's life, but on the story of discovery told by the divers. Yohanna's name and the story of her death inspired authors to produce representations of more general themes, such as the vulnerability of life—"No one saw his eyes/Open briefly/Then shut."

Yohanna's name later caught the attention of Western writers who returned to the disaster after the initial news cycle. Mattathias Schwartz (2014) mentioned Yohanna in his story about the Eritrean priest Mussie Zerai in the *New Yorker* (April 21, 2014). The piece is about the shipwreck from Mussie's point of view, and within the story, Schwartz briefly witnesses Meron Estefanos's interview of Mehbratom. Frances Stonor Saunders (2016) picked up Yohanna's name from Schwartz's story for her essay in the *London Review of Books* about crossing borders and identification. She too, like Meron, had been haunted by the story of the woman who gave birth while drowning. As someone who had witnessed the disaster only at a distance, through the media, she seems distracted by the horrific detail. Saunders couldn't forget the disaster, not because she knew any-one who was on the boat, but precisely because she didn't know anyone, not even one name. She knew one story, or rather, one detail of one story: a woman had died while giving birth. But not knowing the full story, not knowing the woman's name, produced a disturbing relationship with the disaster. Saunders (2016) writes: "All I know is that a woman who believed in the future drowned while giving birth, and we have no idea who she was. And it's this, her lack of known identity, which places us, who are fat with it, in direct if hopelessly unequal relationship to her."

In witnessing the disaster through the media, Saunders is caught in a relationship that is defined by a gap—a gap between dying here in "our" European society and yet as a stranger to us. The female victim does not exist as a person for European institutions or the European public. In her search for a way out of this uncomfortable position as a European who *looks*—witnesses through the media—but is unable to *see* or *know*, after two years of thinking about the woman who drowned, she finally comes across Mattathias Schwartz's article in the *New Yorker* and finds the woman's name: *Yohanna*. Saunders (2016) ends her essay by repeating a detail from Schwartz's story: "Her name, this man said, was Yohanna. In Eritrean, it means 'congratulations.'"

Interestingly, it was not the story of the woman who gave birth while drowning that touched Saunders's heart, to use Meron's phrase, but the fact that she didn't know who the woman was and that she lived in a society where *not knowing* was not an issue. She was unsettled by the institutionalized blankness and the social indifference that was revealed to her by the lack of a name. Therefore, it was perhaps not so much finding out Yohanna's name that relieved Saunders's anxiety, but rather finding out about the attentiveness of others to her identity and story: the efforts of Meron, the act of recalling Yohanna's memory by her partner, Mehbratom, the activist engagement of Mussie, and the investigative reporting of Schwartz.

However, it is necessary to ask, what is the meaning of knowing one name for the publics that witness the disaster through media. Does knowing the name of Yohanna enable us to find an emotional relationship to the 368? Does it fill the uncomfortable gap and generate action that would not treat the dead as strangers? By attending to one name, Meron sought the means to create an emotional relationship to the disaster and emotional knowledge about it. While an individual's emotional response to the disaster does not change depending on whether the number of victims is 366 or 367, knowing one victim by name can trigger an emotional flow. An emotional relationship to Yohanna was also a means of keeping the memory of the disaster alive. The name and the story of one individual victim—that is, knowledge that "touches the heart"—would haunt the public much longer than a number, Meron believed. The referential afterlife of a disaster depends on its capacity to produce emotional responses, and in this process, knowing one victim by name may extend the echo.

While 368 (or 366, 377, 369, or 373) are too many to know and to remember one by one, Yohanna can be remembered. She can become a symbol for the 368 dead, and the presence of her name across platforms and in poems reminds the public that the other 367 have names and stories, too. Her name can invoke the understanding that individual lives were destroyed, in contrast to a focus on the presence of dead bodies. Alan Kurdi, the little boy whose body was found on the shores of Turkey in 2015, became an icon of the deaths of the many refugees and migrants who lost their lives in the Mediterranean Sea during the European refugee reception crisis—one of 3,777 dead, as counted by the IOM in 2015.

Similarly, Anne Frank is remembered as one of the six million Jews killed by the Nazis. Primo Levi (1988, 56) writes in *The Drowned and the Saved*: "There is no proposition between the pity we feel and the extent of the pain by which the pity is aroused: a single Anne Frank excites more emotion than the myriads who suffered as she did but whose image has remained in the shadows. Perhaps it is necessary that it can be so. If we had to and were able to suffer the sufferings of everyone, we could not live."

Nevertheless, an icon of mass death, one name that immediately refers to a certain event or era, may prompt the public to imagine the manifold individual cases of suffering. However, she might also remain the only individual who is remembered. Saunders recognizes the danger that knowing Yohanna by name can lead to her being cast as a "sentimental artifact," an object or a symbol created by others for their own emotional purposes: a sentimental artifact that relieves the concerned European spectator's pain of not knowing and her discomfort at realizing she is living in a fundamentally unequal society.

In the context of humanitarian intervention, the Nigerian American author Teju Cole (2016, 349) writes in a similar vein about "the White Savior Industrial Complex" as "a valve for releasing the unbearable pressures that build in a system developed on pillage." Cole writes that American sentimentality allows one to emotionally engage with "isolated 'disasters'" without connecting the dots or seeing the pattern of power behind them. "All he sees is need, and he sees no need to reason out the need for the need" (Cole 2016, 344). Sentimentality does not require acknowledgment of the multiple forces that in conjuncture produce a disaster.

The List of Names

Immediately after the disaster, three survivors developed the idea of collecting the names of the victims while they were confined in the refugee accommodation center in Lampedusa. Mohamed Kasim, who now lives near Copenhagen, was one of them. He explained to me in an interview that he and the others felt obliged to notify the families of the victims. They all knew how painful it is to remain in the liminal state of not knowing if a person is dead or alive. Every Eritrean has struggled with the uncertainty of disappeared persons.

As survivors of the disaster, Mohamed explained, it was their responsibility to account for the dead and let their family members know. They did not rely on the Italian authorities or the Red Cross, as they thought that Eritrean diasporic networks would be more efficient in disseminating the information. The Lampedusa disaster would become a pilot case for migrant disaster victim identification procedures as I explain in chapter 9, but in the immediate aftermath survivors took the task to account who the dead were. It was important, Mohamed stressed, that the families be able mourn their losses. For the survivors, accounting for the disaster by listing the names was an act of respect for those who remained alive, for those who were missing someone. This was the first act of *survivor citizenship* after the disaster, an identity that I discuss further in chapter 7. Regardless of their legal status, the survivors acted as citizens of Europe by undertaking social duties and claiming rights and justice. Compiling the list of dead emerged from the feeling of responsibility toward those who died and their families.

The journey and its fatal end connected the survivors to the victims in a profound way. While the list of names that Mohamed and his two fellow passengers started to compile made visible the absence of the people who had died and separated the dead from the living, the act of collecting the names re-created a community that comprised both the living and the dead: those who had traveled together on this specific journey. Some had been together since departing from the same village in Eritrea. They had survived the first dangerous crossing together—the prohibited escape from Eritrea. Some had met later on in the journey, in the collection and waiting points governed by smugglers. Some had experienced or witnessed violence together: a few had been kidnapped in Libya, and their relatives had paid $3,500 in ransom for their release. Then there were the families: a brother who lost a sister, a man who lost a cousin, and a husband who lost his wife. But there were also those who had become friends on the boat.

The three survivors re-created the network of relationships by asking the other survivors for information about those they had known on the boat. Who was sitting next to you? What details about those people do you remember? Many others joined the effort and collected information. Using pen and paper, the survivors organized these answers into a table that stretched to nine pages. According to Mohamed there were several versions of the list. The three of them made revisions as the information became more accurate. At first, there were several duplicates in the list of names: two or more people had remembered a name that later turned out to refer to the same person. Although a number preceded each name on the list, establishing the total number of victims was not the goal.

The list that I have seen is the one that was later published on the Eritrean opposition website Assenna.com. It is titled *tselim mezgeb 365 gdayat meqzefti Lampedusa* (The Black List of 365 Victims of the Tragedy of Lampedusa). This list has 367 names, written in neat Tigrinya script and organized alphabetically in straight rows. Two names are crossed out. Only twenty-six names on the list are missing the second name. After each name, the survivors have recorded the victim's gender, nationality, clan, and address. The list includes seven people from Ethiopia; the rest are from Eritrea. Some of the media coverage of the disaster had reported that there were Somalis among the travelers, so I wondered why no Somalis were on the list. When I mentioned this contradiction in reported nationalities to Mohamed, he was puzzled. To his knowledge, there were only Eritreans and a few Ethiopians on the boat. He was sure that the survivors would have remembered and listed every person, no matter their nationality. Their intention was to list everyone—that was why there was a column for nationality.

Finally, the list had a column for additional details. Its initial function was to prevent repeat entries. However, the additional details became a testimony of how the survivors remembered those who did not survive. Through these memories, the dead appear as persons and personalities. One person was a bar owner, another a priest. There was a teacher, remembered for his afro hair style. Although names are important markers of identity and individuality, this list is not only about names. The details that the survivors remembered—professions, clans, the streets or towns where people lived—are evidence of belonging to a community, and as a document, the list also communicates this. In addition, the list of names makes some of their relationships visible. Each name has a number that can be cross-referenced: according to the notes in the "additional details" column, entry no. 367 referred to the child of the person named in entry 274. Number 142 is the mother of numbers 62, 80, and 89. These details recorded on the handwritten document reveal that the person who died mattered to another person who also died.

The list accentuates the dignity of the dead by naming them and by making their relationships visible. The list highlights three kinds of relationships: First, by compiling the list, the survivors made their relationship to the dead visible. They re-created the relational network that existed on the boat before it capsized. Second, the survivors acknowledged that the dead had relationships and by making the list they informed the family members who otherwise might never hear about the fate of their loved ones. Third, they made the relationships between the dead visible by indicating them in the handwritten document. The relationships continued to matter even in death. Each individual existed in relation to other people, dead or alive. Such representation of relationality and interdependence is central to dignity and humanity.

Judith Butler (2004) bases her work on "grievable life" on the relationality of being human, arguing that relationality makes every human vulnerable. Death is the ultimate loss and transforms survivors, as well. We are hurt not only by violence or pain that is directed at us personally, but also by violence toward someone else we have a connection with. Butler says: "On one level, I think I have lost 'you' only to discover that 'I' have gone missing as well. At another level, perhaps what I have lost 'in' you, that for which I have no ready vocabulary, is a relationality that is composed neither exclusively of myself nor you, but is to be conceived as *the tie* by which those terms are differentiated and related" (Butler 2004, 22). At this intimate level, the loss of "the tie" concerns everyone equally, and Butler argues that recognizing this vulnerability, which all human beings share, is a key to justice. However, in public life, she points out, societies recognize and even amplify some deaths, whereas other losses become unthinkable and ungrievable. Public grief is selective, and therefore the act of mourning deaths that are ignored in public life has radical political potential.

The main purpose of listing the names was to help those who were looking for missing relatives. In other words, the survivors of the Lampedusa disaster who compiled the list took moral responsibility as survivors, a position that also constituted their own identities and a sense of a community. It is this awareness of the vulnerability and relationality of being human that makes the creation of the list of names such a powerful moral and political act. The survivors compiled their list of names as an act of forensic civics in the face of public institutions indifferent to the identities of the dead. They did what the Italian authorities and the humanitarian organizations (namely, the Red Cross) would have done in so-called normal circumstances—in disasters where citizens die or where citizens of countries that matter to Italy die. An Eritrean Italian who interpreted for the Italian investigators of the disaster told me in a telephone interview in 2020 that he later typed the list of the dead in the Latin alphabet and handed it over to Italian authorities.

The Circulation of the Names

The list of the dead that was compiled by the survivors did not remain simply a reference used for contacting family members but was soon photographed and digitized and began to spread more widely. It remains unclear to me who initially digitized the handwritten list and started spreading it but there was a demand to know the names in various activist and religious communities. The names were read out on Eritrean radio programs such as *Radio Asenna* and in religious memorial services held by the Eritrean diaspora. They were also recited in religious ceremonies in Italy and in human rights protests in various European cities.

The three survivors who had collected the names were troubled that the list had been spread in various directions. Their intention had been to document the victims only for the people who survived them. They were aware of the relatives' possible wishes of anonymity. Three years later, in 2016, Mohamed Kasim was still concerned about the unethical aspects to spreading the list. Later, he learned that publicizing the names had caused further harm to some of the victims' families. One issue that Mohamed and others mentioned was that some people had heard about the death of a loved one through the radio or social media, breaking the traditional convention of delivering news of a death in person. The second concern, not articulated by survivors themselves but by Eritrean human rights activists I interviewed was the fear of reprisal. Illegal exit, draft evasion, and desertion from the national service are not treated in the judicial system; but punishments are inconsistently imposed by military officials and security forces (EASO 2019, 21). Arbitrariness of punishments may also place family members remaining in Eritrea in danger. Issues of data justice and privacy of the victims and their families are crucial aspects in thinking of representation and memorialization by naming. While anonymity risks sanitizing a disaster and hiding its human consequences, naming the victims can also be problematic.

Two different groups had a specific interest in the names of the victims and their value for activism. First, there were the European-led humanitarian groups, migrant activists, and religious actors who had been raising awareness about deaths in the border zones for several years. Mourning and creative rituals had become a part of their activism, underlining the fatal consequences of the European border regime. Second, Eritrean human rights activists and oppositional political actors in the diaspora also highlighted the deaths, but their activism emphasized the oppressive political situation in Eritrea. For them, the disaster became a symbol of the suffering produced by the Eritrean regime. These two types of activists treated the list of names as documentation of individuals who had lost their lives as a consequence of direct or structural violence and the denial of human rights. Reciting the names and making the names known was crucial for their practice—political or religious.

For the Community of Sant'Egidio,[2] obtaining the list of names of the Lampedusa disaster was a continuation of their ongoing practice. Reciting the names of dead migrants had been an important part of the organization's prayer service *Morire di speranza* (Dying of Hope), which they had been holding in Basilica di Santa Maria in Trastevere in Rome on World Refugee Day since at least 2011

(Sant'Egidio 2011). Each year, some of the names of those who have died at the border are recited, and a candle is lit in their memory. The Dying of Hope prayer vigil is specifically meant for "thinking of each of them"—each of those who died at Europe's border, as Sant'Egidio frames it in their public communications. In order to think of "them" individually, a list of names is read aloud. This practice is intended to remind members of the community to take responsibility and "to look directly at the reality of migration by putting the lives of each person and full respect for human rights in the foreground" (Sant'Egidio 2011).

In Lampedusa, Stefano Nastasi, the parish priest, received the list of names from the Community of Sant'Egidio and read them out in some of the services the parish organized. One took place inside the airport hangar, where some 110 coffins, each adorned with flowers, were organized in straight rows in the arrangement that I discussed in chapter 2. Four years later, Father Nastasi (2017) explained how saying the names of the victims was an important part of this ceremony: it was about "bringing back the presence of the person." The reading of the names counteracted the generic nature of the arrangement by representing the disaster as the absence of individual lives. *Asmat—Names*, a film directed by Dagmawi Yimer (*Asmat* 2015) includes a recitation of all names. He underlines that reciting names brings forward the subjectivity and relationality of those who died. In a public lecture he explained the focus on names in *Asmat*: "Naming our children is a way of telling the world about our hopes, our dreams, our beliefs, or about the people and things we respect. We choose meaningful names for our children, just as our parents did for us" (Yimer 2015, 15). He also argues that saying the names of the victims reveals the political agency of the victims: "These names have defied man-made boundaries and laws, have disturbed and challenged African and European governments" (Yimer 2015, 15).

For several decades, listing the names of those who have died in wars or disasters has been a form of remembering victims. War memorials, sites of terrorist attacks, and memorials of disasters—like the memorial in Stockholm's Galärvarvskyrkogården (Galley Shipyard Cemetery) commemorating the sinking of the *Estonia* in 1994—often list the names of those who lost their lives. After the Christchurch terrorist attack on March 15, 2019, New Zealand prime minister Jacinda Ardern rendered the terrorist "nameless" and refused to mention his name. Instead, in her first speech to parliament after the attack, she urged the public to speak the victims' names (Wahlquist 2019). Naming victims is also a common practice in the antiracist Black Lives Matter movement as hashtags #SayTheirNames and #SayHerName indicate (Khaleeli 2016).

Publicly identifying war victims, including civilians, in memorials has become a common practice since the aftermath of World War I. In Srebrenica, where more than 8,000 men and boys were murdered in 1995 during the Bosnian War, the names of victims are read aloud each year at the annual ceremony where recently identified human remains are reburied. Reading thousands of names is also a ritual in the remembrance of the victims of the Holocaust.

Reading the names of victims who have suffered an unjust death is a public performance of commemoration, which as Klaus Neumann (2000, 136–39) argues, reminds those attending the ritual that the number of victims is a multiplier. Names invite the participant to think of the group of victims as "one individual plus one individual plus one individual plus . . ." In reciting the names in the list compiled by the survivors of the Lampedusa disaster (the one published in Asenna), the figure 365 becomes 365 times one name. Still, 365 names are probably too many for anyone to remember individually. Unless one is waiting for a particular name to be said, it is perhaps even difficult to hear each individual name. Or if the list of names is written or carved in a memorial wall, as is sometimes done, the multiplicity of names turns into a graphic visual element composed of the letters of the alphabet. This transformation of names into a visual element is especially evident for me when I look at the list of names from Lampedusa, which is in Tigrinya: the names are in a script that I cannot read.

Moreover, while the monotonous reading of names, as in Dagmawi's film *Asmat* and on Eritrean radio programs, does communicate that there are *many* names—a long list—it does not necessarily allow the listener to pause to reflect on any *one* of them. In addition, there is repetition in the list, as it is alphabetically ordered and many of the victims had the same first name. The narrator in *Asmat* recites the names as a meditative mantra: "Berahat, Berahat, Berahat, Berahat, Berahat, Berahat." Before moving on to the next name, the English translation is spoken: "Blessing." The translation divides the repetitions of one name from the next. This break allows the listener a moment of reflection: there were six victims by the name of Berahat. Similarly, the hundreds or thousands of names engraved on memorials often appear ornamental when seen from afar, but when one approaches a memorial, there is the opportunity to pause and focus on one name, or on one name at a time.

Arguably, reciting the names of victims aloud is a means of making a number visible, audible, and comprehensible. While the public may understand the figure as a multiplier, it nevertheless reveals nothing of the victims' character. Their differences flatten out, making it difficult to understand the individuals beyond the category of "victims." We don't see their politics, reasons for fleeing, personalities, interests, or hopes. However, we can begin to imagine them. This is crucial for imagining the migrants as being part of the shared world and as having a social life.

Portraits of the Victims

In addition to the names, the survivors began collecting photographs of the victims. Aregai Mehari, one of the survivors of the Lampedusa disaster, set up a Facebook group for the survivors on November 19, 2013; more than one hundred people joined. His intention was to create an online platform where people who had shared the horrific experience could stay in touch after parting ways in Lampedusa. In 2016, Aregai and I met in Sweden and analyzed the photographs that had been posted to the Facebook page. Aregai had learned English in high school and been assigned as a teacher in the national service. He speaks English very well and was the first survivor with whom I could have a conversation directly. He worked as a translator at an asylum-seeker accommodation center in Sweden after his arrival there. Later, Aregai became a bus driver in one of Sweden's larger cities.

When we looked at posts in the Facebook group, I noticed that the first photographs to be shared were of the survivors in Lampedusa soon after the disaster. In the first photograph, a young man stands on the rocks by the sea, looking at the waves. Then, there are photographs of groups of survivors, or of groups consisting of both survivors and Lampedusans. In one photograph, fifty or sixty survivors pose with rows of red funeral candles in front of them. There are two members of the Italian military at one end of the formation. Some survivors posted photographs captured from online news sites: the image of the sunken ship provided to the media by the Italian fire and rescue service and an image of the rows of coffins in the airport hangar (discussed in chapter 2) both appeared in the Facebook group.

The visual flow in the Facebook group changed a month later, when Aregai suggested to the group that survivors post old photographs of the victims. Almost all of the survivors knew someone who had lost their life in the disaster and either had photographs of them or were able to contact their families to get a photograph. Some survivors shared victims' photos in their original form; others edited the pictures, adding the date 3/10/2013, "Lampedusa disaster," "R.I.P.," and the name of the victim. Almost all of the photographs were studio portraits similar to the found photographs discussed in chapter 2, with the subject consciously posing and looking at the camera. Some of the photographs have digital backgrounds, featuring stars, geometric shapes, images of waterfalls, or mountains. Some include studio backdrops and props—one person sits on a fancy chair with draped curtains in the background. Aregai told me that having a portrait taken in a studio is a common practice in Eritrea. While graduations, weddings, or birthdays are some common reasons to have a professional photograph taken, a special occasion is not necessarily required.

The flow of portraits on the survivors' Facebook group represented the victims both as individuals and as a large group of people who had died in the same disaster, similar to how the list of names functioned. The pictures underlined the victims' individuality and personality in two ways: First, because they are portraits, attention is centered on the subject and the subject is aware of and partly in control of the photographic moment. Second, those who posted the photographs also attached names to them, with information about the person's relationships and personality appearing in the comments.

Each posted photograph was greeted by comments from other group members in Tigrinya, Arabic, or English. Aregai and Adal translated Tigrinyan and Arabic comments to me in English, and for the sake of privacy, I do not post direct quotations except for the common phrases. The responses ranged from generic condolences to more personalized messages:

> In loving memory of.
> Erefti selam ygberelom. (Rest in peace, R.I.P.)
> Amen.
> God bless you.
> Yehwatna; Amlak byemanu yiqebelom.
> (Brothers and sisters; may God receive you in Heaven.)
> You were too young to die and are already missed dearly by your loved
>   ones.
> There are no words. We couldn't do anything. He is not here anymore
>   but he is living in our souls. Every single minute.
> The sea took our beloved ones, I comfort the mothers of the victims.
> You prayed during the whole journey, may God receive you in Heaven.

Like the act of compiling a list of names, the sharing of photographs by the group of survivors re-produced the community of those who were on the fatal journey together. Some of them were now dead while others lived. The comments on the photographs often addressed the deceased directly as "you," as if they would still be able to hear the memories: "You prayed during the whole journey." One photograph is of two young women, looking directly at the camera. Their heads meet over a small table. The names of the women are mentioned in the post and someone has commented: "You were friends until death."

Through this memorial engagement, the survivors produced a community— one that shared not only the experience of staying alive, but also of mourning. However, not everyone in the group agreed that sharing photos was the best way to remember the dead. One person commented in Tigrinya, "Since they are in our hearts, please don't post the pictures," and another, "This is not so ethical in our culture, let us keep them in our hearts and connect with them in our souls." Another criticism emerged when the photographs posted in the Facebook group began to appear in Eritrean diasporic media and elsewhere in social media. Like the spreading of the names, the spreading of the photographs potentially violated the privacy of the victims and their families. Like the list of names, the photographs shared in the Facebook group were intended for a specific community and specific purpose, not for other communities or the wider public. Like Mohamed, Aregai did not know how the digitized photographs began to spread.

Whereas the purpose of creating a list of names was identification, so that family members could know the fate of their loved ones, the photographs were collected for memorial purposes. While the list of names was also used for memorializing, the memorializing has been done by others, such as the Community of Sant'Egidio, Lampedusans, and Dagmawi Yimer, the documentary filmmaker. In the case of the photos on Facebook, however, the collection of images and practices of visual appropriation had a memorializing function for the survivors themselves from the beginning. The images were used not only as part of the commemorative ritual that emerged in the online space where photographs, memories, and consolation were shared, but Aregai also appropriated the photographs into collages, for which he cropped the portraits to round shapes and softened them on the edges. He placed six of these images around a picture of candle flames and posted the collages back to the group. In his practice, he was interested in collecting the photographs "so that the victims would not be forgotten," as he later put it in our conversation in Sweden.

Pictures originally intended as a memory token of something else—graduation, friendship, kinship—were transformed into an object of grief and mourning. This appropriation of a digitized photo of a printed photograph is similar to the practice of recontextualizing a photograph at home by placing a candle in front of a framed picture. What is different, though, is that these *digital objects of memorialization* are transnationally spreadable in the contexts where refugees are on the move and families are dispersed on different continents. The practice of sharing and commenting on the photographs among the more than one hundred survivors in the Facebook group produced a mourning community in a situation where the survivors didn't have a home or a community to mourn with. They were either still being detained in Lampedusa or on the road toward Germany, Sweden, or Norway. The Facebook group provided a space where they could come together and mourn.

Some of the same portraits of the victims appeared in the ceremony held in the cathedral in Lampedusa to mark the first anniversary of the disaster. A large poster featuring a grid of portraits stood on the altar: eighty-four photos of individuals and three of mothers with their children. On the right corner of the poster was the date of the disaster in Italian, *3 ottobre*, and *per non dimenticare* (not to forget) in Italian and Tigrinya. After the ceremony members of the Community of Sant'Egidio handed out postcards that had the same grid of portraits printed on them. The back of the card is filled with 360 names, *Beyene-Gebreamlak-Tewelde-Hadeghe-Iyasu-Mihreteab* . . . , and a quote in Italian from Pope Francis's sermon during his visit to Lampedusa in July 2013, three months before the disaster:

> Has any one of us wept because of this situation and others like it? Has any one of us grieved for the death of these brothers and sisters? Has any one of us wept for these persons who were on the boat? For the young mothers carrying their babies? For these men who were looking for a means of supporting their families? We are a society which has forgotten how to weep, how to experience compassion—"suffering with" others: the globalization of indifference has taken from us the ability to weep! (Pope Francis 2013b).

FIGURE 6.   Postcard of photos of the victims, distributed in Lampedusa by Comunità Sant'Egidio, October 3, 2014, and the names of victims on the back of a card distributed in 2018. © Karina Horsti, 2022. Photo by Karina Horsti.

Similar to the Community of Sant'Egidio's practice of reading out the names of dead migrants in their Dying of Hope prayer service, the photographs and names printed on the postcard are a means to resist indifference to the suffering of others. Sant'Egidio remediates the call for weeping for "these persons who were on the boat." The word *person* is the key. People are not visible in a number, but when seeing faces and reading or hearing names one can imagine an individual, a person. From the pews of the church in Lampedusa, it could be seen that there were many faces on the poster on the alter. But to see each face, one had to get closer to the poster or pick up the postcard. As in the reading of the list of names, this was a visualization of *the many* and a commemoration of a collective, the victims of the Lampedusa disaster. But it was simultaneously an opportunity to pause and consider a single individual. The grid of portraits, like the list of names, was a way of knowing *who* died and representing the absence of life, in contrast to representing the victims by a number.

Tadese, the survivor who collected photographs for the postcard, envisioned the purpose of the card as a method to understand the singularity of each victim. He was twenty-eight years old at the time of the disaster and because he was hospitalized after the disaster Tadese is the only survivor who remained in Italy. He became an active member of Community of Sant'Egidio that helped him to settle in Rome. In his speech at the ecumenical commemoration at the Sanctuary of Madonna di Porto Salvo in Lampedusa on October 3, 2018, Tadese said that he wanted to reconstitute the names and the faces of the "*naufragati*," the shipwrecked, so that they would not be forgotten. "Because such tragedy must not happen again," he said. The way in which he justified his presence at the ecumenical service reveals how he sees the connection between one person (face, name, testimony) and the broader issue. "I feel a responsibility to testify how important it is to save a life, *una vita*," he said. Tadese was there alive in front of us who listened to him at the Sanctuary. His presence was a testimony of "*una vita*," a life that was saved. However, he also represented those lives that were *not* saved. His presence animated the eighty-seven adult faces on the card or the total number of the disaster. They too could have been there alive; and if he had not been rescued by the Lampedusan mason Constantino Baratta, he too would be a face on the card.

The postcard would become an important memorial object for the survivors and family members of the victims. As far as I know, privacy of the victims and their families has not been an issue raised among survivors and relatives. One survivor installed it on the memorial sculpture *Le radici nel cielo* (*The Sky's Roots*, discussed in chapter 4) in Lampedusa in 2014 and shared a photograph of it on Facebook. In October 2018, when Sant'Egidio members disseminated the postcards again in the anniversary commemoration in Lampedusa I noticed how survivors held the cards in their hands when they marched in a procession to Porta d'Europa, a sculpture created in memory of migrants who had died in the Mediterranean. In chapter 8, I discuss how the brother of a victim glued the postcard on a grave as part of a memorialization ritual.

The public interest in the faces and names of the October 3 victims—or even in their exact number—is distinctly different from the interest in the victims of other disasters where the dead "mattered," such as the collapse of the bridge in Genoa in 2018 or the crash of Germanwings flight 9525 in Southern France in 2015. In both cases, the media and the authorities were quick to identify the victims, providing names and photographs to the public (see, e.g., Associated Press 2018). The difference in practices is also related to the mode of death. Border deaths are perceived as unfortunate but nonetheless unavoidable, and they are to some extent an expected feature of the European border, whereas a bridge collapse or plane crash is unexpected and avoidable. Death at Europe's border is normalized, as it doesn't concern "me." Following Judith Butler's notion of ungrievability, the lives lost at the border are not conceived as livable lives at all, and therefore, ontologically, cannot be lost.

While these analyses of indifference and ungrievability are powerful, describing well the general response to border deaths, this chapter has taken up the challenge of examining representations that *are* attentive to the individuality and humanity of the victims. Both grievability and respect necessitate attention to the victims as human beings, persons.

Nevertheless, the transformative potential of the focus on individualizing victims, representing them as persons-as-such (Edkins 2011), instead of generalities is not without its pitfalls. As scholars such as Luc Boltanski (1999) have argued, individualizing—or "localizing"—the suffering of others risks depoliticizing it (Boltanski 1999, 6–7). Humanitarianism, for example, often produces ideal victims, individuals or specific categories (like women and children) worthy of our compassion (Ticktin 2011; Fassin 2012; Chouliaraki 2013). Not everyone qualifies as *a person-as-such* that the spectators in the European public sphere, narrowly defined, can relate to. However, this chapter demonstrates that in the case of deaths at the border, a problem that is highly mediatized but dominantly represented in ways that distance European publics from those who suffer and from the mechanisms that produce the suffering, the focus on particularities has critical potential (see also Kobelinsky 2020; Lewicki 2017).

In this chapter, I have discussed three alternative ways of representing the dead: through photographs, by naming one victim as a symbol of the many, and by listing the names of the victims. These representations reveal three important aspects of the afterlife of a disaster and what makes the memory of the disaster evade oblivion in the public domain. First, an afterlife is not a single mediation or reappearance of a disaster. Rather, it forms over multiple mediations, or in fact, re-mediations, each taking shape and energy from the mediations that came before. The disaster has multiple afterlives. In this respect, the list of names compiled by the survivors was the first mediation, the first form of reappearance. As such, the list was initially made for practical purposes, an act of civic forensics. However, it was more than simply a list of names—it was an object that revealed the individuality and relationality of the people listed. Moreover, the list had afterlives of its own—subsequent re-mediations particularly in the domain of memorialization. It reappeared as a representation of the victims in radio programs, commemorative ceremonies, art, and on the back of the Sant'Egidio postcard. The list of names became a memory object that would be significant in the shaping of afterlives through other re-mediations. The name *Yohanna* also had multiple reappearances and sequences as it traveled across Eritrean diasporic and global media platforms. Similarly, the collection of photographs in the survivors' Facebook group had a second, third, and fourth life through re-mediations across different media spaces.

Second, this chapter has demonstrated that afterlives are transnational. In digitized societies, representations increasingly move through mediated networks and cross geographic borders. Interestingly, after relatives and friends of the victims digitized printed studio photographs in order to share them as digitized objects of memorialization on Facebook, the images were converted back to material objects—a postcard and a poster. Digitization afforded the photographs plasticity, so that they could be appropriated into the grid of portraits at the church or the round shapes in Aregai's collage. It also ensured the spreadability of the photographs across different platforms and forms of materiality. The combination of mobile people and digital networks produced transnational afterlives that followed the disaster and its representations and re-representations.

Third, all these re-mediations required agents—people who were driven by a sense of responsibility to engage with the disaster or with the names and photographs serving as representations of the disaster. The survivors, journalists, family members, artists, and religious communities, among many others, felt responsible as direct witnesses or because they had witnessed the disaster through the media. Engagement with the names and the photographs was a response to fundamentally unequal relationships—a relationship produced by death in the case of the survivors, or by indifference and not-knowing in the cases of Frances Stonor Saunders, the writer for the *London Review of Books*, and the religious members of the Community of Sant'Egidio.

While names and faces offer a powerful critique of the distanced and sanitized representation of the victims as a number, they can also result in an object that has a more nuanced and imaginative afterlife. The "List of Deaths" created by the activists of United for Intercultural Action is a case in point. It does not claim to offer accurate numbers, although the total figure (34,361 as in the *Guardian* supplement) appears as a precise fact. Most of the rows have very little information: name unknown, origin unknown. Only the columns reporting the cause of death and source of information are filled in. Nevertheless, this lack of information and focus on counting has prompted several artistic and activist engagements. With its breakdown of the indefinite number, in fact serving more as documentation of not-knowing than of knowing, the list is an object that has prompted meaningful and critical engagement, triggering the curiosity or responsibility to know more about who each individual was.

ADOPTING THE DEAD

When migrants die at sea borders, the bodies often disappear into the waves. Survivors of shipwrecks and drifting boats have reported drownings of their fellow passengers. Locals have found unknown dead bodies on the shores of the Mediterranean Sea and fishermen in their nets. The presence of so many dead bodies and survivors who knew the identities of the victims was therefore exceptional in the October 3, 2013, disaster in Lampedusa. The coffins containing the dead were at the center of public attention (as discussed in chapter 2), but also the burials in Sicily became a public issue in an unprecedented way. The province of Agrigento (to which Lampedusa belongs) asked its municipalities to bury as many victims as they could. Municipalities announced how many vacant slots they were able to provide. When the coffins arrived in Agrigento by a military ship from Lampedusa, to be interred in Sicily's cemeteries, people responded by arranging ceremonies for dignified burials and adopting the dead into their family graves.

In this chapter, I examine how and why Sicilians responded to the disaster by memorializing. This chapter opens the section of the book that focuses on how "others" are memorialized; the people who initiated these memorials and rituals did not have a personal relationship with the victims, nor were the victims members of their community or citizens of their country.

The Failed State Funeral

Italian prime minister Enrico Letta had promised a state funeral for the victims when he visited Lampedusa after the disaster (Kington 2013b). The state funeral was part of the symbolic posthumous citizenship he announced the day after the disaster: "The hundreds who lost their lives off Lampedusa yesterday are Italian citizens as of today" (Ansa 2013). The memorial service at the San Leone tourist harbor in Agrigento on October 21, 2013, was nevertheless not a funeral, much less what would be expected of a state funeral. It turned into what Agrigento mayor Marco Zambuto called "a farce" (Deutsche Welle 2013). The Italian authorities had invited Eritrea's ambassador to Italy to the memorial ceremony, and the Eritrean regime's secret service—according to the Eritrean Swedish human rights activist Meron Estefanos (2016)—photographed the relatives and activists who protested at the event. Fabrizio Gatti (2013) reported in *L'Espresso* that what "opened in front of the few family members who had come was a catwalk of mayors wearing the tricolor band, of emblems, of government representatives, including minister of the interior Angelino Alfano." In addition, the survivors, many of whom were relatives of the victims, were confined in the "reception center" in Lampedusa, suspected of having violated Italian law by crossing the border "illegally," and unable to attend the event.

Some Eritrean human rights activists, including Mussie Zerai and Meron Estefanos, were present and protested with banners saying: "La presenza del regime eritreo offende i defunti emette in pericolo i sopravvissuti" (The presence of the Eritrean regime offends the deceased and endangers the survivors), "Survivors deserve to attend this commemoration," (in English) and "Vittime delle vostre leggi" (Victims of your laws). The official ceremony became a site of conflict between diasporic Eritreans protesting how the ceremony had been organized and the delegation of regime supporters. Meron Estefanos (2016) told me that some Eritreans participating in the ceremony accused her and Mussie Zerai of enticing Eritrean youths to undertake the dangerous journey to Europe. The presence of the ambassador, in particular, was an insult to the victims, she said; the ambassador and his delegation represented the regime that many of the victims had fled.

Nations and communities organize such public memorial services after disasters to overcome a traumatic rupture. These services are a form of necropolitics (Mbembe 2003) that are used to govern death, in this case the deaths of noncitizens, and the meaning of deaths in relation to the state. According to Durkheimian theory on ritual, such a ritualization seeks to reassert social bonds and moral unity. In Gatti's interpretation, the essence of the ceremony were not the dead (who had already been buried in different cemeteries) nor the survivors or the relatives of the victims but the government of Italy, performing benevolence through necropolitics. The social bond that the ritual presumably was intended to reassert was one among "Italians," and between Italy and the regime of its former colony, Eritrea. Those who were most intimately touched by the disaster were excluded from the moral unity of the nation.

The Lampedusa disaster caused a rupture in the Italian society—otherwise, Letta would not have announced a "state funeral." Following Victor Turner's (1980) theory of social drama, it seems that Italy attempted to solve a crisis by performing the public memorial service in Agrigento. This performance was a follow-up to Letta's kneeling in front of the arrangement of the coffins in Lampedusa (discussed in chapter 2). While unity might be a desired function of a ritual, it can also become a site for contestation. A ritual can also bring dissent and simmering social conflicts to the fore (see, e.g., Bell 1992, 33–35; Vinitzky-Seroussi 2002; Wagner-Pacifici and Schwartz 1991). Unity after the disaster was difficult to assert—both among Italians and Eritrean Europeans. Existing political conflicts in the Eritrean diaspora came to the fore in the aftermath of the disaster, as Meron Estefanos (2016) explained to me. Eritrean European human rights advocates also criticized Europe and Italy for their migration policies. In addition, a lack of consensus among Sicilians and Lampedusans on how the dead should be treated and where they should be buried created tension. Many Italians opposed the state's right to mourn in such a performative manner altogether (as I discuss in chapters 5 and 6). The national memorial service became a performance of dissensus, which revealed that the state had not recognized multiple conflicting communities that were touched by the disaster.

Adoption of a Dead Body

Agrigento Notizie, a local online news site, announced the burial of five victims in the small village of Raffadali on the afternoon of October 16, 2013, so that the public could attend. At the ecumenic burial, Imam Yusuf Spoto, Catholic Vicar Giuseppe Livatino, and representatives of the municipality prayed together with local residents. Giuseppe Livatino said that the ceremony was to seek forgiveness for the "social sin" (*peccato sociale*) (Di Benedetto 2013). The cause of the "social sin," according to him, was paradoxically "unforgivable indifference" (Di Benedetto 2013). By using the term "indifference," Livatino connected the burial ceremony to Pope Francis's speech delivered in Lampedusa earlier that year. The pope had then used the phrase "globalization of indifference" in his address on border deaths (Pope Francis 2013b). The care of the dead and the ritual that asked forgiveness, symbolically, aimed to correct the social sin committed by indifference to migrants' distress.

In Agrigento, Amalia Vullo, a woman in her early sixties who worked for the municipality in the department responsible for cemeteries requested that the local administration allow her husband Giuseppe Gelardi and her to bury a victim's body in the Gelardis' family grave. Vullo was shocked by news images showing the cranes in Lampedusa's dock that moved the victims' coffins to the military ship for transport to Agrigento. In 2018, she recalled: "Everything started when we saw images of that saddest day, October 3, five years ago. . . . That was a horrible scene. Already seeing the [images of] coffins was sad and then those cranes, it was horrible seeing them taken by cranes" (Vullo 2018).

Vullo witnessed the scene through the news media, and like the Eritrean Europeans whose response to the scene I discuss in chapter 3, she too thought the treatment of the dead had been undignified. In her view, the state failed to care for noncitizens, and she felt responsible and perhaps even obliged to correct what she could of the injustice. Because of her position in the department that was responsible for cemeteries, she came up with the idea of burying one of the 366 dead bodies with dignity into their family tomb.

The Vullo-Gelardis did not choose the victim they would bury, Vullo explained. However, the coffin that was given to them was like no other: it was one of the few coffins that had been personalized by survivors and relatives in Lampedusa's dock before being loaded onto the ship. The coffin had four large images taped onto it. On top was a large printout representing Jesus Christ. Below that, a full body studio photograph of the woman when she had been alive. Then, number 47, and an enlarged passport photograph of her, and her name, Wegahta (and her father's name) printed on the photo. Another print of the same full body photograph was taped in the space that remained. When the coffin had arrived in Sicily, it had obviously attracted the attention of those who were tasked with managing the dead. This and two other decorated coffins appeared in a photograph published in the local *Agrigento Notizie* newspaper.

In the photo published in *Agrigento Notizie*, three personalized coffins are displayed on a red carpet; bouquets of fresh flowers have been laid around them. The coffins depict not only the individuality of the dead but also the grief of family or friends who knew them. When I look at the photograph of the coffins it reveals to me that Wegahta had been young and Christian, and that she was missed by someone who had decorated the coffin. The grief and the care are visible. In other words, these coffins and the photograph of them produce a visual politics of interdependency—a subversive relationship between the viewer and the people depicted (or symbolized) in a visual image or arrangement (discussed in chapter 2). The viewer is invited to see the dead in relation to the living, bringing the humanity of the disaster to the fore. The coffins and the image of them evoke civil imagination (Azoulay 2012)—a capacity for imagining a connection to those who mourn the dead, and to the dead themselves. The relationship between the viewer and those represented in the image, both the dead and the mourners, can constitute a transgressive citizenship (Rygiel 2014; 2016; Stierl 2016), a relation whereby those excluded from full citizenship are treated as part of a common world.

The Vullo-Gelardis ordered a small stone with a reprint of the passport-style photograph that was attached to the coffin and placed it on top of the tomb. They placed that next to a similar stone remembering their family member. Under the woman's picture was her name and a number, 47. Wegahta had been the forty-seventh recovered body. Though Amalia Vullo did not seek publicity about the burial, journalists soon started covering the story. Through a journalist, she and her husband were able to contact the woman's two brothers. One had settled in Norway, and the other brother had survived the October 3 disaster.

The brothers have visited the grave in Agrigento and met the Vullo-Gelardi family. Both parties have posted photographs of the two families' encounter on their Facebook profiles. Vullo said that they are in touch regularly through WhatsApp. These brothers are now close to the Vullo-Gelardi family through their deceased sister: "We can say she has become part of our family because she is together with our deceased family members," Vullo told me. The relationship between the dead created a familial tie between the Vullo-Gelardis and Wegahta's surviving family members. By "adopting" a dead body as a means of correcting the state's unjust treatment of the dead, the Vullo-Gelardis constituted a transgressive civil relation to Wegahta's living relatives though a transgressive posthumous relation between their own dead and a dead woman they did not know. These two types of relational citizenships, in my view, are outcomes of civil imagination.

The relationship between Wegahta's family and the Vullo-Gelardis seems like one of serendipity, but deliberate actions preceded the connection. First, by decorating and naming the coffin, Wegahta's brother knowingly or unknowingly sent out an invitation to care for his sister's body. Second, those who managed the arrival of the coffins in Agrigento selected the coffin most likely because it was personified (the two decorated coffins in the *Agrigento Notizie* photograph were also "adopted" by another Sicilian family). Third, Amalia Vullo reacted to the news images of the coffins in Lampedusa with sadness, an emotion that spurred her into action.

Their new kinship, "becoming part of our family," as Vullo said, was not based on any particular articulated tie, such as ethnicity, locality, marginality, or sexuality, as is often the case in nonbiological kinships in Euro-American societies (Carsten 2000). Feminist and queer scholars, in particular, have written about such bonds as families of choice (Weston 1997). Such relatedness, founded on a common marginalized position, can either confirm existing social structures or radically challenge them (e.g., Weston 1997; Berlant 2008a; Duggan 2012). In the context of adoption and fosterage, another type of nonbiological kinship, research has shown that a strong sense of kinship can be created through nurturing and care, a conscious process of kinning (Howell 2006). In the case of the Vullo-Gelardis, an intimate relatedness is imagined between the dead—Wegahta and the dead Gelardis—and practiced reciprocally between the living families. Similar to adoption, Amalia Vullo had a choice to "adopt" some body, but she was not able to choose the body.

On February 12, 2017, Amalia Vullo was awarded a special prize given alongside the Dresden Peace Prize in Germany for her "humanitarian action" and "compassion" (Dresdner Preis 2017).[1] The public attention to Vullo's care for the dead woman and her relationship with the living relatives show how European publics have been inspired by the story of care beyond boundaries. In one sense, it is a story of conviviality—caring for the unknown others as participants of a shared world. In another, however, the elevated instance risks to hide what it seems to reveal. Instead of forcing the state to care for the noncitizen dead, the public story of one woman potentially pacifies criticism. In the public domain, the story of the adopted dead and Wegahta's grave risks becoming "sentimental artifacts," similar to the repeated story of Yohanna that I discuss in chapter 3. It risks becoming a symbol created by others for the purpose of relieving the concerned European spectator's discomfort while they realize the fundamental inequality of their society.

Memorials and Their Absence at Cemeteries

When I visited cemeteries in Sicily in 2018, many of the graves of the October 3, 2013, victims seemed untended. I found 116 graves in four cemeteries, and most of them I was able to locate only with the help of cemetery caretakers. In the small inland village of Cattolico Eraclea, there were twelve graves, just one of them marked with a name: Weldu (and the second name). The dates of his birth and death and a photograph on the marble stone indicated that his relatives had positively identified the body and visited the gravesite. The others were unmarked, nor was there any general memorial or signage informing visitors that victims of the Lampedusa disaster had been buried there. It was October 6 when I visited, and there were no candles or flowers that might have indicated that locals or relatives had visited the graves on the fifth anniversary of the disaster.

Later, a woman who was working at a restaurant in the village refuted my conclusion that local residents had failed to tend to the migrant graves. She said that the villagers know where the graves of the October 3, 2013, *naufraghi*—the shipwrecked—are, and that they pray at their graves when they visit their own dead. The locals did not leave a material record of their visits to the cemetery.

FIGURE 7. Unidentified graves of the Lampedusa disaster victims in Piano Gatta cemetery, Agrigento, Sicily, October 7, 2018. © Karina Horsti, 2018. Photo by Karina Horsti.

FIGURE 8.   Unidentified graves of the Lampedusa disaster victims in Piano Gatta cemetery, Agrigento, Sicily, October 7, 2018. © Karina Horsti, 2018. Photo by Karina Horsti.

Thus, they did not feel obliged to encourage others to follow their example, nor did they wish to communicate their actions to others who visit the cemetery. Such spiritual practice for the dead one does not know is practiced also elsewhere in Sicily, and people may even refer to the dead migrants by terms normally used for relatives: *sangumeo* and *ciato di lu me cori*, meaning "my blood" or "breath of my heart" (Mirto et al. 2020, 108). Through the ritual of prayer, the locals adopt the unknown dead within their own community of deceased.

In Castellamare del Golfo, a seaside town west of Palermo, the public response to the victims of the October 3 disaster was completely different from Cattolico Eraclea. There, I met Nicola Coppola, who had been the town's mayor in October 2013. When we met, he had just recently lost his position and had time to show me the cemetery and introduce me to other locals who were active in engaging with the memory of the migrant dead. Coppola (2018) told me how he had responded to the call that went out from Agrigento for burial sites. Castellamare del Golfo is a town living off fishing and tourism in Trapani province. By Sicilian standards, it's barely a midsize town with about 15,000 inhabitants. Thus, it is quite interesting that instead of accepting "one or two" coffins from another province, Coppola wanted a significant number of dead. It was important "to make it a sign of *accoglienza*"—of hospitality, he said. Hospitality was also how Coppola described the welcome of newly arrived asylum seekers in the local reception center. Many inhabitants regularly organized social activities such as communal dinners with them. If the living were welcomed with hospitality, so were the dead.

Coppola was sent nineteen victims of the October 3 disaster and ten victims from another disaster (the date on the graves is October 12, 2013, and the place "Canale di Sicilia"). These were the first unknown migrant dead to be buried by the municipality. Unlike the seaside towns on the southern side of Sicily that face Africa, no dead bodies had washed on the shores of Castellamare del Golfo, which faces the north. Nevertheless, since the victims of the two October 2013 disasters, the town has received more unidentified migrant dead. They are buried in another section of the cemetery than those received in 2013. They are buried in the same manner: individual graves with individual headstones in a specific area of the cemetery reserved only for the migrant dead.

This individualized burial practice is not the case in all Sicilian cemeteries. In Catania's main cemetery, *Cimitero Monumentale di Catania*, the municipality created a memorial for migrant dead, titled *La speranza naufragata*, Wrecked Hope, on March 10, 2015. There are seventeen individual unidentified graves as part of the memorial (Horsti 2019c; Kobelinsky, Furri, and Noûs 2021). However, far from the memorial, at the edge of the cemetery, I found a row of burial mounds that are marked only by coded signs that indicate that three bodies are buried under each mound of earth. There was no sign explaining the site, and so, it was only through talking with a local couple who were taking care of their daughter's grave nearby that I learned that this was the burial ground for *clandestini* "the illegals," as they called them (Horsti 2019c, 195–96). This section of the cemetery is opposite to the part of the cemetery where the dead are known but whose burial expenses are not privately paid.

When the cemetery caretakers in Castellamare del Golfo first buried the dead of the two disasters of October 2013, temporary wooden markers were put on each grave. The municipality organized a ceremony in which verses from the Quran in Italian translation were read out and a Catholic priest recited prayers. They did not know who the dead were and what their religion or customs were, so they invented a "cerimonia di accoglienza," (ceremony of hospitality), Coppola explained. When this was done, Coppola felt that it hadn't been enough. The high number of migrant deaths in the Mediterranean is comparable to the number of war victims, Coppola said. He did not explain further, but at the cemetery the next day, I realized that he had implied that deaths at the border deserve public recognition comparable to that given those who have died fighting for their country.

FIGURE 9.   Castellamare del Golfo cemetery, October 6, 2018. In addition to the victims of the two disasters near Lampedusa in 2013, an identified migrant body was sent from Palermo in 2014 to be buried in this memorial cemetery. © Karina Horsti, 2018. Photo by Karina Horsti.

When I saw the new markers that had been placed on the migrant graves in the Castellamare del Golfo cemetery, the first thing that came to mind was the Catania War Cemetery in Sicily and other American or Commonwealth war cemeteries in Italy. The shape of headstones in Castellamare del Golfo is very similar to the cemetery in Catania. Nevertheless, the thirty identical marble tombstones, arranged in straight rows on a green lawn, is an unusual sight in a Sicilian cemetery, where there is otherwise a great variety in the style and decoration of the tombs. Each Sicilian family personalizes its tomb, and no grave is identical to another.

Immediately next to the memorial arrangement of graves in Castellamare del Golfo stands a sculpture made and donated by a British artist, Mike Power, who has lived part-time near the town regularly since the 1970s. It depicts a human figure, curled up so as to protect itself from something terrible or perhaps bent under the weight of the large pot standing on the figure's back and neck. A mirror in the mouth of the pot stands as an invitation for self-reflection.

The cemetery caretaker explained to me that flowers were not planted on the graves because the burial customs of the victims were unknown. While the locals felt comfortable in combining Muslim and Catholic traditions in the ceremony of inauguration, they were unsure about more permanent material symbols, such as planted flowers. While the arrangement of multiple graves could be addressed in the more generalizing terms of "cerimonia di accoglienza," the single graves were treated as belonging to unknown individual dead and their relatives. The markers state the date and place of the victim's death, either Lampedusa or "Canale di Sicilia." Twenty-six of the thirty headstones identify the dead only by the number given to the body. Four graves list also the deceased's name and date of birth.[2] Three named graves display a photograph of the victim, similarly to many Sicilian graves. In front of the rows of graves, an inscription in both Italian and English is carved into a larger stone:

> Dal tempestoso mare della vita al quieto mare dell'eternità in un infinito abbraccio. La città di Castellamare del Golfo. In memoria delle vittime dei naufraghi. From the stormy sea of life to the quiet sea of eternity. An endless embrace in memory of shipwreck victims. 1 November 2014.

The memorial stone was installed on Ognissanti, All Saints' Day. It is a day when Italians not only visit the graves of their loved ones, but also bring flowers to forgotten graves. An official inauguration service followed in February 2015, when Sergio Mattarella, who had just been elected Italian president, visited the cemetery; his wife and brother are buried there. The mayor took advantage of the opportunity to have him inaugurate the memorial.

The graves and headstones in Castellamare del Golfo are visible as a memorial, particularly with the addition of the sculpture and the marble marker at the head of the arrangement. Nicola Coppola spoke fondly about the memorial and noted that many locals are proud of how well it is maintained. The lawn, in particular, symbolizes dignity and care. It needs constant watering and maintenance in the Sicilian climate, and to have such a green lawn in a publicly maintained cemetery is rare, Coppola pointed out.

When I asked what motivated him to create the memorial, Coppola explained that he felt personally responsible for the proper burial of the migrants:

> We are a country of emigration. My father went to work in America. I am happy that he was welcomed there. He found a job and made a living for us children. And if all this has taught us something, it is clear that we must do something for others. Being the mayor, I was able to do things. (Coppola 2018)

Coppola's actions resonated with the values of the community. There was no open opposition to the memorial. A heritage of emigration is central to the identity of

Sicilians, and it often emerges in conversations about present-day migration (see also Casati 2018). Castellamare del Golfo, much like the rest of Sicily is marked by decades of emigration not only to Northern Italy but also to the United States, Australia, Germany, Switzerland, and France. Most likely, mass emigration of the 1950s and 1960s evoked Nicola Coppola's memory. However, in this context, Castellamare del Golfo is best known for being the birthplace of some of Italy's most notorious emigrants—the La Cosa Nostra mafiosos in New York in the 1920s and 1930s.

While similarities in the migration experience have the capacity to create solidarity, the relationship between past and present is not to be taken for granted, as Noemi Casati (2018) reminds us. In her research on a reception center in a small Sicilian village, Casati (2018, 802–3) found that a structural malfunction in the migration system led to instrumentalizing similarities in history—not for solidarity with migrants but for mistrust and division. Past emigration, in that case, was told as a mythical narrative against which the present-day migrants were depicted as incompetent, dishonest, and lazy (Casati 2018). However, in the case of Castellamare del Golfo, Coppola's parallel with the past and the present created solidarity with migrants. Similarities in history, in this case, evoked an ethical obligation to care for the dignity of present-day migrants, both dead and alive.

The text on the memorial stone in the Castellamare del Golfo cemetery reveals only that the dead memorialized there were victims of shipwrecks. The only community that is identified is that which has created the memorial, the municipality of Castellamare del Golfo. The stone communicates to visitors that the municipality cared about and has commemorated the victims of shipwrecks; the constant watering of the lawn indicates that they continue to do so. This reflects public and social aspects of memorialization. However, the memorial has not been constructed for the local community alone, as the English inscription demonstrates. The creators of the memorial took into account that relatives of the victims might some day visit the site and not speak Italian. Thanks to that consideration, the memorial reaches out to create a transnational and transcultural public memory.

The headstones, some of which were already marked with names by the time the memorial was created in 2014, represent the disaster in a more individualized way. Among the dead lies Amanuel (and the second name), who was twenty-nine years old when he died. He had been born in the small village of Halib Mentel in central Eritrea, and he was a Christian. The text carved on the stone—"You will always be in our hearts. We will never forget you."—is written in English. In the framed oval studio photograph mounted on the marker between the number 189 and a carved cross, the young man smiles. He has a fresh haircut and wears a smart black suit with a white shirt and a red bowtie.

I have to push a large bunch of yellow chrysanthemums aside so that I can read the inscriptions on the tombstone. It is October 6, 2018, and someone clearly visited the grave a couple of days earlier. The chrysanthemums imply that Amanuel, along with two other victims whose graves are adorned with fresh flowers, must have relatives living in Europe. Later, Mariangela Galante (2018), a high school teacher from Castellamare del Golfo, tells me that two women, one from Oslo, Norway, and another from Düsseldorf, Germany, one a sister and the other the widow of a victim, have been visiting the cemetery on October 3 for the past few years.

The anonymity of the other twenty-six graves is emphasized all the more by the few personalized graves in the memorial arrangement. The only distinctive feature among the unnamed headstones is the number that signifies the order in which the bodies were retrieved from the sea in each of the two disasters. These nameless graves are not completely unattended, though—not like the ones in Cattolica Eraclea. At each grave is a red memorial candle, fresh red roses and carnations, and boats folded out of colorful paper. A floral arrangement with a tricolor ribbon placed at the large memorial stone was an indication that the mayor and the administration of Castellamare del Golfo had paid their respects at the memorial on October 3, 2018.

Civil Imagination on October 3

The flowers, candles, and paper boats on the graves in Castellamare del Golfo were laid by local students who had participated in the commemorative ceremony at the cemetery on October 3, 2018. Since 2015, on every October 3, junior high school students, their teachers, representatives of the municipality, and people from the local association Circolo Metropolis had remembered the victims by reading poems and texts related to migration at the cemetery.[3] Mariangela Galante, an active member of Circolo Metropolis, explained to me that this was the third time the school had memorialized the deaths at the cemetery. The law establishing the October 3 as the National Day of Remembrance in 2016 supported the commemorative action that has become a tradition. The Day of Remembrance created a legal obligation to memorialize "victims of migration" in publicly funded state institutions such as schools. These institutions are required to organize ceremonies or initiatives that "raise awareness and educate young people on immigration and reception issues" (Senato della Repubblica 2016).

Memorialization in Castellamare del Golfo served a pedagogical function in addition to its function in local identity politics reproducing the sense of being a community of *accoglienza* and of emigrants, as Coppola (2018) had explained.

In 2018, however, another crucial motivation for memorialization had emerged, which Galante (2018) said made memorializing the migrant dead even more significant than it had been in previous years. After the Italian general elections in March, the far-right Lega party took power together with the populist Five Star movement (the government lasted until August 2019). The leader of Lega, Matteo Salvini, minister of the interior and de facto leader of the government, became infamous for his cruel policies targeting humanitarian sea rescue, asylum seekers, and refugees (e.g., Geddes and Pettrachin 2020). The government closed the ports to rescued migrants and began criminalizing rescue operations at sea. For many people, including the about twenty members of the Circolo Metropolis, the duty to remember the migrant dead became more clearly connected to countering the cruel border politics returning in Italy. Resistance to the deadly border was a continuation of their anti-Mafia action and environmental protection. Originally, the group had been created to resist Mafia after the Capaci bombing in 1992 that assassinated Giovanni Falcone, a judge and prosecuting magistrate in Palermo who worked against the Mafia (Galante 2021).

The form of the ceremony the students carried out at the cemetery in 2018 was shaped by how the locals interested in commemorating experienced the memorial. One feature of the memorial in particular, the numbers and lack of names, produced unease in the locals, which they then processed in the ritual. For example, the numbers had disturbed the members of the Circolo Metropolis over the years. Mariangela Galante told me: "You can treat numbers in any way you like. In concentration camps, they marked people with numbers. When you're a number, you're nothing" (Galante 2018). The presence of the unknown dead bodies of noncitizens complicated the local community's determination to know its population. As Thomas W. Laqueur (2015, 314–17) has argued in his cultural history of death, since the eighteenth and nineteenth centuries, the condition of a society could be judged by how it cared for the poor and their decent burial.

During the memorial ceremony at the cemetery, a student read aloud an Italian translation of the English-language poem "Number 92," by the London-based Eritrean writer Selam Kidane.

> Number 92
> I wonder what she called you, little one?
> Your precious Mama . . .
> Maybe she called you Berhan? . . . my light
> Or did she call you Haben? . . . my pride
> She may have called you Qisanet . . . after rest she yearned
> Or were you Awet? . . . victory . . .
> Tell me little one did she name you after her hope?

Or her aspirations . . . her dream?
Did she call you Amen as end to her prayers?
Did she name you after the saints your Grandma prayed to?
Or were you named after the brother she lost in prison?
Maybe after her father long gone?
Did she name you . . . Sina . . . after the desert she crossed?
Or Eritrea . . . the land she reluctantly left . . .?
Perhaps she named you for the land you were to inherit?
Tell me little one what did your precious Mama call you? . . .
For I can't bear you being called number 92 . . .

Number 92 is not buried in Castellamare del Golfo, but two days later, at Piano Gatta cemetery in Agrigento, I noticed the number in one of the five *tombe* that hold eighty-six victims of the October 3 disaster. A small black-and-white cardboard label reveals that number 92 is a little boy named Esrom (and the second name), who died with his two sisters, Delia and Milen, and his mother, Helen.

As Selam had, the students also imagined what the dead might have been called and wrote conjectured names on the paper boats they placed on the graves: this was "adoption by naming," as Galante (2018) put it. This imaginative work continued over the winter with a creative writing workshop organized by a literary festival *Contaminazioni* and led by author Fabio Stassi. The students wrote short texts imagining who the dead were, what their pasts and dreams were, and what they might say now, were they able to speak. The stories are all written in the first-person singular, and the name of each fictional person has two parts, one foreign and one Italian: Akil Vincenzo, Dahak Elena, Wara Adriana. In the ten stories Galante sent me after the workshop, relationships emerge as a recurring theme. The fictional narrators remember brothers and sisters, the care of their mothers and fathers, and what they did with friends. For the students, death seems most importantly to mean the loss of a friend, parent, or child—the end of social life.

Zara Elisabetta

Hi, I'm Zara and now I'm in the middle of nowhere. My eyes are closed and I imagine myself on a stage—me, alone, singing my songs. My music will enter everyone's mind and no one will forget me. My voice will sing out under the sea and under the earth. I imagine my mother, too, singing. She is my greatest strength. Because she has patience like no other woman has. I remember when my brothers and I were small, and we threw stones at windows. She scolded us, but she did it calmly. I remember the love she put into telling our family stories. Tonight, I'm staring at the sky full of stars. And I think my mom is here, and she keeps me safe and protects me. I perceive the boat moving and people screaming, but I am calm because I have closed my eyes and see my mother. Bye, I'm Zara. And in this moment, I'm in the middle of nowhere

(Students of Castellamare del Golfo).

With their acts of naming and through creative writing, the students imagined themselves as the dead, which facilitated their imagining of the unknown dead as persons-as-such (Edkins 2011). In previous chapters, I have argued that, from management of the dead to the representations of them in the media, treating the dead as persons who had social lives is necessary for justice and for the recognition of the rights of the dead and of living relatives. While naming the dead carries critical potential, it does not automatically translate into transformative politics, as I discussed in chapter 3. Sometimes, as Jenny Edkins (2016, 362) has argued, naming is not about recognizing the person and her politics so much as it functions to dampen the disturbance that an unknown body creates. In analyzing the 9/11 National Memorial in New York, Edkins argues that the listing of names in the memorial "portrays the victims as ordinary, apolitical" (Edkins 2016, 368) and that the function of naming is to integrate the dead into the body of the nation-state (Edkins 2016, 362).

However, in Castellamare del Golfo, imagined names and biographies function differently. A new student cohort next year might imagine other names and other biographies. Instead of closure, imaginative naming may function as a critical opening in at least two ways. First, fictional names and stories make visible the dissonance created by the bodies being buried in "our" ground and not knowing who the people were and why their bodies are "here." The use of imagination resists indifference to or acceptance of the deadly border and the injustice of bordering. It is the same uneasiness, wrought by the recognition of an unequal relationship, that I examined in chapter 3 in relation to Frances Stonor Saunders's essay. The recognition of the unequal relationship drove Saunders to write an essay after she discovered the name of the woman who died in the Lampedusa disaster while giving birth.

Second, the aesthetic approach of working with the imagination opens an alternative communicative space akin to Ariella Azoulay's (2012, 2) notion of the "civil" in her writing on "civil imagination" and "civil discourse." Similarly to Azoulay (2012), I do not limit the term aesthetic to mean judgment of taste, nor do I contrast the aesthetic with the political. Her definition of "civil" is a position from which to move beyond such opposition. Writing in the context of Israel's violence against Palestinians, Azoulay maintains that civil discourse refuses to align with governmental power and to accept uniform categories of people (e.g., "refugees") as separate from "us" and as the Other. In a civil position, one refuses to align with the regimes that "make disasters" (Azoulay 2012, 2). Instead, Azoulay makes way for "the domain of relations between citizens on the one hand, and the subject denied citizenship by a given regime on the other, on the basis of their partnership in a world that they share as women and men who are ruled" (Azoulay 2012, 3). Imagining the victims as persons—particularly through their imagined relationships, as the students did—is not fiction. The students made way for the potentiality of civil encounter with subjects who crossed the deadly border (or died while crossing) and their relatives.

While the motivation for memorializing might be centered on "us" at the scale of the community of Castellamare del Golfo, the memorial and the rituals and imaginative creative writing that engagement with the memorial generated are not exclusively centered on the self. The form of the memorial is not fixed, but instead recognizes the potentiality of its transnational meaning and of civil connections with the victims' relatives: the texts are written in English, and the headstones can be personalized. While the memorial commemorates the local response to the mass deaths—its *accoglienza*—it is also oriented toward the future and open for transformation.

Similarly, the "adoption by naming" undertaken by the students does not mean that the community has incorporated the Other into itself or that it is not open to transformation. In the stories of the students, the dead are not replicas of Italian teenagers, nor are they imagined as people who want to become "us," as was the case in the writings of Italian journalists when they interpreted the studio photographs found at the disaster site (as discussed in chapter 2). The students' writing project included research on Eritrea, and their stories include references to contemporary lives outside Italy. They refer to military conscription in Eritrea and to the *krar*, a musical instrument common in Eritrea and Ethiopia. The students also spoke with migrants from the nearby asylum seekers' reception centers many of whom also have a visible presence in town. They had been invited to the ritual at the ceremony and to the writing workshop.

Transformative Relationships

My analysis of the engagement with migrant dead in Castellamare del Golfo as a form of civility and recognition resonates with recently expanded research about memorialization and migration activism (at Europe's borders see, e.g., Rygiel 2016; Stierl 2016; Gutiérrez Rodríguez 2018; Squire 2020; at the US-Mexico border, see, e.g., De León 2015; Alonso and Nienass 2016a). Activist memorialization is seen as a practice that defies the states and authorities' perceived lack of dignified recognition of the dead. Vicki Squire (2020), in her analysis of grave dressing at Lampedusa's cemetery, identifies a responsible "politics of empathy" in cemetery activism that aims to resist states' indifference toward the dead. Encarnación Gutiérrez Rodríguez (2018) interprets activists' mourning of dead strangers as an inclusive practice, a form of "inclusive friendship" based on the recognition of interdependency between people of different communities. Kim Rygiel (2014; 2016) defines such encounters as "transgressive citizenship"—an alternative relationship from below that contravenes boundaries that nation-states try to impose between people. Engaging with dead strangers, activists can generate a transformative politics, and "a community beyond borders" (Stierl 2016, 173).

The acts of Amalia Vullo and the people in Castellamare del Golfo, like the activism of Mussie Zerai and Meron Estefanos discussed in this chapter, can be interpreted as acts of transgressive citizenship (following Kim Rygiel's terms). The "acts of citizenship" perspective, developed by Engin Isin and Greg M. Nielsen (Isin 2008, 17; 2009; Isin and Nielsen 2008) defines citizenship not as a membership to be awarded or given, but a position claimed through *acting* as a citizen. These acts and articulations of claims-making create sites for struggle and identification different from traditional sites of citizenship like military service or voting. While acts of citizenship can be performed in a place, they stretch across boundaries and involve multiple scales of contestation (Isin 2009, 371).

The dignified relationship that people form toward the migrant dead and the engagements' potential for resistance and contestation of the murderous border policies are central in the analysis of Rygiel, Squire, Gutiérrez Rodríguez, and Stierl. They show how in multiple instances activists resist bordering by correcting what the authorities fail to do and how they make the state's undignified incompetence and ignorance visible. Acts of citizenship that refuse to obey boundaries evidently are central to afterlives of disasters at global borders. Instances discussed in this chapter could be added as evidence to this body of scholarship.

However, the stories in this chapter, in my view, highlight that the care for the dead importantly shapes relationships between the living. While care for the dead can be acts of citizenship that defy the state that fails in its responsibilities, their transgressive politics becomes stronger when a relationship with the living relatives is created. Nevertheless, as the story of Castellamare del Golfo manifested, an awareness—or a capacity for civil imagination in Ariella Azoulay's terms—of the potentiality of such a relationship is the key.

Gerhild Perl (2018) examines the emergence of a relationship between people in two towns connected by a shipwreck where twelve young men from Hansala, Morocco, died near Rota, Spain, in 2003. What started as the Spanish delivering condolences to the villagers developed into amicable bonds, repatriation of the dead bodies, and economic cooperation. Perl shows how "death is a potentially vital moment that politically and morally animates people to forge a different future by creating unknown and unexpected political, economic and amicable bonds" (Perl 2018, 96). Perl tells a story of ordinary people who develop an unusual relationship. Over time the relationship develops to collaboration, a form of translocal solidarity.

In the activist context, Maurice Stierl (2016, 178, 180, 181, 187) touches on the relationship between living relatives of those who died or disappeared at the border and discusses an instance of "failing empathy." He examines a case in which activists imposed their political agenda on a memorializing event and did not pay attention to the different politics and feelings of relatives of the dead. Thus, a countermemorial action divided those it meant to unite. Stierl (2016), similar to Perl (2018), emphasizes that transformative politics emerges from continuous engagement and self-reflection of power dynamics among those involved in memorializing.

In Castellamare del Golfo, the physical memorial, the students' ceremony at the cemetery, and residents' acts of imagination opened up a communicative space where the relationship between locals and the relatives of the victims can develop. The site's transformative potential is the possibility for a civil connection beyond borders to develop between the living who have ties to either the dead as individuals or the cemetery where they are buried. Galante told me that her connection with the women from Düsseldorf and Oslo who visit the cemetery has been growing only gradually because of the language barrier. Recently, she has been able to have a conversation with the woman from Düsseldorf in German, which Galante has studied and the Eritrean woman has become more fluent in. They stay in touch between the anniversaries of the disaster, and in 2020, when international travel was restricted due to the COVID-19 pandemic, the woman in Germany asked Galante to buy a bunch of flowers to leave on the grave. Galante did so and sent the woman photos of the cared-for grave (Galante 2021).

The Essential Unknowingness

The locals in Castellamare del Golfo have invented practices of receiving and memorializing the dead and of communicating with the relatives. Having "strangers" buried in their soil was out of the ordinary, but the ethical model they could refer to from the past was the memory of their relatives having been migrants themselves. The presence of dead strangers evoked the memory of the emigrant, and that allowed them to see the "specter" of the migrant that was buried in their community.

Jacques Derrida's (1994) theory of hauntology offers a useful perspective for understanding the search for proper responses to the disaster and practices for dealing with its memory in Castellamare del Golfo. Why were the people of the town *not* indifferent? Derrida describes specters as guides that disorder the common state of things, that wake us up to seek answers beyond normal boundaries and familiar narratives. Here, a hauntological reading means to understand how people like Mariangela Galante and Nicola Coppola were compelled to engage in the new situation. Coppola referred to his biography of being a son of a labor migrant and Galante to the rise of cruel anti-migrant politics personified in Lega Nord leader Matteo Salvini. The ethics that Galante and Coppola followed when they faced the essential unknowingness of what to do was the cultivation of attentiveness to the dead as *persons-as-such*. They acted upon questions of who the dead were and what would happen if someone in the future arrived in town to look for the dead. Being attentive and open to the specters of the past and the future constituted a position that is the opposite of being indifferent to the dead strangers.

In his essay on responses to migrant deaths at various borders in Australia and Europe, Klaus Neumann (2013) argues that the opposite of indifference is not compassion, which entails a hierarchical relation between the one who has the power to feel compassion and the one who suffers, but that of attentiveness. Referring to Pope Francis's mass in Lampedusa in July 2013, in which the pope condemned "la globalizzazione dell'indifferenza" (the globalization of indifference), Neumann defines attentiveness as being "attentive to the world we inhabit." He identifies two directions from which attentiveness can be cultivated: first, by paying attention to a particular person and experience, and second, by paying attention to one's own self-interest—to "what we, living in the affluent West, think and do" (Neumann 2013). Thus, being attentive to the dead as relational figures is to understand them as "inhabiting" the same world we do—or in Ariella Azoulay's (2012, 3) terms, as being partners in the world we share.

These kinds of relationships that have emerged in Castellamare del Golfo between locals and the relatives who mourn at the victims' graves create a new kind of civil sphere, one that is not bound by the nation-state, language, or ethnicity, but that emerges despite these boundaries that are so often taken for granted. In future, connections with the victims' relatives may transform the memorial and commemorative practices in Castellamare del Golfo. The meaning of the memorial is not fixed, the individuals buried there continue to be imagined, and some of them may yet have their names carved on the headstones, as more relatives find their way to the graves.

In this chapter, I have explored how people and communities in Sicily cared for dead strangers who arrived in the hundreds. They succeeded where the state failed. The official memorial ceremony that turned into a farce failed to unite those who witnessed the disaster through mediation with those who lived through its consequences in their intimate relationships. Unlike the state, the people I met in Sicily recognize the dead strangers as relational persons and as part of the shared world. While engaging with the dead they reproduced identities and communities. They constituted a citizenship based on attentiveness.

The stories I heard in Sicily show how transnational friendships, and even new types of kinship, such as the "family" of the Vullo-Gelardis and the brothers of Wegahta, can develop in this alternative communicative space. Memorials and rituals were central in creating the space and imagining relationships. I've addressed the care for the dead migrants in Sicily in reference to the notion of adoption. Through prayer or imagining names and narratives, communities adopted the dead strangers into the community of their own dead. However, the relationality between the living that the adoption generates strengthens the transformative potential. The burial of Wegahta in the Gelardi family tomb resulted in a process of kinning between her brothers in Norway and the Vullo-Gelardis in Sicily.

Uncertainty and the uncomfortable feeling that something was not right defined the instances of memorialization in which attentiveness toward the victims and one's own responsibility emerged. The specters of the past and the future, as Derrida would see them, cause established certainties such as the nation-state, borders, and the assumed differences between "us" and "them" become irrelevant. The people in Sicily faced an uncertain reality, but instead of being indifferent, they started to find ways of articulating that reality. In the afterlives of a disaster, being attentive to specters—not only those of past figures, such as the Italian emigrants, but also those of the victims' and survivors' descendants—is important in the practice of inquiry itself. In Castellamare del Golfo and Agrigento, the world elsewhere became visible both in the form of dead strangers but more profoundly, in the form of living relatives who returned to mourn the dead. The transformative potential of the attentiveness to the dead as persons importantly connects those who live on.

MEMORIAL INTERVENTIONS

Lampedusan practices to honor unknown dead migrants have centered on death rituals and praying at the cemetery where several migrant bodies have been buried. Memorializing October 3 at graves has been impossible, however, as the 366 coffins of the victims were transported to Sicily nine days after the disaster. Within a month, the municipality created a *Giardino della memoria* (Garden of Remembrance). At the garden's inauguration ceremony, survivors of the disaster who were still staying at the local reception center joined Lampedusans in planting fifty shrubs. Six years later, on October 3, 2019, a monument titled *Nuova Speranza* (New Hope) was erected in the center of town. The bronze, tornado-shaped memorial bears the names of 366 victims.

In this chapter, I examine how and why Lampedusans created memorials after the dead had been taken away. I also discuss what kinds of identities they produced through the creation of material memorials. In the context of war memorials, Reinhart Koselleck has argued that memorials provide a means to identify the dead as heroes, victims, martyrs, or the defeated (Koselleck 2002, 287). Memorials are invitations to remember an event and the people affected by it in a particular way. They may allow for an erasure of some specifics of the event to smooth the transition of difficult narratives as Marita Sturken (1997, 74, 82) writes in relation to the Vietnam Veterans Memorial. In addition, memorials are also an invitation to recognize those who have created them.

There are several public memorials in Lampedusa that commemorate lives taken by the sea in general, including the obelisk *Cassodoro* (1988) by Arnaldo

Pomodoro, and two bronze statues by Gerry Scalso, *Trionfo del Mare* and *Omaggio al Pescatore*. They are located in the center of town, and although I had passed by them several times, I had not paid them any attention. As Austrian author Robert Musil famously wrote, there is "nothing as invisible as a monument." "They are no doubt erected to be seen—indeed to attract attention. But at the same time, they are impregnated with something that repels attention, causing the glance to roll right off, like water droplets off an oilcloth, without even pausing for a moment" (Musil 1987, 61). Remembering is not to be taken for granted, and the forgetting of an event might even be the intention of a memorial.

In addition to these lost at sea memorials, there is also a memorial sculpture in Lampedusa that remembers migrant dead: *Porta d'Europa*. To see it, one must take a twenty-minute walk or a ten-minute drive from the center of town to the shore beyond the airport runway. *Porta d'Europa* is not a conspicuously inconspicuous monument (Musil 1987, 61); there is nothing on the rocky shore except the monument and the ruins of a small bunker dating from World War II. *Porta d'Europa* is a sculpture by Mimmo Paladino that was commissioned by Italian cultural actors in 2008 to commemorate migrants who had lost their lives at the sea border (Bolzoni 2008). The open gateway rises sixteen feet tall and faces Tunisia, which is only sixty miles away. The ceramic surface of the sand-colored gate features small sculptures—hats, broken cups, shoes—that call to mind found objects washed up on the sandy beach (for further analysis of *Porta d'Europa*, see Muneroni 2015; Horsti 2016a). The monument was prompted by the so-called Strage di Portopalo, the Portopalo Massacre, which took place near Portopalo di Capo Passero in Sicily in 1996. At least 283 migrants from Southeast Asia drowned, with only a few survivors. Local fishermen and the local authorities kept quiet about what had happened until 2001, when a fisherman revealed the site of the wreck to Giovanni Maria Bellu, a Rome-based journalist who was investigating rumors of the ship's sinking (Bellu 2004).

However, these existing memorials to deaths at sea did not serve to properly identify those who were lost on October 3, 2013. The generic memorials were not appropriate. It was not the sea that had taken the victims of the disaster, they had been killed by being allowed to drown. *Porta d'Europa* was perhaps not considered suitable to memorialize the victims because it had been prompted by another disaster or because it was not created by Lampedusans. In any case, two memorials have been erected in Lampedusa specifically in memory of the October 3, 2013, disaster. They were not prompted by the continuous presence of dead bodies, but by their absence—and by the struggle over the meaning of the disaster that started with the failed "state funeral" in Agrigento (as discussed in chapter 4).

The *Giardino della Memoria* in Lampedusa

A month after the disaster, on November 4, the Municipality of Lampedusa and Linosa, the region of Sicily, and the environmental association Legambiente inaugurated the *Giardino della Memoria* with the planting of the first fifty of what would eventually be 366 shrubs on the side of the road that runs through the six-miles-long island.[1] While the site is outside of the town, the road is busy during the tourist season: the road leads to the island's main tourist attraction, La Spiaggia dei Conigli. The inconspicuous memorial garden disappears into the barren landscape, and there is no sign along the road that would encourage tourists to stop. Farther from the road, a modest sign matching the others in the natural reserve where the garden is planted tells visitors in Italian that the shrubs were planted "in memory of the victims of the shipwreck of October 3, 2013—'Lest we forget.'" There are no names or even mention of where the passengers on the boat were from or the nature of their journey: they are simply "victims of a shipwreck." There is also no indication that the site of the shipwreck is visible from the Garden of Remembrance. Nevertheless, for those who know, the garden offers a viewpoint for a commemorative gaze toward the precise disaster site in the sea.

The garden was a project that brought together various people and groups on the island, including the anti-capitalist activist collective Askavusa, who created the memorial installation *Le radici nel cielo* (*Roots in the Sky*) for the garden. Giusi Nicolini had invited Askavusa to participate in the making of the memorial. The collective had assisted the municipality after the disaster by meeting Eritrean Europeans arriving at the airport and guiding them in the search for their disappeared relatives (interview with Askavusa 2015). The installation consisted of an uprooted tree that resembled the American land artist Robert Smithson's *First Upside Down Tree* (1969). Askavusa does not explain the memorial work but when I talked about its meaning with different people, I got the sense that the piece could be read as a form of memorial activism, critiquing the border that turns everything upside down: turns decent to indecent, humane to inhumane. It could also be read as a countermemorial in opposition to the memory politics that was beginning to take form through the actions of the political establishment—or perhaps even in opposition to the memorial garden itself. Instead of symbolically burying the dead, the uprooted tree represented lives in disorder and the continuation of injustice.

Mayor of Lampedusa Giusi Nicolini had refused to participate in the memorial service organized by the state in Agrigento and by doing so, demonstrated solidarity with the survivors who had been prevented from participating. The ceremonial planting of the *Giardino* brought together those who should have

FIGURE 10. *Le radici nel cielo*, in *Giardino della memoria*. Askavusa, 2014.
© Karina Horsti, 2014. Photo by Karina Horsti.

been at the "state funeral" but who had not been invited—the Lampedusan civilian rescuers and the survivors. Together they symbolically reenacted the funeral that never was, documenting the event with pictures in which survivors stand beside Mayor Nicolini, civilian rescuers, and other Lampedusans. For Rosario Crocetta, the president of the Region of Sicily who had also boycotted the memorial service but attended the opening of the Garden of Remembrance, the garden was a substitute for a graveyard: "I go to pray on those graves on the *vigilia del trigesimo* [marking thirty days after a death] of October 3, the date when the worst tragedy in the story of global immigration happened," he said at the dedication (Radio Cento Passi Journal 2013).

The initial planting was not only an intervention into memory politics but also a statement on European asylum policies at the time, Nicolini said: "This is a day on which Lampedusa continues to be an example for Italy and Europe which should adopt new and civil migration policies based on the principle of reception and on the respect for human rights" (Radio Cento Passi Journal 2013). Similarly, Crocetta said: "I am here to honor the dead but also to reiterate that we need to change immigration policies, that Frontex has failed, that the policies of rejection do not work. We need to implement a new strategy that doesn't deliver more dead and that shares reception policies at the European level and goes beyond the Dublin agreement" (Radio Cento Passi Journal 2013). Both southern Italian leaders are members of the Democratic Party, which has (at least until 2017) been on the liberal side of immigration and integration politics. In 2013, Nicolini and Crocetta distinguished themselves and the Lampedusans from the European governments that, as they argued, were implicated in the deaths.

Both Nicolini and Crocetta thought of the disaster as globally and historically significant—they were "feeling historical," to use Lauren Berlant's term (2008b, 5). In her essay "Thinking about Feeling Historical" Berlant analyses the performative act of "thinking" in two texts: the African American gay activist Essex Hemphill's poetry and George Bush's speech about the fear of American soldiers dying in Iraq. The performative "thinking" refers to a realization that one is living in a situation that will matter in the future: "A situation is a state of things in which something that will perhaps matter is unfolding amidst the usual activity of life" (Berlant 2008b, 5). In terms of hauntology (discussed in the Introduction and chapter 4), thinking historically is awareness of the specters of the future.

By "feeling historical," Berlant means seeing and sensing an event as something that one assumes will have an afterlife. "We are directed to see not an event but an emergent historical environment that can now be sensed atmospherically, collectively," Berlant (2008b, 5) writes.[2] The awareness of "the emergent historical environment," the emergent and unfolding afterlife of the disaster shaped Crocetta's and Nicolini's actions. Crocetta defined the event as a globally significant moment in a story that continues to be told, as a tragedy in the "story of global immigration." Nicolini envisioned the garden as a permanent feature of the island and for the islanders, including future generations. She envisioned a hospitable future, when today's children would return to the garden as adults and be able to say, "this no longer happens" (Mastrodonato 2013).

Nicolini and Crocetta were motivated first by issues of the present: they wanted to establish Lampedusa as the memory site of the disaster and criticize European border and asylum policies. By October 2013, the island had already become a symbolic site of the European border and migration. Border politics and policies had become spectacularized since the early years of this century, and Lampedusa had turned into a major stage of this performance (Sossi 2006; Campesi 2011; Cuttitta 2014). The symbolic status is also why Pope Francis chose Lampedusa for his first papal trip outside of Rome. His commemoration of migrant deaths during the visit in July 2013 further intensified the symbolic imaginary of Lampedusa. In addition, the locals had memorialized unknown migrant graves at the cemetery (Zagaria 2016), and the municipality under Giusi Nicolini's term had renewed markings of the graves.

In Nicolini's and Crocetta's minds, attempts to move the memorialization of October 3 from Lampedusa to Sicily were wrong. Second, by "feeling historical,"

Nicolini and Crocetta were thinking of the present as a future past—they were mindful of the recoverability of the present in the future. They sought to create a testimony for future generations that their communities had resisted the violence of the border and envisioned a future where the Mediterranean Sea would be safe for all. They attempted to *make* future and take control of the future. This demonstrates how social life has a fluid temporal horizon—both to the past and the future. Barbara Adam (2010) argues that social research often seeks explanations from the past but does not always pay sufficient attention to the futurity of social life—to the fact that individuals and communities alternate between perspectives of anticipated *future presents* and enacted *present futures* (Adam 2010, 362).[3] If Nicolini's and Crocetta's desire to prefigure how their political leadership is judged in the future is informed by the way in which past leaders' actions and inactions are interpreted in the present time they do not articulate what those events might be.

Crocetta presented the issue beyond the local, regional, and national frameworks by connecting the disaster to the global story of immigration. However, neither he nor Nicolini seemed to consider the potential significance of the memory site itself on a transcultural or transnational scale. Their speeches made no mention of what the garden might mean to survivors or to the families of the victims who might come and visit it. Nicolini had invited the survivors to the planting ceremony as guests of the Lampedusan community but failed to see them as citizens who had an interest in shaping the afterlife of the disaster.

While the garden was clearly created as a memorial of a specific disaster, its meaning could transform. The meaning of a memorial is never fixed on the initial identification inscribed by those who created it (see, e.g., Sturken 1997; Neumann 2000; 2020; Koselleck 2002). People who visit and "use" a memorial can add to or even transform its meaning. In fact, on October 10, 2016, an additional plant, carefully circled with stones, appeared in the garden. A small sign next to it informed that the relatives of victims of an unrelated maritime disaster in Italian waters, the 1991 collision of the ferry *Moby Prince* with an oil tanker in Livorno Harbor had planted this small bush in the garden. The collision started a fire and released toxic fumes that killed all but one person on board *Moby Prince*. The rescue effort failed because of inefficiency of the coast guard, and the later inquiries and court proceedings revealed that deaths could have been prevented by an immediate and coordinated rescue operation. Thus, the narrative of the 1991 disaster in many respects resembles the 2013 disaster (Safety4Sea 2019).

According to the small sign in Lampedusa, the plant is "in memory of migrants who have lost their lives." This (nominally) 367th plant is meant to amplify the garden's message. First, it is a gesture of solidarity by those affected by the earlier tragedy. Second, it potentially frames the memorial politically as it reminds visitors that there has been no justice for either those who perished on April 10, 1991, or those who died on October 3, 2013. It therefore sheds a critical light on the efficiency and honesty of the institutional rescue efforts—an issue that is still raised by Askavusa, human rights organizations, relatives of the victims, Eritrean survivors, and Lampedusan civil rescuers.[4] Third, since the sign does not make a reference to the specific disaster of October 3, 2013, the new plant potentially could shift the meaning of the garden toward a memorial for all migrant deaths. However, if that meaning was emphasized, the Porta d'Europa would have been a more suitable location.

Survivors Return to *Giardino della Memoria*

The memorial's sign did not recognize the survivors as creators of the memorial although they participated in the planting of the first shrubs. Neither did the environmental organization Legambiente that was responsible to the Nature Reserve stay in touch with the survivors nor did they develop it in collaboration with them. Nevertheless, over the years, many survivors returned to the *Giardino della memoria* to care for the plants. On October 3, 2018, I accompanied a group of survivors to the memorial garden.

It was getting dark, but I could still make out the disaster site from where I stood in the Lampedusa Island Nature Reserve. One had to know where to look, however, as there was nothing indicating where the boat had sunk. Mobile phone flashlights illuminated the scene. Six Eritrean survivors and two men who had each lost a brother in the disaster knelt on the ground to clear away weeds and straighten the numbered signs that had been planted beside the shrubs. The dead bodies had been numbered according to the order in which they had been retrieved and the plants in the Garden of Remembrance were also numbered. Both of these numbers had become meaningful for relatives and friends, and some of the men and one woman were wandering around looking for specific numbers in the garden. Some of the numbered signs that the environmental organization Legambiente had added the previous year had gone missing, however, and many of the plants had died anyway.

Among the survivors were two men, Amanuel and Ambasager, both of whom now work in health care in Sweden, looking after mostly elderly people in their homes. They had become close friends during the journey that had ended in disaster. From Lampedusa, they had continued together to Sweden and shared a room in the reception center there while they waited for their asylum applications to be processed. Ambasager's wife and young son had arrived safely in Sweden two years after the disaster through the family reunification process. Amanuel had also married, and the two men's families had become friends as well. Ambasager is among the oldest of the survivors. He is a tall, slim man with glasses, about my age—late forties—and has a bit of gray hair at his temples. Amanuel is a bit younger and shyer. When we first met, at an outdoor restaurant in Lampedusa for dinner, he recalled in his soft voice how Vito Fiorino, who had rescued Amanuel in his leisure boat, *Gamar*, had taken off his shirt and given it to him to wear. Ambasager and Amanuel have been regular participants in the various commemorations that have been held in Lampedusa. They organize and pay for their trips themselves and have been hosted by Fiorino, their rescuer.

On every October 3 since the disaster, survivors who were able to return to Lampedusa had taken pictures of the remaining plants in the memorial garden and of each other standing next to them. Some of them had participated in the garden's inauguration ceremony in November 2013, when the first fifty shrubs were planted. As then, they again now took group photos and shared them via their social media networks. Survivors who were not present in Lampedusa responded with crying emojis and greetings from their new countries: Norway, Sweden, Denmark, the Netherlands, Germany.

For the survivors, being together on the plateau overlooking the darkening Mediterranean Sea brought back memories. As we walked back to where the rental cars were parked, Adhanom, introduced in the beginning of this book, told me in Swedish about an episode he and the others had discussed earlier. There had been a woman with crutches at the smugglers' collection point in Libya. She was not meant to be on their boat, but she had begged the smugglers to let her board, claiming that her leg needed medical care. The smugglers relented, but when the boat capsized, she had no chance of survival with her broken leg. The survivors had mused: "If she had stayed, if only the smugglers had not let her jump the queue . . . she might still be alive." These were the types of stories that were shared at the *Giardino* as the survivors tended to the plants.

Contested Memorialization in Lampedusa

Other than the attention received from the relatives of the *Moby Prince* victims, the Garden of Remembrance continued to deteriorate. A storm had blown away Askavusa's installation by the time of my second visit to the garden in 2015. An environmental organization, Legambiente, made plans to rebuild the Garden of Remembrance and in 2018 planted new shrubs and installed numbered plates next to the plants. In 2021, those plants and plates had decayed. The community at large was not involved, and the replanting did not seem to resolve the memorial politics of the disaster. Vito Fiorino, the ice cream maker and captain of the first boat to arrive at the disaster site, continued to envision the return of the bodies to Lampedusa and the creation of a memorial cemetery.

Lampedusans have not been unified in their memorial practices related to migrant deaths, whether before the October 3 disaster or after it. Lampedusans have memorialized unknown migrants on their own or in various groups, motivated by ethics, religion, or politics. Some local groups, namely Askavusa and a solidarity network Forum Lampedusa Solidale have helped relatives organize burials or find graves. The Lampedusa cemetery, located outside of town, behind the airport, is a notable site where material traces reveal the memorializations that have taken place. During my visits to Lampedusa in 2014–2021, I often came across ephemeral traces of memorialization at the cemetery, such as ribbons that had Amnesty International logos printed on them and notes visitors had left by crosses marking unknown migrant graves (see also Zakaria 2016; Squire 2020, 174–76).

Vincenzo, an elderly cemetery caretaker whom my research assistant, Ilaria Tucci, and I often found sitting with other old men on the benches at an intersection on via Roma, told us that he buried the cemetery's first unknown migrant in 1996. He had since buried more than eighty bodies, praying at the graves and marking some of them with simple wooden crosses. While talking with us, he took a small newspaper clipping from his wallet, unfolded it, and revealed a picture of him greeting Pope Francis. It was from a German newspaper, he said. "There are some who recognize what I have done. They've come from Austria, Germany, many countries." But he had grievances about how some Italians and Lampedusans did not respect his deeds. He was disappointed that the crosses he had made had been removed when a group of religious women from elsewhere in Italy had renovated the section for the unknown dead at the cemetery in 2016. The women had collected donations and paid a local carpenter to make new crosses of wood taken from North African fishing vessels that smugglers had used to transport migrants. One of the women writes in her report of the project, which she sent me by email, that they were inspired by the story of Rizpah, who watches over the dead in the Bible (2 Samuel 21). They renovated the section of the cemetery in observance of the Holy Year of Mercy declared by Pope Francis.

In addition to the renovated section, there are numerous graves intermingled with those of the locals. As Tony Kushner (2016, 90) has observed, Lampedusans have made every effort to provide as much detail as possible about the dead. Most graves are unnamed but gender, possible place of origin and age, and the details of a particular disaster (when known) are included in the printed descriptions on the graves. Kushner defines these acts of remembering the unknown dead not only as personal acts but also as "the first act of historicization of a mass movement that in so many cases leaves not a trace" (Kushner 2016, 90).

On the first anniversary of the disaster, Vito Fiorino had opposed public memorialization. In 2014, he and the others who had been on his boat that night published an open letter to announce that as rescuers, they were refusing to participate in the public commemoration of the disaster: "We would have preferred that the institutions continue their silence, the silence that has prevailed for the twelve months since the tragedy and which is now interrupted by an instrumentalized media spectacle, by useless and expensive political parades. Our commemoration remains private, as it has been since the day of the tragedy" (Fiorino et al. 2014; see also Puglia 2014). The institutional silence Fiorino and his friends draw attention to in their announcement refers to the lack of investigation into the disaster and the failed rescue. Fiorino believed that agencies such as the Coast Guard and the Guardia di Finanza and representatives of the Italian government or European Union had no right to memorialize the disaster in Lampedusa. However, Vito Fiorino continued to memorialize in his own, more private way, first by closing his *gelateria* on October 3, posting a notice reading "Chiuso per lutto" (Closed for mourning) and spending time with survivors who had returned to commemorate the disaster. He took survivors out to the disaster site on his boat *Gamar*, a practice he continued even after selling the boat. The purchase agreement he made with the new owner included a provision that Fiorino could use the boat once a year, on October 3. However, in 2017, Fiorino began to take a more public role in memorializing. He gave his first speech at the interfaith commemorative ceremony in Lampedusa on October 3, 2017, standing with a group of survivors at the Sanctuary of the Madonna di Porto Salvo.

Fiorino's memorial activism was motivated by the lack of investigation into the disaster and the absence of the dead victims—the absence of those whom he and the other Lampedusans had not been able to save. Survivors returned to the island for commemorative rituals every year, and they were part of the islanders' everyday life through video calls, messages, and photographs sent by Facebook, Messenger, and WhatsApp. The mediated copresence of the living reminded Lampedusans of the physical absence of the dead. The removal of the dead and their burial in multiple different cemeteries in Sicily was a second disappearance, reminding the rescuers of the first disappearance—the loss of lives.

The civil rescuers were haunted by those who had lost their lives in front of them. During my research in Lampedusa, I often encountered the rescuers' regret about not being able to save everyone. This regret is central to the memory of the disaster as told by Lampedusans. The memory of saving lives is paired with the memory of lives they were unable to save. "The oily arms that slip away, those Christians disappearing in the waves, looking at me, asking" was a scene that tormented Domenico Colapinto for months after the disaster (Cavallaro 2013): "You hear shouting, you save one, and you can't see the other anymore. In the moment you decide to save one, you let another one die. To be God, in that moment. My nephew Francesco shouted, 'Look, there is a woman. Go!' But as I go, there is another one, arm stretched out to me. Can I let him drown? And so, that woman dies" (Domenico Colapinto quoted in Cavallaro 2013). Constantino Baratta told me he refuses to accept the title of hero that the media continues to foist upon him. We had been sitting in Lampedusa's Bar dell'Amicizia, talking about the Italian magazine *L'Espresso*'s selection of him as "Uomo dell'anno," Man of the Year, for 2013. There was nothing heroic in what he had done—it was only what a normal person would do, he said. "I always say to everyone who calls us 'heroes' that I—that we are all ordinary people, simple people. Like last year, I said to [Martin] Schulz and [Federica] Mogherini: 'No, we are not heroes.' For one thing, we felt so bad after the disaster because we couldn't do more. We always regretted having done so little that day." The memory of being unable to rescue was always part of the memory of rescue.

Nuova Speranza—"Dignity to Our Europe"

In 2018, Vito Fiorino traveled to Stockholm to visit survivors who lived in the area. One issue he wanted to discuss with them was the burials. Two men of Eritrean origin whom Fiorino had rescued met him at the airport. They told me later that day in Stockholm that they both wore identical T-shirts they had printed to honor his arrival. The shirts had a picture of *Gamar* overfilled with people, the forty-seven rescued and eight rescuers. Below the photo was a text that read "LAMPEDUSA 3/10/2013."

On the Sunday of Fiorino's weekend trip, he sat with a group of four survivors, three men and one woman, in the yard of Adal Neguse's apartment building in a Stockholm suburb. The conversation progressed through multiple layers of simultaneous interpretation. Ilaria Tucci translated to and from Italian for Fiorino, and Adal translated to and from Tigrinya for the three other survivors. English was the language that Tucci and Adal shared and from which I made my notes. As we sat around a garden table, Fiorino explained his plans for the memorial cemetery. If reburial was not possible, he said, at least a memorial should be created. There should be a place where the dead can be mourned in Lampedusa, he said. One of the survivors reminded him that immediately after the disaster, the survivors had protested the transport of the dead to Agrigento and had gone to the mayor of Lampedusa to request that the dead be buried there, in one place. But there was no space in the cemetery for 366 dead, Giusi Nicolini had responded. Another survivor added that moving the dead back to Lampedusa now would probably not be in the interests of family members who were advocating for sending the bodies to Eritrea. Eritrean custom was to bury the dead in the place where they were from when possible. Interestingly, survivors and relatives had not demanded reburials elsewhere in Europe, for example, in Sweden, Germany, or Norway, where many now lived.

Survivors agreed with Fiorino that a memorial was a good idea, and in fact, they had talked about creating one themselves, to be placed in the Garden of Remembrance. The names of the dead would have to be there, one of the survivors said. The memorial would list the names of the dead on a column of white marble, he envisioned when I asked about the memorial again on another occasion. "As survivors, we have a responsibility," he said. His intention was not so much to evoke the duty to remember in others, such as tourists visiting Lampedusa, or for the memorial to be instrumentalized for any kind of politics. Instead, the memorial was intended for those most affected: "There needs to be a place where the families of the victims can go," the survivor told me. It would have a therapeutic meaning; the top of the pillar would have a place for a candle. The memorial would stand as a symbolic correction to the burial of the victims in unnamed graves in multiple different cemeteries in Sicily. Because only thirty-one victims have been forensically identified as of 2018 (Olivieri et al. 2018, 125), many relatives are unable to visit the graves of their loved ones, even if they are able to travel to Italy. In this sense, the survivors' idea of the memorial as a substitute for the graves was similar to Vito Fiorino's motivation.

To coordinate the survivors, most of whom had settled in Northern Europe, the survivor with the vision for a memorial created a Viber group, which about seventy people immediately joined. After a lengthy discussion, the survivors agreed that the most appropriate site for the memorial would be the Garden of Remembrance. Lampedusa is remote, but as Adhanom had told me when we were at the garden, "It is a place where I can really commemorate my friends and feel connected to them."

Less than a year after the meeting in Stockholm, the monument *Nuova Speranza* (New Hope) was unveiled at Piazza Piave in the center of Lampedusa, next to the post office.[5] Wooden poles about three meters high rise from the center of a brass whirl, which descends in the shape of a tornado to the blue-painted base. Three hundred sixty-six names of victims have been engraved on the monument in the Latin alphabet. The visual motif of the memorial—a tornado and the sea—reflects the disaster in a figurative, concrete way: the boat overturned, and the people drowned. It could also be interpreted as an explanation of the disaster—that it was a natural disaster, and the killer was the sea. However, this potential interpretation

FIGURE 11. *Nuova Speranza* monument, the mural, and the poster of victims' faces at Piazza Piave in Lampedusa, 2021. © Karina Horsti, 2021. Photo by Karina Horsti.

is countered by a sign placed next to the monument, which reads in both Italian and in English:

> "NEW HOPE"
> 3 October 2013
> I wanted to give a name to these human beings,
> women, men and children,
> that after their death have been buried
> in various agrigentino cemeteries and identified only with a number.
> THE INDIFFERENCE of that night
> has made that dawn never came [sic]
> for 366 of them.
> Vito Fiorino

The sign frames the memorial as a critical commentary about the undignified treatment of the dead, including their nonidentification, and the failed rescue operation. The dead are identified by their names on the memorial, but the sign is written in first person and signed by Vito Fiorino. The name of the memorial, *Nuova Speranza*, also refers to his boat, *Gamar*, which had had that name at the time he bought it. In the text, Fiorino is the one who "gives a name" to those who are otherwise known only by a number. The agency of naming was picked up and amplified by Italian author Davide Enia in 2019 in a public social media post:

> It was the stubbornness of Vito Fiorino—who so badly wanted this artwork, seeking funding, finding labor, organizing transport—that finally made it possible for the names of the victims of the shipwreck to exist. Before today, they were not remembered anywhere. Not here, not elsewhere. . . . This list of names on the monument gives a shred of dignity to our Europe, so dramatically distant, so indifferent, so cowardly.

What is said about the names both on the sign and in the commentary, however, is not completely correct.[6] It was the survivors who had done the initial labor of identification: the listing of the names (see chapter 3). Further, the names had already been used in memorialization by others. The names had been recited in Dagmawi Yimer's memorial film *Asmat* and in a memorial service in Lampedusa's airport hangar and had been shared in the Eritrean diasporic online media and printed on the back of the Sant'Egidio postcard (see chapter 3). The agency of the survivors who compiled the list of names is invisible not only in *Nuova Speranza*, but also in these other memorials. The names are taken for granted by those who memorialize, and the work and care that went into the creation of the list is not recognized in the memorializations. Some relatives of the victims had even identified and named graves in Sicily, one by one (see chapters 4 and 8). What Fiorino did, however, was publicize the names in a visual form that had not been done before.

The story of creating *Nuova Speranza* demonstrates how memorials provide a means of identification. *Nuova Speranza* frames the dead as victims of a double indifference—the indifference that let them be killed by the sea (reflected in the tornado shape and the blue base) and the indifference that failed to attend to their dignified burial. But, as is typical of memorials, the sign next to *Nuova Speranza* also identifies those who memorialized: Lampedusans, and specifically, Vito Fiorino. They are the agents who are publicly acknowledged as countering the indifference, and in this way, as Davide Enia maintains, they offer a way to feel "a fragment of dignity" and hope for "our Europe." The memorial offers a space in which Europeans can renounce the indifference that produces mass death at the borders.

While *Nuova Speranza* was inspired by conversations with survivors, it became a memorial that reflected the needs and messages of its creators. This was obvious in the inauguration ceremony as well, which I viewed via mobile phone videos sent to me by Vito Fiorino and survivors on October 3, 2019. I watched the videos in Hamburg with a victim's brother, Teddy (a pseudonym). The attendees included Lampedusans and Italian youth who had come to Lampedusa for the Comitato 3 ottobre's educational program (see chapters 4 and 6). The inaugural program addressed this audience: it was in Italian, and the well-known love song "La cura," by Franco Battiato, was sung together to create a communal atmosphere for commemoration. In Hamburg, Teddy watched the mediation of a ceremony in which others memorialized the disaster's victims, including his brother. While his brother was no longer just a number in a sequence of numbers, for the public gathered around the memorial, he was still only a name in the list of other names. Nothing about him was known to those attending the inauguration—except that he was dead.

This, however, is my interpretation of the scene—I had expected to see survivors and family members involved in erecting the memorial and in its inauguration. But Teddy did not share my reservations about the memorial. He had attended the commemoration organized by the Comitato 3 ottobre in Lampedusa the year before and dined at Fiorino's house. The attention he had received in Lampedusa and the islanders' memorial practices that he had witnessed then and was now observing through mediation created a social tie between him and the Lampedusans. He respected *their* acts of memorialization and was comfortable taking part in them. But Teddy is able to memorialize on his own, as well, with his transnational family or together with survivors and other family members of victims, as he had in Lampedusa the previous year. A similar position was common among the survivors I knew and talked with about the memorial in the following years. They respected the erection of the memorial in Lampedusa, which they call in Tigrinya *hawelti gdayat Lampedusa*, Lampedusa's memorial monument.

The Communicative Space of Piazza Piave

As soon as the creation of any public memorial is announced, a discursive space opens up. As a multimodal ensemble of visual elements and text placed in relation to a specific material and social setting, a memorial invites engagement from others. Sometimes the space is also open for conflict, and memorials often turn into material manifestations of different types of conflicts (see, e.g., Vinitzky-Seroussi 2002; Neumann 2022).

On the Piazza Piave in Lampedusa, multiple layers of identification were already present at the inauguration of *Nuova Speranza*. While the memorial project was initiated by Vito Fiorino, other organizations and individuals were also involved in shaping the site. A freshly planted olive tree on the square is accompanied by a sign which reads in English and Italian: "We remember the people who in Lampedusa have not been indifferent and assumed a responsibility in front of those who died in the Mediterranean Sea. Gariwo, the forest of the Righteous." The sign is attached to a metal frame with two hands reaching out to one another across a piece of wood from a North African fishing boat that was used to cross the Mediterranean Sea. The sign emphasizes the identification of the memorial as a gesture of Lampedusans' attention and responsibility as they encountered the disaster.

Gariwo—Gardens of the Righteous Worldwide is a nonprofit organization based in Milan that has created gardens honoring "the Righteous" of different causes. The term "Righteous" and the design of the main garden in Milan was inspired by the grove of trees at Yad Vashem, the Holocaust Remembrance Center in Israel that acknowledges non-Jews who protected Jews during the Holocaust. One of the categories of the righteous in the garden in Milan are those who have assisted undocumented migrants in the present day. The Coast Guard of Lampedusa and the Eritrean Italian human rights advocate Alganesh Fessaha were recognized by the garden in 2015. Constantino Baratta and Vito Fiorino were recognized in 2018, together with Daphne Vloumidi, a hotel owner from Lesbos, Greece, who assisted migrants who had crossed the Aegean Sea from Turkey. As a result of being recognized by the organization, Vito Fiorino knew the president of Gariwo, Gabriele Nissim, and decided to contact him to ask for a donation for the memorial project. Nissim replied that there would be no need to seek further donations for the project, as Gariwo would cover the entire cost of the monument: 15,000 euros (Fiorino 2021). This collaboration provided Gariwo with access to the scene of memorialization, allowing them to plant the tree and erect the sign on the same square as the memorial.

The second memorial element at the Piazza Piave, on the wall of a building next to the monument, is a large mural depicting a wreath of yellow and white flowers resembling the wreath Pope Francis threw into the sea in Lampedusa in July 2013. A number of humanitarian, cultural, and religious organizations that wanted to participate in the memorial[7] commissioned the Italian street artist Neve (Danilo Pistone) to paint the mural, which adds a religious meaning to the monument. The wreath, visible above the monument, is an aureole that sacralizes the dead who have been named (but also, potentially, Vito Fiorino and the Lampedusans who are mentioned in the signs).

The third element on the square is made of plastic, and thus, its materiality is not as lasting as the other elements. However, its changeability reflects its function. A poster depicting the faces of 137 victims of the disaster is affixed to the wall below the mural. It can be updated annually if Tadese, a survivor who lives in Rome, receives more photographs from relatives. The poster is a revised version of the Sant'Egidio postcard discussed in chapter 3. In this version, in addition to more faces, an image of the wrecked boat on the seabed has been added.

The poster's title text reads, in Tigrinya script "Aykrsakumnye nay guezo btsotey, gdayat 3 tikimti 2013 ab Lampedusa" (I will not forget you my travel companion, the victims of 3 October 2013 in Lampedusa), reflecting that this element is created by the survivors, the travel companions. However, this knowledge is available only to speakers of Tigrinya. In Italian, the poster says: "Per non dimenticare 3 ottobre 2013 Lampedusa" (Not to forget October 3, 2013 Lampedusa) and "Volti e nomi delle vittime del naufragio del 3 ottobre 2013 a Lampedusa" (Faces and names of the victims of the 3 October 2013 shipwreck in Lampedusa). On the right margin of the poster is a word in English: "Eritreans." This adds another identifying element to the memorial: the dead in the photos are from Eritrea. This clue is ambiguous, however. It can be interpreted as an attempt to connect the memorial to a specific nationality (this is a memorial by or for Eritreans), or it can be taken as a critical political message (they died because they had to escape Eritrea). Tadese brought the poster to the memorial inauguration ceremony that was held on October 3, 2019, at 3:30 a.m., the time of the disaster. Since then, it has become a fixed element of the memorial piazza, but its ephemeral material quality suggests it can be revised by adding new faces—and perhaps new meanings.

The way in which a memorial can function as a communicative space and invite further memorialization and additional layers of meaning was confirmed

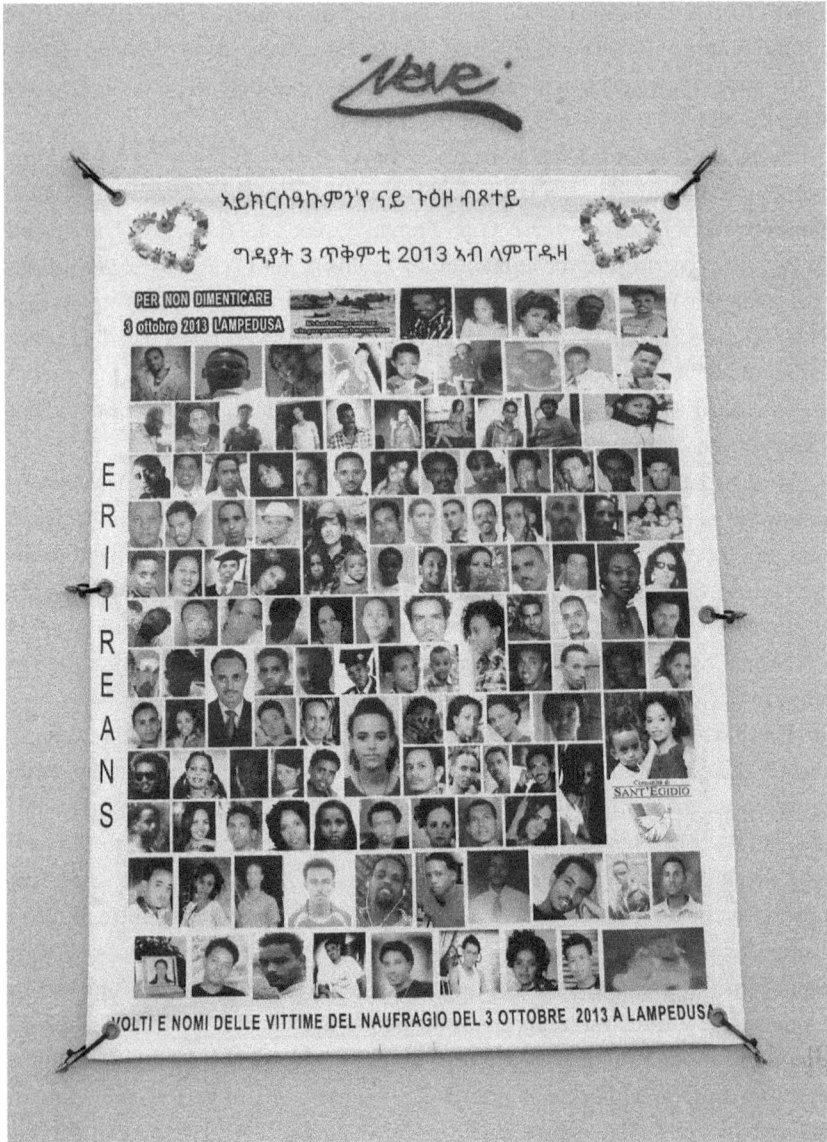

FIGURE 12. "I will not forget you my travel companion, the victims of 3 October 2013 in Lampedusa" the poster title reads in Tigrinya. Photos of 137 victims, created by Tadese. © Karina Horsti, 2021. Photo by Karina Horsti.

in 2021 at Piazza Piave. The memorial service started at 3:30 a.m., and as I arrived a bit late, the singing of "La cura" was just finishing. The small memorial square was full of mainly high school students with their teachers from different

European countries who had been invited to participate in the educational activities organized by the Comitato 3 ottobre (and partly funded by the Italian Ministry of Education). Next to *Nuova Speranza*, survivors had spread out a knitted blanket that Forum Lampedusa Solidale, a local solidarity group, had made from 368 knitted squares that people from various countries had mailed them. Dozens of red candles were lit by the memorial.

A cameraman and journalist were present from RAI, the Italian public broadcasting company, and when the crowd began to dissolve, the television camera turned toward a group of eight Tunisian women. They were mothers and sisters of men who had disappeared during an undocumented border crossing in the sea from Tunisia to Italy. The women held pictures of the disappeared; one showed a photo on her mobile phone, which glowed in the dark of the early morning hour. They formed a row for the cameraman and others, posing right under the memorial poster with the images of the October 3, 2013, victims.

Holding photos of their disappeared while standing beneath photos of the 137 victims of another disaster, the women created a powerful relation between two groups of "non-citizens" and their mourning relatives. The memorialization of one disaster created a communicative space for the representation and mourning of another disaster. The Tunisian women used the event to make claims for their right to know what happened to the disappeared. This was an act of forensic citizenship—a subjectivity they constituted in relation to the state of Italy, but also in relation to people, particularly in relation to those intimately touched by the October 3, 2013, disaster. They made claims for the rights of the dead and the rights of relatives there in Italy, where their sons and brothers had disappeared. As they performed their act at a site and ritual memorializing another incident, they constituted a relational citizenship with the dead, survivors, and relatives of the victims of the October 3, 2013, disaster. Their act also upheld the visibility of the issue of forensics and identification in the context of the October 3, 2013, disaster, an issue that eight years later was still not resolved. The conjuncture of these two types of disasters, which took place in the same sea, accentuated the broader issue of border deaths and their unfinished aftermaths.

In Lampedusa, memorializing the disaster's dead, who were not part of the community, reveals something about the community that does the remembering. Three types of identifications and politics intersect in Lampedusans' physical memorials. First, both memorials, the Garden of Remembrance and *Nuova Speranza*, serve as an intervention into the memory politics of border deaths—how, where, and for whom is it appropriate to remember these deaths? In the immediate aftermath of the disaster, the southern Italian leaders Giusi Nicolini and Rosario Crocetta worked toward establishing Lampedusa as the disaster's memory site, and the new administration has intensified those efforts.

Nuova Speranza is located in the center of town, and the monument's visibility is emphasized by the mural, the olive tree, and the poster of victims' faces. Lampedusans were haunted by the physical absence of the dead, particularly because the specters of the dead lingered in their memories and reappeared with the survivors who visited and remained in their lives through mediated communication. Each survivor brought to their minds a dead victim who could have been rescued.

Second, the community's memorializing takes a political stance against Europe's asylum policies and murderous bordering. From the periphery of Europe, which is the center of its border zone, they contest Europe's politics of bordering, the corporeal and emotional consequences of which they have witnessed with their own eyes. In addition, Vito Fiorino makes a critical statement on the lack of identification of the dead and proper investigation into the disaster. By raising these points, *Nuova Speranza* amplifies survivors' concerns (see chapter 7).

Third, the memorials cannot be owned, even by those who created them. Families of the victims of another disaster, the *Moby Prince* collision, left their mark on the Garden of Remembrance by planting an additional shrub. The garden has also become significant for the Lampedusa disaster survivors who return to care for the plants and envision creating a memorial in the Nature Reserve. On Piazza Piave, Tadese inserted the poster of victims' faces, accompanied by text in Tigrinya and a label, "Eritreans," in English. The Tunisian women entered the memorial scene of the October 3, 2013, disaster and inserted their case of disappearance and claims for investigation and the right to forensic identification. In doing so, they constituted a subjectivity of forensic citizenship, both through claims-making toward the state of Italy, and through relationships with the dead, survivors, and relatives of the October 3, 2013, disaster. The layering of meanings on Piazza Piave open up other ways of understanding *Nuova Speranza*, adding another political scale to the memorial that encourages visitors to ask who the victims were and why they died. Memorials are not fixed. They create a communicative space where the meaning and memory of an event are negotiated and contested.

MEMORY POLITICS

My examination of memorializing has so far focused on local communities in Sicily and Lampedusa, on those who witnessed the disaster's consequences with their own eyes. The presence of physical bodies of the dead—and their disturbing absence—generated an obligation to memorialize. The obligation emerged from a biography, history, political leaning, religion, or ethics that defined the individual or community that memorialized. A citizenship of attentiveness to the dead as individual people with relationships emerged as a critical subjectivity that prevented indifference. This citizenship developed from the capacity for civil imagination, including an awareness of haunting specters of the past and the future.

However, public memorialization of the Lampedusa disaster is not limited only to these southern islands: it has expanded across Italy and Europe. In Villa Celimontana Park in Rome, a square is named as *Largo vittime di tutte le migrazioni* (Square of the victims of all migrations) in the memory of the disaster. In Foligno, Perugia, there is *Piazzetta tre ottobre*. Since 2016, the date, October 3, is observed as the National Day of Remembrance for the Victims of Immigration in Italy. Beyond Italy, examples include the "Lampedusa Cross," supposedly made of wood from the boat that sank on October 3, 2013. The cross was acquired by the British Museum in 2015 and displayed at St. Paul's Cathedral in London during a service on June 19, 2016. In Dresden, photos of victims' graves in Sicily were printed on rugs that were laid out in Theaterplatz in February 2017 to create an imaginary cemetery titled "Lampedusa 361" as part of the anniversary commemoration of the destruction of Dresden during the Second World War.

In this chapter, I analyze memorialization done by others at a distance, people who do not have a direct relationship with the dead nor have concretely witnessed the materiality of the disaster. I expand my analysis to the mediated witnesses, to the scale of the nation and to that of a transnational community, the European Union. The designation of October 3 as the National Day of Remembrance for the Victims of Immigration (*Giornata nazionale in memoria delle vittime dell'immigrazione*) in Italy is an important memorial that has prompted various forms of memorialization, as the ceremony involving the students at the cemetery in Castellamare del Golfo (in chapter 4) demonstrated. The story of the National Day of Remembrance, established through a legislative process in Rome, started in Lampedusa, however.

On the evening of October 3, 2013, Paola la Rosa, a lawyer who had worked with migrants since moving to Lampedusa some fifteen years earlier from Palermo, got together with nine other people to consider questions such as how the disaster would be remembered one year later (La Rosa 2015). What would the legacy of the disaster be? The disaster's magnitude made them think that it would have an afterlife. Their aim was to create what they termed a Day of Memory and Welcome (*Giornata della memoria e dell'accoglienza*), to be observed on October 3. The idea encompassed both the remembrance of the dead and honoring those who rescued and welcomed the migrants. To this end, they created a committee, the *Comitato 3 ottobre*.[1]

When La Rosa explained to me in 2015 the initial purpose of the Comitato, she used the word *riconoscimento*, which translates as recognition, acknowledgment, or identification. According to La Rosa, the original philosophy of the Comitato was to afford *riconoscimento* to the victims in two ways: by commemoration and by identifying the dead though scientific methods. La Rosa had long been concerned that the anonymous dead found by local fishermen and the coast guard and buried in Lampedusa's cemetery remained unidentified. She was active in Forum Lampedusa Solidale and had been among those locals who cared for the graves of unknown migrants at the cemetery and engaged with civic forensics. In the Comitato's view, memorializing the disaster would eventually inspire people to ask who the dead were, ultimately forcing the authorities to seriously address the scientific identification of the dead. They acted upon the obligation to do justice. "It is justice that turns memory into a project; and it is this same project of justice that gives the form of the future and of the imperative to the duty of memory" (Ricoeur 2004, 88).

In one sense, the Comitato's early initiative can be seen as a countermemorial, as the Day of Remembrance would be an acknowledgment of people whose deaths were not usually seen as worthy of public commemoration. The process of initiating the memorial would remind Italians what they have publicly forgotten, and because an official Day of Remembrance requires establishing a law, it would, in fact, challenge the border policies of the sovereign state itself.

In the context of the US-Mexico border, Jessica Auchter (2013; 2014, 129–32) and Alexandra Délano Alonso and Benjamin Nienass (2016a; 2016b) have argued that countermemorialization is a form of continued witness, and that it has the political potential to make and keep injustice visible. Auchter also argues that countermemorialization "in specific contexts" reminds us that the state is something constructed and imagined (Auchter 2013, 310). Paradoxically, however, the Comitato advanced memorialization through the Italian parliament—an institution that was simultaneously involved in making the border.

The Comitato posted a draft for a law establishing the Day of Remembrance as a petition on the website Change.org and began to collect signatures.[2] On November 13, 2013, three parliamentarians proposed the law to the Chamber of Deputies; it was passed by that assembly on April 15, 2015. On March 21, 2016, the law passed in the Italian Senate and October 3 became the National Day of Remembrance for the Victims of Immigration (*Giornata nazionale in memoria delle vittime dell'immigrazione*). By passing the law, the Italian parliament communicated that the deaths at Italy's sea borders were worthy of public remembrance and that it was the duty of Italians to commemorate the victims. The term "victims of immigration" does not, however, point to any potential perpetrator—it instead implies that people suffer because they migrate (also because they choose to do so).

In his introductory speech in the Chamber of Deputies, the parliamentary committee rapporteur Luigi Famiglietti referred to the Lampedusa disaster as the reason for selecting October 3 as the day of remembrance, but that was his only direct reference to the disaster. He refers to the victims of the disaster only by the total number of the dead and does not mention any other details about them or about the disaster, not even the fact that the victims fled from Eritrea. It is somewhat surprising that at the scale of the national debate, Eritrea—a former colony of Italy—plays no role. There is no mention of the present-day problems that urge Eritreans to leave the country nor discussion about how those problems are rooted in European colonialism (discussed in Introduction). There is no awareness of the role the Global North played in the disintegration of European colonialism and in Ethiopian expansionism, in what Awet Tewelde Weldemichael (2013) terms as recolonialization, regional colonialism, and Third World Colonialism.

More important than *who* died is apparently *where* the deaths occurred. When death occurs in what the speakers often refer to as *nostre mare, nostre Mediterraneo* (our sea), the Italians and Italy as a nation become agents responsible for remembering due to their ownership of the site of death. The articulation of the duty to remember reproduces and reaffirms national boundaries.

According to the law, the purpose of memorializing the disaster is to raise awareness and educate young people on immigration. Article 2 of the law defines the aims of the Day of Remembrance: "to raise public awareness of civil solidarity with migrants, respect for human dignity and the value of the life of each individual, integration and *accoglienza* (welcome)" and "to raise awareness and train young people on immigration and issues of reception" (Senato della Repubblica 2016). Memorializing in this case is not about the specific event or the persons involved—not about knowing what happened on October 3, 2013, what led to the disaster, or who the dead were. The disaster is a symbol through which the public is expected to become aware of the phenomenon of migration and "sense"— imagine and know through feeling—what both crossing borders and saving lives are like.

Not only are the Italians the ones who have the duty to remember, they are also the objects of commemoration. The term "victims of immigration" in the title of the law allows the memorial to be broadly defined: it recalls past generations of Italian migrants and encompasses present-day Italian rescuers. The memorial can also be seen as part of a broader phenomenon of emigrant memorialization—*monumenti all'emigrante* and emigrant festivals—that have become popular both in Italy and among Italian Americans in the United States (see Ruberto and Sciorra 2022). In the parliamentary debate, Luigi Famiglietti (2015) invoked the mining disasters in Monongah and Dawson in the United States in the early twentieth century and the Mattmark Dam disaster in Switzerland in 1965 as examples of other disasters that could be remembered on October 3. In addition, he recalled how Italians have also suffered from the lack of the right to cross borders:

> We must not forget the many Italian migrants who after the Second World War tried to enter France clandestinely, subjecting themselves, their women, and their children to very serious risks to their safety and to life itself. In fact, traversing the alpine passes often meant doing so without equipment or knowledge of the mountains and the difficulties they present, malnourished, poorly equipped, with a heavy load. In 1948, the municipality of Giaglione in Val di Susa asked Turin prefecture for help because they didn't have enough resources to bury the illegal Italians. Every night, more than a hundred illegal Italian emigrants

tried to cross the border in that area and there were at least two deaths every month. (Famiglietti 2015)

Through drawing a parallel between the past and the present, Famiglietti persuades his colleagues and the Italian public to act in solidarity with present-day migrants. As with mayor Nicola Coppola in Castellamare del Golfo (discussed in chapter 4), Famiglietti links the duty to remember with the cultivation of Italy's heritage of emigration. Seeking such parallels from the past is typical of making sense of events and for memory. Michael Rothberg (2009) suggests that "we consider memory as multidirectional: as subject to ongoing negotiation, cross-referencing and borrowing: as productive and not private" (Rothberg 2009, 3). In the memorialization of the disaster in Italy, migration plays a crucial part in both local identities and in the Italian national identity. The interaction between past and present migration is productive in two ways. On the one hand, memories of the past evoke understanding and solidarity with present-day border-crossers. On the other hand, present-day migration makes the past relevant and real. As Rothberg points out, there is a "productive and intercultural dynamic" of memories (Rothberg 2009, 3). However, the dynamic and directionality of memory is selective.

The memories that surfaced in the parliamentary debates were those that the supporters of the bill were willing to remember: histories of Italian labor migration and of escape from fascism. These memories highlight the good in past generations and describe their legacy as one of hard work and democratic values. But the memory of Italian emigration *haunts* the present society, to use the terminology of Avery Gordon (1997), who argues that social life is shaped by the "screaming presence" of what appears not to be present. The figure of an unwanted migrant is simultaneously absent (as the Italians no longer fit this category) and present (the migrants do). The shift in the embodiment of the unwanted migrant on the global scale enables the Italians as a nation to mark their social progress.

However, beyond the ghosts of Italian emigrants, there are also other "ghostly matters" (Gordon 1997)—or in psychoanalytic terms, "intergenerational phantoms" (Abraham and Torok in Davis 2005, 373–74)—in play. These ghostly matters are secrets or traumas transmitted from others or "the articulated and often disarticulated traces of that abstraction we call a social relationship of power" (Gordon 1997, 183). They are issues that seem to be missing from the public debate but which could have emerged. If the victims and their families had been centered, for example, the specters of the Italian colonial domination of Eritrea may have become visible. The connections that seem obvious for Eritreans and that are still so apparent in places like Asmara—the capital city built by Italians for Italians—remain hidden. Nor is the imperial expansion and rule during Italian Fascism and the creation of *Africa Orientale Italiana* articulated as the background for the present-day conflicts in the region that continue to force people to flee. The historian Alessandro Triulzi has argued that the Italian public ignores its postcolonial status and migrants' claims to a common past, including the "ancient routes and connections" (Triulzi 2016, 151) that present-day border crossings in the Mediterranean have reopened.[3]

The centering of Italians is also evident in the lawmakers' praise of those who rescue and welcome migrants. The parliamentarians considered Lampedusans to be hospitable and exemplary citizens, "extraordinary" as Khalid Chaouki (2015) described them in his parliamentary speech. In addition, parliamentarians included the Coast Guard, the Guardia di Finanza, the Navy, and the Carabinieri among those to be remembered on the Day of Remembrance—institutions that paradoxically control the border while also rescuing migrants at sea. This military-humanitarian nexus suited the political climate at a time when the center-left coalition led by Prime Minister Matteo Renzi was collaborating with international donation-based rescue operations in the Mediterranean.

Micaela Campana (2015) was one of the parliamentarians who in the debate mentioned Operation Mare Nostrum, the military search and rescue operation that was launched a month after the disaster in 2013. "Mare Nostrum was an important operation not only because of the 150,000 people saved, but also because with this operation, Italy has lifted its head; it is a moment of dignity. With Mare Nostrum, we have demonstrated the greatness of Italy." The memorial is therefore a means to celebrate and further demonstrate the *grandezza dell'Italia*, which according to Campana emerges from the combination of military and humanitarian strength.

In Italy, the Day of Remembrance was instrumentalized for a number of national interests: it produced a mental mapping of national boundaries (of "our sea"), it produced a hospitable identity for Italians—the model being the Lampedusans—and it created humanitarian clout and moral greatness for Italy's military operations. It also marked and demonstrated social progress, as the present-day migrants were signposts of what Italians no longer were: unwanted border-crossers.

The parties that opposed the passing of the law and did not see the national interests in the Day of Remembrance were the nationalist-populist Lega Nord and the counterestablishment Five Star Movement. Cristian Invernizzi (2015) of Lega Nord saw the Day of Remembrance as an invitation for migrants to embark on fatal journeys, which he said would not end the "misery of hundreds of millions of Africans." He claimed that the memorial was a "symbol of hypocrisy" and a "festival of *buonismo*" (righteousness or do-goodism) for the governing parties. The populists' opposition to the Day of Remembrance was primarily political: they opposed the memorializing because from their viewpoint, the governing parties did not have the right to memorialize and to create the obligation to memorialize in Italy.

Memory Politics on the European Scale

In 2014, Italy held the rolling presidency of the Council of the European Union, and migration from third countries—"the migration emergency"—as Italy's presidency program termed it, was one of the key issues Italy wanted to raise. Italy was concerned about the Dublin II policy, which requires asylum applications to be processed in the first member country in which asylum seekers arrive and used the presidency to underline its unfairness to EU countries bordering the Mediterranean: Italy's concern was "the particularly intense pressure on the national asylum systems of some Member States," and it wanted to promote "solidarity at the European level" (Italian presidency of the Council of the European Union 2014). Solidarity in this context does not refer to solidarity with migrants but to sharing the "burden" of asylum seekers among the countries of the European Union.

As part of the EU presidency program, the president of the European Parliament Martin Schulz, the president of the Italian Chamber of Deputies Laura Boldrini, and the Italian minister of foreign affairs Federica Mogherini (who was soon to be high representative of the European Union for foreign affairs and security policy) flew to Lampedusa to participate in a ceremony at the disaster site. On a Guardia di Finanza vessel, Martin Schulz with about forty survivors of the disaster lowered a wreath into the sea. Meanwhile, at the harbor, protesters who had been assembled by Askavusa, an anti-capitalist activist collective in Lampedusa, shouted "*vergogna!*" (shame, disgrace), "hypocrisy!" and "the truth about the third of October!"

At the harbor, I observed the confusion the politicians' memorial had caused among the activists. Some of them had arrived in Lampedusa thinking that it was the *lieu de mémoire* of dissensual commemoration and were prepared to memorialize the disaster as a form of a protest against Italian and European leaders. In a panel discussion of Lampedusa in Festival on September 28, 2014, two activists of Boats4People, for example, explained how they had in previous years organized commemorative solidarity actions along the Mediterranean shore. They had organized vigils for those who had died at the border. The List of Deaths (UNITED 2022), the list of fatal incidents since 1993 at Europe's borders was used in these vigils to make the massive number of deaths imaginable to the public through visualization and reading out loud details of missing and dead migrants. These commemorative performances revealed the murderousness of the European border. They were spectacles to counter the "border spectacle" (De Genova 2013)—the display of enforcement apparatus at the border, such as militarized gear, concertina wire, and detention facilities, whereby migrant "illegality" is made spectacularly visible. However, now the scene of the spectacles had changed. The representatives of the Italian government and European Union—the very individuals whose attention activists had sought in countermemorializing border deaths earlier—were about to memorialize the dead themselves. This shift in the politics of memorializing border deaths is connected to two broader political divisions that were taking shape in Europe's political landscape at the time: the Eurozone financial crisis and the rise of right-wing political parties.

In 2014, Europe was on its way to deeper divisions. After the global financial crisis of 2009, some governments in the European Union, mainly those in the South faced serious fiscal problems, while countries in the North were less affected. In the common currency Eurozone, international cooperation became politically heated (Baldi and Staehr 2016; Schneider and Slantchev 2018). At the same time, the countries struggling with finances were more affected by irregular border crossings. In migration policy, the Dublin II agreement put more pressure on the countries at the southern border as they were responsible for reception and management of migrant arrivals.

Furthermore, nationalist, populist, Eurosceptic, and anti-immigration parties had had unprecedented success in the European Parliament elections in May 2014—just a few months before the commemorations in Lampedusa.[4] Asylum-seeking and the border were issues that divided Europe, a development that has since escalated. The Europe that Martin Schulz represented was not unified, and he made this clear in his speeches during the commemorations. Memorializing dead migrants was an attempt to create cohesion in the divided Europe—unified by dignity, the virtuous from both sides of the division (Schulz of the North and the Italian leaders of the South) gathered at the memory of a mass death. It was a rerun of the commemorative spectacle at the Lampedusa airport hangar the year before when European leaders led by the President of the European Commission José Manuel Barroso commemorated the rows of coffins (discussed in chapter 2).

Speaking at a press conference at the airport in Lampedusa on October 3, 2014, Martin Schulz (2014) referred to three issues from which his duty to remember the disaster stemmed. First, he reminded the public that Europe was not hosting as many refugees as countries closer to conflict zones were, such as Lebanon with its "one million Syrians." Second, he was motivated by fear of rising right-wing nationalism in Europe. And third, he referred to European histories of both protecting refugees and being a source of refugees. Schulz seemed to argue that we have the duty to welcome migrants because we ourselves have migrated and because others host more migrants than we do. We have a duty to protect migrants because our ancestors protected them, too.

"On the third of October one year ago happened a tragedy which was," Schulz paused and gestured toward the Italian leaders who were sitting at the conference, "for all of us, not only a humanitarian disaster. It was against our dignity that on the coast of one of the richest parts of the world hundreds of people must die under such circumstances." Schulz was outraged because mass death was not what should happen in Europe. He defined the disaster in a way that incorporated the whole of Europe. It was not only a violation of the dignity of Others—the victims and the survivors, about thirty of whom sat in the front rows during the press conference—but also "against our dignity."

The losses of the families or the experiences of the survivors had no role in the definition of "us"—they were not part of "Europe" but instead belonged to the "humanitarian" sphere. In his writing on the ethics of remembering war, Viet Thanh Nguyen (2016) argues that ethical outrage at the disproportionate death and suffering inflicted on others "is not enough, even though it may be more than many can allow themselves" (Nguyen 2016, 75). He points out that such outrage still reasserts "the centrality of the person feeling that emotion, which justifies viewing the other as a perpetual victim." In his statement, Schulz characterized the Lampedusa shipwreck as more than just a humanitarian disaster, more than simply 366 deaths. His assessment elevated the disaster to the symbolic level, but in doing so, centered the "European" experience.

Martin Schulz also positioned himself in opposition to the nationalist-populist forces that he implicated in the disaster in his speech: "I want to say to those who criticize us: Yes, I am ashamed. But you should also know the reality in the European Union. I am the president of the Parliament where a fourth of those elected say we have nothing to do with them [the refugees]—they should stay at home and not come to Europe. These are the forces" (Schulz 2014). Despite feeling "ashamed," Schulz did not move toward a restorative politics that would have included acknowledging culpability for the deadly border—for example, in the form of an apology. In Viet Thanh Nguyen's (2016, 73) terms, he failed to recognize his own "capacity to do harm." On the one hand, his presence at the ritual in which the wreath was lowered into the sea communicated the social importance of undocumented border-crossers and underlined that their mass death was a broader European issue and worthy of common remembering. In that respect, he did much more than other European leaders had in terms of taking responsibility for the deaths. On the other hand, memorialization offered a position of righteousness to those who participated in the commemoration and situated "Europeans" and "European" feelings at the center.

Europeanization of the Memorial

After Italy's presidency of the Council of the European Union, Italian politicians continued to push for the memorialization of October 3 on the European scale. In 2015, Luigi Morgano, an Italian member of the European Parliament, proposed an amendment to the European Parliament Resolution on the Situation in the Mediterranean and the Need for a Holistic EU Approach to Migration (LIBE Committee 2015) that would designate October 3 as a European-wide Day of Remembrance. On April 12, 2016, the European Parliament voted in favor of the resolution, which read, in part: "3 October should be recognized as a Day of Remembrance for all the men, women and children who perish while attempting to flee their countries as a result of persecution, conflict and war, as well as all the men and women who risk their lives every day in order to save them." The idea that the memorial would recognize both those who died while attempting to cross borders and those who tried to rescue them originated from the Comitato 3 ottobre. In an email, Luigi Morgano (personal communication 2018) directly referred me to the Comitato 3 ottobre for further information about the aims of the Day of Remembrance. Thus, my interpretation is that his amendment to the EU resolution was intended to expand the Italian Day of Remembrance to the European scale.

The Day of Remembrance was not discussed in the European Parliament; it slipped through without much attention, as one small section of the broader resolution. The debate focused instead on the "internal solidarity" of European Union member countries concerning asylum decisions and the relocation of asylum seekers. The European Parliament had once again concluded that the EU needed a more unified approach to asylum and migration policy, and perhaps parliamentarians hoped that a common memorial would function as a unifying point of reference in this process.

Within the European Parliament, the Committee on Civil Liberties, Justice and Home Affairs (known as the LIBE Committee) and several of its members have been at the forefront in pushing for recognition of October 3 as a European memorial. Center-left Italian members of the committee, in particular, have been prominent in this respect. For example, Cécyle Kyenge, who served as Italy's minister of integration in 2013, requested a minute of silence in the European Parliament plenary session on October 3, 2016.

Another important recognition of the disaster's memory took place on October 3, 2019, when the LIBE Committee held a hearing on search and rescue operations in the Mediterranean. The meeting was devoted to identifying gaps in legislation and policy that prevented or hindered humanitarian rescues. While the representatives organized themselves, MEP Magid Magid from the United Kingdom asked "if there was any point in the meeting today when we would have a minute of silence for the anniversary of the Lampedusa [disaster]" (Magid 2019).

Before the hearing began, the chair of the committee, Juan Fernando López Aguilar, announced that the meeting was dedicated to the memory of "all victims of the tragedies in the Mediterranean Sea" (López Aguilar 2019). The disaster that stood as the symbol for "all victims" was recalled as a reference point against which the ongoing border deaths discussed in the hearing were evaluated. The disaster itself was remembered by recalling the number of victims, its location, and its emotional effect on Europeans. López Aguilar (2019) opened the meeting by referring to the disaster: "It's the third of October. It's a national day in Germany [German Unity Day], but it's also the anniversary of the very shocking sinking of a boat carrying migrants from Libya to Italy. Off the Italian island of Lampedusa, more than 360 human beings perished in that shipwreck in 2013. . . . Six years after being so shocked, many people are still dying in the Mediterranean trying to set a foot on the European coast of the Mediterranean."

Carola Rackete, a captain of the German donation-funded Sea-Watch 3 SAR vessel, offered expert testimony in English at the LIBE Committee meeting. She also marked the Lampedusa disaster as a key moment, starting her remarks by referring to the disaster:

> I am particularly honored and also saddened to hold my speech on the occasion of the sixth anniversary of a famous shipwreck where more than 368 people died right in front of Lampedusa as a result of omission of rescue. Six years have passed, and instead of trying to avoid similar tragedies, the EU member states have engaged in a policy of externalization of responsibilities and a praxis of pushbacks and omissions of rescue, delegating responsibility to a country at war, Libya, in a breach of international law. And yet there is hope, represented by the European civil society at the Mediterranean Sea, defending to respect [sic] everyone's right to life and the rule of law. (Rackete 2019)

The memorializing of the disaster from a European political platform and among civil society actors such as Carola Rackete of Sea-Watch shows how the disaster has become a Europeanized *lieu de mémoire*. The disaster serves an important function for those who memorialize, and the memorial itself provides them a means for identification (Koselleck 2002).

Those attending the LIBE hearing in Brussels had a personal or a professional connection to the disaster that (at least nominally) produced an obligation to memorialize. Members of the European Parliament represented an institution that was partly responsible for the bordering of Europe. Representatives of the European Border and Coast Guard Agency Frontex and the Italian *Guardia Costiera*—who were also heard at the meeting—represented institutions that controlled the borders where the deaths took place. Carola Rackete represented civil society actors who resisted bordering, and she herself had witnessed suffering at the border. Pietro Bartolo, a Lampedusan doctor and eyewitness of the immediate aftermath of the October 3 disaster, was also among the committee members, as a recently elected MEP. At the meeting, he said that the October 3 disaster was the very reason he became a member of the European Parliament.

A recommendation to memorialize border deaths at a European scale, coming from the European Parliament, does not become a practice among Europeans unless there are communities and individuals with whom the idea resonates. The civil society rescue operations in which ordinary citizens participate through donations might create such resonance, as Carola Rakete's speech at the LIBE Committee suggests. As has been the case in Italy, memorialization needs to serve some function for the community that commemorates. The European version of the Day of Remembrance has not, at least to date, been observed in the EU member states to the extent its advocates had hoped. Most likely, if the narrative of October 3 resonated with a given community, the motivation to commemorate and the commemoration's function would be articulated in ways dependent on the local context. Therefore, when considering the scale of the European Union, I must return to the scale of locality to make sense of what memorializing the Lampedusa disaster elsewhere in Europe might mean.

Memorializing Lampedusa in Dresden, Germany

In Dresden, Germany, October 3 resonated as a memorial for migrant deaths in 2016. Those who commemorated there, however, were unaware of the Day of Remembrance in Italy and the resolution in the European Parliament. In fact, their actions emerged from the assumption that deaths at the border were *not* being publicly commemorated. On October 3, 2016, about fifteen people dressed in black went to the banks of the Elbe under the Augustusbrücke with a large black banner that read in white letters: *Deutsche asylpolitik toten* (German asylum politics kill). They pushed eighteen white coffin-shaped pieces of polystyrene foam into the river. "R.I.P." and "3.10.13 LAMPEDUSA" were written on the coffins with black marker (Michaelis 2016).

The performance was part of a wider leftist protest against the Day of German Unity that is celebrated as a national holiday on October 3. In 2016, the main festivities of the national commemoration took place in the formerly communist East German city of Dresden with the theme "Building bridges"; German chancellor Angela Merkel and the president of Germany Joachim Gauck attended. The event attracted two protests stemming from opposite ideological directions. The far-right movement Pegida and the far-right party *Alternative für Deutschland* organized a protest that drew 6,000 to 8,000 people. The antiracist and leftist coalition Solidarity without Limits attracted about 2,500 protesters with a call that made reference to the Lampedusa disaster:

> Bridges are a good thing. You could build many bridges, for example over the Mediterranean to save the lives of tens of thousands of refugees and migrants. Especially on October 3, the third anniversary of the Lampedusa shipwreck, it would be the right time to think about how to make sure all people can cross the Mediterranean safely. This could be the beginning of the end of Fortress Europe. . . . German society is increasingly polarized [and] authoritarian and excluding tendencies are more and more popular. The gap between rich and poor widens. For us, these developments are good reasons for a critical intervention against this German national day on October 3. (Critiquenact 2016)

Three years after the protest, I contacted the Dresden anti-fascists (Undogmatische Radikale Antifa Dresden) to ask more about their motivation to publicly remember the Lampedusa disaster. They responded by secure email:

> We are always disgusted by patriotic festivities—first and foremost (but not solely) because of Germany's past and its crimes—but in this case, we had to act against this cynical slogan [building bridges]. It was cynical and it still is, because people, who are looking for a better life, are still being stopped at the European borders and they are still drowning in the Mediterranean Sea. It is an act of sheer ignorance to speak of "building bridges" on the 3rd anniversary of the boating accident near Lampedusa, where a lot of people lost their lives. (Undogmatische Radikale Antifa Dresden 2019)

The performance at the river Elbe instrumentalized the aesthetics of mourning and funeral (black clothing, coffins) in a protest against the bordering of Europe and social and political developments in Germany. The conflict that the date October 3 created in the local and national context—the irony of celebrating "the fall of the wall" on the same day that could be used to remember an existing fatal border—opened a space for transformative and critical politics. Such an opening may invite others to see border deaths differently and to recognize relationalities between the Germans who suffered from the violent border in the past and those who now suffer from Europe's external border politics. The protesters made visible the relationality between the two borders and their victims across time and space. As one of the participants in the memorial performance said to the local newspaper *Dresdner Neueste Nachrichten*: "How can we celebrate a borderless Germany while building huge border fences across and around Europe where people die? That's obviously a contradiction!" (Michaelis 2016).

The public's ignorance of death at the border and the apparent normalcy of it made the protesters uncomfortable. Another person said: "I shocked myself. On September 21, again many people died in the Mediterranean, but instead of being sad, angry, and upset, I just skimmed the very brief report." And a third explained: "We do not want it to be normal for men, women, and children to drown in the Mediterranean. We do not want to live in a society that is cold when refugees die" (Michaelis 2016). The protesters perceived the situation in the Mediterranean as a matter relevant to them and considered the conditions of the deaths to be unacceptable.

The anti-fascist protesters felt obliged to remember the Lampedusa disaster for the sake of who they were and the type of society they wanted to live in. Their duty to remember stemmed from critical self-reflection and from contextualizing the events and histories of two different border zones. Instead of merely skimming brief news items and accepting the deaths as something normal, the protesters refused to accept indifference and called upon everyone to take responsibility for the deaths that were turning society cold and unlivable. The October 3 disaster symbolized the broader issue of migrant deaths, and the lack of memorializing the disaster symbolized social indifference—"coldness"—toward refugees and their deaths. It made visible Europe's indifference to sharing the world.

In this case, it would be easy to interpret the protesters' actions as centering their own emotions. However, as in the case of the Castellamare del Golfo student performances (discussed in chapter 4), I contest this reading, instead arguing that attentiveness both to others and to one's own actions and position constitute a form of citizenship that contests indifference. The protesters did frame their outrage in terms of political division—division within Germany, division between the rich and the poor, and the rise of nationalist forces. However, they did not transfer inhumanity and responsibility elsewhere (to the smugglers, to the far right, or to Europe) as tends to be the case in the arguments for memorializing at the scale of local governance (such as the Garden of Remembrance in Lampedusa, discussed in chapter 5), the nation (the parliamentary debates in Italy) and Europe (Schulz's statement during his visit to Lampedusa). On the contrary, the protesters recognized their own culpability in the deaths and their own potential inhumanity, their "skimming over" of news about border deaths. They were haunted by specters of their future selves as they considered who they would become if they remained indifferent. Their position is critically different from that of other mainstream positions that seem to advocate for migrants, such as that of Martin Schulz who felt that mass deaths violated the dignity of the society he belongs to. Schulz did not fully recognize his own role in the scenario of border deaths, while the Dresden anti-fascists did.

The Dresden protesters cultivated a form of restorative activism that recognizes one's own responsibility in the production of violence. They constituted a citizenship based on attentiveness to one's own self-interest in the world we inhabit. Viet Thanh Nguyen (2016, 73) argues for an ethics of recognition that "recognizes our capacity to do harm." That recognition is critical in creating potentiality for imagining alternatives. The critical opening in Dresden emerged from the collision of two kinds of memorials. The civil imagination of the protesters was sparked by the multidirectionality of memory, the cross-referencing, but of memories that were out of sync: the celebration of the removal of one border and the simultaneous lack of grief over mass death at another.

The dominant understanding of border deaths has been one of cultural amnesia rather than remembering. The fundamental criticism in recent academic work on border deaths is largely based on Judith Butler's (2009) notion of "ungrievability," arguing that these deaths are ignored and not remembered in a dignified way in Europe and by Europeans except in specific critical activist or artistic settings (e.g., Stierl 2016; Stümer 2018). Like the Dresden protesters, these scholars, artists, and activists consider forgetting to be a continuation of public indifference to border deaths. Memorializing, therefore, becomes an act of public recognition of migrants and is crucial for social power dynamics because representing groups, individuals, or events as worthy of common remembering highlights their social importance. From a Durkheimian sociological perspective, such commemorations communicate the society's shared values, and common points of reference such as these function to reduce social instability and division (Connerton 1989, 49). Activist and local communities' memorialization of border deaths has been interpreted through the lens of countermemorialization—as political acts of continuing witness of injustice that otherwise would be forgotten by publics (e.g., Auchter 2013; Alonso and Nienass 2016a; 2016b; Stierl 2016; Stümer 2018).

The abundance of memorializing at different scales examined in this chapter (and in chapters 4 and 5) raises a number of issues concerning the afterlife of the Lampedusa disaster. First, while the common understanding is that the impetus to memorialize border deaths emerges from a perceived lack of existent memorialization, in fact, most of the instances of remembering that I have examined have been prompted by other memorials and rituals. Public memorialization produces a communicative sphere in which people respond to how others have remembered dead strangers.

Second, the memorials and rituals related to border deaths have thus tended to produce more memorialization rather than attest that the border's victims have gained a certain level of social importance. Writing about the abundance of Holocaust memorialization, Klaus Neumann (2014, 476) points out that the crucial question is not simply what and how much is being remembered, but rather one should ask: Who is remembering whom, and to what end? He reminds us that in Germany, Holocaust memorials are everywhere, but their existence is not a result of demands by survivors. Most memorials are the initiatives of local non-Jewish Germans. Their aim is "not the resuscitation of the dead but the redemption of those living with the shame caused by their association with previous generations of perpetrators" (Neumann 2014, 476).

Third, the communicative sphere of memorialization is produced through re-mediation—one form of memorialization inspires another—and consequently, the afterlives of border deaths are constantly transforming. Memorials attract rituals, and rituals may elicit the need to create longer-lasting memorials. The Day of Remembrance in Italy prompted the recognition of the date in the European Parliament, particularly in the LIBE Committee that works with issues of justice. At local levels, such as in Castellamare del Golfo in Sicily, the community that buried victims of the disaster, the obligation to memorialize stems from both directions—from "above" in the form of the National Day of Remembrance and from "below" from the uncomfortable feeling of having unknown bodies buried at a local cemetery (as discussed in chapter 4).

Fourth, while some selected pasts and present conditions fell into amnesia, across the scales of memorialization discussed in this chapter and in chapters 4 and 5, three kinds of haunting pasts were related to the motivations and functions of remembering: memories of past migration, past borders, and fascism in Italy and Germany. These "ghosts" as Avery Gordon (1997) would call them, haunt the memorializing communities, cause established certainties such as the differences between "us" and "them" to waver, and create a duty to remember.

The figure of the unwanted migrant and Italy's heritage of emigration evoke remembering at the national scale. These specters remind Italians of their own social progress and their present position of power, in which they can be the ones who welcome and protect. At the level of European institutions, the memory of being both a source of and a host to refugees produces a duty to remember and produces a common point of identification for the divided European community— or so the institutions hope. In Dresden, the protesters dressed in black were perplexed by the contradiction contained in the erasure of one violent border while another past border was recognized. This contradiction was revealed to them by the date October 3, which encompasses the memory of two events.

In addition, in Italy, in Dresden, and in the speech of Martin Schulz, the memory of fascism lurks. As people die at Europe's borders and their unidentified bodies are welcomed into Europe's cemeteries, the specters of fascists, bystanders, the persecuted, and the dissidents who fled across the Italian border to France haunt Europe in a more or less visible and articulated form. The memorializing of dead strangers takes place in the memory of what happened in Europe seventy years ago.

What differentiates the Dresden protesters' position on memorialization from the other memorial instances discussed in this chapter, those at the scale of the nation and Europe, was the personal responsibility that the protesters took for the world and their being in it. They instrumentalized memorializing to counter the far right in Dresden and a society that is "cold"—a society where one finds oneself "skimming over" the news about border deaths. The recognition of one's own responsibility in the production of violence nurtures a restorative activism and is central for the capacity to imagine an alternative world in which living together is possible. The protesters in Dresden constituted a citizenship of attentiveness that was based on a haunting awareness of how their potential future selves might judge the present if they chose self-interest over attentiveness to the inequalities of the world. Their approach resisted reproducing the division between "good" citizens, who recognize dead strangers through memorializing, and "bad" citizens, who ignore these deaths.

This chapter concludes the section of three chapters that examines how the disaster has been memorialized by others—people who did not know the dead. In the next chapter, I discuss how those who knew the dead—survivors and relatives of the victims—relate to memorials and rituals created for "Italian" and other "European" audiences. The position of survivors and relatives as witnesses is crucially different. Rituals are always performative, and memorials can be reframed by visitors; neither are ever fixed to an intended meaning. Rituals and memorials often bring dissent and simmering social conflicts to the fore, as discussed in the three chapters of this section. In the next chapter, I examine what people who knew the dead do in the sphere of memorializing created by others. The chapter continues to explore the dynamics that I highlighted in chapter 5 in my analysis of scenes at the *Nuova Speranza* memorial in Lampedusa. I examine what kinds of contestations and politics emerge in the sphere of memorialization, and how survivors and relatives of the victims activate the ritual atmosphere and the existing memorial structures for their own concerns and causes.

SURVIVOR CITIZENSHIP

By October 3, 2014, high tourist season in Lampedusa had passed, and some of the shops along the main road were already closed. But every hotel was booked full, and enough bars and restaurants were open to accommodate the throngs of people who had arrived on the island to commemorate the disaster of the year before. There were Eritrean survivors, family members of the victims, members of the European Parliament, representatives of human rights and humanitarian organizations from all over Europe, journalists, academics, artists, and the simply curious. The day was filled with commemorative programs. Some of them overlapped, and it was impossible to participate in everything.

I rented a bicycle and rode from one event to another in the merciless sun of the mostly treeless island. There was a press conference at the airport with the president of the European Parliament, Martin Schulz, and Italian ministers from Rome. The Lampedusan activist collective Askavusa held a protest outside questioning the right of European and Italian leaders to memorialize a disaster that their policies had produced. And at the port, politicians and other invited guests set out on customs (Guardia di Finanza), coast guard (Guardia Costiera), and gendarmerie (Carabinieri) vessels to lower wreaths into the sea at the disaster site. The divers attached a memorial plaque to the sunken wreck, and the local fishermen's association threw a wreath from their own boat—but as a protest against the Roman establishment, they did it at a different time.

About forty survivors who had returned to the island from their new homes in Northern Europe painted rocks at the harbor with Lampedusan high school students, and a participatory performance for the filmmaker Dagmawi Yimer's memorial film *Asmat* (that I discussed in chapter 3) gathered people who entered the sea wrapped in white sheets. Adal Neguse—with whom I would later collaborate in my research—worked on a mural of handprints with Lampedusan students, and late in the afternoon, the church was filled with locals and guests for an interfaith ceremony. From there, a procession to the *Porta d'Europa* memorial sculpture began.

The survivors could be picked out of the crowds because they all wore identical T-shirts. The shirts had been provided by one of the Italian organizers of the events, the Comitato 3 ottobre, which had also paid for their trips to Lampedusa. "Protect people—Not borders" was printed on the shirts, along with a drawing of a family (man, woman, and a child) sitting in a bottle floating on water. Representatives of organizations such as UNHCR, Save the Children, and Amnesty International wore vests, hats, or shirts marked with their logos. A representative of Frontex wore a blue armband with the circle of yellow EU stars. Italian customs, Fire Brigade (Vigili del Fuogo), and coast guard leaders were dressed in their uniforms. They all seemed like actors, dressed up for the commemorative spectacle.

In this chapter, I ask why Eritrean survivors of the disaster return to sites of memory in Lampedusa and participate in the commemorative rituals—many of which have in fact been created for Italians or Europeans more broadly. Are the survivors in their identical T-shirts a reproduction of their media representation as passive victims to be rescued by the able and caring Europeans? What does memorializing within this context mean for the survivors? What functions does memorializing have for the Eritrean diaspora in Europe, and what kinds of politics does their engagement with the disaster's memory produce? By discussing different kinds of acts of commemoration—both private and public, and their mediations—I explore how the survivors acted upon the assumed responsibility to remember and how they transformed their public identity from a victim to a survivor. I develop the notion of *survivor citizenship* to elucidate how, regardless of their legal status, the survivors acted as citizens of Europe and refused to be passive victims to be rescued or inserted into a celebration of European or Italian greatness. This reflects a new kind of Europeanness, one which is simultaneously about both being at home and being transnationally connected. It is not a citizenship that is granted, but one that is *acted* as responsible members of a society, following Engin Isin's and Greg Nielsen's idea of "acts of citizenship" (Isin 2008; Isin and Nielsen 2008).

By examining memorializing from the perspective of the survivors, I move beyond the critique and deconstruction of Europeans' commemorative performances that have been central in chapters 4, 5, and 6 to a refugee-centered analysis that acknowledges the creative agency, hopes, and politics of refugees. In underlining refugees' agency, I am not sentimentalizing oppression, suffering, or harm, but instead drawing attention to the ability "of social beings to wave alternative, and sometimes brilliantly creative, forms of coherence across the damages" (Ortner 1995, 186). To recognize agency is to see others as human, to "grant the other the same flawed subjectivity we assume for ourselves," as Viet Thanh Nguyen (2016, 73) argues in his work on the ethics of memory after war.

The Therapeutic and Instrumental Functions of Memorializing

The first anniversary of the disaster in 2014 was crucial in setting the scene for memorializing the disaster. The commemoration was part of the rolling presidency of the Council of the European Union that Italy held, and which brought notable politicians to the island: the president of the European Parliament Martin Schulz, the president of the Italian Chamber of Deputies Laura Boldrini, and the Italian minister of foreign affairs Federica Mogherini. In chapter 6, I analyzed how the commemoration shaped European and Italian politics, and vice versa. However, also the survivors and the relatives of the victims were present in the commemorative events, and in this chapter, I focus on what the commemorations meant for them and how they created a subjectivity in the communicative sphere that was created for "Italian" and "European" audiences.

At the press conference held at Lampedusa's airport where Martin Schulz gave a speech (analyzed in chapter 6), the seating arrangements illustrate how European and Italian leaders dominated the event.[1] The politicians were seated at the front, behind a row of desks, while the survivors sat in the audience, albeit in the front row. Behind them were journalists, and representatives of humanitarian and religious organizations.

The organizers of the press conference had asked for a representative of the Eritreans affected by the disaster to speak. "I am the brother of a victim," Adal Neguse began, speaking in English. He stood between the politicians and the audience, off to the side so that he could address both groups. The survivors had decided that he, an Eritrean Swedish health care worker, would "deliver the message," as the survivors explained to me. Some of the survivors knew Adal personally from when he had come to Lampedusa to search for his brother in the days after the disaster. Adal went on:

> The survivors and the families of the victims, we are all here to remember our beloved ones. We are grateful for all the help that we have received so far, that our loved ones have been recovered from the boat

and have been given a place to rest. But all this would be meaningless unless the families are given a chance to identify their loved ones and to replace the number with a name on their gravesite.

We feel that the tragedy could have been avoided, but we are not here to blame someone. We ask you to do everything you can to prevent such tragedy from happening again. We now know that the Italian authorities are working hard on rescue after this big disaster. We would like to express our gratitude for that. We would like to ask other European countries and the European Union to be part of this rescue operation. It's high time we stop this suffering.

By saying "we are all here," Adal Neguse identified the survivors and the relatives of the victims as a community on whose behalf he was speaking. The speech is directed at a "you" who is not to be blamed but is nevertheless responsible for taking action, as it is capable of "preventing such tragedy from happening again." At the end of the speech, Adal joins the "we" and the "you" and creates a different "we"—a we that takes collective responsibility: "It's high time we stop this suffering." The more or less recent migrants from Eritrea, like the other Europeans in the audience, have the capacity to prevent disaster, Adal seemed to be saying. The survivors and the relatives are not positioned as victims in Adal's speech, or noncitizens but as actors who have the capacity and the responsibility to take action for justice, irrespective of their formal citizenship status. They too, like the other Europeans, were susceptible to becoming indifferent to injustice.

Adal Neguse's speech contains four themes that correlate to the two functions of memory that Paul Ricoeur (2004), among others, has identified: therapeutic and instrumental. The personal remembrance of loved ones and the expression of gratitude to those who have helped serve therapeutic functions: they are means for dealing with loss in an ethical way. A therapeutic function does not necessarily produce closure; it can also be a means to live on with the dead—to maintain a relationship with the dead.

Adal also makes claims that are, on the one hand, specific to the Lampedusa disaster (the forensic identification of the dead) and, on the other hand, concern broader refugee rights (the continuation of search and rescue operations at sea). These claims put the disaster in the service of improving the rights both of the relatives and of refugees in general. Such instrumentalization is not, in this case, "co-opting" the memory of the disaster for the benefit of politics that would not have mattered to the victims. The speech opens with a review of past wrongs and good deeds and ends with a reference to future aspirations: the desire to prevent "such tragedy from happening again." The speech presents a structure that the community of Eritrean survivors and relatives have repeated in their public statements during the four subsequent anniversary commemorations that I refer to in this chapter.

Porta d'Europa: A Site for Countermemorialization

After the first anniversary commemorations in 2014, the memory site for the survivors' statement was *Porta d'Europa*, a sculpture created in 2008 to commemorate migrants who had lost their lives at the sea border (Horsti 2016a). *Porta d'Europa*, like the Garden of Remembrance (discussed in chapter 5), represents what Diana Taylor (2003) has termed archival memory. People who have no intention of memorializing border deaths can encounter these memorials and engage with the issue by thinking about it, finding out more, and taking a position. *Porta d'Europa* has an expansionist quality in the sense that it makes no reference to the Portopalo migrant disaster of 1996 that inspired its construction. The only narrative it suggests is that of an open gateway. Unlike new commemorative art inspired by relational aesthetics (Bourriaud 1998; Gibbons 2007), the monument does not encourage interaction (Horsti 2016a). Nevertheless, *Porta d'Europa*'s open gate is available for multiple meanings. This ambiguity has also contributed to it becoming a significant site for the survivors' critical agency, which has developed as they have repeatedly returned to commemorate the disaster in Lampedusa.

FIGURE 13.   *Porta di Lampedusa—Porta d'Europa* (Gateway to Europe) memorial in Lampedusa by Mimmo Paladino. © Karina Horsti, 2015. Photo by Karina Horsti.

The messages that the Eritreans—survivors, relatives, and the Italian Eritrean priest Mussie Zerai—have relayed at *Porta d'Europa* have expressed gratitude to the Lampedusans (for symbolically opening the gate) and simultaneously denying gratitude to the institutional border agents who failed to rescue them (symbolically closing the gate). They have also demanded that European governments secure safe passage for refugees stranded in Libya. The survivors' engagement with the memorial shows how the memory conveyed by a monument is not static, but rather in constant transformation and dialogue with the people who visit the memorial. The survivors have taken ownership of the memorial and its meaning, just as they have with the *Giardino della memoria*, albeit so far not as publicly as with *Porta d'Europa*.

Every October 3, since 2014, ten to forty survivors and relatives of victims, together with high school students from Lampedusa and elsewhere in Italy and Europe, have led a procession to the monument. Up to five hundred other participants have joined them: journalists, humanitarian professionals (recognizable by the logos of their organizations), Catholic nuns and priests, border agents such as coast guard members in their uniforms, more high school students, many of whom have flown in with their teachers from mainland Italy, Muslim and Christian religious leaders, tourists, and a few politicians. The Eritreans sing church hymns in Tigrinya, and some of them, together with students, have carried a banner reading "Proteggere le persone—non i confine" (Protect people—Not borders) produced by the Comitato 3 ottobre, the organizer of the events led by Italian Eritrean Tareke Brhane.

Throngs of students at a memorial ceremony might remind Sicilians of the anniversary commemorations held on May 23 each year in memory of two Mafia terror attacks that took place in 1992 in Capaci (*strage di Capaci*) and on via D'Amelio in Palermo (*strage di via D'Amelio*). Since 2002, the commemoration in Palermo has started with the arrival of about 1,500 students and teachers from all around Italy on *La Nave della Legalita*, the "Ship of Legality." The incorporation of students from across the country (and in the case of Comitato 3 ottobre, from across the European Union) is informed by the haunting of both the past and the future. As the Falcone Foundation, which organizes the May 23 ceremonies, writes on their website: "For a future without a Mafia."

For the survivors of the October 3, 2013, disaster, however, the marching and singing are reminiscent of the day in 2013 when the survivors protested at the Lampedusa "reception center" where they had been detained. They had seen news about the official "funeral" in Agrigento, Sicily, and realized that they had not been invited to the ceremony. The survivors forced the guards to open the gates and marched into town to protest. They sang religious songs along the way and divided into two groups. One group picked wildflowers from the rugged landscape and walked to the sea to pray and commemorate. Another group went to the town hall to demand to know why they had not been invited to the funeral service and why the bodies had not been buried on Lampedusa. These two acts reflect the two functions of memory, the therapeutic and the instrumental, which later structured the survivors' memorializing.

The memories of walking together as a group, singing and stopping traffic, became important to the survivors; many of them later recalled the 2013 protest in conversations with me. Protesting the unjust treatment of the dead in such a powerful embodied performance created a sense of identity and community for the survivors. This sense of responsibility for the dignity of the dead was evoked and strengthened in subsequent years by the march to *Porta d'Europa*. Such repetition of performance—the movement of bodies in a repeated formation—is intrinsic to commemoration (see, for example, Connerton 1989, 59, 72).

In 2014, the procession to the monument was interrupted by a powerful thunderstorm. The television camera crews retreated to their vans and almost everyone else who had joined the survivors during the walk rushed back to town. When a storm sweeps the island, one realizes that Lampedusa is just a large rock in the middle of the sea. The storm could have easily ended the *Porta d'Europa* ceremony altogether and prevented the ritual from becoming significant in future anniversaries, but it had the opposite effect. It transformed the public performance into an intimate and nonmediated ceremony, and later, into a memory that remained significant for those who participated in the event. Unperturbed by the storm, the Eritrean survivors continued to sing religious songs in Tigrinya and to pray. They were led by the then Switzerland-based priest Mussie Zerai, a central critical figure in coordinating calls for sea rescue from migrant boats before European activists stepped in. The following year, he would be nominated for the Nobel Peace Prize for his work with refugees.

Lightning lit up the darkness and for a moment made visible the scene: the monumental gate, the stormy waves in the background, and the group of drenched mourners holding flowers in their hands. The performance continued, improvised; its audience was composed only of survivors, the priest, and two or three people who like me stood there watching. One of the survivors present there participated in a focus group research interview in Stockholm a year later and told me that this had been the most memorable experience of the commemorations. As a religious person, he had felt that "God was with them" and that "the heavens were crying for the victims." It gave him an immense sense of relief, he said, to feel that while he had survived, the victims had been received in heaven by God. The existential experience of commemorating in the storm solidified the survivors' role as carriers of memory and underlined their responsibility to act politically from that position.

The Performance of Selectively Grateful Refugee

In contrast to the previous year, the weather was perfect for the commemorative procession in Lampedusa in 2015. At noon, seventeen survivors led the march from the mayor's office at the New Port to *Porta d'Europa*. The survivors stopped at the monument while Lampedusan students chatted in groups scattered around the area; for anyone outside the inner circle surrounding the survivors, it was impossible to hear the Muslim, Catholic, and Eritrean Orthodox prayers being offered by survivors and religious leaders. Afterward, sixteen of the survivors climbed onto the bunker a few meters away, while the seventeenth, a woman, sat alone on the rocks to the side and gazed toward the sea. They were all wearing identical T-shirts with the Comitato 3 ottobre logo. Standing on the makeshift stage with the survivors was Adal Neguse representing the relatives of the victims, three Lampedusan first responders, Mayor Nicolini, Rosario Crocetta, the leftist president of Sicily, Mussie Zerai, and the Comitato 3 ottobre's Tareke Brhane, who translated from Tigrinya to Italian. None of the Italian speeches were translated into Tigrinya, and therefore most survivors were unable to understand what was being said. The Comitato's commemorative script was clearly aimed at an Italian audience.

Television crews and photographers took their positions in front of the makeshift stage. Mussie held a wooden cross and addressed the authorities in Italian. Standing with the survivors, he amplified and mediated their issues and those of the Eritrean refugee community at large. He raised three matters of concern to the survivors: the lack of investigation into the events leading to the disaster, the delays in identifying the victims, and the unwillingness to repatriate the human remains to Eritrea. He said in Italian: "We are here today not only to remember the dead, but also to remember those families who are still waiting for justice. Those families who are still waiting for the bodies of their loved ones" (Zerai 2015). In addition to these issues specific to the disaster, he also raised the broader issue of the thousands of migrants who were continuing to die along the journey to Europe. The solutions he presented reflect his dual roles as a refugee rights activist and opponent of the Eritrean regime:

> We need to push, to press. The first commitment must be to solve the root problem in the country of origin of these people who flee. This is the first long-term commitment. The second is to protect these people along the migration path. That is, in neighboring countries, in transit countries, to guarantee decent, safe and protected living conditions. The third commitment is to organize resettlement programs, those humanitarian corridors, those humanitarian visas, visas for family reunification.

FIGURE 14.   The bunker next to *Porta d'Europa*, 3 October 2015. A survivor reads a message of gratitude to the people of Lampedusa and prepares to hand out certificates. Mussie Zerai translates, while Tareke Brhane, Giusi Nicolini, Rosario Crocetta, and three civil responders stand with the survivors and family members. © Karina Horsti, 2015. Photo by Karina Horsti.

After his speech, Mussie announced in Italian that the survivors wanted to show their gratitude to the Lampedusan civilian responders on behalf of all 155 survivors and the relatives of the victims. The survivors, who had been standing still during Mussie's speech, relaxed their postures and wrapped their arms around each other's shoulders. They knew what was coming next; the script that followed was theirs.

The previous day, the survivors had gathered at a restaurant in the evening to discuss what to say as a group to the journalists, politicians, and Lampedusans who would be present at the commemoration ceremony. They all agreed that they wanted to show their gratitude to those who had rescued them. Adal Neguse drew a picture of two hands, one pulling the other from what could be the sea or the ground. The motif was similar to that in the underwater memorial that divers working for the coast guard had attached to the wreck during the 2014 anniversary commemorations. A form of the motif reappeared at the memorial constellation at the Piazza Piave in 2019 on the metal pedestal erected by Gariwo (the Garden for the Righteous) as an acknowledgment of those Lampedusans who "assume responsibility." The drawing of the two hands became part of what the survivors called "certificates." They added text to the drawing and had a certificate printed for each Lampedusan rescuer at the local copy shop. The text read in Italian:

Grazie! Questo è per ringraziare voi, che avete fattuno sforzo incredibile il 3 ottobre 2013, salvandoci la vita. Avete un grande posto nel nostro cuore; siamo e vi saremo eternamente grati. Che Dio vi benedica! I sopravvisuti e le famiglie delle vittime del 3 ottobre 2013. (Thank you! This is to thank you who did an incredible deed on October 3, 2013, by saving our lives. You have a great place in our hearts; we are and will forever be grateful. God bless you! The survivors and the families of the victims of October 3, 2013.)

The survivors first intended to present the certificates in the morning when the commemorations began outside the mayor's office. But that scene had been too chaotic—inappropriate for a dignified ceremony. No one could hear what was being said over the chattering of the Lampedusan students eating their breakfasts. Across the street from the mayor's office, local garbage collectors had piled up hundreds of stinking garbage bags. They had been on strike and were protesting because the municipal authorities had not paid them on time. They thought that the commemoration, with its prestigious guests, was an event being put on by and for the mayor. At the chaotic event, with attendees distracted by the stench of garbage, there was no opportunity for the survivors to shift the crowd's attention to themselves. In fact, there was no stage that the survivors could have taken over.

Therefore, the survivors decided to look for a more suitable moment at *Porta d'Europa* to deliver the certificates. Atop the bunker, a survivor who had arrived from his new home in Denmark, spoke about the survivors' gratitude and read out the names of the awardees. There was one certificate for the people of Lampedusa (received on their behalf by Giusi Nicolini) and one for each of the local civil rescuers. The survivors had agreed not to give any certificates to the Carabinieri, the Guardia Costiera, or the Guardia di Finanza, although these organizations had also been involved in the rescue operation and were present at the commemorative rituals that the Comitato 3 ottobre had organized. By explicitly excluding these rescuers, in their presence, the survivors wanted to convey that they did not owe them any recognition because they had failed to respond adequately.

To a certain extent, the performance of gratitude conformed to the role that the "Italian" audiences expected the survivors to play. For the "Italian" and "European" publics, the islanders at the margins of the Italian nation-state and Europe symbolized a lack of culpability and evoked nostalgic memories of the hospitality extended. Handing out the certificates affirmed not only the benevolence of the rescuers, but also the stereotypical notion of the refugee who is grateful for being rescued and given the gift of a new life, protection, and freedom (Nguyen 2012; Espiritu 2014; Hong 2016). Mimi Thi Nguyen (2012) theorizes the grateful refugee as someone who "lives under enduring consciousness" of debt for "the gift of freedom." However, this gift "co-exists with violence or because of violence that appears as something else" (Nguyen 2012, 6). Writing about Vietnamese refugees in the United States, Mimi Thi Nguyen unpacks the powers of the "benevolent empire," such as colonialism, militarization, and imperialism, that produce "the gift of freedom" at the same time as they produce the violence that causes displacement.

This was not the full picture in Lampedusa, however. The survivors refused to offer their gratitude to the institutional rescuing agents who represent the "benevolent empire"—the European border that is simultaneously militarized and humanitarianized. Only named individuals (and the "people of Lampedusa") had a "great place" in the survivors' hearts.

When the reading of the recipients' names began and the survivors were about to hand out the certificates to the civilian rescuers on stage, it became apparent that while three of the recipients were present, at least eight others were missing. This disrupted the script of the ceremony, which the survivors had designed as a surprise to the recipients. The survivors wondered among themselves why the Lampedusans most dear to them, those they had called by name, had not attended the ceremony. They were not aware of the protest against the official commemorations led by the first responder Vito Fiorino and his friends.

After the ceremony, Constantino Baratta, a Lampedusan mason who had rescued twelve people in his seventeen-foot fishing boat and who was present at the *Porta d'Europa* ceremony, told the other civilian rescuers that the survivors wanted to give them certificates. They organized a meeting and invited an interpreter who worked at the local "reception center" to translate between Tigrinya and Italian. In the evening, the survivors quietly left the interfaith ceremony organized by the Mediterranean Hope project at the Sanctuary of Porto Salvo to attend this informal meeting. The rescuers who had not attended the official commemorative ceremonies explained their protest to the survivors, and both survivors and rescuers realized that they shared a concern that the response to the disaster had not been properly investigated.

For two years, the survivors had been asking questions about the coast guard's mismanagement of the rescue operation. In the meeting with the civilian rescuers, the survivors again said that they had seen two large vessels close to their boat when its engine stalled, and that they had shone a spotlight onto the stricken vessel. Vito Fiorino told them that he had been asked by the Guardia Costiera to sign a false statement concerning the time of the emergency call and that they had prevented him from transferring survivors from his boat to their larger vessel so that his crew could continue their rescue work (see Askavusa 2018). Unbeknownst to the survivors, Fiorino's group of rescuers had given media interviews about the lack of an investigation and the inefficiency of the coast guard operation over the course of the previous two years.

The scene at the monument, with its unsuccessful attempt to deliver the certificates as part of the public commemorative program, revealed to the survivors that the remembrance of the disaster was contested in Lampedusa. Learning of their shared critical position made the survivors more confidant and vocal about their concerns, some of which the Comitato 3 ottobre did not prioritize: the return of the dead to Eritrea, and the investigation of the disaster. In addition, the survivors became more critical of the politics of memorialization. After meeting with the rescuers, the survivors began talking about taking more responsibility for how the disaster was remembered in public.

Conflicting Ideas about the Rights of the Dead

In 2016, Tareke Brhane of the Comitato 3 ottobre was ill and therefore unable to coordinate the ceremonies, opening up space for the survivors' own improvisation. At the bunker at *Porta d'Europa*, two survivors spoke to the public, their words translated by Mussie Zerai. A survivor from Denmark delivered what he called "a message to the world" in English. He criticized the fact that there were no survivors on the Comitato, and that none had been involved in planning the commemorations. "The Comitato does not reflect our feelings," he said in English. Another survivor took the microphone and added, also in English: "The people of Lampedusa [are] like our family. [The p]eople of Lampedusa saved us! No rescue team! No military! Only they helped us. And we need to directly communicate with the Lampedusan people."

These feelings had also been articulated in the procession to the monument. Instead of carrying the Comitato's banner, survivors and relatives now carried handwritten signs of their own. The signs were written in Tigrinya, Italian, or English, and in all three languages, the survivors communicated their gratitude to the Lampedusans and their demand that the dead be identified and returned to their families. The signs read: "Grazie a tutta la gente di Lampedusa" (Thank you, people of Lampedusa), "Our families are waiting for the souls of their children," and "Chiediamo che i corpi dei nostri fratelli, delle nostre sorelle e dei nostri bambini vengano riportati a casa" (We ask that the bodies of our brothers, sisters, and children be returned home).

The Comitato 3 ottobre and the participating humanitarian organizations did not publicly engage with the issue of returning the 366 coffins to Eritrea. In my view, their interest was on the border, specifically on the construction of a humanitarian border. In seminars and roundtables, the issue of why even those

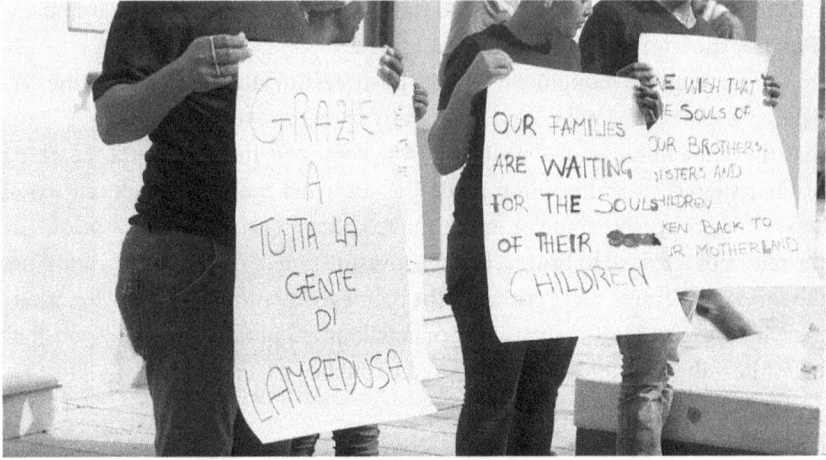

FIGURE 15. The survivors with their handwritten signs, Lampedusa, October 3, 2016. Still image of a video by Anna Blom. © Anna Blom, 2016.

families who had identified their relatives' remains and had the means to do so were prevented from burying the dead where they wished was not addressed. To return the dead "home," to Eritrea, it seemed to me, was absurd from a Eurocentric perspective. European preconceptions about the colonial subject colored the framing of the aspirations of those who had been on the boat: in the Italian imagination, the migrants desired to become one of them (as discussed in the context of journalistic interpretation of the found photographs in chapter 3). A refugee who identifies with his or her country despite having escaped its regime, who seeks human rights, political agency, or political change in their country while in exile, did not fit the humanitarian imaginary that prevailed in the Lampedusa commemorations. These claims did not conform with the European image of a refugee, which has become less and less of a political category in the past two decades (Fassin 2005). My interpretation is that the complexity of the political agendas and emotions of the Eritrean Europeans complicated the frame of a vulnerable and grateful refugee that those involved in organizing the commemorations needed for their agendas.

There were conflicting views also within the broader Eritrean diaspora in Italy and beyond in Europe about the meaning of the disaster and the burials. These conflicts, in my view, would not have helped the Comitato's position in relation to ministries and humanitarian organizations that funded its activities. Its main aim of educating publics about refugees—instrumentalizing the disaster's memory in resistance to European border control—a messy and confusing refugee diaspora would have been problematic.

In the first week or two after the disaster, the oppositional political diaspora advocated for the return of the coffins to Eritrea. The Eritrean Swedish human rights activist Meron Estefanos told me in a research interview (Estefanos 2016) that Eritrean exiles who resisted the regime had hoped that the arrival of 366 coffins in Asmara would start a revolution, as it would make visible the fact that so many young people were attempting to flee the country. However, the regime-friendly diasporic Eritrean community in Italy soon reframed the return of the coffins. They claimed that the disaster was a result of Western countries and exiled Eritrean opposition groups luring young Eritreans into making the dangerous journey. Regime-friendly Eritreans had shouted at Meron Estefanos and Mussie Zerai at the "state funeral" in Agrigento in 2013 (which survivors had been prevented from attending) and blamed the two human rights advocates for the disaster.

The regime-friendly Eritrean community in Italy published a declaration before the first anniversary of the disaster that called for commemorative activities across the country to prevent opposition forces from taking "ownership of our tragedy for purposes offensive to the dignity of our dead or hostile to our beloved nation (Eritrean community in Italy 2014)."[2] The dead, this declaration claimed, were "the victims of a secret policy of the West" that "deceived youth" and "traded on humans" to "monopolize Eritrean land and resources" (Eritrean community in Italy 2014).

The oppositional Eritrean diasporic publication *Awate* framed the memory differently:

> Eritreans all over the world will observe a day of remembrance for the victims of Lampedusa. . . . [Those fleeing Eritrea] will die and suffer as long as the repressive Eritrean regime is in power; as long as the ruling party enslaves the people and monopolizes the economy; as long as an unelected leader continues his brigandage and runs Eritrea as a military garrison. As long as the youth are kept in endless servitude, and as long as citizens are denied basic freedoms, Eritreans will flee away from their country and face great risks in the process. (Awate 2014)

According to the opposition, the repressive Eritrean regime had forced the youth to flee and risk their lives and was therefore responsible for the disaster. Specific forms of repression were cited, such as the unpaid labor and indefinite national service required by the regime. The term "victims of Lampedusa" that is used in the text (as opposed to "victims of *the disaster* in Lampedusa") shows how familiar the disaster is to the Eritrean diaspora. The word "Lampedusa" alone signifies the disaster.

The survivors of the disaster also hold a variety of views regarding the regime in Eritrea. Some identify as part of the opposition, while others are not politically active or are ambivalent about the regime. They might also hold a combination of both critical and understanding views. It can be difficult to distinguish between economic, religious, social, and political reasons for leaving the country because the regime controls all spheres of life.

Most of the survivors do not want to speak publicly against the regime, even if they privately hold critical opinions. Some fear exposing their family in Eritrea or Ethiopia to the risk of persecution or harassment. Others do not want to jeopardize future visits to Eritrea. As long as they pay the required 2 percent "Rehabilitation and Reconstruction Tax" on all income since escaping the country and sign a "Letter of Regret," visiting Eritrea is technically possible, though there is still danger of reprisal from the military. Remaining silent about politics also makes it easier to navigate the Eritrean diaspora in Europe, which includes different political generations. Many of those who fled Eritrea during the war of independence (1961–1991) formed a nationalist identity at a distance—a group that Tricia Redeker Hepner (2009) calls "generation nationalism." During the war, they financially supported the liberation forces, and it has been hard for them to believe that the liberators have since turned oppressors. However, like the recent arrivals, the older diaspora is also divided, and dissenting views are common (Proglio 2020, 45; Hirt and Mohammad 2018). In Victoria Bernal's (2017, 25) terms Eritrean diasporic subjects belong to "a political community under siege, rather than simply sharing cultural affinities or native origins."

Public Feelings at the Disaster Site

While *Porta d'Europa* became the memory site where survivors verbally articulated their claims and negotiated their relationships with other agents, such as the coast guard and the Comitato 3 ottobre, the site of the disaster itself became a significant memory site for nonverbal performances of public feelings. For the survivors, going to the disaster site at sea is a strong existential experience. As part of the anniversary commemorations, survivors and relatives board the vessels of the Guardia di Finanza, Guardia Costiera, and Carabinieri to go to the shipwreck site. Paradoxically, the survivors are transported on the boats of the institutions they criticize—the institutions that control the border and, from their perspective, mismanaged the rescue.

In 2015, I joined journalists, academics, and humanitarian workers on a Carabinieri boat. When we reached the site of the shipwreck, the vessels turned down their engines, formed a circle and by doing so, created a symbolic memorial site. Isola dei gonigli, Rabbit Island, seemed so close that I thought I could swim there. From our vessel we had a direct view of the group of survivors on the Guardia di

FIGURE 16. Memorial ceremony at the disaster site. © Karina Horsti, 2017. Photo by Karina Horsti.

Finanza vessel who threw a wreath of yellow flowers into the sea. I could hear the survivors cry; two men collapsed to their knees.

Seeing the emotional reactions of the survivors affected me. Being with the embodied witnesses of the disaster in the place where it happened created a particular emotional knowledge of the disaster. Diana Taylor (2011, 272–73) has argued for the use of "presence" as an active verb (as in Spanish, *presenciar*) as a means to produce understanding of violent events. One can never experience or fully know another person's experience. However, being with the witness in the place of events, seeing the sites where violence took place and the embodied feelings and reactions of revisiting the place and the memory can produce knowledge through embodied listening, through "presencing." "I participate not in the events but in his transmission of the affect emanating from the events," Taylor (2011, 273) writes in the context of "presencing" the testimony of a torture victim in Villa Grimaldi, Chile.

A month after being at the disaster site, I mentioned this episode to a focus group of survivors. Adal Neguse had helped me organize the session. I wanted to know how the survivors felt about the expression of emotions in public, a situation they had all experienced in Lampedusa. In addition to the traditional analysis of media representation, I wanted to develop a method of "refracting the analytical gaze" (Horsti 2020). This methodological practice is predicated on two obligations of the scholar: first, to open a nonjudgmental and receptive space where knowledge can be produced through collaborative conversation; and second to open a space in the moment of coanalysis (Horsti 2020, 148–49).

I showed press photographs taken from the docks of Lampedusa in 2013 when the coffins were transported to Sicily. Among them was a photograph of the grieving woman who had thrown herself on her brother's coffin (see chapter 2). Adal and three survivors together analyzed these mediated scenes of grief. They told me that they had been aware of being filmed during the ritual at the disaster site. In fact, this was an issue they had discussed extensively, even before the first anniversary in Lampedusa, in their closed Facebook group. Some of the survivors had been concerned that their grief would be politicized and instrumentalized for various Eritrean or European political purposes. One survivor in the focus group said that he had avoided cameras in Lampedusa. But the others wanted to express their feelings in public, in order "to remember our brothers and sisters who left us on that terrible journey," as one of them put it.

By the time the focus group discussed the scene on the Guardia di Finanza boat in 2015, the survivors had been living in Sweden for almost two years, and they understood why I was curious about their expression of emotions in public and that it seemed different from the more reserved Nordic manner. To make his point about the difference in cultural expressions in general, one of the survivors picked up his phone and searched for an English-language meme that read: "Waiting for a bus like a Swede." In the picture, six people stand in the snow by the side of a road, with several meters between each of them. This, he said, contrasted with "our culture." "I am proud of the custom we have in our culture that we come together to mourn the dead and to comfort others. It's a good thing," he said, underlining that grief could be proudly displayed in public.

The loud crying on the boat was a result of genuine feeling, not a "fake" expression, each of the survivors assured me. But it was, nevertheless, a conscious performance of emotion. It was directed not only at the "European" public but also, at least by some, at the Eritrean regime and the regime-friendly diasporic public. Some of the survivors were convinced that the deaths had resulted from the actions of both European governments and institutions and the Eritrean regime that abused the human rights of its people. The survivors explained that in Eritrea, they would not have been able to publicly grieve a person who had fled the country. "The regime in Eritrea does not want the world to know of such incidents [as the shipwreck], and therefore they prohibit public commemoration," one of the survivors said. They told me of two examples they had heard about from relatives in Eritrea. After the disaster, the Eritrean regime had ordered soldiers to guard the Martyrs Cemetery in Asmara to prevent large groups of people from gathering there to mourn the deaths publicly. Police had also removed public death notices for the victims of the October 3 disaster. Another survivor said: "When you look at it from a political point of view, we do these commemorative ceremonies together in exile in the memory of those who died during their escape because we didn't have the right to do so in Eritrea." Performing emotions publicly was a freedom the survivors had gained in Europe, and they wanted to show that to the publics that would be witnessing their grief through the media.

Personal and Collective Grief

Solomon Gebrehiwet is a survivor from Sweden whom I first met in Lampedusa in 2015. He is in his twenties and always stylishly dressed. In Eritrea, he had worked as a DJ for a short time while still in school, but then the state had conscripted him in the national service as a mechanic. In Sweden, Solomon drives a bus between two small towns and enjoys occasional weekend getaways, dancing in a nightclub on the overnight ferry that runs between Finland and Sweden. He spoke openly about his reasons to flee the indefinite national service conscription. It was for freedom, he said. "I was not free in my country. I don't want to live isolated from family and the society. [And w]hen you are oppressed and subjugated, you hate life," he said in 2016.

For Solomon, the experience of the commemorative ceremony at the disaster site had been different each year because his public role there had varied. His experience reflects the interconnections between the intimate and public spheres of commemoration, and the ways in which he has both performed public emotions and been influenced by the emotions of others. The first time he participated in an anniversary commemoration in Lampedusa was in 2015. Solomon had prepared for the boat journey to the disaster site by writing a poem, which he read aloud aboard the vessel, in Tigrinya. Another survivor filmed the reading at sea, and Solomon showed the video to me later. Although the Guardia Costiera boat had stopped alongside the other boats, the engine was audible in the background of the video. Solomon held the text in his hand and recited in a loud, clear voice:

> That time,
> It was horrible, the day turned dark.
> You tore them from my arms and dumped them, you sea!
> You should have known who they were and the problems they had.
> You just swallowed them down, young and old.
> Even though they came to you, you swallowed them.

You should have known their problems and become a bridge instead.
Grief has become a habit in our family.
Before the mourning ends, it is renewed by other sorrows.
As always, mother has been robbed of her children, those young chil-
    dren who didn't live long enough.
They were the hope for the future but now they ceased to exist.
Before doomsday's arrival, have we faced our own doomsday?
I would cry so many tears if I could have you back.
May you live in heaven forever, it is your compensation.
May you live in heaven forever, it is your compensation.

(Excerpt from Solomon Gebrehiwet's poem, 2015,
translated by Adal Neguse)

The poem begins with Solomon's personal memory, "you tore them from my arms," referring to the moment when he was no longer able to hold on to a small boy, whom he had held throughout the journey, and to the boy's mother. Solomon had taken care of the woman and the boy since meeting them on the smuggling route in Sudan, protecting them by pretending to be the woman's husband. Before boarding the smugglers' boat, she had taken sleeping pills because she was afraid of the journey. Incapacitated by the medication, she drowned along with her son. In the poem, this memory is implied, but in other instances later Solomon has talked about the woman and her son directly, for example, in the documentary film *Remembering Lampedusa* (2019) and in Eritrean diasporic media (Tekle 2020). In the middle of the poem, Solomon moves from personal grief to addressing the broader social experience of Eritreans: "Grief has become a habit in our family." State violence, indefinite national service, recurring war operations, and the young who disappear or die along perilous escape routes are permanent sources of distress for many Eritreans. The "family" and the "mother" in the poem could refer to the Eritrean people collectively. In addition to "grief becoming a habit" because of the present-day suffering in Eritrea and when fleeing Eritrea, the poem can also be understood to refer to the decades of collective Eritrean suffering.

When I discussed the recurring theme in the memorialization of the disaster in Eritrean diasporic media—a mother who loses her children—Hadnet Tesfalom who in 2020 translated some of the materials for me explained how the tragic figure of an Eritrean mother who "sacrificed a son or a daughter for the nation," *ade swue* (the mother of a martyr), has been essential in remembering wars among Eritreans. The sacrificial mother evokes sympathy like nothing else, Hadnet said. It is also central in the Orthodox Christianity in the figure of Mary.

The Eritrean War of Independence (1961–1991) and the Eritrean-Ethiopian War (1998–2000) are known for the brutal massacres they entailed. However, those war losses have not been publicly dealt with as individual losses of life. Victoria Bernal (2014, 7, 27–29) has described the aftermath of the wars against Ethiopia as "sacrificial citizenship": personal losses and horror have been silenced by the nationalist discourse that treats the war dead as "martyrs" or "heroes" (see also Ayalew Mengiste 2017, 48–49). Citizenship is expressed through sacrifice to the nation: Isaias Afwerki, the regime leader, urges mothers to celebrate rather than mourn their children who have been killed in the war, for example (Bernal 2017, 30).

In Solomon's poem, the personal and broader social experiences of the suffering of the Eritrean people are entangled in a way that is emblematic of the idea of Eritrean collective suffering. The poem articulates personal experiences of loss; however, these personal feelings and memories are intertwined with the collective suffering of the Eritrean people.

Solomon continued with this combination of the private and the collective in a new memorial poem that he published in his public Facebook profile on October 3, 2020. Because of the pandemic he did not go to Lampedusa but commemorated the disaster in the Eritrean diasporic online media sphere. In the second poem, Solomon creates a parallel between the disaster and the Eritrean-Ethiopian border war (1998–2000) by referring to Badme, the border town that was central in the conflict.

> Oh mother, how bad is your luck.
> Even though you are a mother, you became childless.
> Badme and the sea, one at a time.
> Before she was comforted enough, the second grief caught up with her.
> (Excerpt from Solomon Gebrehiwet's poem,
> 2020, translated by Adal Neguse)

In the first poem, written in 2015, Solomon does not explicitly oppose the regime—it is not clear what the "problems they had" are and he blames the sea for the killing. In the second poem, five years after, he has become more outspoken in his criticism of the regime. He criticizes it for an undignified treatment of the dead and their family members because the Eritrean regime has not made the burial of the dead in Eritrea possible. Later in the poem, he writes: "You denied them the dignity of resting in peace in their country."

Solomon's public reading of his first poem in Tigrinya onboard the coast guard vessel while the official ceremony was conducted in Italian illustrates how intimate and personal memories as well as collective memories of a minority can find a space within public and spectacular commemorations orchestrated by the majority. Solomon carved out an alternative commemorative space in which he expressed his personal emotions and memories and the conflict inherent in survival, in living on with the memory of the boy slipping from his arms. The poem was for the dead, but also for his fellow survivors, and through the spontaneous filming and mediation of Solomon's reading, the poem found its way to the Eritrean diasporic public.

The next time Solomon went to the disaster site, in 2017, he represented the survivors' community in a ceremony in which he threw a wreath into the water with the president of the Italian Senate, Pietro Grasso. Solomon reflected on the experience in an interview:

> Yesterday was very hard, particularly when we went to the place of remembrance. The whole experience, from the moment the boats started to move off the docks together to when we reached the destination. . . . To see the whole process, the movement of the boats side by side, and to see so many people attending—it just makes you feel different. Everything comes back; the feeling of the moment of the disaster returns. Placing the flowers with the president [of the Senate Pietro Grasso] was also very hard. I couldn't control my emotions. And I couldn't help it—the tears came, my head hurt, and I couldn't stand anymore. I had to sit on the deck, and I let the sorrow come out.[3]

The combination of the social and the spectacular in the ritual—the movement of the military police, customs, and the coast guard vessels side by side, the officers in their uniforms and the throngs of people attending—created "a different feeling," the kind of aura that commemorative rituals are designed to produce. This began to intensify when the boats left the dock and culminated in the moment when Solomon released his emotions in public, after the wreath had been thrown into the sea. Everyone's attention was on him and the president of the Senate. Knowing that others were witnessing his grief and his experience of "everything returning" was meaningful for Solomon. It amplified his experience and made him conscious of the publicness of the survivors' expressions of grief. When in the interview he described "letting his sorrow out," it was not a story of losing control or somehow failing in his responsibility as a representative of those who had lost loved ones or survived. On the contrary, he was very sure about his public feelings.

When I had asked about the meaning of public emotions in the focus group interview in 2015, the survivors had emphasized that the emotions were "real." But it is critical to understand that they emerge in a specific context: the date, the disaster site, the company of other survivors, the large boats, and the crowds of people help create the aura of commemoration. The emergence of public emotions is social, situated, and contextual. And while the emotions are "real," the survivors were clearly aware of and very articulate about the fact that public emotions could be utilized, and that they themselves could make use of those emotions. The sharing of emotions by the group of survivors and performing them while being filmed or photographed by the European media or diasporic Eritreans produced additional value. Public emotions produced a sense of community among survivors and mourners that was significant for developing critical politics targeting both the Eritrean regime and the European governments that have created the deadly border. This aspect of public emotions is akin to Sara Ahmed's (2004) notion of affective economies. She has argued that emotions "do things" by aligning and binding individuals with (though also against) others and that they produce affective capital through circulation and repetition. The two functions of memorializing—the therapeutic and the instrumental—are therefore not separate, but intertwined.

Mediation of Rituals in the Eritrean Diasporic Public Sphere

On October 3, 2018, Solomon Gebrehiwet spoke on behalf of the survivors at *Porta d'Europa* and in a panel discussion with representatives of humanitarian and religious organizations. As in previous years, the survivors had had a discussion upon arrival in Lampedusa about what their public "message" would be. They had made a collective decision, which they told me was unanimous. Solomon was to create awareness of the suffering of refugees detained in Libya.

On the march to *Porta d'Europa*, Solomon took up a style of protest common in Eritrean diasporic resistance against the regime. He shouted slogans in Tigrinya, and the others responded, echoing back the same line. "Justice for our brothers in Libya! Justice for our African brothers! Many of them die every day! Remembering is not enough! Journalists, you must report on our brothers suffering in Libya! Italy, it's not right to turn back those who are coming! You have to help those who suffer!" The protest slogans amplified the collective voice and emotional energy of the Eritrean Europeans. Tareke Brhane translated the slogans for the Italian journalists who accompanied the march. Solomon walked at the head of the procession, and like the other survivors, he held in his hand a postcard featuring the photographs of eighty-four victims. It was the memorial object that the Italian lay Catholic Sant'Egidio community had produced in 2014 and since reprinted (as discussed in chapter 3). By holding the picture of the victims, Solomon and his protest gained strength from their legacy, calling attention to the suffering of living refugees in the names of those who had died.

After the ritual at *Porta d'Europa*, Solomon shifted his focus to the Eritrean diasporic public. He began livestreaming on Facebook when the boats left the dock to head to the disaster site. The audience that followed him to the disaster site through social media was sizable. I watched the video three hours later, and by then it had had 3,900 viewers and 65 shares; by January 30, 2019, there had been 18,000 views, 141 shares, and 348 comments. The real-time comments and the more than 300 comments posted later below the video on the Facebook page are mostly emojis that communicate grief: crying faces and broken hearts. Some have added messages, such as "R.I.P." and the common Eritrean condolence in Tigrinya, *amlak byemanu yiqebelom* (May God receive you in heaven). Almost all of those who reacted to the video have Eritrean or Ethiopian names.

Until the moment the wreath is thrown into the sea, the video runs like reportage, with Solomon Gebrehiwet in the role of reporter. He interviews other survivors and explains the scene to the audience. His mobile phone then changes hands, and we see him participating in the commemorative rituals. He speaks Tigrinya and addresses the audience as Eritreans. First, he asks Adhanom Rezene, "What would you like to say, Adhanom?" Adhanom responds by inviting the Eritrean diaspora, "particularly those in Europe," to join them in Lampedusa next year. "We should make a memorial, a monument—the survivors and other Eritreans together," Adhanom announces. Solomon turns the phone's camera onto himself and repeats that they need Eritreans' help to build the memorial and commemorate the disaster together. He shows the postcard with the victims' photos, noting that they do not have pictures of all the victims. "Please send more," Solomon urges the audience.

When the boats arrive at the disaster site, Adhanom's voice becomes somber and his words come out slowly: "Look, this is the exact place. The boats are circling the site. It is here." Solomon recounts that they were in the water for four or five hours and that "366 lives—no, it was 368" lives that were lost, "and not only Eritreans, but also Ethiopians. This is where we capsized. It was here that we lost our beloved ones." The phone's camera is focused on the blue sea before moving to show the boats on the other side of the circle. Solomon reports that the Eritreans on the other boat are *yehwatna* (our brothers and sisters), who had recently arrived from Libya. Unlike in previous years, in 2018, the authorities allowed newly rescued Eritrean refugees to leave the reception center and participate in the commemorations.[4]

Before they came to this ceremony at sea, Solomon says, the survivors talked to the Italian authorities about the situation of refugees detained in Libya. "It is important to come to Lampedusa to commemorate, but it is even more important to help those refugees who are alive and suffering in Libya. We are doing our best. We are meeting our responsibility," Solomon says in Tigrinya.

The video continues with an Italian pastor reciting a prayer through a loud-speaker; then eight survivors and relatives of the victims form a V-shape with its point at the railing of the ship. The survivors themselves had planned this choreography. They take their time positioning themselves; the two in the center hold a wreath of orange and white flowers high in their arms, holding the pose for a few minutes. A Syrian man who had lost a son in another disaster (that of October 11, 2013) films the ceremony with his phone. Solomon has given his phone to someone else and joined the others in the formation. He says, in a more solemn voice, that they will now lay the flowers. Then he stops talking, no one talks, the flowers are held in the air, pictures are taken, and sobbing is barely audible in the video. The two survivors throw the flowers into the water, and the rest release the V-formation and lean on the railing to watch and film the wreath as it moves farther from the vessel.

The way in which the survivors choreographed their performance on the vessel, with the intention of being photographed and filmed, demonstrates that their act of commemoration was intended to be public and mediated. The formation of bodies in a specific shape and the holding of the flowers created a commemorative aura and dignified the moment that culminated in the throwing of the wreath. The wreath was held high in the middle, and a roughly equal number of people stood to each side—arranged so that each of them was visible to those who filmed the ritual. In this collective experience of returning to the disaster site and taking group photographs, filming, and being live on Facebook, they reestablished and strengthened the community of mourners. The V-formation included not only survivors, but also victims' relatives who had not been on the journey themselves. There was no difference between those who were survivors and those who were relatives; as a community of mourners, they were united. In the photographing practice, the survivors and relatives communicated a sense of site-specific presence (we are here in this memory site) and a sense of solidarity (we remember together).

The representatives of the humanitarian and religious organizations and the Guardia Costiera stand separated from the survivors, highlighting the centrality of the Eritrean community experience. By the time the wreath is thrown, the other vessels that had made up the circle of boats have started to return to the port. The mayor of Lampedusa had thrown his wreath of flowers into the water much earlier, and the other fishing boats, like the one I was on, followed the mayor's boat back to shore. The prayers on the survivors' boat had taken more time, as had getting all the survivors and relatives into position for the wreath-throwing ritual.

I watched Solomon's video with Adal in Stockholm a month after the anniversary ceremony. He translated for me what was said in Tigrinya, but he was also interested in observing and commenting on the ritual, which he had participated in himself on three previous occasions. Adal identified a major change in the ceremony: in earlier years, Italian politics had been at the center, he said. But now, the survivors did what they wanted on their own terms. There was no political authority, not even the president of Sicily, Rosario Crocetta, who had been at Giusi Nicolini's side during the mourning rituals in 2013, as well as at the 2015 commemoration when no political authority from Rome had accepted the invitation to participate. The new mayor of Lampedusa, Salvatore Martello, was a longtime leader of the fishermen's association and had decided to attend the commemoration at the site of the disaster on a fishing boat instead of on the Guardia Costiera boat. In an interview with me in 2017, Martello said that he had not liked "the elitist feeling" the ceremony had had during Nicolini's term, when it had centered on the institutional rescuers and high-profile guests from Rome and Brussels. The locals had criticized Nicolini for the national and international visibility she had gained through the topic of migration and for her assumed lack of focus on local issues. Martello did not aspire to politics beyond his constituency. He invited the fishermen and anyone else who wanted to join the commemoration to get on their boats.

In 2018, the change in local politics and the fact that Italy's national leaders no longer were keen on taking part in the ceremony created an opportunity for the survivors and victims' relatives to take more control. There were no Italian television crews filming the proceedings, as had been the case in previous years when politicians had been on board. Nevertheless, as the number of Solomon's Facebook viewers suggests, the ceremony was not without a mediated public. The focus of the ceremony and its mediation was solely on the survivors, the family members, and their diasporic publics.

The interplay between memorial sites and rituals that I have explored throughout this chapter shows how the two kinds of memory that Diana Taylor (2003) has theorized as *archive* and *repertoire* intersect: memorials invite performances and rituals. Rituals are often thought to be ephemeral, whereas monuments seem to carry a memory across time. However, the photographs and videos of the memorializations carried out by the survivors and family members have become digital memory objects that circulate in the Eritrean diaspora's social networks. Solomon Gebrehiwet's Facebook livestream has reached thousands of viewers who have been able to see and share the choreographed wreath-throwing at the disaster site. Rather than being an archival memory in the sense of a memory held in a specific static place (like an archive in a museum), these digital memory objects continue to circulate in mediated social networks.

Andrew Hoskins (2009) has argued for the term "network memory," meaning that in the digital age, archival memory has been replaced by a more fluid data that flows through networks. Digital memory objects are therefore shared and stored in a complex transnational network. Who finds what related to the Lampedusa disaster from the digital network memory depends on algorithms and the network structure. Digital memory objects (such as digital photographs of the wreath) are more fluid than physical objects (such as the wreath itself): they cross borders and can be reframed, multiplied, appropriated, and shared more easily. However, the digital world is regulated both by human and automated connectivities. Algorithms, popularity, and social connections determine accessibility to and the compass of the vast material circulating online (Papacharissi 2010, 164; Van Dijck 2013, 13, 26). Mediated rituals, such as the reading of Solomon Gebrehiwet's poem, the speeches at *Porta d'Europa*, the throwing of the wreath, and the sharing of digital memory objects create a transnational site for the production of a collective diasporic memory.

Survivor Citizenship

In this chapter, I have explored how survivors have negotiated their role and made their claims visible in performances of memorialization. In 2014, when I observed the first anniversary commemoration, it seemed to me that the survivors' role was to produce authenticity for the memorial rituals for the benefit of Italian interests. However, when I got to know the survivors and began to listen to them and analyze the rituals and memorials with them, I began to see their agency and sociality. The complexity and ambiguity of the relationships between the survivors and the different European agents taking part in the commemorations also began to surface. Through memorialization, the survivors have played the role of stereotypical grateful refugees, but they have also defied the expectation that they would remain in that role. The survivors have simultaneously accepted and resisted the presence of the coast guard and militarized border agents at the commemorations. They have simultaneously agreed to carry out their commemorations on Guardia Costiera and Guardia di Finanza vessels alongside their uniformed crews at the same time as they have refused to offer them their gratitude. They have interjected their own politics into the commemoration—their personal memories, political manifestations of Eritrean diasporic politics, and disaster-specific claims about the identification and burial of the dead. They have sought justice for the dead and for the families of the dead. They have made claims for the right to flee oppression and seek protection. Some of these claims for rights have aligned with those of European actors in the commemorations, but others have not resonated with European ideas of refugee-ness.

In terms of Engin Isin and Greg M. Nielsen (Isin 2008, 17; 2009; Isin and Nielsen 2008) the survivors act as citizens, they perform "acts of citizenship," despite their legal citizenship status. "They constitute themselves as those with 'the right to claim rights'" (Isin 2009, 371). This concept is similar to Étienne Balibar's notion of "civility" as he argues for a right to access human rights not on the basis of formal citizenship status but on the basis of happening to be "thrown together" by history and economy with other people and groups. Citizenship, for Balibar, means civility: "an active and collective civil process, rather than a simple legal status" (Balibar 2004, 132).

Nevertheless, rather than a linear process, the survivors' acts of citizenship have been a circuit in which different elements are in constant interaction. Claiming rights entails "responsibilizing" the self (Isin and Nielsen 2008, 1): making oneself responsible for and capable of taking action. There are two crucial interlinked elements in the circuit that forms "survivor citizenship," a position from which one is capable of taking action: moral responsibility and group identity. These are in constant interaction with one another and with the acts of memorialization—both verbal and nonverbal—that claim rights.

Regardless of their legal status, the survivors of the Lampedusa disaster have acted as cultural citizens of Europe. Importantly, this is a transformative kind of European citizenship. It stretches across various European nation-states that produce the deadly border that they resist—often the same nation-states that have protected them from the oppression of the Eritrean regime. The ambivalent status of Europe, the empire that on the one hand produces disasters and on the other hand protects from suffering, is reflected in the survivors' ambiguous relationship with the European agents and individuals present at the commemorations in Lampedusa. The figures of the grateful and ungrateful refugee intertwine in their performances.

In the Lampedusa disaster, public memorialization has been a symbolically powerful site and practice through which the survivors have made political and social claims for the rights of refugees, both dead and living. They have done so through two kinds of public acts: First, there have been verbal articulations such as speeches, conversations and interviews, prayers, poems, songs, protest shouts, and self-made signs. Second, they have made claims through nonverbal performances such as walking, praying, and choreographing the rituals at *Porta d'Europa* and the disaster site in which the display of emotions in public has been central. Survivor citizenship is about both acting politically and finding an existential security about being the one who lives on.

Constituting a subjectivity that I have termed *survivor citizenship*— responsibilizing oneself as a survivor—started before the border crossing and continued to evolve afterward. Those who left Eritrea did so knowing the risks; they risked their lives in order to survive. The Isaias Afwerki regime had annihilated their social, cultural, and political life in Eritrea, and for many, escaping the country to migrate was a means of survival (see also Perl 2016; Betts 2013, 5). The migrants had acted upon their "right to have rights" (Arendt 1951/1973), and after the disaster, some of those who survived acted as citizens of Europe, despite their lack of formal citizenship status.

Solomon reflected on his decision to act publicly by talking about the disaster:

> There are people who blacken my name, and even though everyone doesn't like what we say, we should not gloss over history. Someone needs to take a stance and talk about the tragedies Eritreans are going through. When I'm talking about my brothers and sisters, when I'm talking to the Eritrean people, I'm doing it because others are not. I should be lucky because I can speak on behalf of others. (Gebrehiwet in Global Yiakl 2020)

Acting upon that responsibility entails a specific relation to power: a person or a group must feel powerful enough to act. Solomon says he is "lucky" to have the capacity to speak. Survivors of the disaster generated the capacity and power for acting out of their sense of responsibility by performing public emotions and embodied movements together.

The sites of the survivors' acts were also central for creating survivor citizenship, with scenes of memorialization, including the memorials created by "Europeans," shaping survivors' memorialization practices. Furthermore, the publics that were present at the rituals helped produce what I have called a commemorative aura. For example, for Solomon, the presence of large military and coast guard vessels, uniformed officers, and throngs of people produced a "different feeling" than at other types of memorializations. In addition, the mediated presence of both "European" publics and the Eritrean diaspora generated a sense of publicness for the performances, which the survivors were aware of and took into consideration. There was also, perhaps, the expectation that one performs the role of responsible survivor.

Survivors' ambiguous relationship with Europe demonstrates how survivor citizenship not only depends on the willingness and agency of survivors but is also carried out within a certain framework of expectations and limitations. Survivor citizenship is constructed in a relationship, and not only between the survivors and European states, but also with others in the civil sphere, including the Eritrean diaspora. Survivor citizenship opens platforms and space in both the European public sphere and the diasporic public sphere where one can be heard. This form of citizenship, while enabling in one way, is in other ways limiting. First, a diasporic citizenship in which the sacrificial element (Bernal 2014) is central must be negotiated in relation to identification based on survival. This diasporic citizenship can be contradictory to survivor citizenship. Leaving Eritrea "illegally" can be perceived in the diasporic community and in Eritrea as defying expectations regarding sacrifice to the state. Nonetheless, the regime expects sacrifice for the community and the state even after an "illegal exit." Through its long-arm diaspora governance, Eritrea controls the lives of everyone in its diaspora.

Second, public identification as a survivor-citizen may limit one's role in the community and political agency as a European. Such identification does not necessarily allow in-betweenness, for subjectification as an "almost survivor" or "not-quite survivor." In chapter 8, my analysis of survivors' testimonies will show how survival is ambiguous and a process. The position as a survivor from which one can make public acts of citizenship is not necessarily a certain or permanent condition.

In the context of the aftermath of the 1986 Chernobyl nuclear disaster, Adriana Petryna (2013, xxv) has developed the notion of biological citizenship, a subjectivity that the survivors of the nuclear disaster had to produce in order to access compensation and medical care. Sickness and citizenship fused together as survivors had to remake themselves as "recognized sufferers of the state." This biological citizenship has not been available to everyone who suffers physical symptoms, however. On the one hand, biological citizenship is a limited resource. On the other hand, some survivors hide their symptoms and avoid being classified as Chernobyl victims.

In the case of the Lampedusa disaster, public identification and recognition of survivorship has given survivors access to a position in which they are invited to play public roles in commemorations and to speak through words, gestures, and emotions. However, while some Lampedusa survivors have created a subject position of survivor citizenship as a means to continue their life after the disaster, this was not an option for everyone. In the commemorations, there were always some survivors who did not step up on the bunker at *Porta d'Europa*, who did not wear the identical T-shirts, and who stood instead among the audience. Public identification as a survivor of a disaster at the border is not easy. As Solomon noted, those who become public figures as survivor citizens receive unwanted attention. They are seen as perpetual victims and objects of pity, but they also face hate—they are blamed for not doing enough for those who died or for risking their own lives and escaping Eritrea. These are issues survivors must cope with as they live on after the disaster.

In the next chapter, I continue to discuss survivors' survival, but change my perspective from public performance and engagement to a more intimate level. Acting out of responsibility can sometimes be the result of a personal feeling of guilt, and public actions, such as those performed in annual commemorations, may function as compensation or atonement. In the commemorations, the survivors as a group did not identify their feelings of guilt with culpability: there was no sense that they were guilty because of what they had done or not done, or that they would absolve their guilt by memorializing. However, feelings of shame and regret did emerge in the personal interviews I examine in the next chapter.

SURVIVAL

In Tigrinya, those who were rescued from the October 3 disaster call themselves *wutsae meat*, "survivors of a catastrophe." The Tigrinya term for "survivor" needs a qualifier. One must be a survivor of something: a shipwreck, a tragedy, "Lampedusa." For Eritreans in the diaspora and in Eritrea, "Lampedusa" refers more to the disaster than to the specific place, the island. In this context, the event itself is a crucial definer of survival: those who survived lived on, *beyond* and *after* "Lampedusa." The prefixes in *survivre* in French, *sorvivere* in Italian, and *över-leva* in Swedish, like *survive* and the archaic *overlive* in English, emphasize the meaning of living *over* or *beyond* something. (In Tigrinya, *wutsae* does not have the root related to living.) Rescue is the moment from which the continuation of their life begins.

In this chapter, I examine how those who were rescued from the sea experience survival. What does survival mean for the survivors? Though authorities were able to report soon after the disaster that 155 people "survived," not all of those who stayed alive necessarily survived—not immediately, anyway. How were they affected by the disaster and how do they continue living on in a meaningful way? Others died, and they too could have died, but instead they somehow stayed alive. Then, I examine the role of others in the experience and meaning of survival. How does recognition of those who were rescued as persons in the common world shape their survival? This perspective to the disaster's afterlife allows me to further develop what Didier Fassin has discussed as "the anthropological consequences of the concept of survival" (Fassin 2010, 83) that is, to scrutinize what human beings make of their lives, and how their lives question what it is to be human.

In philosophical inquiries into what it is to be human and live a human life, the aspect of survival is central. Life is survival, Jacques Derrida observed in his last interview: "I have always been interested in this theme of survival, the meaning of which is *not to be added on* to living and dying. It is originary: life *is* living on, life *is* survival [la vie *est* survie]" (Derrida and Birnbaum 2007, 26). Survival is living on, continuing to live. Derrida's understanding of survival is informed by his reading of Walter Benjamin's (2009) work on translation in which Benjamin defines survival first as *überleben*, living beyond a death, like a child who survives the death of his parents, and second as *fortleben*, continuing to live on (Derrida and Birnbaum 2007, 26). These two definitions of survival are not separate as the analysis of the aspect of living beyond losing a loved one in a specific type of death, death at the border, will be illustrated in chapter 9. The second meaning of Benjamin's definition of survival, the continuing to live on (*fortleben*), is also relevant in understanding survival of death of another.

There are two ideas in Walter Benjamin's (2009) theorization that are pertinent in understanding survival of a migrant disaster. First, for Benjamin the active verb, *living*, is central to survival. This is the insight that Derrida emphasizes in his interview when he underlines that "life is survival." Both of these theorists maintain that survival is not about staying alive physically, nor is it a continuation of the same life. What survives, lives on, but it continues to transform in the manner of any living organism: it does not remain the same.

Benjamin does not conceive of life as merely a physical or material condition. In reference to works of art, he writes: "organic corporeality was not the only thing to which life could be attributed" (2009, 31). Life is more than the physical existence of something, more than an "element of the animal" (Benjamin 2009, 31). It is only on the basis of history "that the sphere of life must ultimately be defined," Benjamin maintains. Life, therefore, needs to be understood in the wider sphere of history. Survival is the continuation of life in its social, cultural, and political form rather than its mere physical existence.

In the theoretical work on survival as life, the Holocaust has been a defining event. In her influential discussion of human rights in *The Origins of Totalitarianism*, Hannah Arendt explains how before the physical killing in the death camps, the Nazis destroyed much of the social, political, and cultural lives of those they perceived as not worthy of human life. Though some stayed alive physically, their lives as participants in the common world were ended. They did not survive.

Humans are capable of a life that has meaning in a cultural and political sense. Hannah Arendt's work in this respect is perhaps the most influential. *The Human Condition* discusses her central idea of the human condition, that of pluralism: each person is distinct and unique, and each human life is made of particular events. Humans are capable of new beginnings, of taking an initiative and setting something unique in motion (1998, 177). Each person has a "biography," and therefore, this part of human life, *bios*, can be distinguished from mere biological life *zoe* (Arendt 1998, 79).

Giorgio Agamben (1999, 132–33), following the work of Hannah Arendt, defines survival in the concentration camps in *Remnants of Auschwitz* in two ways. He distinguishes a biological form of life as the first form of survival. In reference to a *Muselmann* (a slang term used in Nazi concentration camps to refer to a prisoner who was still biologically alive but no longer had any personhood), Agamben argues that survival means "the inhuman capacity to survive the human" (Agamben 1999, 133). The prisoner has passively let go of the will to live a human life while remaining biologically alive. This is the first sense of survival. In the second sense, a person actively becomes a survivor by fighting not only biological but also social death—that is, the inhumanity into which a *Muselmann* has fallen. In doing so, a survivor maintains his or her personhood. Agamben's distinction is based on concentration camp testimonies. The destruction of a social, cultural, and political life took time, and therefore falling into the state of a *Muselmann* took time.

While the condition of the camps has often (including in the work of Agamben) been paralleled with present-day asylum "reception centers" (including the one in Lampedusa; for a discussion, see Neumann 2019, 17), survival of a disaster at sea is a different matter. One of the key differences is that the perpetrators and structures of violence that are visible in the camps are invisible at the sea border: the natural force of the sea is the apparent killer. Thus, survival in a camp is not entirely analogous to surviving mass death at the sea border. The first sense of survival—staying alive physically while one's social and cultural life is annihilated—does not directly apply to the survival of a disaster at sea. Nevertheless, Agamben's idea of the second sense of survival offers an important opening to understanding the survival of a migrant disaster. This meaning of survival underlines an active and processual resistance against the death of a social, cultural, and political life.

If human survival is living on, as Derrida (Derrida and Birnbaum 2007, 26) argues, what kind of experience is it? I examine this question by analyzing witness testimonies, interviews, and my field notes of time spent with survivors. The core of the material is four survivor testimonies that resulted from interviews conducted by Adal Neguse in 2017 for the documentary film project

Remembering Lampedusa (2019). Each interview was conducted in Tigrinya at a survivor's home, filmed by Anna Blom and Ditte Uljas, and transcribed and translated into English. Each interview lasted one to two hours. I was present at Solomon Gebrehiwet's interview and earlier at the first meeting of the four survivors, Adal Neguse and Anna Blom, where we spent the day at a survivor's home to discuss and plan the documentary project.

Analysis of the material reveals that there are three important facets of survival that support Derrida's key insight that survival is life. First, survival is about creating a new self and a new life. Second, the capacity to feel shame and to come to terms with unsettling ethical situations is crucial in this process of survival. Third, interaction with others and the awareness of others to whom a survivor is responsible for bearing witness of the disaster are central to survival. Survival is life; it is a transformative, social process.

Survival as a New Life

In interviews, Vito Fiorino and Constantino Baratta, the two Lampedusans who have spoken most prominently about their role as civic rescuers on October 3, 2013, always mention that the rescued call them "father." Vito and Constantino also refer to the rescued in familial terms—as "sons," "daughters," "*ragazzi*" (boys and girls) or by their first names, such as Adhanom, Marawi, Luam, or Solomon. Rosa Maria, Constantino's wife, speaks of them as "*i miei figli*," my children. Once when traveling back from Lampedusa with Amanuel and Ambasager, who live near Stockholm, I asked them why they call Vito father. Amanuel responded that by rescuing him, Vito gave him a new life. "He is a father to me. *Abona.* I have two fathers," Amanuel said. Ambasager's oldest daughter's birthday is October 3, and he told me: "She turned ten when I started from year zero." They both used the phrase that they were reborn that day, and Vito, as the captain of *Gamar*, became their father.

Describing Vito and Constantino as "fathers" and the disaster as "year zero" suggest that the survivors perceive the disaster as a new beginning, which demands a new identity. Yet despite the survivors' "rebirth," the disaster is nevertheless not a moment that erases the past and resets the clock. Amanuel has not forgotten his first father, nor has Ambasager forgotten his ten-year-old daughter. "Year zero" is a rupture in the survivors' lives rather than the beginning of a completely new life. There is a before and after, an old life and a new life, but both parts—the old and the new—belong to the same life. When the survivors speak of their rescue as having been born again, they are referring to receiving a second chance to live a physical life. In the new life, they received a new relationship—Amanuel becomes the son of an Italian ice cream maker. This extension of family suggests that there is more to survival than just not dying.

The disaster and living beyond it restarts the lives of the survivors in a new form. The issue of how this new life differs from the old, the new self from the old self, surfaces strongly in the testimonies of four survivors that Adal Neguse, the brother of a victim, elicited in Sweden in 2017 as part of the research for this book and the *Remembering Lampedusa* documentary film project he worked on with the filmmaker Anna Blom. Toward the end of survivor Bisrat's retelling of the disaster, Adal asks her: "Did this change your attitude toward life?" She responds: "Yes. It is very hard to witness so many lives wiped out right in front of your eyes. As long as you live, you have to go on with love and sympathy in everything you do. I escaped death and created a second life. There is nothing worse than what I have already seen." Similarly, Adal asks Solomon Gebrehiwet: "Did this change you as a person?" Solomon replies: "Compared to someone who comes here directly from Eritrea, I, who have come through many problems, and him—we are not the same. We are different like the earth and the sky. He could know about the problems only through [hearing] a story, but not like me who has gone through it. I have gotten a lesson out of it: patience. I have become more patient."

The self-recognition of personal transformation—that neither Bisrat nor Solomon is the same person four years after the disaster—is an obvious characteristic of the process of survival. Their experience of the disaster shapes their lives and gives their lives a particular meaning. Bisrat describes her experience of witnessing mass death by saying "there is nothing worse." This experience has created meaning for her life—she has the incentive to live with love and sympathy in everything she does. Solomon underlines that having endured many problems defines who he is now. "Many problems" can mean the disaster and what he experienced during his journey, but also, perhaps, the time afterward. His survival is also something to go through, and this process has evidently made him a different kind of Eritrean in Sweden compared to those who have come "directly." The journey he took without papers and the disaster he survived are detours that fundamentally changed him as a person. While becoming a refugee in Sweden can always be said to be the beginning of a new life, Solomon insists on a difference between himself, who experienced the disaster, and those who didn't. Like Ambasager and Amanuel, Solomon does not think that his life started from zero, that his old life and old self were erased. His new self, shaped by the experience of the disaster and by survival, can still be compared with that of Eritreans who come directly. It is not the same, but it is comparable.

Interestingly, when Solomon tells Adal about his experience of the disaster and his survival, he points out that those who have not gone through these experiences can only learn about them "through a story." Solomon's capacity for witnessing (seeing the disaster) and bearing witness (telling about it) is different from those who were not there, who were not in the water struggling with those who died. Solomon's understanding of knowledge is similar to Yuval Noah Harari's (2009) notion of "flesh witnessing"—that only by experiencing, by understanding via one's own flesh, can certain knowledge can be gained. It follows that this sensible, experiential knowledge can never be fully communicated to anyone because only by being there and experiencing the disaster can one fully understand it. Solomon acknowledges that another could gain knowledge, though "only" through listening to a story, resulting in knowledge that is less than his own, incomplete. Complete knowledge, Solomon seems to suggest, is available only to the flesh witness. Thus, survival of a flesh witness must also be specific.

The remaking of oneself that both Bisrat and Solomon describe in their interviews is familiar from other narratives of surviving various types of traumatic experiences. Susan Brison (2002, 39) discusses how narratives of trauma frequently return to the issue of no longer being able to find the self one once was. She quotes trauma literature to illustrate this point, giving examples such as: "I died in Vietnam" or "One can be alive after Sobibor without having survived Sobibor" (Brison 2002, 39). Near-death experiences and witnessing the death of others undoes the self. Survival, then, requires an active remaking of the self and envisioning one's world and future anew.

A survivor is a haunted subject—haunted by the disaster and the dead, but also by the future and the remade self. In *Haunted Subjects*, the literature scholar Colin Davis (2007, 117–18) writes, in reference to Emmanuel Levinas's lectures on surviving the death of another person, that the dead "constitute me as survivor of their death" (Davis 2007, 118). Thus, while the dead cannot directly speak to the living, and there is no actual dialogue between the living and the dead, the dead do "signify"—produce signs—"since the survivor continues to be the uncomprehending addressee of signs which cannot be attributed to any living subject" (Davis 2007, 117).

Memorializing disaster is one crucial means of attending to such "signs," and therefore also central in the process of survival. In chapter 7, I explained how survivors who return to Lampedusa for the annual commemoration of the disaster act upon their responsibility as survivors and for the benefit of other refugees, making claims for the rights of refugees more broadly. Bisrat describes it as doing something in the name of the dead. Memorializing the dead in a public or more private way is one important aspect of survival. Through acts of memorializing, survivors not only create relationships among the living—among themselves, the relatives of victims, the Lampedusan civil rescuers, and others present at the rituals—they also create a relationship with the dead. They act upon the world in the name of the dead, which also helps the memory of the dead survive. The memory of the deceased continues to live on through acts of commemoration. Bisrat told Adal: "When I meet the people who were rescued with me, I feel joy. We meet not to forget, but to carry on with our relationship. We also want to do something. As long as we live in this world, we want to do something in their [the deads'] name." In chapter 7, I examined survivors' acts of memorialization and argued that commemorating together and presenting themselves as a group was important. Here, Bisrat talks about that same power of peer support. Meeting other survivors and doing something in the name of the dead are instrumental in the process of living on in her new life. Survival, for her, is a collective, relational process. She survives together and in interaction with others, particularly those who were rescued with her and are in the same position as witnesses. They share an embodied knowledge that no one else can know in the same way.

Nevertheless, as much as remembering the disaster is central to survival, so is forgetting. Survival comes across in the interviews as a continuous balancing act between remembering and forgetting. Later in the interview with Adal, Solomon reflects that his memories of the disaster cause him stress if they enter his mind in his daily life, such as while he is at work driving a bus: "You need to live a new life. The bad and dirty things, you need to leave them behind. You have to decide what your new life should look like. If everything keeps coming back, you are in danger." To survive—that is, to "live a new life" in Solomon's words—one also needs to forget, or to be able to manage one's emotions when "everything comes back." If Solomon remembers the disaster at the wrong time, he is unable to live his new life. While survival involves the collective and relational work of remembering, it also involves the solitary management of those memories and being able to forget.

Survivors' articulation of the rescue as "being born again" or having "a second life" underlines that survival is about a new beginning—this is an aspect that is fundamental to human condition, and to a full human life. Both remembering and forgetting are action and speech, and both are necessary for a new beginning. Deliberate silence or forgetting—the leaving behind of bad and dirty things—is an act, just as speaking or doing something in the name of the dead are acts of remembering. Life is survival, as Derrida said, and survival is a beginning, life set in motion.

The Ethical Complexity of Survival

The need to forget is related to the ethical complexity of the disaster and to the difficult and ambiguous emotions, such as shame, guilt, and regret, that emerged afterward. What conduct was right and what was wrong? The answer was not obvious to the survivors. Adhanom Rezene, who also narrated his testimony to Adal in Stockholm, speaks about the ethical uncertainty of his own and others' actions during the disaster. Humanity and inhumanity, compassion and ignorance are entangled in his memories of his time in the water. Though he does not try to forget these difficult scenes, his choice of words suggests that he nevertheless creates a certain distance between himself and the events:

> While we struggled to survive, others died. You move away from people. In the darkness, if you hear someone nearby, you swim in the other direction. You flee from death. . . . When you are swimming and someone comes next to you and asks for help, you flee, change your route. . . . Then you might see your close friend—you can't leave him. . . . Those who had some strength said to others: "Keep moving, we are very close, the rescue team is coming." I didn't have the strength to speak, I was vomiting. . . . But some people gave hope to others.

Adhanom's description of the event remains vague: *someone* came next to someone else, "you" (not "I") fled from those who called for help. Certainty and detail seem to be unspeakable; the "rules" of interaction in the disordered disaster scene are described in a distanced manner. However, after describing the scene generally, Adhanom does speak about himself directly, acknowledging that he was unable to even "give hope to others." Nevertheless, while talking about action and nonaction, Adhanom does not suggest that he or any of the other passengers on the migrant boat are guilty. Ethical judgment is suspended, it is impossible.

Similar memories of existing at the limits of humanity and ethics also appear in the other three survivor testimonies. Yusef (a pseudonym), who was the youngest of the survivors, thirteen years old at the time of the disaster, recalled how he and a friend stayed alive in the water. This memory also included uncertainty about ethical action. When the sun rose over the migrants struggling in the sea, Yusef recognized a boy in the water nearby, a friend from his village in Eritrea. He swam toward the boy, though it was not how one was supposed to behave at the scene of the disaster. "I approached only him. Otherwise, you don't do that," he says, referring to swimming toward another person. Like Adhanom, Yusef speaks of swimming away from people who might hold on to "you" (in a general sense) and pull you under when describing the disaster scene. It was the order of the disaster, at least in the narratives of those who remained alive to give an account of the disaster. The ethical order of those who died we cannot know. Yusef doesn't directly identify any particular person whom he or someone else left behind. But the fact that he swam toward the friend and not away from him, and that the other boy allowed Yusef to swim toward him and did not flee, reveals a special relationship between the two boys. They were friends and trusted one another.

Yusef had found a plastic bottle floating in the sea that he was using to help stay afloat. He and his friend started to swim together. They talked and "encouraged each other," Yusef says.

> He asked me to share the plastic bottle with him. But the bottle was very small—you couldn't share it. I told him he could have it—our hope must come from God, not plastic—but he refused to take it. His idea was that we could both hold on to it from opposite ends. My idea was that he could take it for a while and then give it back to me. But he didn't take it. We were both rescued and arrived safely. He is now in Germany, and we stay in touch.

Adal, the interviewer, wants to know more about how the two boys survived together and asks: "Were you swimming together? Could you see each other [the whole time]?" Yusef starts to become uncertain about the moral of his story, which to this point has been about mutual encouragement, trust, friendship, and willingness to share, to endanger one's own safety for a friend.

> YUSEF: Yes, but because I had the plastic bottle, I couldn't swim very fast. I was moving more slowly. He was swimming faster. That's why he didn't want the plastic bottle. He wanted to swim, and no one can swim [fast] holding a plastic bottle. Or you have to swim like this. You stay where you are unless the wind takes you elsewhere. So, he went further, far further than me.
>
> ADAL: But weren't you rescued together?
>
> YUSEF: Yes, after I was pulled from the sea, I found him on the same ship.

Yusef's and Adhanom's memories reveal that actions and inaction create a sense of ethical ambiguity. Adhanom, for example, acknowledges that he was not able to provide hope to others. Their distanced manner of speaking suggests that both Adhanom and Yusef feel uncomfortable about, and perhaps even ashamed of, having seen and been part of ethically ambiguous situations in which right and wrong were not clear choices. Should one swim toward someone who calls for help and perhaps be pulled under? Which one of the boys was right about the bottle? Do they feel shame because they might have compromised morally? To stay alive, did they momentarily give up their capacity for social and cultural action? In Agamben's terms, did the inhuman (biological life) survive the human (political, cultural, and social life)? Such a trajectory is not clear in Adhanom's and Yusef's testimonies, but it is definite that no personal action of compromise is necessary for a survivor to feel shame. Simply seeing and being at the scene of a disaster creates a sense of shame when one examines oneself while describing the scene to a listener, when one imagines being seen by others. Witnessing and bearing witness both contribute to the emotion of shame.

Survival as a Capacity to Feel Shame

The sense of being seen by others as having stayed alive while others died is apparent in Bisrat's and Solomon's interviews when they describe the days after the disaster. The most difficult emotions emerged when they became aware of their need to bear witness. In her interview, Bisrat recalls her decision to leave Eritrea and pursue the dangerous journey to Europe. When she set out, she thought she would either arrive safely or vanish at sea: "You were not crossing legally, either you would make it or perish." She had escaped Eritrea where her future was compromised. Conscription in the national service was indefinite and family life was suspended. In order to live a full human life, she had to risk also her biological life. "You would make it or perish." But she had not thought of the possibility of surviving a disaster and having to bear witness to mass death. Bisrat recalls how she pushed dead bodies away as she tried to swim toward the light of the Lampedusa lighthouse. She was nearly unconscious when the coast guard rescued her, and only later did she realize that none of her family or friends had survived. She said to Adal: "When I regained consciousness, I could not find those who were with me. I had lost them all. Then, I regretted that I was rescued. I mean that at that time it was very hard for me to be the only one [from my group] who was rescued. They were my friends, my family, people from my neighborhood." She regretted that she was rescued when she became aware that no one else in her group made it. It meant she would have to relay the news of death to the relatives of the others.

In her testimony, Bisrat tells Adal how the survivors were given phone cards at the reception center in Lampedusa so they could call family. This was meant to be a joyful event—to call family and tell them you have made it to Europe. But Bisrat did not call, and many other survivors also put off making the calls. Bisrat mentions twice that her throat was "clogged" from swallowing sea water and fuel that had leaked from the boat into the sea. Her physical inability to speak is given as one explanation for not calling her family: "I had not gotten my voice back. I mean my throat was not okay." However, she also says: "Even if you wanted to speak, you couldn't. There was no strength." The physical condition of having lost her voice is entangled with the emotional difficulty of calling relatives to let them know she had survived. The phone call upon arrival, which for migrants is often the high point of the journey to Europe, was now a situation that required great effort, and as Bisrat suggests, her circumstances were, in fact, unspeakable. In her conversation with Adal, it is obvious how difficult it is for Bisrat to find words to describe why she didn't make the call. The unspeakability of one's survival remains unspeakable even afterward.

> **Bisrat:** We were feeling so bad that we weren't able to make those calls.
> **Adal:** Do you mean that you did not want to call?
> **Bisrat:** Yes. It was very hard. You feel for [the victims'] families.
> **Adal:** What was the reason you didn't want to call?
> **Bisrat:** My family would ask about the others, and I had nothing but bad news.

Bisrat's use of "we" rather than "I" at first when talking about the phone cards suggests that she hesitates to take sole responsibility for not calling. It was not just her, but others too, she indicates. Adal pushes further on this issue and asks Bisrat to clarify whether she and the others *couldn't* call or didn't *want* to call. Solomon speaks about the same situation and the emotional difficulty of calling family:

> Wasn't the disaster on Thursday? I didn't call on Thursday. It was Friday evening when I called. They gave us a phone card so we could call our relatives. But, you know, I felt ashamed that I had survived, to say that I have survived. I didn't call. I kept quiet. I didn't tell my family, anyone. But my brother had heard somehow that I was on that ship and people had already started to console him. He thought I was dead. Some others had already called [their families] on Thursday. Then I called [on Friday] and said "Hello Mulie." My brother said "Selie" and fainted. He was gone.

Bisrat talks about her regret over staying alive and says that "feeling bad" prevented her from calling. Solomon names his uncomfortable feeling "shame." For many on the boat, calling family to let them know they were alive meant also having to bear witness to the death of others. Most survivors had been traveling in a group of cousins, friends, or neighbors, so there was no avoiding having to communicate that someone else had died. Bisrat did not find the strength to call, and four years later it is still difficult for her to relate the memory of staying silent in her narrative about the disaster.

Neither Bisrat nor Solomon talks about regret or shame in the sense of feeling guilt about one's own actions or inaction during the disaster. Their feelings are not about the guilt of culpability. Shame is a self-conscious feeling as well as a social emotion (Shapiro 2003, 1134). Both Solomon and Bisrat describe their difficult feelings in the context of becoming aware of themselves and their condition *in relation to others*. Bisrat regrets her survival when she becomes aware that her friends and family have died. Solomon postpones calling when he imagines the moment he would need to report who died. Shame emerges particularly at the moment of the phone call, and the memory of this difficult moment continues to haunt them four years later. The emotion of shame requires exposure and visibility, appearing before another and before oneself. To feel ashamed is to be a spectator of oneself. One imagines and evaluates oneself and one's humanity. Shame is not about the fear of being found guilty for one's actions.

It is not surprising that regret, shame, and memories of ethically complex situations appear in the testimonies of all four of the interviewed Lampedusa survivors. In fact, difficult emotions such as shame and guilt are also central in Holocaust survival testimonies and in the literature on surviving the concentration camps. "Guilt is a locus classicus of literature on the camps," Giorgio Agamben (1999, 89) argues in *Remnants of Auschwitz*. For Buchenwald survivor Bruno Bettelheim, survival does not mean merely staying alive but transforming as a person through "the ability to feel guilty" (1976, 34). In his *New Yorker* essay "Surviving," Bettelheim argues that guilt is "a most significant aspect of survivorship" (1976, 45) and states that "one cannot survive the concentration camp without feeling guilty that one was so incredibly lucky when millions perished, many of them in front of one's eyes" (1976, 45). Bettelheim also refers to scholarship on the survivors of the bombing of Hiroshima, suggesting that Bettelheim believes that guilt at having survived is a common condition among survivors of an event resulting in mass death.

Primo Levi also identifies the emotions of guilt and shame as central for survival. Like other concentration camp survivors, Levi speaks of guilt and shame rather interchangeably. Discussion as to the difference between these two emotions in concentration camp experiences appears only later in academic literature examining survivor testimonies (see Agamben 1999; Shapiro 2003; Leys 2007). Primo Levi (1988, 72–73) maintains that it is "absurd" and "paradoxical" that shame was so common among the survivors of the camps because rationally, those who felt it knew that they had not caused the cruelty. In pointing out this absurdity, Levi recognizes that the feeling of shame does not require wrongful action.

In the context of the violent border of Europe, the perpetrators of violence are external to the scene. But even if they had been on the scene, capable of taking action to stop the cruelty or choosing not to do anything, the feeling of shame would nonetheless be unavailable to them. Shame is an emotion shared by those who witness events but are not directly implicated in them. David Shapiro argues that subjugation, the inability to resist, and feelings of helplessness are reasons for shame in the context of experiencing or witnessing violence. Those who were rescued in Lampedusa feel ashamed of their survival because they witnessed mass death from a position in which there was very little they could do for others.

To some extent, the same can be said about those who witnessed the disaster through mediation. Pope Francis's "*vergogna*" and its echoes in the headlines of European newspapers and across the global media (discussed in chapter 1) were not the confessions of people who identified as perpetrators or felt culpable of mass death. Shame in the context of mediated witnessing can mean two things. First, shame can be understood as "shame on you," a shaming of those responsible for Europe's migration policy and for producing the violent border. Second, the mediated witnesses may be announcing their own feeling of shame, which triggers a response inspired by a sense of responsibility toward what is taking place in the Mediterranean. Attentiveness to one's own self-interest in the structures and practices that produce violent bordering is connected to this type of shame. In chapter 6, I discussed the shocking feeling of shame felt by Dresden activists when they realized how easy it was to ignore news about border deaths. The emotion of shame demands that one act upon the wrong, despite a lack of direct or personal involvement. Thus, shame is intrinsic to attentive citizenship. Through mediation, one has entered the scene, become aware of the violent border, and understands that one is implicated through being a citizen of Europe.

In *The Drowned and the Saved*, Primo Levi says that the emotion of liberation from the camps was shame, not joy (Levi 1988, 70–72). Levi devotes an entire essay in his book to the topic of shame, expounding on a scene in which Russian soldiers arrive to liberate the prisoners in Auschwitz. This perspective reveals that shame is primarily an emotion felt while witnessing violence that is being done or has been done by others.

> It was the same shame which we knew so well, which submerged us after the selections, and every time we had to witness or undergo an outrage: the shame that the Germans never knew, the shame which the just man experiences when confronted by a crime committed by another, and he feels remorse because of its existence, because of its having been irrevocably introduced into the world of existing things, and because his will has proven nonexistent or feeble and was incapable of putting up a good defense. (Levi 1988, 72–73)

There are four important aspects of the shame of survival in this memory that help us to think about survival in Lampedusa. First, the feeling of shame that was familiar to the camp survivors due to their position as witnesses during prisoner selections arose again at liberation. Though the survivors in Lampedusa saw other people drown, it was only after their rescue that they felt shame. The emotion emerged when they became aware of who had died and had to start making phone calls.

Second, in Levi's memory, shame is related to the inability to act upon wrong-doing. The prisoners could not prevent the selections and liberating soldiers who arrived in the camps could not immediately remove the harm that had been done to the prisoners. In Lampedusa, the inability to help others—for example, to share the water bottle or even to give hope, as Adhanom recalled—created complicated emotions, including shame.

Third, Levi describes what "the just man experiences when confronted by a crime committed by another." He refers to the prisoners who were capable of feeling shame as "just men." They had not done anything to cause the crime whose consequences they were witnessing. This aspect differs from the scene in Lampedusa, as I have discussed earlier. In Lampedusa, the perpetrators were invisible and unidentifiable. The sea was the apparent killer. There were no identifiable unjust actors at the scene of the disaster, no actors whose conscious cruelty one could witness and feel ashamed about. Agency is far removed from the scene of violence in Lampedusa. The European policy makers and the Italian authorities, the coast guard that arrived too late, and any other actors who might have done something to prevent the disaster are external to how the scene of the disaster is perceived. Khaled Bensalem, the Tunisian "captain" of the boat who was sentenced to eighteen years in prison in Sicily, is the only individual that the Italian authorities identified as a perpetrator. It was only due to human rights lawyers and activists who took the crew of a Sicilian fishing vessel *Aristeus* to the court in a civil case, that resulted in seven fishermen receiving sentences of five to eight years in prison for failing to provide assistance or notify authorities about a boat in distress (Tribunale di Agrigento 2020, 3–4). All others implicated in the disaster seem more like "just men."

Fourth, Levi argues that shame is social and connected to exposure. One sees the horror and one's seeing is seen by others. One is aware of oneself as a spectator. Through seeing, the horror of the crimes committed by another joins the "existing things" of one's world. This insight expressed in the famous quote above is also central in the context of survival after Lampedusa. The scene of mass death in Lampedusa introduced something previously inconceivable to the "world of existing things" among many of the survivors. Life and the world as the survivors knew them were ruptured. Afterward, they needed to create a new self and a new form of belonging in the world.

Seeing death with one's own eyes is one thing, but having to tell about it is another, as Bisrat's and Solomon's difficulty with the phone calls demonstrates. Survivors became a particular type of witness in Lampedusa. Their sense of responsibility for bearing witness, to tell what happened and who died, was far-ranging. As I described in chapter 3, immediately after the disaster, the survivors began collecting the names of the dead. They remembered the dead in a Facebook group, they collected photographs of the dead to produce a postcard and a poster (for the memorial in Piazza Piave), and they demanded rights for the dead in commemorative rituals in Lampedusa.

Arguably, this sense of survival can be extended to other categories of witnessing as well, beyond the immediate category of flesh witnesses. Lampedusans who chanced upon the disaster scene, the locals who managed the dead bodies, and the Sicilians who buried the dead were eyewitnesses of the corporeality of the disaster (as discussed in chapters 4 and 5). Mediated witnesses across Italy, Europe, and beyond encountered the disaster from a distance through television, photographs, and reading the news. Many felt shame that prompted them to respond. Memorialization and the alternative forms of representation that I've examined throughout this book are examples of responses that grew out of a sense of shame and responsibility that were felt after facing the mediated representation of the disaster.

Survival as a Shared Process: Awareness and Recognition

The testimonies gathered by Adal Neguse reveal a transformation from victim not yet in a position to bear witness, to survivor with the capacity and responsibility to bear witness. So far, I have focused on the experience and meaning of survival, which is clearly a process. Is there something between the state of being a victim, alive but naked in the water, not sure whether one will stay alive, and the state of being a survivor who has reestablished one's self and one's full human life? Adhanom reflects on the shift from victim to a liminal state of not-yet-survivor in his memory of being rescued by a coast guard search and rescue ship:

> They placed us on the deck, and we saw the dead bodies floating everywhere. They covered us with foil blankets, and it felt good. It was good to see other people being rescued, too. But when we saw the dead in the sea, we started to cry. Everyone was crying, yelling. Some called for their loved ones. You felt like diving back into the sea to join those you lost, but you had no strength to do that. Thank God so many were rescued.

Adhanom's emotions during the rescue were ambiguous: the moment he knew he had stayed alive and saw others being rescued felt good. Simultaneously, however, he and the others who had been rescued started to cry. He would have gone back into the sea with the dead, if only he had had the strength. Adhanom had not yet fully survived. He felt the urge to join the dead, not yet to do something in the name of the dead, as Bisrat described the sense of her survivorship.

On the coast guard vessel's deck, Adhanom was still at the boundary between life and death, although now more on the side of life. In the water, the boundary had been less obvious: "I wasn't sure I would make it." On the deck, he was alive physically, but not yet socially or politically; he was not yet participating in the common world. Survival was not guaranteed. He was still partly a victim, naked, covered in foil, unable to participate in the activity around him or even to jump into the water. For Adhanom, four years after the disaster, seeing the scene from these two positions creates a complex memory. There is, on the one hand, the promise of a future where he can live on, bear witness, and act responsibly in respect to what he has experienced and seen. On the other hand, he is still a victim, not yet a survivor, who wishes to join the dead.

Transformation from victim to almost-survivor is central to Adhanom's narration of survival. He underlines the blurriness and ambiguity of survival, describing a process between death and life. The position of witnessing is important: from the deck, wrapped in foil and having reached physical safety, Adhanom and a few others are able to see the disaster in the water. Nevertheless, being on deck is not yet a position he can feel completely good about. I have seen no images of half-naked survivors wrapped in foil on the crowded deck of the coast guard vessel among those circulated by the survivors. News photographs of the coffins arranged at the hangar, mobile phone photos of commemorative rituals and posed groups of survivors, and images of Lampedusan rescuers are the themes most commonly shared and posted as Facebook profile pictures. These pictures represent survivorship. Representations of the state of almost-survivorship are not publicly disseminated. It seems not to be a state that survivors want to publicly identify with.

I was therefore a bit puzzled when I noticed in Lampedusa in 2018 that a couple of survivors and Vito Fiorino and some other Lampedusan civil rescuers were wearing identical black T-shirts with a photo of Vito's boat, *Gamar*, approaching Lampedusa's harbor. Below the photo was a text that read "LAMPEDUSA 3/10/2013." In the photo, the *Gamar* was overfilled with people, the forty-seven rescued and the eight rescuers. A member of the crew stands on the roof, wearing only shorts or swimming trunks. Ambasager told me that he and Amanuel printed the shirts to honor Vito's first visit to Stockholm earlier that year. When they arrived in Lampedusa later that year, they gave similar shirts to the other seven rescuers who had been on the boat. Ambasager and Amanuel chose the image from a USB stick Fiorino had given them during an earlier visit to Lampedusa. The stick had a collection of hundreds of photographs of the disaster and its aftermath that Fiorino had received from press photographers.

If Adhanom's experience on the coast guard vessel was so unsettling, why were Ambasager and Amanuel eager to display a photograph of a similar situation on their T-shirts? One explanation is that Adhanom has not had a chance to know the coast guard men in the way that Ambasager and Amanuel have created a familiar relationship with Fiorino and his friends. The matching T-shirts symbolized and reinforced the unity between the rescuers and the rescued. In the photograph, they arrive at the port together. They are not two completely separate groups of people. The rescued are not covered in foil, making them appear otherworldly as those on the coast guard ship were. They wear swimsuits or have towels wrapped around them; some have shirts that the rescuers have given them to wear. Similarly, the rescuers are also only partially clothed. Their relationship is already at that moment of arrival less distant than the one between the coast guard and the rescued.

The two different groups of actors in the scene of arrival to the port depicted on the T-shirts are united through a shared experience of their world being shattered by a previously inconceivable horror. The shame of having seen mass death connects the rescuers and the rescued. While they are different types of witnesses—the Lampedusans' lives were not threatened—they share the position of primary witnesses of a scene of mass death. The matching T-shirts signify this shared experience and the familial relationships that developed after the rescue—those who wear the T-shirts are a family. The gesture of giving the T-shirts five years after the disaster demonstrates how survival is a shared process, not only among the rescued, but also between the rescued and the civil rescuers. The image in the shirt and the fact that both rescuers and rescued wore the shirts for the commemoration represents mutual recognition.

In *The Origins of Totalitarianism* (2017), Hannah Arendt wrote about the centrality of recognition to survival: it is not only up to an individual to acquire the capacity to participate in the common world when others have the capacity to prevent one from participating. Arendt's perspective was the political life, and she demonstrated how participation in it is not necessarily accessible to every human being. Practices of differentiation render some people into the abstract nakedness of being human in the sense of being alive physically but not otherwise: "They begin to belong to the human race in much the same way as animals belong to a specific animal species" (Arendt 2017, 395). Stateless people and the prisoners in the extermination camps exemplified for Arendt the great danger of being nothing but human. Only through citizenship, granted by a sovereign nation-state, could one become a political subject with rights. And only through others' recognition of one's profession, opinions, identity, and unique individuality could they become significant as persons in society and recognized as part of "the common world" (Arendt 2017, 395).

While Arendt's perspective is on a larger scale, recognition at the level of individual encounter was significant in the process of transforming from a victim to a survivor. The story about the T-shirt illustrates this. For Amanuel, giving the

T-shirt to Fiorino had a personal significance as well. When I first met Amanuel at a restaurant in Lampedusa in 2017, he was looking forward to meeting Fiorino and wondered if he would remember him. "Does he remember how he took off his shirt and gave it to me when I was naked?" Amanuel said. He shared this memory with me and wanted to recall it again when he met Fiorino. It was a gesture of humanity and a moment of recognition as an individual, a person, that was meaningful for him. In Fiorino's eyes, Amanuel was a man with dignity in need of clothing, not an anonymous, naked victim. Fiorino recognized him as a person, as a participant in the common world. Fiorino had written a message on the back of the shirt, "something like a wish for a good life," Amanuel told me. He kept the shirt but later lost it when he left the reception center in Sicily to continue his journey to Sweden. Fiorino and Amanuel recalled the story of the shirt again when I had dinner with them later in 2018 in a Greek restaurant in a suburb of Stockholm. Fiorino touched Amanuel's cheek and said, "But you have had a good life!"

The Return as a Reflection of Survival

When I read the translations of Adal's interviews with Adhanom, Bisrat, Solomon, and Yusef I was dazed how I had not read or heard much about the experience of surviving disasters at Europe's borders. I had analyzed mediated representations of the phenomenon, also before the October 3, 2013, disaster. During my research on the Lampedusa disaster, I had collected a catalogue of more than fifty cultural productions—films, plays, literature, artworks, journalism—that connected with the disaster. The experience of the survivors' process of survival was largely missing. The three dimensions of the process of survival that emerged in Adal's interviews and during my conversations with the survivors—survival as a new life, survival as a capacity to feel shame, and survival as a mutual recognition—were not topics that interested those who told stories about the disaster.

From journalistic productions to works of film, literature, and theater that touch on the October 3 disaster, the dominating theme of mediated representations is the experience of the Lampedusans. European cultural producers are fascinated by what is seen as the archaic morality of the people of Lampedusa, who live in a place imagined to be at the periphery of Europe, still innocent and pure. One explanation for the lack of attention to the process of survival may be that most European artists created their cultural productions soon after the disaster. Because the experience of survival beyond staying alive takes time, it had not yet become relevant at the time when most of the cultural representations were made. In addition, while memorialization opens a space for the public performance of survivor citizenship, such rituals do not center on the experience of survival. Rather, they focus on the rights of other potential victims.

I found three instances in the literature and film on migration and Lampedusa in which reflection on a survivor's sense of self appears in some interesting form. The island of Lampedusa as a site of self-reflection is a central theme in Zakaria Mohamed Ali's short film *To Whom It May Concern* (2013). Zakaria, a Somalian Italian journalist, arrived in Europe via Lampedusa in 2008, and in returning to Lampedusa he demonstrates that though he was once treated as a nonperson at the border, he is now able to return as a "free man," as Zakaria puts it. In the film, he returns to the gate of the Lampedusa reception center and questions those working for the border regime. "Do you know where they threw my friend's wedding photo?" he demands. The guards' complete ignorance and nonunderstanding of his questions reveal to the viewer how irrelevant asylum seekers' social and cultural lives are to the border system and how they are treated as mere physical beings. Wedding photographs or school certificates that Zakaria asks for mean nothing at the border. To return to Lampedusa as a "free man" is to demonstrate one's transformation from a passive and anonymous victim to a survivor with a remade self.

In 2015, I met Zakaria in Rome to discuss his film. Lampedusa is not just a border that he crossed, he told me. It is also a place where he transformed. It was a moral test to return to the island and think about what he has become. Zakaria explained, "Lampedusa is the place where you finally feel free. It's the place where you call your family. You start your life. You think about what you were, what you will become, what you will become after Lampedusa." It is a place to be haunted by one's future ghost.

Italian author Davide Enia's (2017) book *Notes on a Shipwreck* has a strong focus on the October 3 disaster as Enia arrives in Lampedusa with the disaster on his mind and on the minds of the locals he interviews. His book centers on the experience of Lampedusans as they witness and respond to the October 3 disaster, one of many migrant disasters they have witnessed. While he does not meet any survivors of the October 3 disaster, Enia writes briefly about an encounter with an Eritrean refugee named Bemnet at a beach in Lampedusa. Bemnet has returned to Lampedusa twice since he was rescued by the Italian coast guard in 2009. Enia retells Bemnet's horror at witnessing his fellow travelers' deaths at sea and how while on the migrant boat that was floating for days, seeing the others die one by one, he tried to memorize the names of the dead. Enia frames Bemnet's horror as the result of the ignorance of the European authorities. Bemnet testifies that while at sea they encountered Maltese coastguardsmen, who instead of rescuing them steered them into Italian waters and left them there. The scene ends with what Lampedusa means to Bemnet.

"I touched dry land on August 20. That day became my second birthday. I was reborn here." Twenty-one days of shipwreck.

Eighty of them set out.

Seventy-five of them died.

"I don't know why I survived. I'm one of the last five who saw these
people alive and yet, if I went back to my village, I really wouldn't
know how to tell the story of their death. I was only seventeen years
old."

Bemnet pointed to the sea.

"All my friends are out there."

He said nothing more.

(Excerpt from Davide Enia's *Notes on a Shipwreck*,
2017, 158, translated by Antony Shugaar[1])

Through Bemnet's story, Enia shows Lampedusa to be not only the place where
Bemnet was reborn, but also the place to which he returns to remember the dead
so he can continue to live on in his new life. The "return" depicted in both Davide
Enia's book and Zakaria Mohamed Ali's film forges a contrast between the temporal ground zero of the disaster and the new present. Returning to Lampedusa,
where the sea is visible from almost everywhere, survivors are moved to reflect
on who they have become in their new lives.

The third example is related to the interviews Adal did with Bisrat, Adhanom, Solomon, and Yusef that I have examined in this chapter. The ethical
complexity of survival and the remaking of the self that these four testimonies
bring to the surface are themes represented in the documentary film series
Remembering Lampedusa that Adal Neguse and Anna Blom directed and
edited on the basis of these survivor testimonies. Central in the film project is
the role of Adal as the listener to whom the survivors tell their stories. Each of
the survivors became friends with Adal during anniversary commemorations
of the disaster in Lampedusa. The return to Lampedusa and the space of reflection it provides has been important in cultivating trust and closeness with Adal.
His motivation to know about the disaster is personal: his younger brother died
in the disaster, and in listening to the four different stories, he proceeds in his
own process of surviving his brother. The return to Lampedusa is also a point
of personal reflection for Adal. In chapter 9, I discuss in more detail the meaning of survival for the relatives of victims. The testimonies in *Remembering
Lampedusa* are shaped in part by the fact that Adal wanted to know about the
event for his own survival of the loss. The disaster had a singular meaning for
Adal—it was not merely a symbol of thousands more deaths at the border, or
of the phenomenon of border death in the Mediterranean. For him, listening

was a means of living on with the loss of his younger brother Abraham, and this connected him intimately with the survivors.

Literature on testimony, such as the work of Shoshana Felman and Dori Laub, emphasizes the role of the listener (Felman and Laub 1992, 70; Felman 1991; see also Brison 2002, 46). Adal and his follow-up questions are pivotal in teasing out memories of difficult and paradoxical emotions as is evident in the quotes of the interviews in this chapter. The ambiguous and complex figure of a survivor that appears through these testimonies and in the documentary films is not visible in European news representations of the disaster (which are discussed in chapters 1, 2, and 3). It is also not visible in public memorializations, where the political subject—the survivor-citizen—is prominent (as discussed in chapter 7). The ambiguous figure of a survivor who holds contradictory memories of shame and self-respect, care and indifference, is a figure that is challenging to listen to. The framing of a hero that can be celebrated or a victim that can be protected is easier for different publics—such as "European" or Eritrean diasporic—to relate to.

The essential elements of the interview setting that made the survivor testimonies possible were the survivors' willingness to speak and the testimonies' "joint, participatory context that assured both confidence and empathic listening," as Triulzi (2013, 215–17) described similar work undertaken by the Archive of Migrant Memories in Rome (see also Gatta 2019). Adal had created relationships with the four survivors both while in Lampedusa for commemorations and in Sweden, where he assisted many of the survivors in their new lives. In addition, Solomon remembered Adal from the days following the disaster, when Adal had traveled to Lampedusa to search for his brother, who had been traveling alone. None of the survivors had had contact information for Abraham's relatives, so they had been unable to call.

The memory of seeing Adal searching for his brother among the survivors appears in Solomon's testimony, demonstrating how bearing witness is a process that includes the listener. After describing his difficulty calling his brother to tell him he had survived, Solomon is reminded of Adal searching for his brother with a photograph in his hand: "And then, soon after, you came with your brother's photo. I felt your emotion so strongly, and I saw my brother in you. We should forget, but honestly, this is what I always remember. When I remember my brother, I remember you and your brother." Solomon returns to the issue of forgetting: survival is both remembering and forgetting. The pain of loss that was so evident in the figure of Adal, holding his brother's photograph, is what Solomon wants to forget in order to survive in his new life. And yet the image is simultaneously what he needs to remember.

In this chapter, I have examined how survivors describe their experience of staying alive when most of the other passengers on the boat died. As one outcome of the collaborative work of testimony undertaken by the survivors and Adal, I have presented three important insights about survival. First, survival is a process that develops in stages and involves a remaking of oneself and life. Second, the capacity to reflect on ethically unstable events and deal with difficult emotions, namely shame, is crucial in the process of survival. Third, the process of survival is social: relationships and mutual recognition among the survivors and with different other types of witnesses are important.

Staying alive is merely the first stage in the process of survival in the fullest sense of the term. Survival does not mean simply remaining physically alive, although that is of course necessary for the making of a politically and socially meaningful life. The process of surviving a disaster at the border begins from the state of victim at the borderline between physical life and death, not sure if one can make it.

At the point when Adal and I talked with the survivors about their experiences, they were in a position from which they could reflect on the disaster and their survival. They had achieved a legal status and established their lives in Sweden and organized trips to Lampedusa to commemorate. They had jobs and children who had been born since the disaster. They had learned Swedish and created a foundation for their new lives and new selves. They were part of the world in which they lived. They had achieved survival through acting upon the world. However, as their narratives demonstrate, survival is not a condition that can be taken for granted once one has achieved it. Solomon mentions twice that he needs to continuously work on both remembering and forgetting. Living with love and sympathy is crucial for Bisrat's survival and is a continuous practice in her daily life. Survival is living, constantly becoming a participant in the world. However, this transition from victim to survivor is not an immediate shift. Before full survival, before being capable of participating in the common world, there is the liminal state of almost-survivor, in which one is alive but not yet capable of acting upon the world.

These insights on survival required listening and being present with those who survived the disaster, in the full meaning of the term *survived*. The empathic listening context that was created over four years of regular meetings in Lampedusa and Stockholm was central to being able to hear the survivors' memories and reflections. Bisrat, Adhanom, Solomon, and Yusef, who narrated their memories in Tigrinya-language conversations with Adal, as well as Ambasager and Amanuel, with whom I conversed in Swedish and English multiple times during this research, were all motivated to discuss, to recall, and to think through what the disaster has meant in the course of their lives since. This perspective illuminates how the consequences of disasters haunt all of us in Europe, including those of us who have witnessed the disasters only through mediation. Survivors continue their lives in our common society in Europe. Their memories of the disaster and experiences of survival live on with them, and because they are Europeans, these processes are the concern of everyone in Europe.

I have argued in this chapter that shame is not necessarily a passivizing emotion. Shame can generate a new self and prompt a new kind of action on the world. The acts of citizenship prompted by shame can also involve other emotions, such as anger, that are more clearly channeled toward demanding rights and calls for taking responsibility. Love and care, in contrast, connect different actors as participants in the same world and generate a form of relational citizenship based on attentiveness to others, both dead and alive. When visible, the emotion of shame felt by the survivors can make those more distant from the scene of the disaster reflect on their own emotions as well. Mediated witnesses can also feel shame, and shame can connect different kinds of witnesses in action to prevent similar events from happening again.

The survivors of the October 3 disaster with whom I have collaborated in this research are not victims: they have proceeded from that position by actively participating in the world around them. They are also not heroes to be celebrated. Both of these representations reduce a person to a singular aspect. This analysis of survival has demonstrated a nonreductive understanding of those who have lived on and made their new lives in Italy, Germany, the Netherlands, Denmark, Norway, or Sweden. Attention to their survival ensures they can be recognized in Europe as participants in the common world—as humans, in all of our complexity, ambiguity, and uncertainty. Understanding survival through the lens of attentiveness is therefore central in the critical process of transforming the violent border of Europe. It is central in the thinking and actions that aim to ensure that such disasters are no longer created. Achieving the capacity to participate in the world is not only the responsibility of those on the path to survival—it is the responsibility of everyone.

SURVIVING THE DEATH OF ANOTHER

In the preceding chapters, I analyzed how and why the Lampedusa disaster survived oblivion in the domains of memorialization and representation. Individuals and communities in Lampedusa, Sicily, and beyond—in Germany and elsewhere in Europe—have acted out of responsibility and engaged with the disaster's memory. They have created memorials and rituals, and represented the events in plays, poems, journalism, songs, and visual images. In this way, they have continued to live on after the rupture caused by witnessing the mass death. In chapters 7 and 8, I discussed how shaping memorializations and representations has also been important in the process of survival among those who survived the disaster. The effects of the rupture differ in terms of their severity for different communities, producing afterlives of the Lampedusa disaster. They have continued to shape the individuals and communities that witnessed it, whether as flesh witnesses, eyewitnesses, or mediated witnesses. The disaster's afterlives serve both therapeutic and instrumental functions, and the process of survival has produced identities, relationships, and politics.

Survival figures into the afterlife of the disaster in one additional important way: as surviving the death of another. This book has defined survival as a continuation of life, as living on or beyond a rupture. Surviving a loved one requires surviving the end of a relationship and continuing life in a new constellation of relationships and identities. As the phenomenologist Claude Romano argues, the death of another "has the sense of an event that happens to the survivors; it is a phenomenon that is shared by those who remain" (2009, 115). According to

Romano, the death of a person is a fact that becomes an "event" through the experience of the living. The literature scholar Colin Davis (2007, 116–17) reaches a similar argument by examining Emmanuel Levinas's lectures on death. For Levinas, relationships with others play a constitutive role in one's own existence; in death, the self is the *survivor* of the death of the other. "Death is, after all, a relation with the other," Davis (2007, 116) writes. In this chapter, I focus on this aspect of survival—living beyond the death of a loved one in the specific context of border deaths.

Thinking of death as something that happens to the living and dead as others who continue to "impinge on the world of the living" as Davis (2007, 116) puts it, means that the duration and the intensity of the experience of death of another varies. Death is not a sudden occurrence, but "a transitory state of a certain duration" (Hertz 2018, 31). As Robert Hertz wrote:

> The image of the recently deceased is still part of the system of things of this world, and loses itself from them only gradually by a series of internal partings. We cannot bring ourselves to consider the deceased as dead straight away: he is too much part of our substance, we have put too much of ourselves into him, and participation in the same social life creates ties which are not to be severed in one day. (Hertz 2018, 31)

Romano's examination of bereavement focuses on intimate experiences and the transformation of the self. However, death is also fundamentally a social phenomenon—it transforms relationships and the social fabric that is constituted in those relationships (Hertz 2018; O'Rourke 2007). Sharing the experience of death with others who remain is a crucial element of surviving the death of another. The transformation of relationships that necessarily results from a person's death requires social markings of transitions—what the ethnographer Arnold van Gennep (2019) termed "rites of passage."

On the one hand, death as a social and individual phenomenon is a universal experience. Death of a person who was part of our life is always to some extent ambiguous, a question mark, a surprise that haunts the living (Davis 2007, 117). On the other hand, however, it is fundamentally conditioned by the particular facts of the death. Death at Europe's border is a specific way of dying, and therefore those who survive the border death of a loved one share a certain sense of death as an event that is not shared by those who survive a loss resulting from another kind of death.

During my research at cemeteries in Sicily, in diasporic online spaces, and among Eritrean European families in Sweden, the United Kingdom, and Germany, I encountered vernacular and creative responses to border deaths that revealed the specificity of these deaths for friends and relatives of the deceased. In this chapter, I focus on the interconnected elements of uncertainty that make border deaths specific. First, I examine two cases in which relatives living in Europe were able to definitively identify their loved one. I contrast these cases to the ambiguous loss of disappearance and discuss border deaths in the context of other situations of disappearance and mass death globally. I then follow Teddy (a pseudonym) as he travels from Hamburg to Sicily to search for his brother's grave to illustrate how he creates and performs death rituals in the crossroads of various uncertainties. Finally, I share Semhar Ghebreselassie's experience in Eritrea, where families found a way to mourn without bodies after having received news of the deaths. These experiences show how even in the exceptional case of the Lampedusa disaster, in which many, if not all, of the dead were retrieved, families still had to invent death rituals. They relied on their communities and on vernacular knowledge when the institutions and organizations that were meant to secure the rights of the relatives of the dead failed.

"It Is Not the Same"

I spent October 3, 2016, in London with two sisters, Helen and Genet (pseudonyms), whose brother had died in the Lampedusa disaster. Helen was then in her thirties and had two children. Ten years earlier, she had arrived in Italy from Libya in a smuggler's boat. She had been on her way to the United States with false papers, but ended up staying in the United Kingdom, where she married a fellow Eritrean refugee whom she had first met in Libya. Her sister Genet was in her twenties and had just recently migrated to the United Kingdom after years in Uganda. She was studying to become a health care professional and living with her sister's family. While we enjoyed the long Eritrean coffee-making ritual, videos, edited pictures, poems, and messages continued to appear in the two women's social media accounts. They referenced not only the Lampedusa disaster, but deaths and disappearances during migration journeys in general. October 3 had become an unofficial day of remembrance for the Eritrean diaspora.

Helen told me about the days after the disaster in 2013 when they were unsure if their brother had been on the boat. She described how the survivors had told them he had died, and how one of the siblings had done a DNA test and interview to identify the body in Italy. All of this was difficult for the family, particularly because they had given in to his desire to follow them to Europe and paid the smugglers for his trip. They had tried to persuade him to be patient and wait for refugee resettlement, but he would not stay longer in Ethiopia.

Helen dressed in black for two months after the disaster, and in the first weeks, her Eritrean and Ethiopian friends in the United Kingdom came to console her. They brought food and prayed and cried with her, typical Habesha mourning practices that remained important in the diaspora. A bereaved family is never left alone, Helen told me. When someone dies, friends and community participate in mourning and in organizing the funeral. It is not necessary to have known the person you mourn. Linda Lystig Holt (2001), in a study of Christian Eritreans and Ethiopians in the United States, has shown how the rhythm of mourning and the unrestrained expression of grief are important for the community. The emotions that are shared reflect the stages of the mourning process: mourning starts with crying and screaming together, but can end in happiness, giving a sense of closure (Holt 2001, 150).

After the mourning period, Helen wanted to control where and when she mourned, but found this difficult. Migrant disasters seemed to enter her daily life via television and her smartphone at unexpected moments. Helen changed the television channel if migrant disasters were in the news. She held her phone at arm's length as she demonstrated to me how for months after the disaster, she was afraid she might see a photograph of her brother or something related to the disaster in her social media feed.

At some point, I told Helen about losing my younger brother, who had died of a brain tumor in 2012, just days after his thirty-fifth birthday. Memories of him had kept returning to me in my everyday life, and I was afraid I would suddenly cry when something reminded me of him. Helen was empathetic but said: "It's not the same." I had heard this response before. During my research, I had often felt the need to share my own experience of loss when asking other people to tell me about theirs and had often received a similar comment in reply.

It was obvious that the circumstances leading to the early deaths of Helen's brother and my brother were not the same. But this was not what Helen really meant. Our conversation had not been about the circumstances of the death or why it had happened, but about mourning, death rituals, and managing the emotion of grief. Her point was about living with the loss, about surviving the death of another, a death that was different from other deaths. This specificity continued to perplex me: why did Helen think surviving her brother's death was unique, different in some way than surviving other deaths?

The Uncertainty of Border Deaths

The complicated specificity of families' experiences in the context of border deaths directed me to the issue of survival—not of surviving the disaster itself, but of surviving a loss and the disruption of a relationship. Parents, siblings, children, spouses, and friends survive the death of another person. For those who knew the dead, the afterlife of the disaster is about living on without that relationship and losing the part of oneself that existed within that relationship. As Romano says, "if bereavement is . . . an unparalleled event that strikes me in the heart like no other and upends me most intimately, this is because this event is a matter of my selfhood" (2009, 120). Death at the border is not only a physical event, but a social one that affects those connected to the dead person, as any death does. However, it is also a specific death, unlike any other.

Border deaths are a specific kind of death because of two interwoven elements of uncertainty that expand the temporality of the event. First, the context of migration creates various ambiguities. Entering Europe without documents has been criminalized, which can complicate sharing the experience of surviving the death of a relative in the community in which one lives. In the context of Eritreans, the additional criminalization of exiting Eritrea shapes how border deaths are perceived in Eritrea and the diaspora. Sacrificial citizenship (Bernal 2014, 7, 27–29), according to which Eritreans are expected to sacrifice their lives for the nation, complicates how the deaths of those who made an illegal exit are perceived. Furthermore, family members in Europe have often paid for migrants' journeys and set an example of migration. Those remaining in Eritrea might have hoped the migration of their family member would bring them remittances. The role of peers and family members in Eritreans' migration decisions has been demonstrated in the literature (Ayalew Mengiste 2018; Belloni 2019).

Second, uncertainties related to death rituals and accessing the dead body also make border deaths a specific kind of death. Often, dead bodies are not retrieved from the sea. If a body is retrieved, identification procedures are rarely successful. The Deaths at the Borders database (Last 2015) shows that almost two-thirds of the people found dead at the southern EU border from 1990 to 2013 have not been identified by the local authorities charged with investigating their deaths. The lack of identification suggests that for European authorities, unknown bodies categorized as "migrant bodies" remain simply victims, without a persona. As I discussed in chapters 1 and 2, the humanitarian framework prevailed in the representation of the disaster. In the words of the Italian president, Giorgio Napolitano, the disaster was "a massacre of innocents" (Breda 2013). Seeing the migrant bodies as victims alone fits the humanitarian framework, which contents itself with anonymous burials. In another sense, however, even migrant dead bodies are categorized bureaucratically as "missing persons," meaning that their identities are a puzzle that needs attention.

The Lampedusa disaster became a pilot case in which the Italian state attempted to use the identification procedures that apply in other mass disasters where citizens die or disappear (about these procedures in Italy before 2013 and after, see Grotti and Brightman 2021). DNA samples were taken, physical attributes were recorded, and clothes and other material objects were collected as evidence of identity. These processes and "forensic care work" (M'charek and Casartelli 2019) have not been very successful, however. Only thirty-one of the 366 bodies retrieved after the Lampedusa disaster have been scientifically identified by 2018 (Olivieri et al. 2018, 125). Despite the use of Interpol's Disaster Victim Identification (Interpol 2021) protocol and attempts to "reinvent forensics anew" (Cattaneo quoted in M'charek and Casartelli 2019, 739), obstacles to identification remain, including the collection of antemortem data that only the living relatives of victims can provide (Piscitelli and Cattaneo 2016; Piscitelli et al. 2016; Romano 2016, 11; Olivieri et al. 2018). Though international organizations, activists, and governments have launched additional projects and committees since 2013, the low success rate of identification remains an issue (e.g., ICMP 2021; Nuovi Desaparecidos 2021).

When a body is not found, or is found but not identified and named, a person disappears (Kobelinsky 2017; Schindel 2020). That this is the most common outcome in the case of border deaths reflects how those who disappear were "already missing, displaced from their established location and without documentation or recognition by the authorities" (Edkins 2016, 369). They are not missing from the polis where they were found, however, and so, in many cases, authorities pay less attention to their identification and systematic burial than they would in the case of their "own" missing persons (Grant 2016, 33–35; Kovras and Robins 2017, 167).

After the disaster in Lampedusa, the survivors compiled a list of the dead for the purpose of informing their families (see chapter 3), sparing them the burden of not knowing if their relative was alive or dead. They also visually identified bodies. In 2020 and 2021, Adhanom began to systematically visit cemeteries in Sicily with other survivors to locate graves so that relatives would be able to find them based on the number assigned to a body. These acts were born of survivors' sense of responsibility toward the victims' families and their civic duty. Eritrean transnational families in general have firsthand experience of, or know of someone who suffers from, the disappearance of a loved one. This knowledge informed the survivors; disappearance was the condition they feared most (Kasim 2017).

Some of the survivors and relatives who were able to come to Lampedusa were able to identify the deceased from photographs of the dead bodies: 184 people were identified through such visual methods (Piscitelli and Cattaneo 2016, 44). In these cases, the number assigned to the body is known, and the grave can be located by asking other survivors and family members who have visited the cemeteries. As of 2018, only thirty-one families had received a death certificate based on DNA identification (Olivieri et al. 2018, 125). While many of the dead were related to survivors or had relatives in Europe, they were not necessarily full siblings or biological children or parents. At the time of the disaster, DNA technology was not sensitive enough to identify cousins or half-siblings (Parsons 2019). The numbers—the 366 names of the dead, 184 visual identifications, and 31 scientific identifications—reveal that various degrees of certainty and uncertainty remain, even in this atypical border disaster in which so many bodies were retrieved.

Repatriation of the Dead

The Eritrean Italian priest and human rights activist Father Mussie Zerai (2019) explained to me that for both Orthodox Christian and Muslim Eritreans, the dead body and its dignified treatment are central in death and funeral rituals. Many in the Eritrean diaspora prefer to send remains back to Eritrea for burial, and this was what Mussie and the survivors advocated after the disaster. Nevertheless, bringing the body *home*, as Eritreans say, is complex in the case of border deaths because the person has usually fled Eritrea.

The wish to repatriate the dead is not unique to Eritrean migrants. Gerhild Perl (2016) has analyzed postmortem repatriations in the context of undocumented crossings between Morocco and Spain, showing how Moroccan families are prepared to endure bureaucratic difficulties and economic costs in order to bring their dead relatives home. Repatriation pacifies the bereaved and reaffirms the deceased person's belonging to the family and community (Perl 2016, 202). Similarly, Jason De León (2015, 238–64) has documented the significance of the repatriation of remains in South America. While doing ethnographic research in the Sonora Desert at the US-Mexico border, he found the body of a dead woman. He later traveled to Ecuador, where the woman was from and her body had been buried. Although the husband and children of the woman had already confirmed her identity through DNA, the arrival and burial of her human remains made her death more real (De León 2015, 253).

To my knowledge, none of the thirty-one victims of the Lampedusa disaster who have been scientifically identified have been sent back to Eritrea for burial. The Isaias Afwerki regime has been reluctant to receive the bodies of that symbolic disaster. On October 9, 2013, the Eritrean embassy in Rome lowered the flag to half-mast and released an unsigned statement to regime-friendly websites claiming that it was collaborating with the Italian government to repatriate the bodies of the disaster victims to Eritrea. This did not happen, however. Two human rights activists I interviewed, Meron Estefanos (2016) in Stockholm and Elsa Chyrum (2016) in London, said the embassy only claimed to be concerned with returning the dead to Eritrea to end a campaign that opposition activists had launched demanding the repatriation of the bodies. The return of so many dead to Eritrea would have had revolutionary potential, Meron said.

In 2017, I met a man in Lampedusa who had come from Germany where he had lived for several years. He had been among the first relatives who identified a victim of the disaster through DNA. This man (who wishes to remain anonymous) told me he had traveled to Sicily a few times, first to give his DNA sample and then to install a headstone on his younger brother's grave in a small inland village. Each time he visited Sicily in the first years after the disaster, the man tried to organize the repatriation of his brother's body to Eritrea, without success. The Italian authorities in Agrigento told him to come back in a few months. He came back, but again, nothing happened. Finally, he gave up.

Ambiguous Loss

I sometimes heard from relatives of victims of the Lampedusa disaster that they considered their family lucky because their loved one's death was certain. Among Eritrean communities, it is common for families to have to deal with disappearance. Father Mussie Zerai (2019) gave me an example of how uncertain deaths continue to affect the diasporic community in Europe: he has remarried widows without official documentation that their previous marriage had ended due to the death of a spouse. In the absence of scientific proof and official documentation, the Eritrean diasporic community has created vernacular mechanisms to obtain a degree of certainty where there are otherwise only probabilities. Eyewitness testimony of death on the journey to Europe is usually the best available evidence for allowing a new marriage to take place.

Uncertainty about death can have severe consequences for the family and friends of the disappeared (Boss 1999, 61; Robins 2010; Crocker, Reineke, and Ramos Tovar 2021). The uncertainty can haunt relatives for years and prevent them from living on, in legal, social, and psychological terms. It creates embodied symptoms that testify to painful social circumstances that are often unevenly distributed depending on class, gender, and nationality as Crocker, Reineke, and Ramos Tovar (2021) show in their study of relatives of those who disappeared in the US-Mexico border. In the context of Tunisian migrants, Simon Robins (2022, 959) argues that this uncertainty is particularly difficult for women whose husbands have disappeared. That their husbands are neither dead nor alive affects the women's own identities: they are neither wives nor widows. Women existing between these categories challenge social norms.

The psychologist Pauline Boss has coined the term *ambiguous loss* to theorize the condition in which the families of the disappeared live (Boss 1999; 2004). Ambiguous loss is a condition of uncertainty in which a person is simultaneously "there" and "not there." Psychologically, it is the most stressful kind of loss (Boss 1999, 6; Boss 2006, xvii). When a death is certain, death rituals can be performed, and the bereaved can resituate themselves in the world and in relationship to others. This allows the surviving family members to refigure identities, status, and relationships. These transitions and markings are not possible with ambiguous loss. Death is an event that at some stage has a conclusion: the dead transition to "not here." Ambiguous loss is not an event—it persists, and therefore freezes the grieving process (Boss 2006, xvii).

In such circumstances, there is a tendency to continue one's relationship with the disappeared longer than in confirmed losses. When a person disappears, one's relationship with them can be maintained as if they were alive but absent. In a study among Tunisian relatives of missing migrants, a significant number of family members believed their missing relative was alive, despite a lack of supporting evidence (Ben Attia et al. 2016; see also Robins 2022). For example, mothers tended to rely on affective and sensory explanations to justify their belief that their sons were alive (Ben Attia et al. 2016).

Ather Zia (2019) has described how the mothers and wives of disappeared Kashmiri men cultivate a continuous relationship with the disappeared. Mourning, for them, is about living on with the disappearance and with the disappeared living on in them. Zia (2019) also shows how the women have transformed their grief into political agency. Protests in city spaces displaying the photographs of the disappeared and the creation of personal archives documenting disappearances are works of private mourning that turn into public performance and political resistance against India's military control and arbitrary violence.

Tunisian mothers took similar action in 2011, as Federica Sossi (2013) has described. After their sons disappeared during the sea crossing to Italy, the women demanded answers from European governments about their sons' whereabouts. Their demand was visual: the women were photographed in Tunisia holding photos of their sons. While the women themselves were prevented from crossing the border to search for their sons, the visuality of the women holding the photographs succeeded in traveling across borders to Europe.

In 2021, in Lampedusa, I met a group of eight Tunisian women who were mothers and sisters of other men who had disappeared. They had gained visas to visit Lampedusa and Sicily, where they met with lawyers and gave DNA samples for forensic identification. In Lampedusa, the women posed with photographs of the missing men for journalists who had come to cover the October 3, 2013, memorialization. "Fedi, 17.2.2021, dove sei?" (Fedi, 17.2.2021, where are you?) was written in one photo. For these relatives of men who had disappeared, as for those in Kashmir, resistance through visibility and publicity produced a subjectivity that allows for survival in the condition of ambiguous loss.

In 2019, I again talked to Mussie Zerai about the return of the bodies of the Lampedusa victims to Eritrea. By then, he had given up hope that that would happen. But it was not too late to identify the dead, he emphasized. The identification of the bodies remains an objective in his advocacy—to find "justice for the dead and for the relatives," as he puts it (Zerai 2019). The term *justice* in relation to the identification of remains is crucial. Mussie does not refer to identification as a humanitarian act, but as an act of justice. The identification of the dead found at the border is central to overcoming the state of disappearance. It is central to the rights of the families of the victims to know the fate of their loved ones. Iosif Kovras and Simon Robins (2017, 166–67) argue that as long as the deaths of migrants are framed as accidents, their burial is seen as an act of benevolence. Their argument resonates with my analysis of Italian and European political leaders' commemorative performances in chapters 2 and 5. The humanitarian framework favored by European leaders centers dignified performances by benevolent actors. In contrast, identifying the dead would be an act of solidarity and justice treating the dead and their relatives as persons who have "the right to have rights," to use Hannah Arendt's famous term.

Mussie Zerai's persistence for almost ten years now on the issue of identification as a matter of justice can be compared to what scholars in various contexts have conceptualized as forensic citizenship (Reineke 2022) or civic forensics (Schwartz-Marin and Cruz-Santiago 2016). Where authorities have failed to identify the dead or investigate disappearances, civil society—often led by relatives of the victims—may take responsibility and action, pressure the authorities, and even create new forensic practices and forms of knowledge. For example, organized civic engagement with forensic science, challenging the state, has been examined in different Latin American contexts, from Mothers of the Plaza del Mayo in Argentina to, more recently, the drug war and organized crime in Mexico and Colombia (see Schwartz-Marin and Cruz-Santiago 2016) and migrants who have disappeared at the US-Mexico border (Reineke 2022). The term forensic refers not only to scientific knowledge and techniques but also to their application in law, court proceedings, and the mediated public sphere (Reineke 2022, 28). Thus, forensics has become central for human rights struggles (Gabriel Gatti 2013). The handwritten list of names created by survivors at Lampedusa's reception center immediately after the disaster and the documentation of graves in Sicily by survivors starting in 2020 are also acts of civic forensics.

The discourse and practice of both civic and expert forensics is related to a broader movement of scholars, human rights activists, and lawyers who have argued for extending existing international agreements on missing persons and enforced disappearances to the context of border deaths (Schindel 2020; Distretti 2020; Nuovi Desaparecidos 2021). In armed conflicts, international human rights law recognizes the "the right of families to know the fate of their relatives" (United Nations 1977). The UN Convention on Enforced Disappearances obliges states to actively investigate the fate of the disappeared even if the state was not itself involved in the disappearance (Schindel 2020, 401). Approaching border deaths through these global frameworks would be a step away from mere benevolence and toward justice.

The use of the term *disappeared* in the context of border deaths is another important move in this direction. It resonates with the term *enforced disappearances*, which acknowledges the state as the main entity responsible for the disappearance. It also resonates with the *desaparecidos* of Latin America, the so-called original disappeared, particularly those disappeared during Argentina's civil-military dictatorship between 1976 and 1983 (Gatti, Irazuzta, and Martínez 2020). While European states do not directly or deliberately enforce disappearances, they do so indirectly. The International Convention on Enforced Disappearances names states as responsible, whether directly or indirectly, by action or by omission, of the crime of enforcing a disappearance (Schindel 2020, 391). In comparison, the category "missing persons" does not necessarily imply a similar state responsibility. "Missing persons" is often used in the context of those missing in action in armed conflicts, for example, in the context of transnational justice in the Balkans, as in the Missing Persons Institute of Bosnia and Herzegovina. In 2019, the International Commission on Missing Persons started to extend their work on identifying human remains to the domain of border deaths in Europe. Despite differences in the implication of responsibility, both terms—*disappeared* and *missing*—are transnationalized: they create an association with conflicts, protests, and the struggle for justice elsewhere. These associations and parallels across time and space produce the critical potential to move beyond indifference or the differential treatment of dead migrants and their survivors.

In the context of the Lampedusa disaster, the term *disappearance* is warranted by two critical observations. First, Italy is responsible for the low number of identified dead, justifying the use of the term *enforced disappearance*. Only thirty-one of the 366 victims of the Lampedusa disaster have been scientifically identified by 2018, which leaves 335 victims de facto disappeared. Second, disappearance puts emphasis on the experience of the relatives. Disappearance is not the same as death. There are 335 families who continue to live in various degrees of uncertainty. The following two stories illustrate the creativity and resilience of victims' relatives as they cope with uncertainty.

The Significance of the Number 120

In 2018, I accompanied Teddy, a twenty-four-year-old Eritrean refugee, on his search for his brother's grave in Sicily. Teddy had crossed the Mediterranean Sea in 2015, and three years later, he had established his life in Germany to the point that he was able to travel to Sicily. He had a job in a factory north of Hamburg, making cables for the shipping industry, and had learned some German. I met him in Lampedusa at the fifth anniversary commemoration of the disaster. He was traveling with a small cross-body bag that had "The City of Hamburg" printed on it. Hamburg had become his new home, not by choice, but by chance. The crew of a Swedish ship had rescued him in the Mediterranean Sea. For him, this was a good sign: Sweden was where his aunt lived, and his intended destination. But the police caught him in Germany, so under EU rules, he had to apply for asylum there. Now he proudly identified with Germany—or actually, with Hamburg.

When I had talked with Teddy in Lampedusa, I had been impressed with his determination to find his older brother's grave. Once he had received a residence permit in Germany and saved enough money for the trip, he bought a ticket and returned to Sicily, the part of Europe he had been so eager to leave just three years earlier.

In Lampedusa, Teddy had invited me to accompany him to Sicily, where his brother was buried. A day after I arrived in Sicily, I received a WhatsApp message from Teddy: "He is in Cattolico Eraclea. I'll take a bus there at 8:30 a.m. tomorrow. It's an hour from here." In the morning, Teddy sent a photo of the road, taken from the bus: "Guten Morgen! I'm on my way." He had gone to the police headquarters, the *questura*, in Agrigento, hoping to find out the location of his brother's grave. All he knew was what the survivors of the disaster had told him: the number assigned to the body, 120. Ilaria Tucci, my research assistant, had already tried to get the locations of the 366 buried bodies from the *questura*, but had had no success. So I had doubted the police would disclose the details of a grave of a victim who had not been positively identified. But I was wrong. Teddy was able to convince the people at the *questura* that he was the brother of victim number 120.

The cemetery where Teddy's brother is buried is located outside the town of Cattolico Eraclea and is similar to other Sicilian cemeteries I have visited. Surrounded by high walls, it is accessible through a gate that is open only during certain hours. The town itself is small, but the cemetery feels as urban as the ones in larger towns. The dead are, for the most part, not buried in the ground, but interred above ground in different kinds of constructions. There are large and elaborate family chapels and tombs holding the dead of multiple generations. Most graves, even the plainer ones, have a small photo of the person buried there. Along the rows, there are also less impressive constructions: multistory concrete vaults, like high-rises for the dead.

When we reached the cemetery, Teddy was already up on a ladder at one of those multistory vaults, decorating a grave. He had bought a bunch of artificial flowers and four funeral candles and placed them on the sill. The number 120 was written with a marker on the white painted surface of the rectangular tomb. To the right of the number, Teddy had glued a photograph of his brother, Temesgen. It had been taken in a studio somewhere along the way, perhaps in Sudan, where Temesgen had stayed after leaving Eritrea. Temesgen had posted it on his Facebook profile, and Teddy had had the picture printed in a photo shop for this express purpose.

Teddy came down from the ladder to greet us. He obviously had the situation under control and had managed to negotiate with the cemetery workers despite the lack of a common language. In my eyes, Teddy seemed different now from when I had come to know him in Lampedusa, where he had attended the commemorations with his uncle, a survivor of the disaster who was now based in Sweden. Teddy's boyish appearance had transformed to that of an adult. The caretaker told us that Teddy should have presented a document from the *questura* to prove the identity of the body and his relationship with the dead. However, the caretaker had felt sorry for the young man who had come all the way from Germany and let him glue the photo on the grave. But for a more permanent installation, an engraved marble stone with a photograph, Teddy would have to officially identify the body.

There are twelve victims of the October 3 disaster buried in different four-story concrete constructions in Cattolico Eraclea. Unlike in the cemeteries in Castellamare del Golfo and Agrigento (discussed in chapter 4), the disaster's victims here are not buried together in one place. Instead, they have been placed among the local dead, in random vacant graves. There is no sign indicating that anonymous migrant dead are buried here, as there is at the cemetery in Castellamare del Golfo. Only one of the victims' graves is identified with a marble headstone. It bears a name, Weldu (and the second name), an oval-shaped black-and-white photo of Weldu wearing a shirt with a Superman logo, his date of birth,

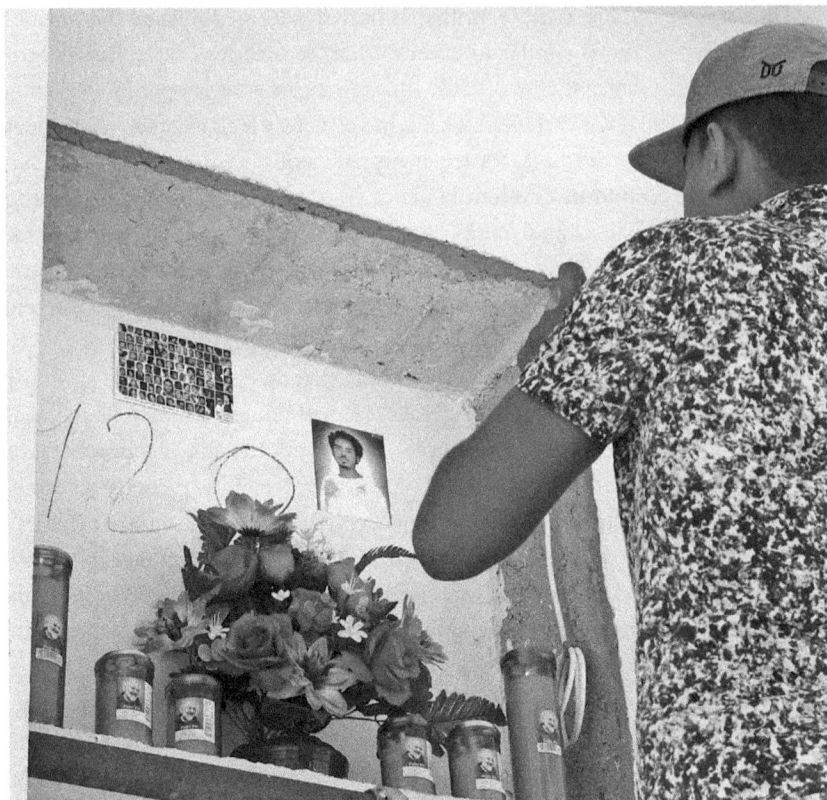

FIGURE 17. Teddy photographing his brother Temesgen's grave in Sicily. © Karina Horsti, 2018. Photo by Karina Horsti.

and his date of death, October 3, 2013. Two bunches of artificial flowers and a metal crucifix on the sill are evidence that someone traveled here to mourn his death not long ago. Teddy had noticed the Eritrean name and date of death before we arrived and placed a candle next to the crucifix.

We became aware of the ten other graves of Lampedusa victims only when the caretaker pointed them out to us: "*naufraghi*," the shipwrecked, he said, as we walked by the unmarked squares among the local Italians' graves, which had names and photos on them. The unidentified graves had at first seemed like vacant slots, but when we heard that they were the graves of the *naufraghi*, they began to represent not death but disappearance—the disappearance of a person, or of a body someone would want to bury and memorialize. Most likely, there was a family somewhere whose son or daughter had died, but they did not know for certain, or they did not know that the body was here, in a remote cemetery in Sicily.

According to the cemetery register, body number 120 was unidentified. In the book, under the heading *"Nato,"* birth, the row for body 120 said *"naufragio,"* shipwreck; under *"Nome,"* name, read *"120 di Lampedusa."* These entries were written in small handwriting, however, so as to leave space for the name and date of birth to potentially be added in the future. It seemed that from the cemetery officials' point of view, nonidentification was a temporary condition, as if they were waiting for people like Teddy to one day arrive at their small office by the gate.

Survivors had visually identified Teddy's brother after the disaster. They were asked to look at photographs of the dead taken before the body bags were closed. Viewing the pictures was voluntary, and those who did had the opportunity to speak with a psychologist, as Adhanom Rezene, one of the survivors, stressed when he told me about the procedure. Survivors and relatives who had seen the photographs told me it was emotionally stressful to look at them and difficult to actually identify a person. Many of the faces were disfigured and swollen. Adal Neguse, for example, said to me that after one hundred photographs, he had to stop looking. His brother was one of the last to be recovered from the hold of the boat, and Adal was unable to go through the photos as far as that number. The images blurred to each other, and even if his brother's face had appeared on the screen, he would not have been able to be sure that it was him. Adal's brother Abraham was eventually identified by a matching DNA sample.

Visual methods of identification, through photographs, clothing, and artifacts found on the body, tend to be unreliable. They can be important for relatives, however, as Jason De León (2015, 202–6) argues: visual confirmation might feel more real than a scientific report on matching DNA (see also Jugo 2017). Visual methods can be seen as vernacular forensic care work, like the list of the dead compiled by the survivors. They are an important manifestation of care performed in conditions where the state fails to carry out its duties. Nevertheless, as a method of identification, visual means depend on subjective observation and cognition, which in disaster situations are particularly unstable (Jugo 2017). According to the international standards for disaster victim identification established by Interpol, visual methods are to be used only in conjunction with the scientific methods of DNA and dental medical records analysis (Interpol 2021; Nuzzolese and Di Vella 2007).

Nevertheless, Teddy trusted the word of the survivors, and the number 120 became meaningful for him. It was the clue he had followed from Hamburg all the way to Cattolico Eraclea. When he turned the unidentified grave into a memorial, he did not cover the number that was written on the concrete, but instead arranged the photograph and the flowers so that it remained visible. The number is also an element in the design for a marble headstone that he drafted at the cemetery caretaker's office before he left. He drew the design on a piece of paper, in case he one day could go through the DNA identification process[1] and get an official permit to install a marble headstone similar to what he had seen at Weldu's grave. Teddy thought that grave was dignified and appropriate.

A Material Sense of Ritual

Materiality was crucial for Teddy's acts of remembrance. The photograph he attached to the grave was printed expressly for this purpose, and he bought silk flowers and candles to decorate the grave. Anthropologists maintain that a central aspect of rituals is "the sense of ritual" (Bell 2009, 74; Willerslev, Christensen, and Meinert 2013, 6–8). Rituals are sensed as something that happens outside ordinary space and time. The flowers and candles created a funereal atmosphere, the feeling of a sacred ritual. The previously blank concrete spot was transformed into a personalized and dignified memorial.

The material objects put on the grave were not "alive" or "vital" in themselves, to use the terms of new materialists (Bennett 2010). Their aliveness and transformation from mundane things to sacred objects of memorialization necessitated connections between the objects, the place, and the people who saw and made meaning of them. Cemeteries are a place where death and the status, identity, and relationships of those who died are made visible through material objects (Hallam and Hockey 2018, 56). The photograph attached to the grave proved that body number 120 was an individual, a person-as-such, like the local dead. The candles and the flowers—similar to those on the local graves—showed how number 120 was a relational human being, missed and memorialized by someone who knew him. The familiar grave objects and identification via photograph integrated the body of a stranger into the community of the dead.

However, the people for whom the objects on the grave would be most meaningful were not there, except for Teddy. He took photographs with his mobile phone of the memorial arrangement, both on the ladder and from below. He also asked me to take pictures of him on the ladder next to the grave. The photographs would later be shared with relatives. He then asked me to go up and attach the Sant'Egidio postcard depicting eighty-four victims of the October 3 disaster (discussed in chapter 3). Teddy pointed out a face in the middle of the grid of portraits on the card and told me: "That's my brother." He took additional pictures of this second arrangement that included the postcard.

The grid of 84 portraits added a broader, public dimension to the memorial. The first arrangement of objects had been a more private form of memorialization. Beyond the number on the grave, the material memorialization as such didn't reveal to anyone else the story behind the death. The arrangement with the postcard, however, connected the individual to a specific disaster and also to the broader issue of migrant deaths at the border. It revealed to anyone visiting the cemetery or seeing Teddy's documentation of the grave that the man in the photograph on the grave had died alongside others. His buried body represented those of all 84 faces—or all 366 names written on the other side of the postcard. The function of the grave paralleled that of the naming of one victim, Yohanna (discussed in chapter 3). It would be impossible to know 84 or 366 graves individually, but it was possible to focus on one grave. Thus, the singular grave made the postcard more comprehensible (while the postcard itself had also worked to make the figure 366 more comprehensible). Through the postcard, this particular grave and its signifiers (the number 120 and the person's photograph) gained an additional meaning: this was a victim of a well-known and globally mediatized disaster that symbolized border deaths and the violence of the border.

Teddy had perhaps become particularly sensitized to the public significance of the disaster by attending the public commemorations in Lampedusa just a couple of days earlier. Perhaps my presence at the cemetery and my questions about the unidentified graves of the victims of the October 3 disaster, as well as our conversations with the cemetery caretakers, had also added a public dimension to his ritual. Though the ritual was initially intimate, it was transformed to address the particular disaster and broader issue of migrant deaths.

Teddy created a sense of ritual not only by situating objects within the physical space of the cemetery, but also by dividing the time spent there into less or more sacred ritual time. When we had spent more than an hour at the grave together, I told Teddy I would go back to the caretakers' office at the gate to see if they would show me the books where the burials are registered. Teddy stayed at the grave to pray alone, returning to an intimate ritual space.

Media Technology in Transnational Mourning

The material artifacts Teddy left at the grave would indicate to the residents of Cattolico Eraclea that a previously unidentified grave had been turned into a memorial. But this was not Teddy's main purpose. Documenting the memorialized grave by photographing it with his mobile phone was at least as important as the memorializing itself. Teddy's mother, siblings, and friends were implicitly present at the ritual he performed. They entered the circle of memorialization through mediation, though at a temporal and spatial distance. Teddy's ritual at the cemetery became social through the documentation and its mediation.

However, Teddy did not livestream the ritual; there was no mediated copresence of his family, though media technology existed that might have afforded such a presence. Media scholars have demonstrated that a connective presence or copresence, an experience of emotional intimate proximity with persons physically distant, is important in maintaining family and care across distances (see, e.g., Wilding 2006; Witteborn 2014; Madianou 2016; Twigt 2018; Alinejad 2019). In this case, however, at least two conditions prevented a real-time intimate presence. First, mobile phone coverage and Internet connections in Eritrea are unreliable. Second, Teddy had not told his mother about the trip to Lampedusa and his search for the grave. He was not sure what the trip would be like and whether it would be successful. He told her about his journey only after he had completed the trip and was back in Germany. He had similarly protected her from worry when he crossed the sea border between Libya and Italy in 2015, the same crossing where his older brother had died two years earlier. "I told her we would leave a few days later than we actually did. Then I called her from Italy to let her know that I was safe. That was the day she thought I would be crossing the sea," Teddy told me. He had a reason for sharing these two stories about protecting his mother from worry with me. It was what I liked to hear, of course, as was obvious from my spontaneous affirmative responses. He knew that I have three daughters, the oldest of whom is around the same age as he. I expressed that I was impressed and touched by his sense of family responsibility. My response probably affirmed Teddy's new position as the eldest son, capable of taking responsibility for others and their well-being.

For Teddy, his mother is a central figure in the community of mourners. It was she to whom he sent the phone he had traveled with to the disaster site in Lampedusa and the cemetery in Sicily, the phone that contained the documentation of his momentous journey. Teddy sent the phone with someone who was able to travel from Germany back to Eritrea. When he told me about this, I was surprised. Why send photographs on a phone rather than in a Dropbox folder, via WhatsApp messages, or even by printing them and making an album?

Perhaps the phone itself had acquired meaning during Teddy's travels to the memory sites. I find it particularly significant that in his inability to send the physical body to his mother in Eritrea, Teddy chose to send the physical phone with images of the memorialized grave and the disaster site in Lampedusa. Or perhaps his mother had other uses for the phone. It was a new smartphone, after all. She could perhaps use the phone's editing tools to modify the photographs of the grave, as Teddy had. He had added stars along the edges of some of the photos. Teddy's response to my surprise was that he had simply thought the phone functions well as a photo album. It is good for viewing both photos and videos: one can enlarge the images and examine details, for example. And yes, his mother now uses the phone in her daily life. It was a good gift, he said. The phone is an album and much more. The expensive phone also demonstrates that Teddy is successful in his new life and that his mother does not need to worry about him.

The contents of the phone are significant, too. The album it contains was curated from photos of Teddy's journey to the two significant memory sites related to the death of his brother, Lampedusa and Cattolico Eraclea. The images are evidence that Teddy has become a responsible eldest son and successfully performed death rituals on a foreign continent. Sending these digitized photographs and videos on a mobile phone to Eritrea underlines the significance and value of these particular visuals.

Teddy also sent the visuals to friends and other family members via Facebook Messenger and other social media platforms. In Eritrean funeral customs, including in the diaspora, family members are expected to travel long distances to attend a funeral, and it is considered shameful if a relative does not make that effort. The size of a funeral gathering demonstrates the importance of the deceased and their remaining family (Holt 2001). Teddy's experience demonstrates how media technology enables some sense of sociality for a transnational family divided by borders, in a situation where a physical funeral and mourning together are impossible.

In my research, I heard about and saw evidence of many situations similar to Teddy's, in which people could not attend a funeral or perform other death rituals because of border restrictions and long distances. Relatives and friends of the victims of the Lampedusa disaster shared photographs and videos of graves and commemorative rituals performed at cemeteries in Facebook and Viber groups. Others participated by sharing memories and condolences in the comments. I sometimes noted that people who I knew had visited a grave in Sicily had not posted about it on their public Facebook or Instagram accounts. They might have shared the ritual in a more intimate network, but they had not made it public. Weddings, births, and first birthdays are often mediated publicly, but the social mediation of deaths—both border deaths and otherwise—is selective.

This selectiveness in creating a mediated community around intimate events concerns not only refugees or transnational families, but families more broadly. For example, Anna Haverinen (2015), in her research on memorializing death on

Facebook in the United States and Finland, shows how people can have opposing views about digitized mourning. She argues that while social media can create a feeling of togetherness that helps the bereaved in their mourning process, it can also create grievances and feel inauthentic. Raelene Wilding (2006), in a study of transnational families and care, shows how already in the early years of the 2000s, email and inexpensive telephone calls produced an imagined proximity that felt like a miracle for her research participants. However, she found that the sense of togetherness was easier to achieve when life was going well: these were "sunny-day" technologies (Wilding 2006, 134). At times of illness or death, a phone call did not provide sufficient care.

Teddy's use of media technology was carefully controlled. He curated and edited his documentation of the grave and of the rituals he performed in Lampe-dusa and Cattolico Eraclea, and he shared his documentation selectively. At the cemetery, he chose not to use technology that would have afforded copresence. While a group video call might have been possible with family members in the diaspora, the most central person in the community of mourners, his mother, was in Eritrea, where Internet connections are unreliable. More important than the simultaneity of the ritual was its careful representation, the curated docu-mentation of the ritual he performed, which added a layer of respect and dignity to the mediated memorialization.

Nevertheless, the pictures could be shared digitally among family and friends, and a community of mourners could be formed across distances. People could access the digital memory objects at any time and in any place, allowing them to manage their own rhythm of memorialization. While he was memorializing the grave, Teddy was mindful of those who could not be present in person. His family and friends were implicitly present through his imagination, and that presence made mourning possible. Mourning, after all, is a social practice, and particularly so among Eritreans, as Helen had emphasized.

Materiality was central in Teddy's memorialization, but so too was the mediation of materiality. Teddy made death visible not only through material objects, into which he invested emotional and social meaning, but also through digitized images of the arranged objects. The pictures Teddy took are visual assemblages that can be edited and shared easily across distances through digi-tal means: they are what I have called *digital objects of memorialization* (Horsti 2019b). The circuit of transformation between digital and material elements is crucial for digital objects of memorialization. The digital images can be modi-fied with editing tools, allowing one to add a personal touch before sharing the memorial object with others. Digital images can also be printed and attached to physical memorials (which can again be photographed). Creative appropria-tion and the circulation of both digital and physical materialities bring certainty to the otherwise uncertain experience of surviving the death of another. Both death and mourning become visible in and through mediation, allowing families to avoid the complicated emotions that are typical in situations where a death is uncertain.

Freudian theory emphasizes that mourning is a necessary phase in finding closure after the death of a loved one. Mourning is a phase that is supposed to come to an end, and if not, Sigmund Freud (1964) argued, one is left in a psychologically damaging state of melancholia. However, in the case of border deaths, where varying stages of uncertainty prevail, such clear-cut closure is unlikely. Jacques Derrida (1986) offers another model of mourning, departing from the Freudian search for emotional closure. Derrida sees mourning as an ongoing engagement with the dead. Those who are no longer "with us" can be "in us," and mourning is about living on by keeping our relationship with the dead alive (Derrida 1986; see also Kirkby 2006).

Finding the grave, praying there, memorializing it, and documenting these acts were of utmost importance to Teddy. Through the photographs, his family was able to reach a level of certainty regarding the death of his brother that they were then able to share socially. In 2022, Teddy was able to complete the official scientific identification by giving a DNA sample and an interview for the University of Milan's Laboratorio di Antropologia e Odontologia Forense (LABANOF) scientists who were present in Lampedusa during the October 3 commemorations. Until then, the family relied on vernacular knowledge of the number 120 and the spontaneous ritual that Teddy performed, documented, and shared through photographs. The mediated ritual, and finally, the DNA identification completed a process that had begun with the sad news the survivors had delivered. The family knew that Temesgen had died, but that knowledge had not been complete. He had not made the transition from "here" to "there." Being able to experience this distinction is what makes rituals important for human social life; it is through them that life can evolve after moments of transformation and disruption. Without such transitions, living with loss becomes difficult.

Six Beds in Rural Eritrea

In Eritrea, the mourning and memorializing that are such social processes were difficult after the disaster. The regime did not acknowledge that the victims were mainly from Eritrea, and the authorities restricted rituals, particularly in Asmara, the capital.

When the disaster happened, Semhar Ghebreselassie was twenty-five years old and living in Asmara. She was in hiding after having deserted her conscripted job as a high school teacher the year before. While clandestinely working at an Internet café, she became involved in the underground resistance and the diasporic political opposition. She has since become a human rights activist in Sweden, where she is involved in Eritrean opposition politics and is a reporter for the diasporic media outlet Global Yiakl.

I spoke with Semhar in 2020, in a Zoom meeting she attended from Stockholm. Ten days earlier, on October 3, she had convened a memorial livestream discussion on the Facebook page of Global Yiakl about the disaster. She told me her memories from Asmara around the time of the Lampedusa disaster: "In Asmara, we have walls where we remember the dead [by posting death notices]. At the time, there were pictures of those who had died in Lampedusa. I remember the streets were full of people looking at the photographs of all those young people who had died," she recalled.

Semhar asked me if I had seen the clip from the state-owned Eri-TV news broadcast where the anchor reports on the Lampedusa shipwreck, saying "almost 400 illegal Africans died." I had. Helen had shown it to me in London, and since then, I had seen it being shared among survivors and other Eritrean Europeans every year on the October 3 anniversary. It was framed as proof that the Eritrean government had avoided recognizing the dead as their own people. Remembering the injury this nonrecognition had caused the survivors and relatives of the victims was part of memorializing the disaster for some diasporic Eritreans. The news item had been broadcast in the international news segment, not with the domestic news, which Semhar pointed out as further proof of the regime's denial. The death notices posted by relatives on the walls of Asmara nevertheless informed the public in Eritrea's capital city about who had died in the disaster. The families had received the news through the survivors and the list of the dead they had compiled.

The families in Eritrea had wanted to organize funeral rituals, even without the bodies. Secondary burials had become common in cases when someone died abroad and their body was not repatriated or did not arrive in time for a scheduled ritual. The government prohibited these substitute rituals at Asmara's cemeteries, however, and families had to mourn in private. Nevertheless, a public memorial for the victims of the disaster was planned to take place at Asmara's Martyrs' Cemetery in November 2013. Rumors circulated across the Eritrean diaspora that the government had deployed soldiers to guard the cemetery and prevent any memorial services (Asmarino 2013). On the opposition website Asmarino, an anonymous eyewitness reported from the capital that "Asmara is caught between the people trying to assert their wish and the government trying to maintain control" (Asmarino 2013). In rural communities, however, public mourning was less strictly controlled. Semhar's cousin who died in the disaster was from a rural village, and there, people were able to organize a secondary funeral.

Semhar's experience of the memorial was twofold: on the one hand, it was a private family matter in which the lack of bodies was circumvented by the six beds; on the other hand, her cousin's death was a public matter. The regime's denial of responsibility, its unwillingness to let families repatriate the dead, and its attempts to prevent secondary death rituals increased the painfulness of the event. Both levels of surviving the death of another, the private and the public, strengthened her resistance to the regime.

The six beds carried out for the funeral represented the bodies that could and should have been there. However, the absence of the bodies in itself was not the main cause of the mourners' additional pain. The diasporic condition had become the norm in Eritrea, and communities had developed a dignified tradition of dealing with death rituals for absent bodies. The pain, for Semhar, was that the six beds outside represented the regime's continued oppression, even after death.

Listening to the experiences of Helen, Teddy, and Semhar revealed to me how border deaths are different than other deaths. Most importantly, surviving a migrant death involves living with various uncertainties. Not knowing the whereabouts of relatives is common among the Eritrean refugee community, and the memorialization of known deaths takes place in this context. The survivors of the Lampedusa disaster engaged in civic forensics when they compiled the list of the dead and visually identified bodies. Later they started to document the graves in Sicily. The opportunity to mourn and memorialize—in one way or another—is uniquely precious in a context in which many families never hear any news of their missing loved ones. The fear of total disappearance is a socially shared concern, and even though visual identification and the listing of names cannot give full certainty, as a scientific identification would, they are meaningful. Importantly, they are a sign of care for the rights of the dead and their relatives. Although the Lampedusa disaster attracted special attention from the community of forensic experts, most of the Lampedusa victims remain not fully included in the common world. Instead, these victims continue to be relegated to the spheres of uncertainty and ambiguity: the categories of "the missing" and "the disappeared." The civic forensic acts of citizenship that Mussie Zerai and survivors continue to practice bring the injustice of disappearance into the public agenda. Their acts allow the burial of border dead to be seen through the lens of forensics and the rights of the dead and their relatives, rather than as acts of humanitarian benevolence.

In this chapter, I have detailed some of the ways in which families have shaped their survival, whether through uncertainties or with the certainty of having lost a loved one in the specific circumstances of border deaths. When the cultural practices of burial and visiting graves are interrupted by the failed responsibilities of the authorities, alternative rituals may repair some of the damage. These new rituals and practices are nevertheless rooted in existing and traditional practices. For example, participating in a funeral is central, and these social responsibilities are fulfilled to the extent possible, even if there is no body or access to a grave. Material artifacts at cemeteries, photographs of these artifacts turned into digital objects of memorialization, and the six empty beds in an Eritrean village make death real. This visualization of death allows relatives to share in the process of mourning and to continue to live with their loss together. The creativity of memorializations among the relatives of the Lampedusa victims demonstrates how death is fundamentally a social phenomenon and how death rituals are important for the social network the deceased person is a part of.

The intimate mourning and memorializing by individuals and families that I have examined in this chapter also have a significant public dimension. In chapters 2 and 3, I argue for the critical potential of representing the dead as persons-as-such (Edkins 2011), which makes apparent their relationality with the living. This focus on the individuality of the dead contributes to broader demands for investigation of the disaster, for the rights of the dead and their relatives, and for political change that would make such disasters less likely to happen again.

Helen, Teddy, and Semhar cultivate their own survival of the loss of another. They produce their subjectivity in relation to their loss and to other family members, the community, the state, and the world. As survivors, they are constituted by the dead and by uncertainties related to the dead bodies and death rituals, and to the particular conditions of migration. Helen survives by reenacting Eritrean mourning rituals in diaspora, supported by her friends and community in London. Teddy's memorializing is affected by his mother in Eritrea as he takes on the role of the responsible eldest son. Semhar's oppositional and human rights activism is shaped by the experience of having mourned her cousin without a body. By sharing the stories of these survivors, I do not want to romanticize the creativity of transnational refugees. Rather, I hope to acknowledge the capacity of individuals and communities for critical action—critical in the sense that they survive their specific, complicated loss with the resources available. In doing so, they refuse to become paralyzed as they experience the violence of the border in their intimate and social lives.

KEBRAT'S STORY

This book project was set in motion by my curiosity about how the October 3, 2013, disaster lives on and evades oblivion through two domains of afterlife, representation, and memorialization. My study showed that the disaster's memory haunts Europe, and as it circulates in these two domains, it *does* things: the afterlives of the disaster are *productive*. Politics and identities are produced in response to the disaster's memory at multiple scales: the Eritrean diaspora, local communities, national governments, and Europe.

Analyzing how and why the disaster remained in the public domain prompted me to ask further questions about survival. The book has therefore also examined how people continue their lives after a rupture; memorialization and representation played a role in their processes of survival after witnessing the disaster and its aftermath. Survival emerged in my research in four different contexts: the survival of those who witnessed the disaster as eyewitnesses or through mediation; the survival of "flesh witnesses" (Harari 2009)—that is, those who "went through" the disaster, to use the words of Solomon Gebrehiwet; and the survival of relatives and friends who survived the death of another. The nature of these experiences of witnessing varied—they ranged from a distant mediated witnessing to an intimate experience of survival, from Martin Schulz's shock at the shattering of European "dignity" and the distress of students in Castellamare del Golfo at not knowing who the dead in their local cemetery were, to Teddy's struggle to find certainty about his brother's death and Bisrat's and Solomon's emotional difficulty in calling the victims' families.

This book has centered on the idea of survival, with survival being defined as the continuation of life—living on or beyond a rupture. This understanding of survival as the continuation of life derived from the works of Walter Benjamin (2009), who theorized survival in the context of artistic work, and Jacques Derrida, who, just before his death, said "life is survival" (Derrida and Birnbaum 2007). The works of Hannah Arendt (2017) and Giorgio Agamben (1999) added important insights into how human life—and human survival—is more than just a biological state. One can be alive and yet not part of the common world in a cultural, social, and political sense. The notion of haunting added insights to theorizing survival: that a survivor constitutes him- or herself in relation to the dead (Davis 2007, 117–18) and that specters haunting the present can be from the past or the future (Davis 2007; Gordon 1997). The not-yet realized future and the demand that something be done are aspects of haunting that drive the process of survival.

The ruptures that people and communities affected by the Lampedusa disaster survived are dissimilar in their effects and unequal in their severity. It is important, however, to acknowledge the full range of ruptures and responses, as they make visible how the consequences of border deaths cannot be externalized to migrants' countries of origin nor confined to the islands in the border zone where the dead disappear or are buried. Rather, these ruptures affect communities in countries of origin and of transit, across Europe and beyond, wherever survivors and the relatives of victims live, and wherever people witnessed the disaster in and through the media. The consequences of border deaths continue to live on. In the future, they may reappear to haunt Europeans—both those of us who survived a disaster or the death of a loved one, and those of us whose governments killed by allowing people to die.

This book has taken a holistic approach to examining the afterlives of the disaster of October 3, 2013, drawing on the experiences of different types of witnesses and their various engagements with the memory of what happened. The disaster's afterlives produced different forms of citizenship, which I understand as acts or practices constituted in relationships between different constellations of individuals, social groups, communities, and states. These forms of citizenship constitute subjectivities that are significant in the processes of bearing witness and survival. My analysis of the research materials and scientific literature led me to identify forms of citizenship that contest indifference toward border deaths.

First, *forensic citizenship* is constituted of acts of civic forensics, such as the survivors' acts of listing the names of the dead, documenting cemeteries, visually identifying the dead, and calling the relatives of the dead. The Italian Eritrean priest Mussie Zerai's activism, which has kept the rights of the dead and their relatives on the public agenda and demanded justice through forensic investigation of the disaster and of the identities of the dead, has been critically important. Other forms of forensic citizenship have included the civil investigations into the events leading to the mass death that cultural producers and activists, such as the Lampedusan Askavusa have conducted. Forensic experts, such as those at LABANOF in Milan and at the International Committee on Missing Persons in The Hague, practically and symbolically raise the issue of forensics in the context of border deaths. All these acts and practices of forensic citizenship contribute to the understanding of border deaths in terms of international law and as an issue of justice (Reineke 2022; Schwartz-Marin and Cruz-Santiago 2016; Schindel 2020; Distretti 2020). Forensics as a concept and practice goes beyond treating life as a biological form of being or a form of biological citizenship (Petryna 2013). Investigation into what happened and to whom brings the question of responsibility and the disaster's human consequences to the fore.

Second, I have discussed *attentiveness* as a form of citizenship that encourages transgression of assumed boundaries between citizens/noncitizens and in-group/out-group (see also findings in Rygiel 2016; Stierl 2016; Perl 2018; Kobelinsky 2017; Squire 2020). The capacity for "civil imagination" (Azoulay 2012) foregrounds attentive engagements with the dead, the living, and the memory of the disaster. The visibility of such acts in the public domain on the one hand supports or invites civil imagination in others, but on the other hand, risks turning attention to those who act attentively as opposed to the victims themselves. In the public domain, figures such as the Lampedusan rescuers and the Sicilians who care for the unknown dead are celebrated and turned into heroes, which relieves the pain and consciences of European spectators.

Therefore, an attentiveness to one's own "capacity to harm" (Nguyen 2016, 73) and self-interest (Neumann 2013) in the structures that produce violence at the border is crucial for attentiveness to be transformative. Some journalists, authors, and activists, such as Frances Stonor Saunders, Meron Estefanos, and the Askavusa collective articulate such attentiveness as they engage with the memory of the disaster. Amalia Vullo in Sicily and the people in Castellamare del Golfo care for the dead with an attentiveness to the relatives who come or may yet come to remember their own. I also discussed attentiveness to one's own capacity to harm in the context of Dresden's anti-fascist activists and some LIBE Committee members of the European Parliament. Through civic forensics, new kinships, and mutual support in the process of survival, forms of attentive citizenship emerge that transgress boundaries and inspire civil imagination.

Third, I have examined a *survivor citizenship*, a subjectivity that stems from the responsibility of having survived the disaster when others died. This new kind of Europeanness is not based on citizenship granted by a state, but rather on taking action as a responsible member of society. Witnessing and surviving a disaster at the border makes one responsible for and capable of taking action. Through acts of survivor citizenship, survivors' process of survival, of living a full human life in the cultural, social, and political sense, has continued. Nevertheless, it is important to recognize that this position is not available to everyone, and it can be politically or socially confining. Survivor citizenship can be compatible with diasporic citizenship or in conflict with it. The Eritrean diasporic community is divided in their understanding of citizenship and the Eritrean state's long-arm governance over the diaspora. Sacrificial citizenship (Bernal 2014, 33) has been part of Eritrean diasporic citizenship, but is evolving. The human rights violations of the Eritrean regime, ethnic, religious, and class relations, and citizenship in countries of settlement shape Eritreans' understanding of sacrifice and Eritreanness. Survivor citizenship is navigation through and negotiation of the various expectations of European and Eritrean actors, such as the grateful refugee or sacrificial citizen.

The survivors' continuation of life after the disaster, in particular, offers new perspectives to the study of border deaths and the conceptualization of survival. Thus, in this concluding chapter, I would like to return to the story of Kebrat, one of the six women who survived the disaster. Kebrat first appeared in the public domain when Romina Marceca, a journalist working for the Italian newspaper *La Repubblica*, interviewed Kebrat at a hospital in Palermo immediately after the disaster. Kebrat's interview provided one the first public voices of survival. Almost all of the other survivors were confined in the "reception center" in Lampedusa and were beyond the reach of journalists. Marceca's (2013) story is written in question-and-answer format, a style that produces a sense of a directness for Kebrat's voice.

Kebrat was flown to Palermo by helicopter after being resuscitated at the clinic in Lampedusa. In her story, Marceca wrote that Kebrat answered her questions through an oxygen mask, her lungs having been injured by inhaling a mix of gasoline and seawater. In the interview, Kebrat describes the scene of the disaster. She remembers seeing dead bodies in the water and hearing screams. She was afraid of death and swam with all her might. She told Marceca she was happy to be alive, and that she hoped to "make it." Kebrat was alive but had not yet survived. She was not yet aware who else was alive and who had died, and she did not yet know how she would continue her life after the disaster. However, she was able to articulate that she had risked her life in hopes of survival: "I have lived for years in fear. We are all looking toward the future in a world without war, where there is peace. I fled my land for this, even left my family."

Kebrat's description of the disaster scene and explanation for leaving Eritrea were among the few available quotes from survivors and circulated in the international news media. Her interview was quoted, for example, in the British *Guardian*

(Kington 2013a), the Australian *Sydney Morning Herald* (Squires 2013), and the German tabloid *Bild* (*Bild* 2013). Her impressions continue to reappear in the public domain as part of Antonio Riccò's 2014 play *Ein Morgen vor Lampedusa*, which has been performed almost four hundred times in readings at schools, churches, and elsewhere in Germany and Italy (Riccò 2014; Horsti 2021). By reading aloud the experiences of those who lived through the disaster, communities that perform the play enter the scene of the disaster—or better, they bring the scene of the disaster into their own familiar spaces. In the play, the character named Kebrat says: "First the flames and then nothing but darkness. When I was in the water, I swam with all my strength. Next to me, I saw many die. I can only remember a little. The screams, yes, I remember them. Then I passed out."[1]

In the play and in journalistic texts based on Marceca's interview, Kebrat appears as a subject with a voice. Accompanying the story in *Bild* is an Associated Press photograph taken at the hospital, possibly at the time of the interview. Kebrat lies on a stretcher, wearing an oxygen mask, surrounded by two nurses and a woman who is talking to her—the woman is not identified, but could be Romina Marceca or perhaps a translator. In the picture, Kebrat is looking at and listening to the woman who is speaking. The visual structure reproduced in the image creates a hierarchy between refugee and caring Europeans. Kebrat's agency, which is apparent in the text of Marceca's article, is not visible in this image.

Kebrat appeared again in the public domain when Lampedusan doctor Pietro Bartolo started to tell the story of her rescue and the significant role he played in her survival. Bartolo became an internationally acclaimed public figure after he appeared as one of the lead characters in Gianfranco Rosi's film *Fuocoammare* (Fire at Sea), which won the Golden Bear at the Berlin International Film Festival in 2016. That same year, Bartolo published a memoir, *Lacrime di sale*, which was translated into English, German, Spanish, Catalan, and French within a year. Three years later, he was elected to the European Parliament.

In Bartolo's story, Kebrat is the woman he saved from death. Her eyewitness account or views on Eritrea do not feature in his telling of the events. Her function in the public domain thus shifted from a witness with a voice to an unconscious victim in someone else's story. Kebrat was pulled from the sea by Domenico Colapinto and the crew of his fishing boat *Angela*. They thought she was dead. In his memoir, Bartolo recalls Kebrat lying on the boat's fishing nets alongside three dead bodies: "Rigor mortis had not yet set in, which could mean that she had died very recently. Then I felt a pulse. . . . That was definitely a heartbeat—it was almost imperceptible, but I had felt it. Then another one. She was not dead" (Bartolo and Tilotta 2017, 190). The story of her return from near-death continued to be told in the media, but its details changed. In some later versions, Kebrat was said to have been already in a body bag when Bartolo discovered her alive. This was the version told on Bartolo's elected-official Facebook account on February 17, 2020, in a post that included a picture of Bartolo and Kebrat embracing in the European Parliament, where she had gone to meet Bartolo with Tareke Brhane of Comitato 3 ottobre:

> Many of you know this story well because it stayed in my heart and I never stopped telling it. It's the story of Kebrat, a girl who arrived on the pier of Lampedusa without a pulse, no heartbeat, after the shipwreck on October 3, 2013. She looked dead, she was already in a bag, with the zipper closed. All I had to do was pronounce her death. And yet, I felt something, I listened better. It was a race against time, clinic, first aid, helicopter transport to the nearest CPR. It wasn't over for Kebrat.

Lying among the dead on Colapinto's fishing vessel—or on the pier—Kebrat was not dead, but she was not yet alive, either. The story of her miraculous rescue that emerged as part of Bartolo's heroic narrative depicted her as a victim and grateful recipient of Europeans' benevolence and care. Bartolo's Facebook post received an outpouring of admiration and gratitude from his followers. In his new role as a member of European Parliament, however, Bartolo channels his celebrity humanitarian status into a political force opposing the violent bordering of Europe. Refugee rights are at the center of his political work, for example, in his role as vice-chair of the parliament's Committee on Civil Liberties, Justice, and Home Affairs. In the parliament's plenary debate on May 18, 2021, Bartolo said today's politicians would one day be judged for border deaths: "Every new tragedy in the Mediterranean is followed by this ridiculous rite of pain. There will be a new Nuremberg but, unlike in the past, today we know everything" (Bartolo 2021).

Bartolo's memoir, like Marceca's interview, prompted re-representations of Kebrat in the cultural sphere. Neapolitan singer-songwriter Nando Misuraca released a song named "Kebrat" in March 2020, saying that it was inspired by Bartolo's book. The song is about the hope of surviving and can be interpreted to convey both a Christian meaning of salvation and a civic meaning of convivial belonging. "There will be something better beyond this falsehood / Beyond all the words that are said / There will be a home, a bit of peace / The hope of a tomorrow that leads us to the future," Misuraca sings. While "falsehood" could be interpreted as a critique of the divisions of the world and "all the words" to refer to the hypocritical legitimation of bordering, the song nevertheless ends with the figure of a grateful refugee. A verse by Senegalese Italian rapper Assane Babou embedded in the song offers the Italian listener a position of benevolence: "I say thank you, and thank you very much / Sicily, Lampedusa, and all of Italy / Thank you so much."

Nevertheless, Kebrat has not always remained in the role of victim or grateful refugee that has been assigned her, but instead has spoken publicly about issues important to her, including issues that do not necessarily fit her perceived refugeeness. After her time in Palermo, she sought refuge in Sweden. Like many other survivors, she has returned to Lampedusa and demonstrated the capacity to speak and act for justice. By inserting her views and politics into memorializations and representations, she has constituted *survivor citizenship.*

Kebrat returned to Lampedusa for anniversary commemorations of the disaster in 2016, 2017, 2020, 2021. Her presence in Lampedusa, near the place she was almost killed but stayed alive, makes visible both survival and the loss of life. Her presence demonstrates how the victims, too, could have been there and continued their lives.

In 2020 and 2021, Kebrat traveled to Lampedusa with her husband and two young sons. Returning to Lampedusa with her family not only demonstrated her continuation of life, but strengthened the new kinships that have developed between survivors and Lampedusan rescuers. In my view, Kebrat was like a daughter who had returned to visit her parents. Public narratives describing these familial encounters—which transcend linguistic and other boundaries—expand the ideas of friendship and kinship, and in doing so, produce a civil imagination of a convivial future for Europe. Kebrat's public appearance with her sons in Lampedusa also exemplifies that survival is a transnational and future-oriented process; memories of disasters at borders cannot be confined to one location or one generation. The visuality of her holding the hands of her Swedish-born sons while walking the docks of Lampedusa demonstrates how survival is about the continuation of life. Her children are Swedes of Eritrean descent who carry the memory of their mother's survival in the Mediterranean Sea.

In her public speech in 2020 Lampedusa commemorations, Kebrat said that survivors of the deadly border live a specific kind of life. Like Solomon, Kebrat distinguished between those who have experienced a disaster and those who have not. Survival means continuing to live a life that is connected to the memory of those who died: "Even though we are among you and seem to live a normal life, there is an unforgettable scar in our hearts. When a person is treated correctly and nicely as a human being, it is good, but [nevertheless], we have a severe injury. Those who were with us are always in our thoughts." The survival process involves a remaking of one's self and one's life. However, this life, which might outwardly seem normal, requires the capacity to reflect on difficult emotions and to live with "an unforgettable scar in our hearts." No one can survive alone, Kebrat seems to say, and so, it is everyone's responsibility to treat others with respect. This responsibility includes understanding that experiencing border violence has serious consequences. There is no "normal life" to return to; life must be remade and transformed. The transformations in Kebrat's life have included taking it upon herself to speak publicly for the rights of the dead and their relatives, as well as for those of the refugees attempting border crossings today.

On October 3, 2017, Kebrat told me how the year before, during her first trip back to Lampedusa in 2016, she had become aware of her position as a survivor whom others listened to. At the commemoration in 2016, she had participated in the protest against Comitato 3 ottobre, who had organized the anniversary events. She held a sign that read, in English: "Our families are waiting for the souls of their children." Her mission then was to seek justice for the dead and for their families, who wanted forensic identification and the bodies to be repatriated to Eritrea. But in 2017, when she served as the survivors' designated spokesperson, she focused instead on what was then the most pressing human rights issue related to European bordering: the suffering of refugees on their way to Europe, particularly in Libya. Like other survivors, Kebrat had received numerous horrific calls for help through Facebook and Viber. Kidnappers in Libya had invented a new practice: they took photographs of tortured refugees and shared them digitally with the victims' families, demanding payment for the refugees' release through social media.

Though their discourse was humanitarian, Italy and other European countries were all the while facilitating the kidnappers' cruel business model (Amnesty International 2017; Pusterla 2021). Italy and Europe were vigorously enforcing the securitization of the border, a process that foreshadowed the nationalist-populist turn that would culminate in Italy's parliamentary elections the following year. This was the issue Kebrat and the other survivors decided to raise in the public space they carved out in the Lampedusa commemorations in 2017. They had discussed what their joint message should be and decided to focus on the future rather than the past. "The Europeans should know about the consequences of their collaboration with the Libyans," Kebrat told me. Her intention was to talk about the violence of bordering and to make its human consequences known to Europeans, who had externalized border controls to Libya, a former colony of Italy.

The horrific stories and images circulating on social media had prompted the survivors of the Lampedusa disaster to recall their own experiences in Sudan and Libya. Many of those on the boat had also been kidnapped and held for ransom. When I asked Kebrat why she had decided to shift attention from the specifics of the Lampedusa disaster to the broader issue of refugees stranded in Libya, she replied: "The dead are already dead." While she deemed the issues of identification, burial, and neglected responsibilities important, she felt obliged to speak out on behalf of today's refugees. She had put aside her criticism of the Comitato.

These changes reflect how Kebrat, along with the other survivors who returned to Lampedusa, negotiated the relevance of their political claims and adjusted their alliances with the other actors taking part in the commemorations. Being a survivor, particularly one with an unusually mediated story, as well as being a woman, afforded Kebrat a certain status in commemorative performances, and she used that status to advocate for those whose lives could still be saved.

As a woman, and later as a mother, Kebrat is a figure that fits European uses of the disaster's memory. In the Eritrean context, however, I observed a more contested and complicated terrain. In my research, I became aware of gender expectations among Eritreans: women were often expected to take a less prominent role in the public domain compared to men. Interestingly, however, many Eritrean human rights activists in Europe are women. Regardless of gender, survivors who speak publicly about the disaster, and particularly those who voice critical views of the Eritrean regime, can expect to receive also negative responses from Eritreans in diaspora. Kebrat's negotiations with publicity and acts of survivor citizenship reflect these conditions, within which she must constitute her survivorship. In my view, she sometimes played the role of the grateful refugee or the submissive Eritrean woman, but at other times, she resisted being cast in those roles. At memory sites originally constructed for European visitors, Kebrat and the other survivors used memorialization to produce and transform public knowledge of border deaths and the afterlife of the October 3 disaster within the spheres that were negotiable.

Creating a subjectivity of survivor citizenship—responsibilizing oneself as a survivor—started before the border crossing and continued afterward. Those who left Eritrea did so knowing the risks; they risked their lives for the chance to survive. The Isaias Afwerki regime had annihilated their social, cultural, and political lives in Eritrea, and escape was their means of survival. They acted upon their "right to have rights" (Arendt 2017), and after the disaster, some of those who stayed alive acted as citizens of Europe, regardless of their formal citizenship status. In fact, survival of the murderous border responsibilized Kebrat and others; their process of survival grew out of their capability for acting as citizens. First, they resisted the Isaias regime that had prohibited the memorialization of border deaths, therefore acting as responsible diasporic Eritreans by using their freedom to memorialize the disaster. Second, survivors created a civil relationship with Europe and Europeans. As survivors of the murderous border produced by Europe, they felt responsible for speaking in the name of those whom Europe had killed and on behalf of the refugees stranded in Libya, those whom Europe was allowing to suffer and potentially ready to kill by allowing to drown. By staying alive and transforming themselves from victims to survivors who returned to the site of violence to speak out in words, gestures, and emotions, they demonstrated they were capable of transforming both Eritrea and Europe.

While survivors' acts of citizenship are directed toward Eritrea, Italy, and the European Union, they have also created civil relationships between people, citizens and noncitizens alike. Importantly, they have been attentive to the rights of the dead and the relatives, and through civic forensic practices they have constituted their survivor citizenship. They imagine themselves part of Europe and part of a common world, and their actions invite others to respond convivially. For example, in readings of the play *Ein Morgen vor Lampedusa*, participants, who have been spectators of a distant event, become, if only for a moment, protagonists, while both re-mediating and becoming witnesses of the retelling of the disaster.

Similarly, the anniversary memorializations of the disaster point to an interconnected and convivial future for Europe. Survivors return to Lampedusa from all across Europe; they return as Germans, Swedes, Norwegians, Danes, and Dutchmen. Disasters do not fall into oblivion, nor can they be contained in a liminal peripheric sphere such as "Lampedusa"—an island perceived as not-quite Europe. Disasters return to haunt us in the present and future Europe where we live interdependently.

This book has shown that while the dead may be central in representations and memorializations related to the disaster, the transformative potential of its afterlife is dependent on the living. The dead have certain rights, but those rights are given and claimed by the living. The transformative power of representations and memorializations of border deaths is manifest in the lives and actions of survivors.

Notes

INTRODUCTION

1. This account is based on accounts of those who survived the disaster and were on the deck when the boat capsized. The boat itself was not on fire, contrary to what has often been reported in mediated accounts (Gebrehiwet 2020). The boat rests on the seabed at the disaster site, and footage taken by the firefighters who retrieved corpses from the boat is available online (Vigili del Fuoco 2013).

2. Adal received compensation for his translation work from the Academy of Finland project funds, and a scholarship from Kone Foundation for the *Remembering Lampedusa* documentary film project.

CHAPTER 1. WORDS

1. Chapter epigraph: the audio was communicated only later in media reporting, for example, in *La neve, la prima volta*, Dossier, TG2, April 6, 2014, and *I giorni della tragedia*, 03 ottobre 2013 Lampedusa, Libera Espressione, October 3, 2016, directed by Antonio Maggiore.

2. In this widely photographed moment, however, Brandt is on both knees.

3. I thank advocate Gaetano Mario Pasqualino for updates on the case.

CHAPTER 2. IMAGES

1. Italy's minister of the interior, Angelino Alfano, and the president of the Region of Sicily, Rosario Crocetta, were also present but are left out of the frame. An unnamed woman stands beside Barroso.

2. "Famiglie delle vittime" (Malmström) and "famiglie delle persone che hanno perso la vita nella tragedia della settimana scorsa e ai loro cari" (Barroso).

3. Hadnet Tesfom translated the Global Yiakl live discussion programme for me from the Tigrinya to the English.

4. Other examples of alternative visual structures include the *Guardian*'s short clip of Reuters footage of the scene that included the mechanical sound of the cranes transferring the coffins and two Eritrean women crying and throwing themselves on coffins. https://www.theguardian.com/world/video/2013/oct/14/lampedusa-ceremony-burial-dead-migrants-video.

5. His experience in the disaster's immediate aftermath transformed Adal Neguse and he became an outspoken public activist for refugees in Sweden.

6. There are a handful of examples in the European mediascape of instances in which journalists have done extensive investigative work to report on the victims of migrant disasters with the same kind of detailed and individualized attention as is paid to other disasters. These investigative reports generally appear somewhat later in the media cycle. For example, on November 14, 2013, the front page of the weekly magazine *L'Espresso* displayed forty-five photographs of those who died in a disaster in the Mediterranean on October 11, 2013.

7. Two survivors, one of them a woman, were flown immediately to Palermo for medical care and were not photographed.

8. The Italian journalist associations Association of Carta di Roma and the Federazione Nationale Stampa Italiana sent a public notice to the professional community on October 7, 2013, indicating that the media should not publish the names or identifiable photographs of the Eritrean survivors. They noted that the people on the boat had escaped a regime that might seek to punish their relatives remaining in Eritrea (Rossi and Suber 2013).

CHAPTER 3. ENUMERATION, NAMING, PHOTOS

1. For example, United for Intercultural Action's "List of Deaths," since 1993 (UNITED 2022); the Deaths at the Borders Database compiled at VU University Amsterdam (Last 2015); and the International Organization for Migration's Missing Migrants Project database, since 2014 (IOM 2022).

2. The Community of Sant'Egidio (Comunità di Sant'Egidio) is an ecumenical Christian lay association founded in Italy, which has since expanded across the world. Their fundamental aim is to pray, help people in need, and promote peace. Advocacy for migrants is an important part of their work, and the organization has sponsored the resettlement of refugees in Italy since 2016.

CHAPTER 4. ADOPTING THE DEAD

1. The actual prize that year was given to the mayor of the Italian town of Riace, Domenico Lucano, who was celebrated for the town's refugee and migrant integration projects.

2. In addition to the twenty-nine headstones of those who died in Lampedusa or Canal of Sicily, the arrangement also includes the grave of Moussa Toukara, born in Mali, who died in Palermo in 2014.

3. Other key members of Circolo Metropolis are Paolo Arena, Rossella Barbara, Antonella Fontana, Maria Rita Navarra, and Adriana La Porta.

CHAPTER 5. MEMORIAL INTERVENTIONS

1. Some of the observations and analysis of *Giardino della memoria* were presented in an article I coauthored with Klaus Neumann. We compared the *Giardino* with the SIEV X memorial in Canberra, Australia (Horsti and Neumann 2019).

2. She builds this argument with reference to Michael Taussig's collection of essays, *The Nervous System* (1992).

3. Barbara Adam (2010) builds the distinction between present future and future present on the work of Reinhart Koselleck (2017) and Niklas Luhmann (1982, 281) who "suggested that the present future is rooted in a utopian approach which allows for prediction while the future present is technologically constituted and as such enables us to transform future presents into present presents" (Adam 2010, 375).

4. Italian human rights organizations Gandhi, Comitato verità e giustizia peri nuovi desaparecidos, and Progetto Diritti were involved in taking the crew of *Aristeus*, a fishing vessel from Mazzara del Vallo to court.

5. The monument was designed by Gaia Rossi in collaboration with Vito Fiorino.

6. In Italian, the sign reads "Ho voluto dare un nome a questi esseri umani."

7. The memorials in Piazza Piave received additional support from the European Union, Amnesty International, Unser Herz schlägt auf Lampedusa, Consorzio Communità Brianza, Associazione Senza Confini, Federazione delle chiese evangeliche in Italia (including Mediterranean Hope), Archivio Storico Lampedusa, Parrochia San Gerlando Lampedusa, and LapisBio6.

CHAPTER 6. MEMORY POLITICS

1. The initial group was made up of Italian journalists who had long covered migration, Vittorio Alessandro, a former coast guard spokesperson, and Tareke Brhane, an Eritrean Italian activist who had worked for humanitarian organizations in Lampedusa. Mayor Giusi Nicolini was an honorary member. Within the first two years, all but Valerio Cataldi, a journalist from Rome, and Tareke Brhane had left the group. Cataldi and Nicolini left the Comitato when Nicolini was not elected for a second term in 2017. They instead became active in Museo Migranti, an organization that utilizes the memory of the October 3 disaster by exhibiting objects from the disaster site in temporary exhibitions. As of writing, Cataldi is involved together with Mussie Zerai and Adal Neguse (who also continue to collaborate with the Comitato) in creating a memorial museum in Palermo for the memory of October 3, 2013, disaster. As of 2018, Tareke Brhane was the only original member remaining on the Comitato, which has subsequently shifted to a nonprofit organization focused on educational programs "aimed at raising awareness on integration and reception of migrants" as the Comitato's website noted in 2020 (Comitato 3 ottobre, n.d.).

2. It was signed by 30,256 people.

3. In addition to Triulzi, Gianluca Gatta (2018, 47–48) and Gaia Giuliani (2018, 70) have also resisted cultural amnesia and articulated the connections between the colonial subjects of the past and present migration.

4. Such parties won 22.7 percent of seats in the European Parliament. These groups include ECR (9.3 percent), EFDD (6.4 percent) and NI (7.0 percent) (European Parliament 2014).

CHAPTER 7. SURVIVOR CITIZENSHIP

1. The politicians included Martin Schulz, the president of the European Parliament; Laura Boldrini, the president of Italy's Chamber of Deputies; Maria da Assunção Esteves, the president of the Assembly of the Republic of Portugal; Rosario Crocetta, the president of Sicily; and Italy's foreign minister, Federica Mogherini.

2. The letter is titled "Commemoration of Lampedusa boat victims" and signed "Eritrean community in Italy, September 26, 2014."

3. This interview was given in Tigrinya and filmed by Anna Blom, a Finnish Swedish filmmaker, and Adal Neguse on October 4, 2017, for their documentary film project *Remembering Lampedusa*.

4. In fact, they were free to leave the island and continue their journey north because they refused to give fingerprints to the Italian authorities in order to avoid being sent back to Italy under the European Union's Dublin Regulation. A couple of days later, the recently arrived refugees were at the Agrigento train station in Sicily, where they were waiting for their relatives to send money for onward travel.

CHAPTER 8. SURVIVAL

1. Copyright © 2017 Sellerio editore, via Enzo ed Elvira Sellerio 50 Palermo. Originally published in Italian as *Appunti per un naufragio* in 2017 by Sellerio Editore, Palermo, Italy. English translation copyright © 2019 Antony Shugaar. Reprinted by permission of Other Press.

CHAPTER 9. SURVIVING THE DEATH OF ANOTHER

1. I contacted the Red Cross in Hamburg to ask if they could help with the DNA identification. A case worker responded that they could only help fill out a Personal Description Document and send it to the Italian authorities through the Red Cross office in Italy.

Teddy would still have to travel to the University of Milan's Laboratorio di Antropologia e Odontologia Forense (LABANOF) to give the sample. Finally, in 2022 he was able to do that in Lampedusa where the scientists of LABANOF came. The Red Cross's activity was mainly limited to facilitating the restoration of family ties through an online platform where migrants could post photographs of their disappeared relatives.

EPILOGUE: KEBRAT'S STORY

1. Antonio Umberto Riccò's play is translated by Thomas Borgard, Lisa Palm, and Jessica Riccò and titled *That Morning on Lampedusa*, 2014.

References

Adam, Barbara. 2010. "History of the Future: Paradoxes and Challenges." *Rethinking History* 14 (3): 361–78. https://doi.org/10.1080/13642529.2010.482790.

Agamben, Giorgio. 1999. *Remnants of Auschwitz: The Witness and the Archive.* Translated by Daniel Heller-Roazen. New York: Zone Books.

Ahmed, Sara. 2004. "Affective Economies." *Social Text* 22 (2): 117–39. https://doi.org/10.1215/01642472-22-2_79-117.

Albahari, Maurizio. 2015. *Crimes of Peace.* Philadelphia: University of Pennsylvania Press.

Alinder, Jasmine. 2012. "Underexposed: The Controversial Censorship of Photographs of US War Dead." In *Outrage: Art, Controversy, and Society*, edited by R. Howells, A. Deciu Ritivoi, and J. Schachter, 175–206. London: Palgrave. https://doi.org/10.1057/9781137283542_8.

Alinejad, Donya. 2019. "Careful Co-Presence: The Transnational Mediation of Emotional Intimacy." *Social Media + Society* 5 (2). https://doi.org/10.1177/2056305119854222.

Alonso, Alexandra Délano, and Benjamin Nienass. 2016a. "Deaths, Visibility, and Responsibility: The Politics of Mourning at the US-Mexico Border." *Social Research* 83 (2): 421–51. https://www.jstor.org/stable/44282194.

Alonso, Alexandra Délano, and Benjamin Nienass. 2016b. "Introduction: Borders and the Politics of Mourning." *Social Research* 83 (2): xix–xxxi. https://www.jstor.org/stable/44282186.

Amnesty International. 2021. *Eritrea.* London: Amnesty International.

Amnesty International. 2017. *Libya's Dark Web of Collusion: Abuses against Europe-Bound Refugees and Migrants.* London: Amnesty International.

Andersson, Ruben. 2014. *Illegality, Inc.* Oakland: University of California Press.

Anderson, Bridget, Nandita Sharma, and Cynthia Wright. 2011. "Editorial: Why No Borders?" *Refuge: Canada's Journal on Refugees* 26 (2): 5–18. https://doi.org/10.25071/1920-7336.32074.

Andreina Papa, Rebeca. 2014. "Il naufragio di Lampedusa: Una nuova rappresentazione dell'immigrazione?" *Comunicazione Punto Doc: Rivista della Scuola di Dottorato Mediatrends della Sapienza Università di Roma* 9:77–89. https://fdocumenti.com/document/comunicazione-punto-doc-2016-9-8-milano-n-134-del-20-03-2009-issn-2282-0140.html?page=4.

Ansa. 2013. "Letta Declares Lampedusa Shipwreck Victims Italian Citizens." Ansa English, 4 October. https://www.ansa.it/web/notizie/rubriche/english/2013/10/04/Letta-declares-Lampedusa-shipwreck-victims-Italian-citizens_9410976.html.

Arendt, Hannah. 1998. *The Human Condition.* Chicago: University of Chicago Press.

Arendt, Hannah. 2017. *The Origins of Totalitarianism.* London: Penguin Books.

Arendt, Hannah. 1958/1998. *The Human Condition.* Chicago: The University of Chicago Press.

Askavusa. 2018. *Lampedusa, 3 ottobre 2013: Il naufragio della verità.* Lampedusa: Askavusa.

Askavusa. 2015. Interview with Karina Horsti and Ilaria Tucci. October 6. Lampedusa.

Asmarino. 2013. Eritrea: A Message regarding the Public Memorial for Lampedusa Victims at the Martyr's Cemetery in Asmara, November 9, 2013. http://asmarino. com/press-releases/1888-report-from-the-rome-delegation-information-for-all-eritreans-regarding-the-lampedusa-tragedy.

Asmat: Names in Memory of All Victims of the Sea. 2015. Film directed by Dagmawi Yimer. Rome: Archivio Memorie Migranti.

Associated Press. 2018. "A Partial List of Victims in the Genoa Bridge Collapse." Associated Press, August 15. https://www.apnews.com/904d2db57dee4ea8b92df25fb78 1318b.

Auchter, Jessica. 2014. *The Politics of Haunting and Memory in International Relations.* Interventions. London: Routledge.

Auchter, Jessica. 2013. "Border Monuments: Memory, Counter-Memory, and (B)Ordering Practices along the US-Mexico Border." *Review of International Studies* 39 (2): 291–311. https://doi.org/10.1017/S0260210512000174.

Augé, Marc. 2004. *Oblivion.* Minneapolis: University of Minnesota Press.

Austin, John L. 1975. *How to Do Things with Words.* Oxford: Clarendon.

Awate. 2014. "The Lampedusa Tragedy: A Chronicle." Awate, last modified October 2. Accessed December 23, 2020. http://awate.com/the-lampedusa-tragedy-a-chronicle-2/.

Ayalew Mengiste, Tekalign. 2019. "Precarious Mobility: Infrastructures of Eritrean Migration through the Sudan and the Sahara Desert." *African Human Mobility Review* 5 (1): 1482–1509. https://doi.org/10.14426/ahmr.v5i1.874.

Ayalew Mengiste, Tekalign. 2018. "Refugee Protections from Below: Smuggling in the Eritrea-Ethiopia Context." *Annals of the American Academy of Political and Social Science* 676 (1): 57–76. https://doi.org/10.1177/0002716217743944.

Ayalew Mengiste, Tekalign. 2017. "Struggle for Mobility: Diasporic Practices and High-Risk Migration Pathways of Refugees from the Horn of Africa towards Europe." PhD diss., University of Stockholm.

Azoulay, Ariella. 2012. *Civil Imagination: A Political Ontology of Photography.* London: Verso.

Bak Jørgensen, Martin. 2019. "'A Goat That Is Already Dead Is No Longer Afraid of Knives': Refugee Mobilizations and Politics of (Necessary) Interference in Hamburg." *Ethnologia Europaea* 49 (1). https://doi.org/10.16995/ee.817.

Baldi, Guido, and Karsten Staehr. 2016. "The European Debt Crisis and Fiscal Reactions in Europe 2000–2014." *International Economics and Economic Policy* 13 (2): 297–317. https://doi.org/10.1007/s10368-014-0309-4.

Balibar, Étienne. 2004. *We, the People of Europe?* Princeton: Princeton University Press.

Balzarotti, Leda, and Barbara Miccolupi. 2016. "La strage di natale e le vittime dimenticate di Capo Passero." *Corriere della Sera,* December 23. https://www.corriere.it/extra-per-voi/2016/12/23/strage-natale-vittime-dimenticate-capo-passero-659e a926-c92f-11e6-bac6-8c33946b31a6.shtml.

Barroso, José Manuel. 2013. Statement at a Press Conference in Lampedusa. October 9, 2013. https://ec.europa.eu/commission/presscorner/detail/en/SPEECH_13_792.

Barthes, Roland. 1977. "Rhetoric of the Image." In *Image—Music—Text.* Edited by Roland Barthes, 152–63. New York: Hill and Wang.

Bartolo, Pietro. 2021. Speech at the European Parliament Plenary debate on "Recent Deaths in the Mediterranean and Search and Rescue at Sea." May 18, 2021. https://www.europarl.europa.eu/doceo/document/PV-9-2021-05-18-ITM-004_ EN.html.

Bartolo, Pietro. 2019. Speech at the LIBE Committee Hearing on Search and Rescue in the Mediterranean. Brussels: European Parliament.

Bartolo, Pietro, and Lidia Tilotta. 2017. *Lampedusa: Gateway to Europe*. Translated by Chenxin Jiang. London: Maclehose Press.

Basaran, Tugba. 2014. "Saving Lives at Sea: Security, Law and Adverse Effects." *European Journal of Migration and Law* 16(3): 365–87. https://doi.org/10.1163/15718166-12342061.

Baster, Timothy, and Isabelle Merminod. 2013. "Photo Essay: For the Eritrean Migrants, There Is More Dignity in Death." *New Internationalist*, October 18. https://newint.org/features/web-exclusive/2013/10/18/eritrea-migrants-lampedusa-europe.

BBC. 2011. "Tunisia Migrants Prompt Italy 'Humanitarian Emergency.'" BBC *News*, February 2. https://www.bbc.com/news/world-europe-12441613.

Bell, Catherine. 2009. *Ritual Theory, Ritual Practice*. Oxford: Oxford University Press.

Belloni, Milena. 2019. *The Big Gamble: The Migration of Eritreans to Europe*. Oakland: University of California Press.

Bellu, Giovanni Maria. 2014. "Carta di Roma, un codice deontologico e professionale." *Comunicazione Punto Doc: Rivista della Scuola di Dottorato Mediatrends della Sapienza Università di Roma* 9:17–20. https://fdocumenti.com/document/comunicazione-punto-doc-2016-9-8-milano-n-134-del-20-03-2009-issn-2282-0140.html.

Bellu, Giovanni Maria. 2004. *I Fantismi di Portopalo*. Milano: Mondadori.

Ben Attia, Frida, Tara Brian, Adrian Carrasco Heiermann, Stefanie Grant, Catriona Jarvis, Iosif Kovras, Frank Laczko, Giorgia Mirto, Katerina Polychroni, Simon Robins, Ann Singleton, and Amal Shaiah. 2016. "'Like a Part of a Puzzle Which Is Missing': The Impact on Families of a Relative Missing in Migration across the Mediterranean." London: Mediterranean Missing Project. https://openaccess.city.ac.uk/id/eprint/17794/1/Report-on-Families-of-Missing-Migrants.pdf.

Benjamin, Walter. 2009. "The Task of the Translator." In *Walter Benjamin: One-Way Street and Other Writings*. Translated by J. A. Underwood, 29–45. London: Penguin Books.

Bennett, Bruce. 2018. "Becoming Refugees: *Exodus* and Contemporary Mediations of the Refugee Crisis." *Transnational Cinemas* 9 (1): 13–30. https://doi.org/10.1080/20403526.2018.1471181.

Bennett, Jane. 2010. *Vibrant Matter*. Durham: Duke University Press.

Bensalem, Khaled. 2014. "Lo scafista del 3 ottobre." Interview by Valerio Cataldi. *Rai Tg2*, June 9. Accessed 27 June 2022. https://www.youtube.com/watch?v=OXXy5AXwD2M.

Bereketeab, Redie. 2016. *Revisiting the Eritrean National Liberation Movement, 1961–91*. London: Red Sea Press.

Bereketeab, Redie. 2009. "The Eritrea-Ethiopia Conflict and the Algiers Agreement: Eritrea's Road to Isolation." In *Eritrea's External Relations: Understanding Its Regional Role and Foreign Policy*, edited by Richard Reid, 98–130. London: Chatham House.

Berlant, Lauren. 2008a. *The Female Complaint*. Durham: Duke University Press.

Berlant, Lauren. 2008b. "Thinking about Feeling Historical." *Emotion, Space and Society* 1 (1): 4–9. https://doi.org/10.1016/j.emospa.2008.08.006.

Bernal, Victoria. 2017. "Diaspora and the Afterlife of Violence: Eritrean National Narratives and What Goes without Saying." *American Anthropologist* 119 (1): 23–34. https://doi.org/10.1111/aman.12821.

Bernal, Victoria. 2014. *Nation as Network: Diaspora, Cyberspace, and Citizenship*. Chicago: University of Chicago Press.

Bertoglio, Barbara, Pierangela Grignani, Paola Di Simone, Nicolò Polizzi, Danilo De Angelis, Cristina Cattaneo, Agata Iadicicco, Paolo Fattorini, Silvano Presciuttini, and Carlo Previderè. 2020. "Disaster Victim Identification by Kinship Analysis: The Lampedusa October 3rd, 2013 Shipwreck." *Forensic Science International: Genetics* 44:102–56. https://doi.org/10.1016/j.fsigen.2019.102156.

Bettelheim, Bruno. 1976. "Surviving." *New Yorker*, July 25, 1976.

Betts, Alexander. 2013. *Survival Migration: Failed Governance and the Crisis of Displacement.* Ithaca: Cornell University Press.

Bild. 2013. "Flüchtlingsdrama vor Lampedusa: Kebrat (24) überlebte das Todesschiff." *Bild*, October 5. https://www.bild.de/news/ausland/lampedusa/woher-kommen-die-fluechtlinge-32677226.bild.html.

Bleiker, Roland, David Campbell, Emma Hutchison, and Xzarina Nicholson. 2013. "The Visual Dehumanisation of Refugees." *Australian Journal of Political Science* 48 (4): 398–416. https://doi.org/10.1080/10361146.2013.840769.

Block, Laura. 2015. "Regulating Membership: Explaining Restriction and Stratification of Family Migration in Europe." *Journal of Family Issues* 36 (11): 1433–52. https://doi.org/10.1177%2F0192513X14557493.

Boltanski, Luc. 1999. *Distant Suffering: Morality, Media and Politics.* Cambridge: Cambridge University Press.

Bolzoni, Attilio. 2008. "La porta che guarda l'Africa in ricordo di chi non è mai arrivato." *La Repubblica*, June 26. https://www.repubblica.it/2008/06/sezioni/cronaca/sbarchi-immigrati-1/porta-immigrati/porta-immigrati.html.

Boss, Pauline. 2006. *Loss, Trauma, and Resilience: Therapeutic Work with Ambiguous Loss.* New York: W. W. Norton.

Boss, Pauline. 2004. "Ambiguous Loss Research, Theory, and Practice: Reflections after 9/11." *Journal of Marriage and Family* 66 (3): 551–66. https://www.jstor.org/stable/3600212.

Boss, Pauline. 1999. *Ambiguous Loss: Learning to Live with Unresolved Grief.* Cambridge, MA: Harvard University Press.

Bourriaud, Nicholas. 1998. *Relational Aesthetics.* Dijon: Les Presses du Réel.

Brambilla, Chiara. 2015. "Navigating the Euro/African Border and Migration Nexus through the Borderscapes Lens: Insights from the LampedusaInFestival." In *Borderscaping: Imaginations and Practices of Border Making*, edited by Chiara Brambilla, Jussi Laine, and Gianluca Bocchi, 129–40. London: Routledge.

Brambilla, Michele. 2013. "Vajont, cinquant'anni fa la tragedia." *La Stampa*, October 9. https://www.lastampa.it/cronaca/2013/10/09/news/vajont-cinquant-anni-fa-la-tragedia-1.35965963.

Breda, Marzio. 2013. "Il quirinale le mosse del capo dello stato: E Napolitano porta i migranti nell'agenda dei paesi del Nord." *Corriere della Sera*, October 10.

Brioni, Simone. 2014. "Across Languages, Cultures, and Nations: Ribka Sibhatu's Aulò." In *Italian Women Writers, 1800–2000: Boundaries, Borders and Transgression*, edited by Patrizia Sambuco, 123–42. Madison: Fairleigh Dickinson University Press.

Brison, Susan. 2002. *Aftermath: Violence and the Remaking of the Self.* Princeton: Princeton University Press.

Buccarello, Mauro. 2015. Interview with Karina Horsti. October 2. Lampedusa.

Buccini, Goffredo. 2013. "La tragedia di Lampedusa: Le vittime, i sorrisi con fidanzate e parenti l'album delle foto dei fantasmi." *Corriere della Sera*, October 4.

Butler, Judith. 2009. *Frames of War: When Is Life Grievable?* London: Verso.

Butler, Judith. 2004. *Precarious Life: The Powers of Mourning and Violence.* London: Verso.

Caccia, Beppe, Charles Heller, and Sandro Mezzadra. 2020. "Mediterranea: Thinking through a Political Invention in Tumultuous Times." *Parse* 10. https://parsejournal.com/article/mediterranea-thinking-through-a-political-invention-in-tumultuous-times/.

Campana, Micaela. 2015. Speech at the Italian Parliament Camera dei Deputati. April 13. Rome: Camera dei Deputati.

Campana, Paolo. 2018. "Out of Africa: The Organization of Migrant Smuggling across the Mediterranean." *European Journal of Criminology* 15 (4): 481–502. https://doi.org/10.1177%2F1477370817749179.

Campesi, Giuseppe. 2011. *The Arab Spring and the Crisis of the European Border Regime: Manufacturing Emergency in the Lampedusa Crisis.* Florence: European University Institute.

Carsten, Janet. 2000. "Introduction: Cultures of Relatedness." In *Cultures of Relatedness: New Approaches to the Study of Kinship*, edited by Janet Carsten, 1–36. Cambridge: Cambridge University Press.

Carta di Roma. "Carta di Roma." Accessed 22 November 2020. https://www.cartadiroma.org/chi-siamo/.

Casati, Noemi. 2018. "How Cities Shape Refugee Centres: 'Deservingness' and 'Good Aid' in a Sicilian Town." *Journal of Ethnic and Migration Studies* 44 (5): 792–808. https://doi.org/10.1080/1369183X.2017.1354689.

Catrambone, Christian. 2020. "Christian Catrambone." Accessed 23 November 2020. https://www.christophercatrambone.com/about/.

Cavallaro, Felice. 2013. "Lampedusa, l'uomo che non pesca più 'Dovevo salvarli tutti, li rivedo affogare.'" *Corriere della Sera*, 28 November 2013. https://www.corriere.it/cronache/13_novembre_28/lampedusa-l-uomo-che-non-pesca-dovevo-salvarli-tutti-li-rivedo-affogare-596fea54-57fc-11e3-8914-a908d6ffa3b0.shtml.

Cennetoğlu, Banu. 2018. "25 Years of the Refugee Crisis: Interview." Supplement to *Guardian*, June 20.

Cetin, Elif. 2015. "The Italian Left and Italy's (Evolving) Foreign Policy of Immigration Controls." *Journal of Modern Italian Studies* 20 (3): 377–97. https://doi.org/10.1080/1354571X.2015.1026149.

Chaouki, Khalid. 2015. Speech at the Italian Parliament Camera dei Deputati. April 13. Rome: Camera dei Deputati.

Chouliaraki, Lilie. 2013. *The Ironic Spectator: Solidarity in the Age of Post-Humanitarianism.* Oxford: Polity.

Chyrum, Elsa. 2016. Interview with Karina Horsti. November 22. London.

Chouliaraki, Lilie. 2006. *The Spectatorship of Suffering.* London: SAGE Publications.

Cole, Teju. 2016. *Known and Strange Things.* New York: Random House.

Comitato 3 ottobre. Accessed December 17, 2020. https://www.comitatotreottobre.it.

Connerton, Paul. 1989. *How Societies Remember.* Cambridge: Cambridge University Press.

Coppola, Nicola. 2018. Interview with Karina Horsti and Ilaria Tucci. October 6. Castellamare del Golfo.

Cosentino, Raffaella. n.d. "Il racconto della morte: Tra escalation dell'orrore e sprazzi di umanità." *Questione d'immagine.* http://www.questionedimmagine.org/argomento/immigrazione/sbarchi/il-racconto-della-morte-tra-escalation-dellorrore-e-sprazzi-di-umanita/.

Crawley, Heaven, and Brad K. Blitz. 2019. "Common Agenda or Europe's Agenda? International Protection, Human Rights and Migration from the Horn of Africa." *Journal of Ethnic and Migration Studies* 45 (12): 2258–74. https://doi.org/10.1080/1369183X.2018.1468393.

Crawley, Heaven, Franck Düvell, Katharine Jones, Simon McMahon, and Nando Sigona. 2016. *Destination Europe? Understanding the Dynamics and Drivers of Mediterranean Migration in 2015.* MEDMIG Final Report.

Critiquenact. 2016. "Solidarity without Limits—Nationalism Is No Alternative!" Critique'n'act-blog. Accessed December 18, 2020. http://critiquenact.blogsport. eu/2016/08/08/solidarity-without-limits-nationalism-is-no-alternative/?lang=en.

Crocker, Rebecca M., Robin C. Reineke, and María Elena Ramos Tovar. 2021. "Ambiguous Loss and Embodied Grief Related to Mexican Migrant Disappearances." *Medical Anthropology* 40 (7): 598–611. https://doi.org/10.1080/01459740.2020.18 60962.

Cusumano, Eugenio, and Matteo Villa. 2020. "From 'Angels' to 'Vice Smugglers': The Criminalization of Sea Rescue NGOs in Italy." *European Journal on Criminal Policy and Research* 27 (1): 23–40. https://doi.org/10.1007/s10610-020-09464-1.

Cuttitta, Paolo. 2018a. "Delocalization, Humanitarianism, and Human Rights: The Mediterranean Border between Exclusion and Inclusion." *Antipode* 50 (3): 783–803. https://doi.org/10.1111/anti.12337.

Cuttitta, Paolo. 2018b. "Repoliticization through Search and Rescue? Humanitarian NGOs and Migration Management in the Central Mediterranean." *Geopolitics* 23 (3): 632–60. https://doi.org/10.1080/14650045.2017.1344834.

Cuttitta, Paolo. 2015. "La frontière Lampedusa: Mises en intrigue du sécuritaire et de l'humanitaire." *Cultures et Conflits* 99–100: 99–115. https://doi.org/10.4000/conflits.19101.

Cuttitta, Paolo. 2014. "'Borderizing' the Island: Setting and Narratives of the Lampedusa 'Border Play.'" *ACME: An International E-Journal for Critical Geographies* 1 (2): 196–219. https://www.acme-journal.org/index.php/acme/article/view/1004.

Davis, Colin. 2007. *Haunted Subjects: Deconstruction, Psychoanalysis and the Return of the Dead*. Basingstoke: Palgrave Macmillan.

Davis, Colin. 2005. "État présent: Hauntology, Spectres and Phantoms." *French Studies* 59 (3): 373–79. https://doi.org/10.1093/fs/kni143.

DDA. 2014. Decreto di fermo disposto dal P.M. May 30. Palermo.

De Genova, Nicholas, ed. 2017. *The Borders of "Europe": Autonomy of Migration, Tactics of Bordering*. Durham: Duke University Press.

De Genova, Nicholas. 2013. "Spectacles of Migrant 'Illegality': The Scene of Exclusion, the Obscene of Inclusion." *Ethnic and Racial Studies* 36 (7): 1180–98. https://doi. org/10.1080/01419870.2013.783710.

De León, Jason. 2015. *The Land of Open Graves*. Oakland: University of California Press.

Derrida, Jacques. 1994. *Specters of Marx: The State of the Debt, the Work of Mourning and the New International*. London: Routledge.

Derrida, Jacques. 1986. *Memoires for Paul de Man*. New York: Columbia University Press.

Derrida, Jacques, and Jean Birnbaum. 2007. "Learning to Live Finally: The Last Interview." In *Learning to Live Finally*, 19–52. Basingstoke: Palgrave Macmillan.

Deutsche Welle. 2019. "Christchurch Terror Attacks: What You Need to Know." December 9. https://www.dw.com/en/christchurch-terror-attacks-what-you-need-to-know/a-47942310.

Deutsche Welle. 2013. "Dozens of Survivors Protest Lampedusa Ship Disaster Funeral." Deutsche Welle, October 21. https://www.dw.com/en/dozens-of-survivors-protest-lampedusa-ship-disaster-funeral/a-17174143.

De Waal, Alex. 1997. *Famine Crimes: Politics and the Disaster Relief Industry in Africa*. London: James Currey.

Di Benedetto, Salvo. 2013. "Cinque immigrati sepolti oggi a Raffadali." *Agrigento Notizie*, October 16. http://raffadali.agrigentonotizie.it/immigrati-tragedie-naufragi-morti-sepolture-raffadali-16-ottobre-2013.html.

Didi-Huberman, Georges. 2002. "The Surviving Image: Aby Warburg and Tylorian Anthropology." *Oxford Art Journal* 25 (1): 59–70. https://www.jstor.org/stable/3600420.

Distretti, Emilio. 2020. "Enforced Disappearances and Border Deaths along the Migrant Trail." In *Border Deaths,* edited by Paolo Cuttitta and Tamara Last, 117–30. Amsterdam: Amsterdam University Press. https://doi.org/10.2307/j.ctvt1sgz6.

Draper, Susana. 2012. *Afterlives of Confinement: Spatial Transitions in Post-Dictatorship Latin America.* Illuminations: Cultural Formations of the Americas. Pittsburgh: University of Pittsburgh Press.

Dresdner Preis. 2017a. "Dresden's Peace Prize Goes to Italy." Dresdner Preis. Accessed December 16, 2020. http://dresdner-friedenspreis.de/dresdens-peace-prize-goes-to-italy/?lang=en.

Dresdner Preis. 2017b. "Sonderpreis für Sizilianisches Ehepaar." Dresdner Preis. Accessed December 20, 2020. http://dresdner-friedenspreis.de/sonderpreis/.

DSP. 2017. "The 2% Tax for Eritreans in the Diaspora: Facts, Figures and Experiences in Seven European Countries." Tilburg: Tilburg School of Humanities, Department of Culture Studies. https://www.dsp-groep.eu/wp-content/uploads/The-2-Tax-for-Eritreans-in-the-diaspora_30-august-1.pdf

Duggan, Lisa. 2012. "Beyond Marriage: Democracy, Equality, and Kinship for a New Century." Scholar and Feminist Online 10 (1–2). https://sfonline.barnard.edu/a-new-queer-agenda/beyond-marriage-democracy-equality-and-kinship-for-a-new-century/.

Durham Peters, John. 2001. "Witnessing." *Media, Culture and Society* 23 (6): 707–23. https://doi.org/10.1177%2F016344301023006002.

EASO. 2021. *Latest Asylum Trends.* Valletta: European Asylum Support Office.

EASO. 2019. Eritrea: National Service, Exit and Return. Valletta: European Asylum Support Office. https://coi.euaa.europa.eu/administration/easo/PLib/2019_EASO_COI_Eritrea_National_service_exit_and_return.pdf.

Edkins, Jenny. 2016. "Missing Migrants and the Politics of Naming: Names without Bodies, Bodies without Names." *Social Research* 83 (2): 359–89. https://doi.org/10.1353/sor.2016.0034.

Edkins, Jenny. 2011. *Missing: Persons and Politics.* Ithaca: Cornell University Press.

Enia, Davide. 2017. *Notes on a Shipwreck: A Story of Refugees, Borders, and Hope.* Translated by Anthony Shugaar. New York: Other Press.

Eritrean Community in Italy. 2014. "Commemoration of Lampedusa Boat Victims." Dehai News, September 27. http://www.dehai.org/archives/dehai_news_archive/2014/sep/0411.html.

Esperti, Marta. 2020. "Rescuing Migrants in the Central Mediterranean: The Emergence of a New Civil Humanitarianism at the Maritime Border." *American Behavioral Scientist* 64 (4): 436–55. https://doi.org/10.1177%2F0002764219882976.

Espiritu, Yến Lê. 2014. *Body Counts: The Vietnam War and Militarized Refugees.* Oakland: University of California Press.

Estefanos, Meron. 2016. Interview with Karina Horsti. April 29. Stockholm.

European Parliament. 2014. "Results of the 2014 European Elections." European Parliament. Accessed December 17, 2020. https://www.europarl.europa.eu/elections2014-results/en/country-introduction-2014.html.

Eurostat. 2017. First Instance Decisions by Outcome and Recognition Rates, 30 Main Citizenships of Asylum Applicants Granted Decisions in the EU-28, 4th Quarter 2017. Luxembourg: Eurostat.

Famiglietti, Luigi. 2015. Speech at the Italian Parliament Camera dei Deputati. April 13. Rome: Camera dei Deputati.

Fassin, Didier. 2012. *Humanitarian Reason: A Moral History of the Present Times.* Oakland: University of California Press.

Fassin, Didier. 2010. "Ethics of Survival: A Democratic Approach to the Politics of Life." *Humanity* 1 (1): 81–95. https://doi.org/10.1353/hum.2010.0000.

Fassin, Didier. 2005. "Compassion and Repression: The Moral Economy of Immigration Policies in France." *Cultural Anthropology* 20 (3): 362–87. https://www.jstor.org/stable/3651596.

Felman, Shoshana. 1991. "In an Era of Testimony: Claude Lanzmann's *Shoah*." *Yale French Studies* 79: 39–81. https://doi.org/10.2307/2930246.

Felman, Shoshana, and Dori Laub. 1992. *Testimony: Crises of Witnessing in Literature, Psychoanalysis and History*. London: Routledge.

Ferguson, James. 1994. *The Anti-Politics Machine: "Development," De-Politicization, and Bureaucratic Power in Lesotho*. Minneapolis: University of Minnesota Press.

Fine, Gary Alan, and Terence Mcdonnell. 2007. "Erasing the Brown Scare: Referential Afterlife and the Power of Memory Templates." *Social Problems* 54 (2): 170–87. https://doi.org/10.1525/sp.2007.54.2.170.

Fiorino, Vito. 2021. Personal communication with Karina Horsti, January 21.

Fiorino, Vito. 2017. Interview with Karina Horsti and Ilaria Tucci. October 4.

Fiorino, Vito, Grazia Migliosini, Linda Barrocci, Marcello Nizza, Alessandro Marino, Anna Bonaccorso, Rosaria Racioppi, and Carmine Menna. 2014. "Oggetto: Rifiuto alla partecipazione della cerimonia organizzata dal comune di Lampedusa e dal Festival 'Sabir.'" October 3. Lampedusa.

Fleming, Melissa. 2013. *UNHCR Urges Countries to Enable Safe Passage, Keep Borders Open for Syrian Refugees*. Geneva: UNHCR.

Freud, Sigmund. 1964. "Mourning and Melancholia." In *The Standard Edition of the Complete Psychological Works of Sigmund Freud*. Vol. 14. Edited by James Strachey and Anna Freud, 243–58. London: Hogarth Press.

Friese, H. 2019. "Framing Mobility: Refugees and the Social Imagination." *ISR-Forschungsberichte* 49: 25–41.

Friese, H. 2010. "The Limits of Hospitality: Political Philosophy, Undocumented Migration and the Local Arena." *European Journal of Social Theory* 13 (3): 323–41. https://doi.org/10.1177/1368431010371755.

Frosh, Paul, and Amit Pinchevski. 2014. "Media Witnessing and the Ripeness of Time." *Cultural Studies* 28 (4): 594–610. https://doi.org/10.1080/09502386.2014.891304.

Frosh, Paul, and Amit Pinchevski. 2008. "Introduction: Why Media Witnessing? Why Now?" In *Media Witnessing*, edited by Paul Frosh and Amit Pinchevski, 1–19. London: Palgrave Macmillan.

Galante, Mariangela. 2021. Phone interview with Karina Horsti. May 8.

Galante, Mariangela. 2018. Interview with Karina Horsti. October 6. Castellamare del Golfo.

Galeazzi, Giacomo. 2013. "Immigrazione le reazioni il papa: Lo sfogo di Francesco, 'una vergogna.'" *La Stampa*, October 4.

Gamson, William A., and Andre Modigliani. 1989. "Media Discourse and Public Opinion on Nuclear Power: A Constructionist Approach." *American Journal of Sociology* 95 (1): 1–37. https://www.jstor.org/stable/2780405.

Gatta, Gianluca. 2019. "Self-Narration, Participatory Video and Migrant Memories: A (Re)Making of the Italian Borders." In *The Politics of Public Memories of Forced Migration and Bordering in Europe*, edited by Karina Horsti, 101–20. Cham: Palgrave Macmillan. https://doi.org/10.1007/978-3-030-30565-9_7.

Gatta, Gianluca. 2018. "'Half Devil and Half Child': An Ethnographic Perspective on the Treatment of Migrants on Their Arrival in Lampedusa." In *Border Lampedusa*, edited by Gabriele Proglio and Laura Odasso, 33–51. Cham: Palgrave Macmillan. https://doi.org/10.1007/978-3-319-59330-2_3.

Gatta, Gianluca. 2014. "Lampedusa, 3 ottobre 2013: Vita, morte, nazione e politica nella gestione delle migrazioni." *Studi Culturali* 11 (2): 323–32. https://doi.org/10.1405/77809.

Gatti, Fabrizio. 2013. "Morti di Lampedusa, gli hanno rubato anche il funerale." *L'Espresso*, October 21. https://espresso.repubblica.it/attualita/2013/10/21/news/morti-di-lampedusa-gli-hanno-rubato-anche-il-funerale-1.138381#gallery-slider=undefined.

Gatti, Gabriel. 2013. "Moral Techniques: Forensic Anthropology and Its Artifacts for Doing Good." *Sociología y technociencia/Sociology and Technoscience* 3 (1): 12–31. https://www.proquest.com/openview/bc4eacc93b274dabad9a21d00f144d26/1?pq-origsite=gscholar&cbl=237700.

Gatti, Gabriel, Ignacio Irazuzta, and María Martínez. 2020. "Inverted Exception: Ideas for Thinking about the New Disappearances through Two Case Studies." *Journal of Latin American Cultural Studies* 29 (4): 581–604. https://doi.org/10.1080/13569325.2020.1839869.

Gebrehiwet, Solomon. 2020. 3 October 2013 Memorial Discussion, moderator Semhar Ghebreselassie. Global Yiakl, October 3.

Geddes, Andrew, and Andrea Pettrachin. 2020. "Italian Migration Policy and Politics: Exacerbating Paradoxes." *Contemporary Italian Politics* 12 (2): 227–42. https://doi.org/10.1080/23248823.2020.1744918.

Gibbons, Joan. 2007. *Contemporary Art and Memory: Images of Recollection and Remembrance*. London: I. B. Tauris.

Gilligan, Chris, and Carol Marley. 2010. "Migration and Divisions: Thoughts on (Anti-) Narrativity in Visual Representations of Mobile People." *Forum: Qualitative Sozialforschung* 11 (2):Art. 32. http://nbn-resolving.de/urn:nbn:de:0114-fqs1002326.

Giubilaro, Chiara. 2018. "(Un)Framing Lampedusa: Regimes of Visibility and the Politics of Affect in Italian Media Representations." In *Border Lampedusa: Subjectivity, Visibility and Memory in Stories of Sea and Land*, edited by Gabriele Proglio and Laura Odasso, 103–17. Cham: Palgrave Macmillan. https://doi.org/10.1007/978-3-319-59330-2_7.

Giuliani, Gaia. 2018. "The Colour(s) of Lampedusa." In *Border Lampedusa*, edited by Gabriele Proglio and Laura Odasso, 67–85. Cham: Palgrave Macmillan. https://doi.org/10.1007/978-3-319-59330-2_5.

Global Yiakl. 2020. Live Streamed Online Discussion on the October 3, 2013, Disaster. October 3. https://www.facebook.com/GlobalYiakl/videos/694251544529571.

Goffman, Erving. 1990. *The Presentation of Self in Everyday Life*. London: Penguin.

Goffman, Erving. 1981. *Forms of Talk*. Philadelphia: University of Pennsylvania Press.

Goffman, Erving. 1972. *Frame Analysis*. Boston: Northeastern University Press.

Gordon, Avery F. 2008. *Ghostly Matters: Haunting and the Sociological Imagination*. Minneapolis: University of Minnesota Press.

Grant, Stefanie. 2016. "Identification and Tracing." In *Fatal Journeys*. Vol. 2, *Identification and Tracing of Dead and Missing Migrants*, edited by Tara Brian and Frank Laczko, 31–74. Geneva: IOM. https://publications.iom.int/books/fatal-journeys-volume-2-identification-and-tracing-dead-and-missing-migrants.

Grotti, Vanessa, and Marc Brightman. 2021. "Introduction: Mediterranean Migrant Hospitalities." In *Migrant Hospitalities in the Mediterranean*, edited by Vanessa Grotti and Marc Brightman, 1–14. Cham: Palgrave Macmillan. https://doi.org/10.1007/978-3-030-56585-5_1.

Gutiérrez Rodríguez, Encarnación. 2018. "Political Subjectivity, Transversal Mourning and a Caring Common: Responding to Deaths in the Mediterranean." *Critical African Studies* 10 (3): 345–60. https://doi.org/10.1080/21681392.2019.1610010.

Hallam, Elizabeth, and Jenny Hockey. 2018. "Remembering as Cultural Process." In *Death, Mourning, and Burial: A Cross-Cultural Reader*. 2nd ed., edited by Antonius C. G. M. Robben, 52–63. Hoboken: Wiley Blackwell.

Harari, Yuval N. 2009. "Scholars, Eyewitnesses, and Flesh-Witnesses of War: A Tense Relationship." *Partial Answers* 7 (2): 213–28. https://doi.org/10.1353/pan.0.0147.

Hartman, Saidiya. 2007. *Lose Your Mother: A Journey along the Atlantic Slave Route.* New York: Farrar, Straus and Giroux.

Hatton, Timothy. 2021. "Asylum Recognition Rates in Europe: Persecution, Policies and Performance." IZA DP No. 14840, IZA Institute of Labor Economics, 1–57. https://www.iza.org/en/publications/dp/14840/asylum-recognition-rates-in-europe-persecution-policies-and-performance.

Haverinen, Anna. 2015. "Facebook, Ritual and Community: Memorialising in Social Media." *Ethnologia Fennica* 42: 7–22. https://doi.org/10.23991/ef.v42i0.59284.

Hegde, Radha Sarma. 2016. *Mediating Migration.* Cambridge: Polity.

Heller, Charles, and Antoine Pécoud. 2020. "Counting Migrants' Deaths at the Border: From Civil Society Counterstatistics to (Inter)Governmental Recuperation." *American Behavioral Scientist* 64 (4): 480–500. https://doi.org/10.1177%2F000 2764219882996.

Heller, Charles, and Lorenzo Pezzani. 2018. "Forensic Oceanography: Mare Clausum; A Report." London: Goldsmiths, University of London. https://content.forensic-architecture.org/wp-content/uploads/2019/05/2018-05-07-FO-Mare-Clausum-full-EN.pdf.

Hertz, Robert. 1960/2018. "A Contribution to the Study of the Collective Representation of Death." In *Death, Mourning and Burial: A Cross-Cultural Reader*, edited by Antonius C. G. M. Robben, 19–33. Oxford: Wiley Blackwell.

Hirsch, Marianne. 1997. *Family Frames: Photography, Narrative, and Post Memory.* Cambridge, MA: Harvard University Press.

Hirt, Nicole, and Abdulkader Saleh Mohammad. 2018. "By Way of Patriotism, Coercion, or Instrumentalization: How the Eritrean Regime Makes Use of the Diaspora to Stabilize Its Rule." *Globalizations* 15 (2): 232–47. https://doi.org/10.1080/1474773 1.2017.1294752.

Höfner, Susan, and Zara Tewolde-Berhan. 2017. "Crimes against Humanity: The Commission of Inquiry on Eritrea." In *Human Trafficking and Trauma in the Digital Era: The Ongoing Tragedy of the Trade in Refugees from Eritrea*, edited by Mirjam van Reisen and Munyaradzi Mawere, 350–69. Langaa RPCIG. muse.jhu.edu/book/50493.

Holt, Linda Lystig. 2001. "End of Life Customs among Immigrants from Eritrea." *Journal of Transcultural Nursing* 12 (2): 146–54. https://doi.org/10.1177%2F104365960101 200209.

Home Office. 2021. "Eritrea: National Service and Illegal Exit." Country Policy and Information Note, version 6.0. London: Home Office. https://assets.publishing.service.gov.uk/government/uploads/system/uploads/attachment_data/file/1020555/ERI_CPIN_National_service_and_illegal_exit.pdf.

Hong, Mai-Linh K. 2016. "Reframing the Archive: Vietnamese Refugee Narratives in the Post-9/11 Period." *Melus* 41 (3): 18–41. https://www.jstor.org/stable/441 55260.

Horsti, Karina. 2021. "Civil Investigation of a Migrant Disaster as a Cultural Intervention against Injustice." *Studi culturali* 18 (2): 263–82. https://doi.org/10.1405/101885.

Horsti, Karina. 2020. "Refracting the Analytical Gaze: Studying Media Representations of Migrant Death at the Border." In *The SAGE Handbook of Media and Migration*, edited by Kevin Smets, Koen Leurs, Myria Georgiou, Saskia Witteborn, and Radhika Gajjala, 142–55. London: SAGE.

Horsti, Karina. 2019a. "Curating Objects from the European Border Zone: The 'Lampedusa Refugee Boat.'" In *The Politics of Public Memories of Forced Migration and*

Bordering in Europe, edited by Karina Horsti, 53–70. Cham: Palgrave Macmillan. https://doi.org/10.1007/978-3-030-30565-9_4.

Horsti, Karina. 2019b. "Digital Materialities in the Diasporic Mourning of Migrant Death." *European Journal of Communication* 34 (6): 671–81. https://doi.org/10.11 77%2F0267323119886169.

Horsti, Karina. 2019c. "Transnational Mediated Commemoration of Migrant Deaths at the Borders of Europe." In *The Handbook of Diasporas, Media, and Culture*, edited by Jessica Retis and Roza Tsagarousianou, 193–205. Hoboken: Wiley.

Horsti, Karina. 2018. "Live Free or Die Motionless: Walking the Migrant Path from Italy to France." *Cultural Studies Review* 24 (2): 56–66. https://doi.org/10.5130/csr.v24i2.5923.

Horsti, Karina. 2016a. "Imagining Europe's Borders: Commemorative Art on Migrant Tragedies." In *Migration by Boat*, edited by Lynda Mannik, 83–100. New York: Berghahn. https://doi.org/10.2307/j.ctvpj7hqz.9.

Horsti, Karina. 2016b. "Visibility without Voice: Media Witnessing Irregular Migrants in BBC Online News Journalism." *African Journalism Studies* 37 (1): 1–20. https://doi.org/10.1080/23743670.2015.1084585.

Horsti, Karina. 2012. "Humanitarian Discourse Legitimating Migration Control: FRONTEX Public Communication." In *Migrations: Interdisciplinary Perspectives*, edited by Renée Schroeder and Michi Messer, 297–308. Vienna: Springer. https://doi.org/10.1007/978-3-7091-0950-2_27.

Horsti, Karina, and Klaus Neumann. 2019. "Memorializing Mass Deaths at the Border: Two Cases from Canberra (Australia) and Lampedusa (Italy)." *Ethnic and Racial Studies* 42 (2): 141–58. https://doi.org/10.1080/01419870.2017.1394477.

Hoskins, Andrew. 2009. "Digital Network Memory." In *Mediation, Remediation, and the Dynamics of Cultural Memory*, edited by Astrid Erll and Ann Rigney, 91–106. Berlin: Walter de Gruyter. https://doi.org/10.1515/9783110217384.1.91.

Howell, Signe. 2006. *The Kinning of Foreigners*. New York: Berghahn.

Human Rights Watch. 2021. *Eritrea: Events of 2020*. New York: Human Rights Watch. https://www.hrw.org.

Hyndman, Jennifer. 2007. "Feminist Geopolitics Revisited: Body Counts in Iraq." *Professional Geographer* 59 (1): 35–46. https://doi.org/10.1111/j.1467-9272.2007.00589.x.

ICMP. 2021. International Committee on Missing Persons. Accessed June 23, 2021. https://www.icmp.int/.

Il Fatto Quotidiano. 2016. "Giustizia and impunità: Naufragio Lampedusa, prima sentenza in Italia per traffico di esseri umani." *Il Fatto Quotidiano*, February 8. https://www.ilfattoquotidiano.it/2016/02/08/naufragio-lampedusa-prima-sentenza-in-italia-per-traffico-di-esseri-umani/2445211/.

International Organization for Migration (IOM). 2022. "Missing Migrants Project." Accessed 23 June 2022. https://missingmigrants.iom.int/.

Interpol. 2021. "Disaster Victim Identification." Interpol. Accessed January 10, 2021. https://www.interpol.int/How-we-work/Forensics/Disaster-Victim-Identification-DVI.

Invernizzi, Cristian. 2015. Speech at the Italian Parliament Camera dei Deputati. April 15. Rome: Camera dei Deputati.

Isin, Engin F. 2009. "Citizenship in Flux: The Figure of the Activist Citizen." *Subjectivity* 29 (1): 367–88. https://doi.org/10.1057/sub.2009.25.

Isin, Engin F. 2008. "Theorizing Acts of Citizenship." In *Acts of Citizenship*, edited by Engin F. Isin and Greg Marc Nielsen, 15–43. London: Zed Books.

Isin, Engin F., and Greg Marc Nielsen. 2008. "Introduction." In *Acts of Citizenship*, edited by Engin F. Isin and Greg Marc Nielsen, 1–12. London: Zed Books.

Italian presidency of the Council of the European Union. 2014. *Europe—a Fresh Start: Programme of the Italian Presidency of the Council of the European Union.* Italian Presidency of the Council of the European Union. italia2014.eu.

Jeholm, Sofie, and Mons Bissenbakker. 2019. "Documenting Attachment." *Nordic Journal of Migration Research* 9 (4): 480–96. http://doi.org/10.2478/njmr-2019-0039.

Jugo, Admir. 2017. "Artefacts and Personal Effects from Mass Graves in Bosnia and Herzegovina: Symbols of Persons, Forensic Evidence or Public Relics?" *Les Cahiers Sirice* 19 (2): 21–40. https://doi.org/10.3917/lcsi.019.0021

Kahsay, Warka Solomon. 2022. "Eritrea—Recent History." In *Europa Regional Surveys of the World: Africa South of the Sahara, 2022.* 51st ed., 419–26. London: Routledge.

Kebrat. 2021. Song by Nando Misuraca. Naples: Suono Libero Music.

Keetharuth, Sheila B. 2013. Report of the Special Rapporteur on the Situation of Human Rights in Eritrea, Sheila B. Keetharuth, Human Rights Council, United Nations General Assembly, 28 May 2013.

Khaleeli, Homa. 2016. "#SayHerName: Why Kimberlé Crenshaw Is Fighting for Forgotten Women." *Guardian*, May 30. https://www.theguardian.com/lifeandstyle/2016/may/30/sayhername-why-kimberle-crenshaw-is-fighting-for-forgotten-women.

Kibreab, Gaim. 2009. "Forced Labour in Eritrea." *Journal of Modern African Studies* 47 (1): 41–72. http://www.jstor.org/stable/30224923.

Kidane, Selam. 2020. "Number 92." International Cities of Refuge Network. https://www.icorn.org/article/poem-no-92.

Kidane, Selam. 2014. "Ode to Yohanna's Baby." *Asmarino*, April 4. https://asmarino.com/writers-corner/2052-ode-to-yohannas-baby.

Kington, Tom. 2013a. "Lampedusa Rescuers Describe Struggle to Save Drowning Migrants." *Guardian*, October 4. https://www.theguardian.com/world/2013/oct/04/lampedusa-rescuers-migrant-boat-survivors.

Kington, Tom. 2013b. "Lampedusa Shipwreck: Italy to Hold State Funeral for Drowned Migrants." *Guardian*, October 9. https://www.theguardian.com/world/2013/oct/09/lampedusa-shipwreck-italy-state-funeral-migrants.

Kirkby, Joan. 2006. "'Remembrance of the Future': Derrida on Mourning." *Social Semiotics* 16 (3): 461–72. https://doi.org/10.1080/10350330600824383.

Kobelinsky, Carolina. 2020. "Who Cares about Ouacil? The Postmortem Itinerary of a Young Border Crosser." *American Behavioral Scientist* 64 (4): 525–39. https://doi.org/10.1177%2F0002764219882993.

Kobelinsky, Carolina. 2017. "Exister au risque de disparaître: Récits sur la mort pendant la traversée vers l'Europe." *Revue Européenne des Migrations Internationales* 33 (2–3): 115–31. https://doi.org/10.4000/remi.8745.

Kobelinsky, Carolina, Filippo Furri, and Camille Noûs. 2021. "The Place of the Dead in the Mediterranean: A Sicilian Experience." *Migration Letters* 18 (6): 711–19. https://doi.org/10.33182/ml.v18i6.1243.

Koselleck, Reinhart. 2017. *Vergangene Zukunft.* Frankfurt: Suhrkamp.

Koselleck, Reinhart. 2002. *The Practice of Conceptual History: Timing History, Spacing Concepts.* Translated by Todd Samuel Presner et al. Stanford: Stanford University Press.

Kovras, Iosif, and Simon Robins. 2017. "Missing Migrants: Death at Sea and Unidentified Bodies in Lesbos." In *Migrating Borders and Moving Times: Temporality and the Crossing of Borders in Europe*, edited by Donnan Hastings, Madeleine Hurd, and Carolin Leutloff-Grandits, 157–75. Manchester: Manchester University Press. https://doi.org/10.7765/9781526116413.00015.

Kushner, Tony. 2016. "Lampedusa and the Migrant Crisis: Ethics, Representation and History." *Mobile Culture Studies: The Journal* 2: 59–92. http://doi.org/10.25364/08.2:2016.1.6.

L'Ancora Online. 2013. "Lampedusa e Vajont le scuse dello stato." L'Ancora Online, October 10. http://www.ancoraonline.it/2013/10/10/lampedusa-e-vajont-le-scuse-dello-stato/.

Landini, Francesca, and Sabina Suzzi. 2020. "New Atlantia CEO Apologizes for Bridge Disaster, Seeks Talks with Government." *Business Insider,* January 24. https://www.businessinsider.com/new-atlantia-ceo-apologizes-for-bridge-disaster-seeks-talks-with-government-2020-1?r=DEandIR=T.

Laqueur, Thomas Walter. 2015. *The Work of the Dead: A Cultural History of Mortal Remains.* Princeton: Princeton University Press.

La Repubblica Palermo. 2013. "Strage del 3 ottobre, ancora morti strappati al mare 359 cadaveri." *La Repubblica Palermo,* October 12.

La Rosa, Paola. 2015. Interview with Karina Horsti. October 2. Lampedusa.

Last, Tamara. 2015. "The Deaths at the Borders Database." The Deaths at the Borders Database. Accessed May 12, 2021. http://www.borderdeaths.org/?page_id=425.

La Stampa. 2013. "I sopravvissuti indagati per la Bossi-Fini grasso: 'Inumana conseguenza della legge.'" *La Stampa,* October 6.

Lauria, Emanuele. 2017. "Giusi Nicolini: 'Non sono carrierista, ho detto molti no e sono stata punita.'" *La Repubblica,* June 13. https://palermo.repubblica.it/cronaca/2017/06/13/news/giusi_nicolini_non_sono_carrierista_ho_detto_molti_no_e_sono_stata_punita_-167996062/?refresh_ce.

Letta, Enrico. 2013a. "A Lampedusa una tragedia immane, l'Italia chiede scusa." October 10. https://www.enricoletta.it.

Letta, Enrico. 2013b. Lampedusa, QandA con i giornalisti—Di Letta, Alfano, Barroso, e Malmström. Palazzo Chigi.

Levi, Primo. 1988. *The Drowned and the Saved.* New York: Simon and Schuster.

Lewicki, Aleksandra. 2017. "'The Dead Are Coming': Acts of Citizenship at Europe's Borders." *Citizenship Studies* 21 (3): 275–90. https://doi.org/10.1080/13621025.2016.1252717.

Leys, Ruth. 2007. *From Guilt to Shame: Auschwitz and After.* Princeton: Princeton University Press.

LIBE Committee. 2015. Motion for a Parliament Resolution on the Situation in the Mediterranean and the Need for a Holistic EU Approach to Migration. Brussels: European Parliament Committee on Civil Liberties, Justice and Home Affairs.

Longo, Grazia. 2017. Phone interview with Karina Horsti and Ilaria Tucci. September 13.

Longo, Grazia. 2013. "Il quelle foto le vite spezzate." *La Stampa,* October 4.

López Aguilar, Juan Fernando. 2019. Speech at the LIBE Committee Hearing on Search and Rescue in the Mediterranean. October 3, 2019. Brussels: Multimedia Center, European Parliament. https://multimedia.europarl.europa.eu/en/webstreaming/libe-committee-meeting_20191003-0900-COMMITTEE-LIBE.

Luhmann, Niklas. 1982. *The Differentiation of Society.* New York: Columbia University Press.

M'charek, Amade, and Sara Casartelli. 2019. "Identifying Dead Migrants: Forensic Care Work and Relational Citizenship." *Citizenship Studies* 23 (7): 738–57. https://doi.org/10.1080/13621025.2019.1651102.

Maccanico, Yasha. 2009. "Italy: The Internal and External Fronts; Security Package and Returns." *Statewatch Analysis* 19 (3). https://www.statewatch.org/media/documents/analyses/no-100-italy-internal-external-fronts.pdf.

Madianou, Mirca. 2016. "Ambient Co-Presence: Transnational Family Practices in Poly-media Environments." *Global Networks* 16 (2): 183–201. https://doi.org/10.1111/glob.12105.

Magid, Magid. 2019. Question at the LIBE Committee Hearing on Search and Rescue in the Mediterranean. October 3, 2019. Brussels: Multimedia Centre European Parliament. https://multimedia.europarl.europa.eu/en/webstreaming/libe-committee-meeting_20191003-0900-COMMITTEE-LIBE.

Malkki, Liisa H. 1996. "Speechless Emissaries: Refugees, Humanitarianism, and Dehis-toricization." *Cultural Anthropology* 11 (3): 377–404. https://www.jstor.org/stable/656300.

Malmström, Cecilia. 2013. Speech at Press Conference in Lampedusa, October 9.

Mann, Itamar. 2020. "The Right to Perform Rescue at Sea: Jurisprudence and Drown-ing." *German Law Journal* 21 (3): 598–619. https://doi.org/10.1017/glj.2020.30.

Marceca, Romina. 2013. "Kebrat: 'Io data per morta e stesa tra le salme.'" *La Repubblica*, October 4. https://www.repubblica.it/cronaca/2013/10/04/news/la_strage_di_lampedusa_intervista_kebrat_isola_dei_conigli_di_romina_marceca-67887262/.

Marina Militare. 2020. "Mare Nostrum Operation." Accessed 23 November 2020. https://www.marina.difesa.it/EN/operations/Pagine/MareNostrum.aspx.

Mason, Charlotte. 2020. "These Photos Show the Coffins of Victims of a Boat Disaster in 2013." Agence France Press, March 27. https://factcheck.afp.com/these-photos-show-coffins-victims-boat-disaster-2013.

Mastrodonato, Claudio. 2013. "A Lampedusa il Giardino della memoria." Ambient and Ambienti, November 7. http://www.ambienteambienti.com/a-lampedusa-il-giardino-della-memoria/.

Mazzara, Federica. 2019. *Reframing Migration: Lampedusa, Border Spectacle and the Aesthetics of Subversion*. Oxford: Peter Lang.

Mbembe, Achille. 2019. *Necropolitics*. Durham: Duke University Press.

Mbembe, Achille. 2003. "Necropolitics." *Public Culture* 15 (1): 11–40. https://doi.org/10.1215/08992363-15-1-11.

McNevin, Anne. 2011. *Contesting Citizenship*. New York: Columbia University Press.

Mezzadra, Sandro, and Brett Neilson. 2013. *Border as Method, or, the Multiplication of Labor*. Durham: Duke University Press.

Michaelis, Paul Felix. 2016. "18 weiße Särge auf der schwarzen Dresdner Elbe." *Dresdner Neueste Nachrichten*, October 3.

Mirto, Giorgia, Simon Robins, Karina Horsti, Pamela J. Prickett, Deborah Ruiz Ver-dusco, and Victor Toom. 2020. "Mourning Missing Migrants: Ambiguous Loss and the Grief of Strangers." In *Border Deaths*, edited by Paolo Cuttitta and Tamara Last, 103–16. Amsterdam: Amsterdam University Press. https://doi.org/10.2307/j.ctvt1sgz6.10.

MOAS. 2014. "Annual Report." Accessed 23 November 2020. https://www.moas.eu/wp-content/uploads/2015/12/MOAS-Administration-Report-2014.pdf.

Moeller, Susan D. 1999. *Compassion Fatigue: How the Media Sell Disease, Famine, War and Death*. New York: Routledge.

Mohamed Ali, Zakaria. 2013. *To Whom It May Concern*. Short film. Rome: Archivio Memorie Migranti.

Mohammad, Abdulkader Saleh. 2021. "The Resurgence of Religious and Ethnic Identi-ties among Eritrean Refugees: A Response to the Government's Nationalist Ideol-ogy." *Africa Spectrum* 56 (1): 39–58. https://doi.org/10.1177/0002039720963287.

Morgano, Luigi. 2018. Email communication with Karina Horsti. January 30.

Mountz, Alison. 2020. *The Death of Asylum: Hidden Geographies of the Enforcement Archipelago*. Minneapolis: University of Minnesota Press.

Mudde, Cas. 2016. *On Extremism and Democracy in Europe*. Abingdon: Routledge.

Muneroni, Stefano. 2015. "Memorialization and Representation of Immigrants in Contemporary Italy: The Case of Mimmo Paladino's Monument 'Gateway to Lampedusa/Gateway to Europe.'" Crossings 6 (2): 233–45. https://doi.org/10.1386/cjmc.6.2.233_1.

Murphy, Connor. 2017. "Theresa May Apologizes for Response to Grenfell Tower Fire." *Politico*, June 21. https://www.politico.eu/article/theresa-may-apologizes-for-response-to-grenfell-tower-fire/.

Musarò, Pierluigi. 2017. "Mare Nostrum: The Visual Politics of a Military-Humanitarian Operation in the Mediterranean Sea." *Media, Culture and Society* 39 (1): 11–28. https://doi.org/10.1177%2F0163443716672296.

Musil, Robert. 1987. *Posthumous Papers of a Living Author*. Translated by Peter Wortsman. Hygiene, CO: Eridanos Press.

Nastasi, Stefano. 2017. Phone interview with Karina Horsti and Ilaria Tucci. March 6.

Negash, Tekeste. 1987. *Italian Colonialism in Eritrea, 1882–1941*. Uppsala: Uppsala University Press.

Neugebauer, Ruben. 2016. Interview with Karina Horsti. March 15. Berlin.

Neumann, Klaus. 2022. "Black Lives Matter, a Princess from Zanzibar, Bismarck, and German Memorial Hygiene." *German Politics and Society* 40 (1): 77–103. https://doi.org/10.3167/gps.2022.400105.

Neumann, Klaus. 2020. "The Appeal of Civil Disobedience in the Central Mediterranean." *Journal of Humanitarian Affairs* 2 (1): 53–61. https://doi.org/10.7227/JHA.034.

Neumann, Klaus. 2019. "True Camps of Concentration? The Uses and Abuses of a Contentious Analogy." In *The Politics of Public Memories of Forced Migration and Bordering in Europe*, edited by Karina Horsti, 15–35. Cham: Palgrave Macmillan. https://doi.org/10.1007/978-3-030-30565-9_2.

Neumann, Klaus. 2014. "History, Memory, Justice." In *A Companion to Global Historical Thought*, edited by Prasenjit Duara, Viren Murthy, and Andrew Sartori, 466–81. Chichester: Wiley Blackwell.

Neumann, Klaus. 2013. "Attentiveness and Indifference." *Inside Story*, July 22.

Neumann, Klaus. 2000. *Shifting Memories: The Nazi Past in the New Germany*. Ann Arbor: University of Michigan Press.

Neumann, Klaus, and Janna Thompson, eds. 2015. *Historical Justice and Memory*. Madison: University of Wisconsin Press.

Nguyen, Mimi Thi. 2012. *The Gift of Freedom: War, Debt, and Other Refugee Passages*. Durham: Duke University Press.

Nguyen, Viet Thanh. 2016. *Nothing Ever Dies*. Cambridge, MA: Harvard University Press.

Nicolini, Giuseppina. 2012. Open Letter from the Mayor of Lampedusa to the European Union. November 15, Lampedusa.

Nikunen, Kaarina. 2019. *Media Solidarities: Emotions, Power and Justice in the Digital*. London: SAGE.

Nixon, Rob. 2011. *Slow Violence and the Environmentalism of the Poor*. Cambridge, MA: Harvard University Press.

Nuovi Desaparecidos. 2021. "Justice for the 'Disappeared People' of the Mediterranean Sea." Nuovi Desaparecidos—Verità e giustizia per i nuovi desaparecidos del Mediterraneo. Accessed January 2, 2021. http://nuovidesaparecidos.net/?page_id=197&lang=en.

Nuzzolese, Emilio, and Giancarlo Di Vella. 2007. "Future Project Concerning Mass Disaster Management: A Forensic Odontology Prospectus." *International Dental Journal* 57 (4): 261–66. https://doi.org/10.1111/j.1875-595X.2007.tb00130.x.

Oliver-Smith, Anthony, and Susanna M. Hoffman. 2002. "Introduction: Why Anthropologists Should Study Disasters." In *Catastrophe and Culture: The Anthropology of Disaster*, edited by Susanna Hoffman and Anthony Oliver-Smith, 3–22. Oxford: James Currey.

Olivieri, Lara, Debora Mazzarelli, Barbara Bertoglio, Danilo De Angelis, Carlo Previderè, Pierangela Grignani, Annalisa Cappella, Silviano Presciuttini, Caterina Bertuglia, Paola Di Simone, Nicolò Polizzi, Agata Iadicicco, Vittorio Piscitelli, and Cristina Cattaneo. 2018. "Challenges in the Identification of Dead Migrants in the Mediterranean: The Case Study of the Lampedusa Shipwreck of October 3rd 2013." *Forensic Science International* 285: 121–28. https//doi.org/10.1016/j.forsciint.2018.01.029.

O'Rourke, Diane. 2007. "Mourning Becomes Eclectic: Death of Communal Practice in a Greek Cemetery." *American Ethnologist* 34 (2): 387–402. https://www.jstor.org/stable/4496813.

Ortner, Sherry B. 1995. "Resistance and the Problem of Ethnographic Refusal." *Comparative Studies in Society and History* 37 (1): 173–93. https://www.jstor.org/stable/179382.

Pallister-Wilkins, Polly. 2015. "The Humanitarian Politics of European Border Policing: Frontex and Border Police in Evros." *International Political Sociology* 9 (1): 53–69. http://doi.org/10.1111/ips.12076.

Pannia, Paola. 2021. "Tightening Asylum and Migration Law and Narrowing the Access to European Countries: A Comparative Discussion." In *Migrants, Refugees and Asylum Seekers' Integration in European Labour Markets*, edited by Veronica Federico and Simone Baglioni. IMISCOE Research Series. Cham: Springer. https://doi.org/10.1007/978-3-030-67284-3_3.

Papacharissi, Zizi. 2010. *A Private Sphere: Democracy in a Digital Age*. Cambridge: Polity.

Papadopoulos, Dimitris, and Vassilis S. Tsianos. 2013. "After Citizenship: Autonomy of Migration, Organisational Ontology and Mobile Commons." *Citizenship Studies* 17 (2): 178–96. https://doi.org/10.1080/13621025.2013.780736.

Parsons, Thomas. 2019. Presentation of the ICMP Laboratory. November 25. The Hague.

Pellander, Saara. 2021. "Buy Me Love: Entanglements of Citizenship, Income and Emotions in Regulating Marriage Migration." *Journal of Ethnic and Migration Studies* 47 (2): 464–79. https://doi.org/10.1080/1369183X.2019.1625141.

Perkowski, Nina. 2018. "Frontex and the Convergence of Humanitarianism, Human Rights and Security." *Security Dialogue* 49 (6): 457–75. https://www.jstor.org/stable/26979674.

Perl, Gerhild. 2018. "Lethal Borders and the Translocal Politics of 'Ordinary People.'" *Anthropological Journal of European Cultures* 27 (2): 85–104. https://doi.org/10.3167/ajec.2018.270206.

Perl, Gerhild. 2016. "Uncertain Belongings: Absent Mourning, Burial, and Post-Mortem Repatriations at the External Border of the EU in Spain." *Journal of Intercultural Studies* 37 (2): 195–209. https://doi.org/10.1080/07256868.2016.1141758.

Petryna, Adriana. 2013. *Life Exposed: Biological Citizens after Chernobyl*. Princeton: Princeton University Press.

Pezzani, Lorenzo, and Charles Heller. 2013. "A Disobedient Gaze: Strategic Interventions in the Knowledge(s) of Maritime Borders." *Postcolonial Studies* 16 (3): 289–98. https://doi.org/10.1080/13688790.2013.850047.

Piscitelli, Vittorio, and Cristina Cattaneo. 2016. "Identification Efforts Following the Lampedusa 2013 Shipwrecks." In *Fatal Journeys: Identification and Tracing of Dead and Missing Migrants*, edited by Tara Brian and Frank Laczko, 43–45. Geneva: International Organization for Migration.

Piscitelli, Vittorio, Agata Iadicicco, Danilo De Angelis, Davide Porta, and Cristina Cattaneo. 2016. "Italy's Battle to Identify Dead Migrants." *Lancet Global Health* 4 (8): 512–13. https://doi.org/10.1016/S2214-109X(16)30106-1.

Plaut, Martin. 2016. *Understanding Eritrea: Inside Africa's Most Repressive State.* Oxford: Oxford University Press.

Polchi, Vladimiro. 2013. "Kyenge: 'Avrei potuto essere sul barcone affondato.'" *La Repubblica*, October 4. https://www.repubblica.it/cronaca/2013/10/04/news/ ccile_kyenge_intervista_la_bossi-fini_tragedia_lampedusa_isola_dei_conigli_ europa_immigrazione_di_vladimiro_polchi-67878124/.

Pols, Jeannette. 2016. "Analyzing Social Spaces: Relational Citizenship for Patients Leaving Mental Health Care Institutions." *Medical Anthropology* 35 (2): 177–92. https://doi.org/10.1080/01459740.2015.1101101.

Pope Francis. 2013a. Address of Pope Francis: To Participants in a Conference Sponsored by the Pontifical Council for Justice and Peace Celebrating the 50th Anniversary of "Pacem in Terris." Vatican: Libreria Editrice Vaticana.

Pope Francis. 2013b. Visit to Lampedusa. Homily of Holy Father Francis. Vatican: Libreria Editrice Vaticana.

Proglio, Gabriele. 2020. *The Horn of Africa Diasporas in Italy: An Oral History.* Cham: Palgrave Macmillan.

Puglia, Alessandro. 2014. "Lampedusa, soccorritori non partecipano al festival Sabir: 'E'un teatrino.'" *La Repubblica*, October 3. https://www.repubblica.it/solidarieta/ immigrazione/2014/10/03/news/strage_lampedusa_sabir_soccorritori-97206625.

Pusterla, Francesca. 2021. "Legal Perspectives on Solidarity Crime in Italy." *International Migration* 59 (3): 79–95. https://doi.org/10.1111/imig.12740.

Rackete, Carola. 2019. Speech at the LIBE Committee Hearing on Search and Rescue in the Mediterranean. October 3, 2019. Brussels: Multimedia Center European Parliament. https://multimedia.europarl.europa.eu/en/webstreaming/libe-committee-meeting_20191003-0900-COMMITTEE-LIBE.

Radio Assenna. 2013. "The 365 Lampedusa Victims and Our Duty to Them." Radio Assenna, October 10. https://www.youtube.com/watch?v=0SEKqp7phCQandlist= ULjhIV_Z27dywandindex=1354.

Radio Cento Passi Journal. 2013. "Strage di Lampedusa: Nasce il 'Giardino della memoria.'" Radio Cento Passi Journal, November 4. http://100passijournal.info/strage-di-lampedusa-nasce-il-giardino-della-memoria/.

Redeker Hepner, Tricia M. 2009. *Soldiers, Martyrs, Traitors, and Exiles: Political Conflict in Eritrea and the Diaspora.* Philadelphia: University of Pennsylvania Press.

Reid, Richard. 2009. "Introduction." In *Eritrea's External Relations: Understanding Its Regional Role and Foreign Policy*, edited by Richard Reid, 10–23. London: Chatham House.

Reineke, Robin C. 2022. "Forensic Citizenship among Families of Missing Migrants along the U.S.-Mexico Border." *Citizenship Studies* 26 (1): 21–37. https://doi.org/1 0.1080/13621025.2021.2018675.

Remembering Lampedusa. 2019. Short films directed by Anna Blom and Adal Neguse. Helsinki: Jamedia Production.

Remes, Jacob A. C. 2016. *Disaster Citizenship: Survivors, Solidarity, and Power in the Progressive Era.* Champaign: University of Illinois Press.

Reuters. 2020. "False Claim: Photo Shows Coffins of Coronavirus Victims in Italy." Reuters, March 28. https://www.reuters.com/article/uk-factcheck-italy-coffins/false-claim-photo-shows-coffins-of-coronavirus-victims-in-italy-idUSKBN21F0XL.

Ribattuta, Cordes. 2013. "L'Anniversario messaggio di Napolitano: Il quirinale sul Vajont; La strage conseguenza di precise colpe umane." *Corriere della Sera*, October 10.

Riccò, Antonio. 2014. *Ein Morgen vor Lampedusa*. Hannover: Unser Herz schlägt auf Lampedusa.

Ricoeur, Paul. 2004. *Memory, History, Forgetting*. Chicago: University of Chicago Press.

Ritaine, Évelyne. 2016. "Lampedusa, 3 ottobre 2013: Letture politiche della morte." *Intersezioni* 5 (1): 101–12. https://halshs.archives-ouvertes.fr/halshs-01348514/document.

Robins, Simon. 2022. "The Affective Border: Missing Migrants and the Governance of Migrant Bodies at the EU's Southern Frontier." *Journal of Refugee Studies* 35 (2): 948–67. https://doi.org/10.1093/jrs/fey064.

Robins, Simon. 2010. "Ambiguous Loss in a Non-Western Context: Families of the Disappeared in Postconflict Nepal." *Family Relations* 59 (3): 253–68. https://doi.org/10.1111/j.1741-3729.2010.00600.x.

Roghi, Vanessa. 2020. "La strage di bologna aspetta ancora il lavoro degli storici." *Internazionale*, August 2. https://www.internazionale.it/opinione/vanessa-roghi/2020/08/02/strage-di-bologna.

Romagnoli, Gabriele. 2013. "Il vuoto, la paura, la fatica negli occhi dei 153 invisibili." *La Repubblica*, October 5.

Romano, Claude. 2009. *Event and World*. New York: University of Fordham Press.

Romano, Serena. 2016. The Italian Legal Framework for the Management of Missing Persons and Unidentified Dead Bodies, and the Rights of the Relatives. Mediterranean Missing Project. https://missingmigrants.iom.int/sites/g/files/tmzbdl601/files/publication/file/Mediterranean-Missing-Italian-legal-memo.pdf.

Rossi, Giovanni, and Pietro Suber. 2013. Attenzione alle immagini dei sopravvissuti alla tragedia di Lampedusa. Rome: Associazione Carta di Roma, October 7. https://www.cartadiroma.org.

Rothberg, Michael. 2009. *Multidirectional Memory*. Stanford: Stanford University Press.

Ruberto, Laura E., and Jospeh Sciorra. 2022. "Disrupted and Unsettled: An Introduction to Monuments, Memorials, and Italian Migrations." *Italian American Review* 12 (1): 1–35. https://doi.org/10.5406/26902451.12.1.01.

Ruchatz, Jens. 2008. "The Photograph as Externalization and Trace." In *Cultural Memory Studies: An International and Interdisciplinary Handbook*, edited by Astrid Erll and Ansgar Nünning, 367–78. Berlin: Walter de Gruyter.

Rygiel, Kim. 2016. "Dying to Live: Migrant Deaths and Citizenship Politics along European Borders; Transgressions, Disruptions, and Mobilizations." *Citizenship Studies* 20 (5): 545–60. https://doi.org/10.1080/13621025.2016.1182682.

Rygiel, Kim. 2014. "In Life through Death: Transgressive Citizenship at the Border." In *Routledge Handbook of Global Citizenship Studies*, edited by Engin Isin and Peter Nyers, 62–72. London: Routledge.

Safety4Sea. 2019. "Moby Prince: Italy's Worst Maritime Disaster since World War II." Safety4Sea. Accessed February 25, 2021. https://safety4sea.com/cm-moby-prince-italys-worst-maritime-disaster-since-world-war-ii/.

Sant'Egidio. 2011. Morire di speranza: I nomi e le storie dei migrant morti nei viaggi verso l'Europa ricordati nella veglia di preghiera a Santa Maria in Trastevere, June 17. https://archive.santegidio.org.

Saucier, P. Khalil, and Tryon P. Woods. 2014. "Ex Aqua: The Mediterranean Basin, Africans on the Move, and the Politics of Policing." *Theoria* 61 (141): 55–75. https://doi.org/10.3167/th.2014.6114104.

Saunders, Frances Stonor. 2016. "Where on Earth Are You?" *London Review of Books* 38 (5): 7–12.

Scarabicchi, Caterina. 2020. "Performing Community: Lampedusa in Festival against the Border Spectacle of Mediterranean Migrations." *Journal of European Studies* 50 (4): 373–88. https://doi.org/10.1177%2F0047244120965749.

Schindel, Estela. 2020. "Deaths and Disappearances in Migration to Europe: Exploring the Uses of a Transnationalized Category." *American Behavioral Scientist* 64 (4): 389–407. https://doi.org/10.1177%2F0002764219883003.

Schneider, Christina J., and Branislav L. Slantchev. 2018. "The Domestic Politics of International Cooperation: Germany and the European Debt Crisis." *International Organization* 72 (1): 1–31. https://www.jstor.org/stable/26569460.

Schulz, Martin. 2014. Speech by the president of the European Parliament, October 3. Lampedusa.

Schwartz, Mattathias. 2014. "The Anniversary of the Lampedusa Tragedy." *New Yorker*, October 3.

Schwartz-Marin, Ernesto, and Arely Cruz-Santiago. 2016. "Pure Corpses, Dangerous Citizens: Transgressing the Boundaries between Experts and Mourners in the Search for the Disappeared in Mexico." *Social Research: An International Quarterly* 83 (2): 483–510. https://doi.org/10.1353/sor.2016.0038.

Senato della Repubblica. 2016. Instituzione della Giornata nazionale in memoria delle vittime dell'immigrazione, 24 May 2016.

Shapiro, David. 2003. "The Tortured, Not the Torturers, Are Ashamed." *Social Research* 70 (4): 1131–48. http://www.jstor.org/stable/40971964.

Sibhatu, Ribka. 2016. "In Lampedusa." Translated by André Naffis-Sahely. *Modern Poetry in Translation* 50 (1). http://modernpoetryintranslation.com/poem/in-lampedusa/.

Sontag, Susan. 1977. *On Photography*. London: Penguin Books.

Sossi, Federica. 2013. "Migrations and militant research? Some brief considerations." *Postcolonial Studies* 16 (3): 269–78. https://doi.org/10.1080/13688790.2013.850045.

Sossi, Federica. 2006. "Lampedusa: L'isola che non c'è." In *Migrazioni, Frontiere, Diritti*, edited by Paolo Cuttitta and Fulvio Vassallo Paleologo, 251–60. Naples: Edizioni Scientifiche Italiane.

Spagnolo, Chiara. 2013. "Emiliano: 'Seppelliamo noi le vittime di Lampedusa'; La tragedia." *La Repubblica Bari*, October 5.

Squire, Vicki. 2020. *Europe's Migration Crisis: Border Deaths and Human Dignity*. Cambridge: Cambridge University Press.

Squires, Nick. 2013. "Sinking a 'Scene from the Titanic.'" *Sydney Morning Herald*, October 6. https://www.smh.com.au/world/sinking-a-scene-from-the-titanic-20131005-2v16m.html.

Stierl, Maurice. 2016. "Contestations in Death: The Role of Grief in Migration Struggles." *Citizenship Studies* 20 (2): 173–91. https://doi.org/10.1080/13621025.2015.1132571.

Stümer, Jenny. 2018. "The Dead Are Coming: Border Politics and Necropower in Europe." *Cultural Politics* 14 (1): 20–39. https://doi.org/10.1215/17432197-4312856.

Sturken, Marita. 1997. *Tangled Memories: The Vietnam War, the AIDS Epidemic and the Politics of Remembering*. Oakland: University of California Press.

Tait, Sue. 2011. "Bearing Witness, Journalism and Moral Responsibility." *Media, Culture and Society* 33 (8): 1220–35. https://doi.org/10.1177/0163443711422460.

Taussig, Michael. 1992. *The Nervous System*. London: Routledge.

Taylor, Diana. 2011. "Trauma as Durational Performance: A Return to Dark Sites." In *Rites of Return: Diaspora Poetics and the Politics of Memory*, edited by Marianne Hirsch and Nancy K. Miller, 268–79. New York: Columbia University Press.

Taylor, Diana. 2003. *The Archive and the Repertoire: Performing Cultural Memory in the Americas*. Durham: Duke University Press.

Tazzioli, Martina. 2020. "Governing Migrant Mobility through Mobility: Containment and Dispersal at the Internal Frontiers of Europe." *Environment and Planning C: Politics and Space* 38 (1): 3–19. https://doi.org/10.1177%2F2399654419839065.

Tazzioli, Martina. 2015. "The Politics of Counting and the Scene of Rescue." *Radical Philosophy* 192. https://www.radicalphilosophy.com/commentary/the-politics-of-counting-and-the-scene-of-rescue.

Tekle, Henok. 2020. *Erisat*, October 4. https://www.youtube.com/watch?v=FYaEvJV3G WQandfeature=shareandfbclid=IwAR3DANj48vdhns6uDlu36cHkFxb5BsC9Kp1 Qowtc_tSHyYkgiNyEhUw6VCY.

Those Who Feel the Fire Burning. 2014. Film directed by Morgan Knibbe.

Ticktin, Miriam Iris. 2011. *Casualties of Care: Immigration and the Politics of Humanitarianism in France*. Oakland: University of California Press.

Till, Karen E. 2008. "Artistic and Activist Memory-Work: Approaching Place-Based Practice." *Memory Studies* 1 (1): 99–113. https://doi.org/10.1177%2F1750 698007083893.

Tondo, Lorenzo. 2019. "Eritrean Man Released from Jail in Italian Mistaken Identity Case." *Guardian*, July 12. https://www.theguardian.com/world/2019/jul/12/ eritrean-man-released-from-jail-in-italian-mistaken-identity-case.

Tribunale di Agrigento. 2020. Sentenza 9 December 2020.

Triulzi, Alessandro. 2016. "Working with Migrants' Memories in Italy: The Lampedusa Dump." *Crossings: Journal of Migration and Culture* 7 (2): 149–63. http://doi.org/ 10.1386/cjmc.7.2.149_1.

Triulzi, Alessandro. 2013. "'Like a Plate of Spaghetti': Migrant Narratives from the Libya-Lampedusa Route." In *Long Journeys: African Migrants on the Road*, edited by Alessandro Triulzi and Robert Lawrence McKenzie, 213–32. Leiden: Brill. https:// doi.org/10.1163/9789004250390_012.

Tronvoll, Kjetil, and Daniel R. Mekonnen. 2014. *The African Garrison State: Human Rights and Political Development in Eritrea*. Suffolk: James Currey.

Tumarkin, Maria. 2005. *Traumascapes: The Power and Fate of Places Transformed by Tragedy*. Melbourne: Melbourne University Publishing.

Turner, Victor. 1980. "Social Dramas and Stories about Them." *Critical Inquiry* 7 (1): 141–68. https://www.jstor.org/stable/1343180.

Twigt, Mirjam A. 2018. "The Mediation of Hope: Digital Technologies and Affective Affordances within Iraqi Refugee Households in Jordan." *Social Media + Society* 4 (1). https://doi.org/10.1177%2F2056305118764426.

UN. 1982. Convention on the Law of the Sea. https://www.un.org/depts/los/convention_ agreements/texts/unclos/unclos_e.pdf.

Undogmatische Radikale Antifa Dresden. 2019. Email communication with Karina Horsti. December 27.

UNHCR. 2021. Resettlement Data Finder. Geneva: UNHCR.

UNHCR. 2019. Eritrean, Guinean and Sudanese Refugees and Migrants in Italy. Geneva: UNHCR.

UNHCR. 2018. Resettlement at a Glance: 2017 in Review. Geneva: UNHCR.

UNITED. 2022. "List of Deaths." Accessed 23 June, 2022. http://unitedagainstrefugeedea ths.eu/wp-content/uploads/2014/06/ListofDeathsActual.pdf.

United Nations. 1977. Protocol Additional to the Geneva Conventions of 12 August 1949, and Relating to the Protection of Victims of International Armed Conflicts (Protocol I). Geneva: United Nations.

United Nations Office of the High Commissioner for Human Rights. 2019. Special Rapporteur Sheila B. Keetharuth's reports to the Human Rights Council. http://ap. ohchr.org/documents/dpage_e.aspx?m=201.

van Dijck, Jose. 2013. *The Culture of Connectivity: A Critical History of Social Media*. Oxford: Oxford University Press.

van Gennep, Arnold. 2019. 2nd ed. *The Rites of Passage*. Chicago: University of Chicago Press.

Vassallo Paleologo, Fulvio. n.d. "La strage più grande: Ecco come è maturato il massacro di Lampeudsa." Progetto Melting Pot Europa. https://www.meltingpot.org/La-strage-piu-grande-Ecco-come-e-maturata-la-tragedia-di.html#.XA5nShmxXR1.

Vatican. 2013. Visit of Holy Father to Lampedusa—the Program. Vatican City: Libreria Editrice Vaticana.

Vigili del Fuogo. 2013. "Strage di Lampedusa, il barcone inabissato: Le immagini subacquee." *La Repubblica*.

Vinitzky-Seroussi, Vered. 2002. "Commemorating a Difficult Past: Yitzhak Rabin's Memorials." *American Sociological Review* 67 (1): 30–51. https://doi.org/10.2307/3088932.

Violi, Patrizia. 2012. "Trauma Site Museums and Politics of Memory." *Theory, Culture and Society* 29 (1): 36–75. https://doi.org/10.1177%2F0263276411423035.

Vullo, Amalia. 2018. Interview with Karina Horsti and Ilaria Tucci. October 7. Agrigento.

Wagner-Pacifici, Robin, and Barry Schwartz. 1991. "The Vietnam Veterans Memorial: Commemorating a Difficult Past." *American Journal of Sociology* 97 (2): 376–420. https://www.jstor.org/stable/2781381.

Wahlquist, Calla. 2019. "Ardern Says She Will Never Speak Name of Christchurch Suspect." *Guardian*, March 19. https://www.theguardian.com/world/2019/mar/19/new-zealand-shooting-ardern-says-she-will-never-speak-suspects-name.

Warburg, Aby. 1910/1999. "The Mural Paintings in Hamburg City Hall." In *The Renewal of Pagan Antiquity: Contributions to the Cultural History of the European Renaissance*, edited by Aby Warburg, 711–16. Los Angeles: Getty Research Institute for the History of Art and Humanities.

Weber, Leanne, and Sharon Pickering. 2011. *Globalization and Borders: Death at the Global Frontier*. Transnational Crime, Crime Control and Security. London: Palgrave Macmillan.

Weldemichael, Awet Tewelde. 2013. *Third World Colonialism and Strategies of Liberation: Eritrea and East Timor Compared*. Cambridge: Cambridge University Press.

Weston, Kath. 1997. *Families We Choose: Lesbians, Gays, Kinship*. New York: Columbia University Press.

White, Nathaniel. 2018. Phone interview with Karina Horsti. August 21.

Wilding, Raelene. 2006. "'Virtual' Intimacies? Families Communicating across Transnational Contexts." *Global Networks* 6 (2): 125–42. https://doi.org/10.1111/j.1471-0374.2006.00137.x.

Willerslev, Rane, Dorthe Refslund Christensen, and Lotte Meinert. 2013. "Introduction." In *Taming Time, Timing Death: Social Technologies and Ritual*, edited by Dorthe Refslund Christensen and Rane Willerslev, 1–16. Aldershot: Ashgate.

Witteborn, Saskia. 2014. "Forced Migrants, Emotive Practice and Digital Heterotopia." *Crossings* 5 (1): 73–85. http://doi.org/10.1386/cjmc.5.1.73_1.

Yardley, Jim, and Elisabetta Povoledo. 2013. "Migrants Die as Burning Boat Capsizes off Italy." *New York Times*, October 3. https://www.nytimes.com/2013/10/04/world/europe/scores-die-in-shipwreck-off-sicily.html.

Yimer, Dagmawi. 2015. *Names and Bodies: Tales from across the Sea*. San Diego: Department of Literature, University of California.

Zagaria, Valentina. 2016. "Vita e morte alla Porta d'Europa: Riflessioni sulle tombe dei morti di frontiera nella Provincia di Agrigento." *Intrasformazione* 5 (1): 80–100. https://doi.org/10.4474/DPS/05/01/DMM221/21.

Zerai, Mussie. 2019. Personal communication with Karina Horsti. November 25. The Hague.

262   **REFERENCES**

Zerai, Mussie 2015. Speech at the Porta d'Europa. October 3. Lampedusa.
Zerback, Thomas, Carsten Reinemann, Peter Van Aelst, and Andrea Masini. 2020.
"Was Lampedusa a Key Event for Immigration News? An Analysis of the Effects
of the Lampedusa Disaster on Immigration Coverage in Germany, Belgium,
and Italy." *Journalism Studies* 21 (6): 748–65. https://doi.org/10.1080/14616
70X.2020.1722730.
Zia, Ather. 2019. *Resisting Disappearance: Military Occupation and Women's Activism in
Kashmir*. Seattle: University of Washington Press.

Index

grievability, 80, 89
guilt. *See* emotion: guilt
Gutiérrez Rodríguez, Encarnación, 108–109

hadega, 38
haunting, 14–15, 61, 75, 132–133, 191, 201, 228
    specters from the future, 117, 147, 149, 155
    specters from the past, 64, 110, 137, 148, 155, 210, 227
hauntology. *See* haunting
Holocaust, 77, 83, 105, 128, 145–148, 181–185, 191–193
hospitality, 8, 100, 102, 104, 108, 159
humanitarian discourse, 9, 89, 138, 207, 212, 225, 232
humanitarian practice, 9, 97, 212
humanitarian security nexus. *See* securitization: and humanitarian nexus
Hyndman, Jennifer, 73

identification of dead migrants, 11, 153, 157, 161, 205–208, 212–213, 228, 234
    See also forensics
imagination
    of alternative futures, 15, 37, 147, 149
    See also civil imagination; journalistic imagination
indifference
    of bystanders, 4, 33, 38–39, 42, 149
    globalization of, 32–33, 69, 87, 94, 111
    social and institutional, 76, 80, 90, 111–112, 126, 145–146, 213
interdependency in visual politics, 47, 58, 60, 63, 68, 95
International Organization for Migration (IOM), 4, 70–73
Isin, Engin, 16, 109, 151, 176
Italian Navy, 9, 57, 138
Italy
    as benevolent and hospitable, 43, 136, 138, 160
    as a country of emigration, 14, 25, 102, 104, 110, 136–137, 148
    fascism and anti-fascism in, 19, 25, 137–138, 149
    as former colonial power, 14, 19, 60, 64, 67, 93, 135–137
    and Presidency of the Council of European Union, 139, 142, 152

journalistic imagination, 61, 63, 65
joy. *See* emotion: joy

justice and injustice, 34, 37, 52–53, 80–81, 134–135, 212–213, 229
    See also data justice

Kasim, Mohamed, 77–79, 81, 86
Kidane, Selam, 75, 105–106
kidnapping, 7, 78, 184, 234
kinning. *See* familial tie
Kushner, Tony, 121
Kyenge, Cécile, 31, 142

Lampedusa
    as a memory site of border deaths, 8, 117, 198
    as a symbol of the border, 8–10, 24, 117
    as a symbol of hospitality and benevolence, 8–10, 138
Lampedusa disaster
    civil rescuers in, 119, 122, 159, 183, 229
    in comparison to other disasters, 89, 118, 135, 154–155, 178, 185, 209–212
    corporeality of, 47
    investigation of, 39–40, 157, 160–161, 193
    as a symbol, 30, 136, 143
La Rosa, Paola, 134
Lesbos, 8, 128
Letta, Enrico, 17, 31, 33–36, 43, 50–54, 92–94
Levi, Primo, 77, 191–194
Libya
    migration route through, 39, 78, 234
    refugees in, 155, 171, 234
    smugglers from, 6, 18, 39
list of victims' names. *See* names
Longarone. *See* Vajont Dam disaster
Longo, Grazia, 59, 63–64

Malmström, Cecilia, 33, 50–54
Mare Nostrum operation, 9, 138
Marina Militare. *See* Italian Navy
Marino, Alessandro, 28–29, 122
Maritiman Maritime Museum. *See* Sweden: Maritiman Maritime Museum
Martello, Salvatore, 55, 174
Mbembe, Achille, 43, 50, 93
Mcdonnell, Terence, 13–14
media representation of refugees, 31–35, 45–46, 48, 57–58, 60, 79–80
    ethics of, 32, 68, 73, 81
mediated copresence, 122, 220
mediated witness. *See* witnessing: mediated witness

Schwartz, Mattathias, 75–76
Sea-Watch e.V, 10, 65, 143
search and rescue,
    civil, 10–11, 31, 105, 134, 142–144, 159
    institutional, 9, 45, 138, 153, 159
securitization, 2, 8–9, 32, 40, 54, 140, 234
    and humanitarian nexus, 9, 31, 53, 160
sentimentality, 77, 79, 97, 152
shame. *See* emotion: shame
shipwreck. *See* disaster
slow violence. *See* violence
smugglers, 39–40, 42, 120
social life, 14–16, 118
solidarity, 10, 212
    across space, 37, 110, 118, 146
    across time, 37, 103, 137
    between European countries, 139, 142
    with refugees, 51–52, 103, 115, 136–139
    survivors' sense of, 17, 173
Soviet Union
    collapse of, 20
specter. *See* haunting
Squire, Vicki, 8, 10, 108–109, 121, 229
state funeral, 34–35, 52, 92–94, 111, 114–116,
    155–156, 163
Stierl, Maurice, 10, 17, 69, 95, 109–110
story. *See* narrative
strage. See disaster
Strage di Lampedusa. See Lampedusa disaster
Strage di Portopalo, 31, 114, 154
Strait of Sicily, 4
studio photographs
    as a genre, 64–65, 85
    as horizontal gaze, 66
    as mediated relics of the disaster, 66
    in memorialization, 84, 95, 103
    as objects, 64–66
    as timeless past, 64
Sudan
    refugees in, 6–7, 11, 18
    relations with Eritrean resistance, 20
    route through, 3, 168, 215, 234
survival, 15, 26, 180–181, 194, 201, 203,
    228
    ethical ambiguity of, 188, 195, 199, 200
survivor citizenship. *See* citizenship: survivor
    citizenship
survivors
    in Denmark, 8, 120, 159, 202
    in Germany, 188
    in Sweden, 3, 84, 86, 119–120, 166–167, 184,
    201, 233
survivorship, 5, 26, 194, 199–200, 233

Sweden
    family members in, 6, 60
    Maritiman Maritime Museum
    (Gothenburg), 2–3
    See also survivors: in Sweden

Taylor, Diana, 13–14, 154, 165, 174
testimony, 88, 165, 182, 200–201
    listener of, 199–200
tragedy. *See* disaster
transgressive citizenship. *See* citizenship:
    transgressive citizenship
transnational families
    disappearances in, 11, 208, 210–214, 225
    mourning in, 59, 127, 205, 219–226
trauma, 8, 93, 137, 185
Triulzi, Alessandro, 138, 200
ungrievability, 25, 69, 89, 147
    See also grievability

United Nations, 20
United Nations Convention on the Law of the
    Sea, 29
unspeakability, 177, 187, 190

Vajont Dam disaster, 35–37
victims
    enumeration of, 69–73
    identification of. *See* forensics
    naming of, 69, 73–80, 88–91
    photographs of, 69, 84–91
    represented as individuals, 17, 66, 73–74, 79,
    89–91, 107–111
violence, 42

Warburg, Aby, 12, 14
White, Nathaniel, 71
Wilding, Raelene, 220, 222
witnessing
    bearing witness, 16, 183, 185, 190, 193–195,
    228
    embodied witness, 165, 184–188, 194, 203,
    227
    eyewitness, 40, 90, 132, 144, 194, 203, 227
    mediated witness, 75–76, 90, 95, 192–194,
    201–203, 227–228

Yimer, Dagmawi, 7, 82–83, 86, 126, 151
Yohanna, 23, 74–77, 90, 97, 219

Zerai, Mussie, 75–76, 93, 109, 155–158,
    161–163, 209–121, 225, 228, 239
Zia, Ather, 60, 211

www.ingramcontent.com/pod-product-compliance
Lightning Source LLC
Chambersburg PA
CBHW030348270326
41926CB00009B/1005